Unless you are a new Christian, you ha.... ....
times. Perhaps your very first reading of that Gospel led you to believe that Jesus
is the Christ, the Son of God (John 20:31). Afterward you have often read chapters or verses from it. Discovering, perhaps, Don Carson's commentary, you were
astonished at the richness of the Gospel—seeing what Jesus did, hearing what He
said, finding in Jesus the Way, the Truth, and the Life. Yet the full power of the
Gospel comes when you hear it preached. The heart-piercing address of Jesus
Himself comes home to you in preaching. The Holy Spirit uses the preached Word
to show Jesus. Pray as you read, and experience the difference preaching makes,
even in written form. As you read, you will hear Skip Ryan in the pulpit voicing
the message of the Gospel of John through the power of the Spirit.

      —EDMUND P. CLOWNEY
          Theologian in Residence, Trinity Presbyterian Church,
          Charlottesville, Va.

Skip Ryan makes the Gospel beautiful. While giving wise insight into John's gracious truths, Skip lavishes these pages with the riches of his own pastoral experience. The result is a book that equips us to face earth's grittiest challenges with
sure belief in the greatness of our Savior's comfort, strength, and victory.

      —BRYAN CHAPELL
          President, Covenant Theological Seminary

These elegant, theologically rich, yet very accessible expository sermons on John
are a delight to read. They also constitute an especially good model for preachers
who want their messages to have a very broad appeal for both seekers and solid
believers, for both old and young.

      —TIM KELLER
          Senior Pastor, Redeemer Presbyterian Church
          of New York City

Skip wrote to me about this book, "It's not all that good, I'm afraid. But it may
help some seeking something between a scholarly commentary and a Sunday
School outline."

    That's Skip—God's humble yet phenomenal servant. "It's not all that good"?
Baloney—it's great!

      —RAYMOND C. ORTLUND
          President, Renewal Ministries

Skip Ryan's ministry pulsates with an infectious enthusiasm for Christ, for the
Gospel of John, for people, and for communicating the gospel. Here is theology
in a popular dress—clearly expressed, practically applied, full of grace and good
news—and, in addition, it's a great read!

      —SINCLAIR B. FERGUSON
          Professor of Systematic Theology,
          Westminster Theological Seminary, Dallas

Skip has done us all a huge favor in sharing this book with us. His thoughtful, passionate, and scholarly concern to know and follow Jesus Christ echoes from every page. Tremendously helpful to pastors and lay folks alike! This book is a keeper.

> —JOHN YATES
> Rector, The Falls Church

Skip Ryan's sermons on the Gospel of John demonstrate why the Lord has so blessed his ministry. In these pages, the words and the Word of the Fourth Gospel come alive, beckoning us powerfully to believe that Jesus is the Christ and, believing, to have life in His name. Simply stated, this is superb exegesis and application!

> —SAMUEL T. LOGAN, JR.
> President and Professor of Church History,
> Westminster Theological Seminary

THAT YOU MAY BELIEVE

STUDIES IN THE GOSPEL OF JOHN

THAT YOU MAY
BELIEVE

New Life in the Son

JOSEPH "SKIP" RYAN

CROSSWAY BOOKS

A DIVISION OF
GOOD NEWS PUBLISHERS
WHEATON, ILLINOIS

Library of Congress Cataloging-in-Publication Data
Ryan, Joseph F., 1947–
   That you may believe : new life in the Son : studies in the Gospel of John / Joseph "Skip" Ryan.
     p. cm.
   Includes bibliographical references and index.
   ISBN 1-58134-353-1 (TPB : alk. paper)
   1. Bible N.T. John—Textbooks. 2. Bible. N.T. John—Devotional literature. I. Title.
BS2615.55 R93   2003
226.5'06—dc21   2002013476

VP		13	12	11	10	09	08	07	06	05	04	03
15	14	13	12	11	10	9	8	7	6	5	4	3	2	1

CONTENTS

Preface   9

PART I
THE INCARNATION OF THE SON OF GOD

1   The Beloved Disciple (John 20:30-31; 21:24-25; 13:23)   15
2   The Word (1:1-8)   23
3   The True Light (1:9-13)   33
4   The Word Made Flesh (1:14-18)   43

PART II
THE WITNESS OF THE SON OF GOD IN WORD AND WORKS

5   The Voice of Witness (1:19-34, 18)   55
6   "Come and See" (1:35-51)   65
7   The New Wine (2:1-11)   73
8   The New Temple (2:12-22)   83
9   The New Birth (2:23–3:21)   95
10 The (Real) New Age (3:22-36)   109
11 Water, Worship, Witness (4:4-42)   119
12 A Signpost to Home (4:43-54)   133

PART III
THE OPPOSITION TO JESUS AS THE SON OF GOD

13 The Conflict (5:2-3, 5-9, 14-24, 27, 30, 44)   143
14 A Sign of Provision (6:1-15)   155
15 "The Will of Him Who Sent Me" (6:38-40)   165
16 The Past, Present, and Future with Jesus   175
        (6:28-35, 51-59)
17 Rivers of Living Water (7:10-13, 37-39)   181
18 "I Am" (from chapters 6–8)   193

19	Truth That Frees . . . and Makes You Odd!	201
	(8:18-19, 31-36, 43-47)	
20	Blinding Light (9:1-41)	217
21	The True and Good Shepherd (10:1-18)	227
22	"Lazarus, Come Forth" (11:1-6, 17-27, 38-44)	236
23	The Anointing (11:45-47, 53; 12:1-8)	247
24	"Behold, Your King Comes" (12:12-16)	255
25	The Hour of Glory (12:20-28)	263
26	A Long Obedience in the Same Direction	273
	(12:27-36)	

PART IV
THE MINISTRY OF THE SON OF GOD TO HIS DISCIPLES

27	The Order of the Towel (13:1-17)	291
28	A Place Prepared (13:33–14:6)	301
29	The Disclosure (14:15-27)	311
30	"That They May All Be One" (17:20-26)	325

PART V
THE PASSION AND RESURRECTION OF THE SON OF GOD

31	Last Words (19:23-30)	337
32	Joseph of Arimathea (19:38–20:10)	345
33	The Three Marys (20:1-2; 11-17)	355
34	The Glorified Body (20:10-18)	363
35	The Stranger on the Shore (21:1-19)	371
36	A Pattern for Beloved Disciples (20:24-31)	381
Notes		387
General Index		393
Scripture Index		397

PREFACE

JOHN LEAVES LITTLE ROOM for doubt or confusion concerning his purpose in writing his Gospel. He tells his readers near the book's conclusion, " . . . these are written so that you may believe that Jesus is the Christ, the Son of God, and that by believing you may have life in his name" (John 20:31, ESV). As a preacher and pastor, I spend my time seeking to understand the "belief structure" of people's hearts—why they believe what they do, what motivates their beliefs, and, particularly, what helps people believe in the Lord instead of functionally trusting (which is what belief is) in many other things. In other words, what helps people turn from idols to serve the living and true God (1 Thess. 1:9)

For it is idols people serve. The evidence for such rampant idolatry abounds in the postmodern West. We are children of this age who rely on the best the world has provided for our sources of meaning and hope. We live by these things. Christians are not immune; the world defines us much more than we recognize—until we leave the familiar and travel to some place where the gospel is breaking out with new and powerful freshness. It has been said that in the church in the West, we have turned the biblical adage on its ear: instead of being in the world but not of the world, we are of the world but not in the world. We share the world's values and pull them into our Christian gatherings. We are not *in* the world enough to be salt, nor are we sufficiently *not of* the world to be light. We have brought the idols into the church but, most often, don't even recognize that we've done so.

The structure of idolatry in our hearts must be one of the pastor's chief concerns. We give ourselves to many things, and most of them do not help us have life. This was surely John's concern. As an aged apostle, but ever the pastor, he ends his letter we call First John with this pithy admonition: "Little children, keep yourselves from idols" (1 John 5:21, ESV). Our idols take the place of Christ's life, love, and gospel, even for the "believer." How desperately we must learn to believe again that Jesus is the only Savior, and to know again how to have real life in His name.

Twice, for the better part of a year each time, I preached sermons on John's Gospel that are revised in this volume. Many preachers have for sound reasons gone on much longer in John's Gospel, but I sought to give an overview so that we could more succinctly have a sweep of the whole, wrestle together with our idols, and learn to believe the gospel more deeply. We all have a long way to go, but it has been a great delight to see my own "belief structure" be more shaped by the gospel as the people of, first, Trinity Presbyterian Church and, in the last decade, Park Cities Presbyterian Church have grown to believe more firmly and cherish more dearly the wonder of the life given in His name.

There are many fine scholarly works on John's Gospel, most notably D. A. Carson's very rich and important recent commentary, *The Gospel According to John* (Eerdmans, 1991). Having read and reread Dr. Carson's clear, theologically toned, and worshipful book, I have wondered what this present volume might add. Perhaps just this: some might find here an accessible appetizer to the larger feast of his work. For that, I would be glad.

And there are many fine professors, preachers, and pastors who have portrayed well John's call to true belief in the Son of God. Dick Gaffin taught me the framework of the New Testament when I was a student at Westminster Seminary, a framework I have relied upon for every New Testament sermon I've preached in the last twenty-seven years. I am delighted to acknowledge my debt to Tim Keller, pastor of Redeemer Presbyterian Church in New York, to whom I owe most of the content and structure of chapters 11 and 23. And always in the background of every message is the voice of Edmund Clowney, whose role in my life for thirty years has moved fluidly between teacher, friend, and father.

There would be no volume in your hands were it not for Terri Speicher, who, for the vision of making this material accessible, labored with affection to make some sense of my scrawling and notes. Her zeal for the project was my continual source of inspiration. Nancy Schmidt works with me every day to bring some order to my schedule and ministry life and after eleven years still is able to be my cheerful colleague and encourager. And reaching way back, it was Colleen Koppert Holby who was the human instrument of my coming as a teenager to believe in Jesus as the Son of God; her prayers and care opened to me life in His name.

My new best friend is Bill Deckard, associate editor at Crossway Books. I can't believe his patience.

It has been the greatest joy and challenge to help Chris, Carey Beth, and crazy Bekah believe in the gospel as the source of their lives and their living. My wife Barbara and I have learned the gospel together again and again through raising them and through the wonder of married life. Collaborator, fan, critic, lover, counselor, friend—she is, more often than anyone else, the source of my delight and my smiles. I love watching Barb believe in and love Jesus as the One who gives her life.

—Skip Ryan
Dallas
May, 2003

PART I

*The Incarnation of
the Son of God*

1

THE BELOVED DISCIPLE

Many other signs therefore Jesus also performed in the presence of the disciples, which are not written in this book; but these have been written that you may believe that Jesus is the Christ, the Son of God; and that believing you may have life in His name (John 20:30-31).

This is the disciple who bears witness of these things, and wrote these things; and we know that his witness is true. And there are also many other things which Jesus did, which if they were written in detail, I suppose that even the world itself would not contain the books which were written (21:24-25).

There was reclining on Jesus' breast one of His disciples, whom Jesus loved (13:23).

WE CAN LEARN MUCH about the Gospel of John by looking at the disciple himself. What was John like? What was his background and how did he see himself? Who was he writing to and why did he write this book? Let's develop a profile of John at the very beginning of this study.

JOHN'S PROFILE

Apparently John was an upper-middle-class Jewish businessman from Palestine, the son of a businessman named Zebedee. He had a brother named James. Together James and John were called the Sons of Thunder (Mark 3:17), perhaps because they once asked the Lord if they should call fire down from heaven on a particularly disrespectful and unbelieving Samaritan village (Luke 9:54). Zebedee and Sons, Inc., was a fishing company. These were not itinerant or poor fisherman throwing lines off a dock somewhere; they probably had a substantial business. They owned their own boats (Luke 5:3) and employed others (Mark 1:20).

It appears that John was a well-educated Jewish layman. He wasn't a rabbi or a prophet, but he was particularly knowledgeable in the texts of the Old Testament. He repeatedly quotes from the Old Testament in his writings. He refers to Father Abraham, to the tabernacle, the temple, the feasts, Jacob's ladder, Jacob's well, manna, and the Sabbath. He consistently refers to things that a Jewish layperson who has taken his or her Bible seriously would understand.

John probably spoke three languages. Speaking multiple languages was not that uncommon for people living in the ancient world, as it is not that uncommon for many in the world today. We Americans are somewhat disadvantaged in this regard. Until recently, our particular borders, the oceans on both sides, and our particular history have promoted the use of one language.

John spoke Aramaic, the everyday speech of his time, as a first language; but he also spoke Hebrew, the ceremonial religious language. Greek was the *lingua franca* of the day, used in commerce and business all over the ancient world. Greek was also the language that would have linked John to the Mediterranean world of his day. Some who had contact with the Roman army or administration might even have known a little Latin.

John was a man of his world. He grew up in Galilee and lived in Judea—in Jerusalem—for a time. Most scholars believe that after the destruction of Jerusalem in A.D. 70, when Jews were scattered throughout the world, John lived for a time in the city of Ephesus, in the western part of Asia Minor, which today is Turkey. Then his final years were spent in exile on the island of Patmos, off the coast of western Turkey.

Moving around as John did sounds more modern than ancient. We usually think people in ancient times lived in one place and never moved, but John traveled a good bit. It's like being born in Pittsburgh, growing up in New York, going to school in Boston and Philadelphia, then living in Virginia and Texas (as I have). In this sense, John's life was more modern than ancient.

JOHN'S WITNESS

How did John see himself? How did he understand his role? First of all, John saw himself as a *truthful* witness to the events and meaning of Jesus Christ's life, death, and resurrection. At the very end of the book of John he claims that his testimony is true. He says, "We know that his witness is true" (John 21:24). That statement is interesting because it is written in the third person, but that is characteristic of John. Never once in his Gospel does John speak of himself in the first person.

He also says (21:25) that his witness is *selective*. He says that if everything was written down that could be written about Jesus Christ, there would be no library in the world that could contain it all. So John picks and chooses for his purposes.

Apparently John was well acquainted with the Gospels of Matthew, Mark, and Luke because his Gospel was written later. But his writing is very different than that of the Synoptic Gospels. Even a casual reading of these four Gospels will tell you that John's cadence and emphases are different. For example, in Matthew, Mark, and Luke there are many accounts of Jesus doing battle with the demons. There is not one such account in all of John's Gospel. Instead, in John we find a "theology of the devil." In John 8 there is a big discussion as Jesus interacts with the Jewish leaders about the nature of the devil as a father of lies. Apparently John is not interested just in the action that Jesus undertook with the demons. Perhaps he assumes that his readers have already read Matthew, Mark, and Luke. He takes it a step further for his purposes and goes into more analysis about why and how and what it means for Jesus to cast out a demon.

John wasn't just truthful and selective; he was also *passionate*. Truth without passion is like light without heat; you can learn a lot of truth, but it is of little use if it doesn't affect, warm your heart, and move you to action. Any other kind of truth is dry. Does that describe the kind of sermons you hear on Sunday mornings, or do they have both light and heat? Every good sermon should have a lot of light, a lot of truth, a lot of understanding of what the Word is saying, inviting you to use your brain. But every good sermon should also have a fair amount of heat. It should warm your heart, move you to conviction, compel you to action, and motivate you to something new and different.

Other sermons have a lot of heat but not much light. You may be in tears at the end of the sermon, but five minutes later you don't know why. We need a good balance.

John was truthful in a passionate way. He was not neutral about Jesus Christ. The Gospels are not dispassionate history. Some might say that the truth of one's testimony or account is compromised if too much passion is involved. The truth, however, does not have to be dispassionate. In fact, the truth should not be dispassionate. Imagine the first witnesses to Auschwitz after World War II as they came upon that horror and told about it later. Would you expect them to be dispassionate? It would be obscene if they were. To be dispassionate about the truth of Christ is almost blasphemous, because the truth of Christ should move us, as it moved John. / *Amen*)

JOHN'S AUDIENCE

John was an evangelist to culturally diverse people. His purpose is stated directly in John 20:31: "These have been written that you may believe that Jesus is the Christ, the Son of God; and that believing you may have life in His name." Perhaps a better rendering of this verse would be, "These things have been written that you may believe that the Christ, the Son of God, is Jesus." Reversing the subject and the object clarifies John's emphasis. John's basic question is not, Who is Jesus, but, Who is Messiah? Who would ask that question? Who is John trying to reach? There has been a lot of scholarly blood spilled about who John's target audience is. Many say he is more or less ignoring Jews and seeking to reach Greeks. But who would ask the question, Who is Messiah? A Jew or a Greek? A Jew, of course. John's primary audience is the Jews who have been scattered throughout the Greek world by virtue of the destruction of Jerusalem in A.D. 70. They are the ones who would be looking for the Messiah. John sees himself as an evangelist to a cosmopolitan culture where people with different religious backgrounds are expecting the Messiah. John is pressing them to ask, Is Jesus the One we seek? So John's target audience is Jews who know the Old Testament because of their family background but who are now living in a Greek city such as Ephesus, which is ruled by the Romans. They speak two or three languages and are urban, educated people.

Along with them, John wants to reach the Greeks or Romans who live in the same cities and in the same environment as the Jews. Perhaps what is going on here is what Paul alluded to in his first chapter of Romans when he said that the gospel is to be preached first to the Jew and then to the Greek. This is what John and Paul may be suggesting: don't discount the Greek, but go first to the Old Testament believers in this multiple-culture setting.

I spent a few days in Santa Fe, New Mexico, last summer. It is a beautiful place, but what a complex culture! There is the old Spanish culture, the Native American culture, the Mexican culture, the Old West–cowboy culture, and the modern, New Age, neo-pagan culture. Santa Fe is spiritual potpourri. Could an evangelist in Santa Fe ignore the fact that the Mayan Indian selling jewelry in the town square is wearing a cowboy hat? Could he ignore the fact that the Mexican American is greatly influenced in his understanding of his own culture by the old Spanish culture and the New Age cultures all around him, as well as by his own Mexican roots? Multiple cultures affect the way the evangelist would talk about Christ. Multiple cultures affect John as he writes his Gospel account.

To use a musical metaphor, John is transposing the gospel into another cultural key. The reader of John must stand amid these multiple cultures with John and see him persuade especially Jews but also the Greeks in the world to which the Jews were scattered. John stays mindful of the fact that these Jewish people are now displaced. For example, he uses the Greek word for Messiah, *Christos*. Why? Because he knows that the Jewish people living in a Greek culture are more likely to use the Greek word for Messiah, not the old Hebrew word. He calls the Sea of Galilee (its Jewish name) the Sea of Tiberias. John knows that these Jews living in a Greek world would come to accept the name Tiberius for that lake because that is what the Greeks around them called it.

When you move to a new place, you learn a new vocabulary. Eleven years ago, before I moved to Texas, I had never once heard the expression, "That dog don't hunt." But now I say it all the time because now I'm a Texan and I have learned to speak like a Texan. I have taken on the vocabulary of the culture in which I live.

JOHN'S PASSION

John is not just a witness; he is a passionate witness who wants to communicate cross-culturally in order to get people to believe in Christ. That is why various forms of the term *believe* appear a hundred times in this Gospel and only about fifty times in the other three Gospels combined.

John is not just a witness; he is not just an evangelist. Above all else he is the beloved disciple. John never directly refers to himself, but four

amazing

times in this Gospel he speaks of himself in the third person as the disciple whom Jesus loved. The first time is in John 13:23: "There was reclining on Jesus' breast one of His disciples, whom Jesus loved." Customarily, those attending a formal meal in New Testament times would put the left elbow on a cushion and lean onto the table. Today we are always telling our children to get their elbows off the table, but it was acceptable in that day. The diner would actually be leaning to the left, so that his head would come close to the person on his left. To be immediately to the right of the Lord was not only a place of honor, it also provided an opportunity for a private conversation between John and Jesus.

Doesn't it seem a bit odd at first that John says, in effect, "I am the disciple whom Jesus loved"? To speak of one's self that way seems a little self-centered, and there is a subtle suggestion that maybe Jesus doesn't love other people as much! But that is not at all what John is suggesting.

For a Christian to think of himself as someone whom Jesus loves is not to suggest that other Christians are loved less; he is simply making it personal. It is the same thing that Paul does in Galatians 2:20 when he says that Jesus loved him and gave Himself for him. Every Christian needs to realize that remarkable truth.

There is a wonderful psychological dynamic in John's claim. D. A. Carson, in *The Gospel According to John,* says, "[T]hose who are most profoundly aware of their own sin and need, and who in consequence most deeply feel the wonders of the grace of God that has reached out and saved them, *even them,* are those who are most likely to talk about themselves as the objects of God's love in Christ Jesus."[1] John is deeply aware that he is loved.

I was thinking about being beloved of Christ and talking about it with one dear woman in our church. She said, "Oh, I need to hear that because I keep doubting it; I keep wondering, I keep questioning whether I'm doing enough, and I need to be released from that bondage and know that the Lord loves me—not only in spite of my sin but in the midst of it." The Lord wants us to grow into disciples and to grow away from all our folly and sin. But it is because we are so beloved in Him that He will change and transform us.

John saw himself as a Son of Thunder who would become the

John the

Apostle of Love. His response wasn't arrogance; it was amazement. He was simply overwhelmed by Jesus' love for him in the midst of his sin. We need to be overwhelmed, because we need to become more truthful and more passionate in our witness to Jesus Christ. Shallow understanding makes weak witnesses. We need to believe not just that the gospel is true but that it is true *for us.* That will make us passionate believers who will be transformed and who will then speak out of overflowing hearts as we dig deep into the content of the Word.

John shapes his whole Gospel with this theme: Jesus was and is the eternal Son of God who came from the Father, who bears the unique name, I AM, and who is the Father's special representative in this world. He came to bring lost sinners to the Father, out of death into life, out of darkness into light, out of hate into love. *Theme of JOHN*

We need to become culturally aware communicators at the outset of this new millennium. The evangelical church in America is becoming more culturally complex than ever. It is not your father's Oldsmobile; it is not the church that it was even ten years ago. It is not and never will be again.

That cultural complication will help us all hear the gospel better. When I see a brother listening to the gospel who doesn't look like me, act like me, or come from the same background as I do, it helps me hear the gospel better. I look at him and ask, *How is he hearing what that preacher is saying?* If we are all the same, then all we are doing is hearing it through the grid of our own established, hardened, cultural biases. The danger is that we won't hear the gospel at all.

From a church in another city, a large church considered wealthy and culturally homogenous, comes this account. One Sunday morning the church was very full and the pastor had just started his sermon. Everyone in the church looked nice, buttoned down, and clean-cut. Then a man entered the rear of the sanctuary who didn't fit. He wore blue jeans, an old ragged shirt, and an earring, and his hair was wild. Someone had been a passionate and truthful witness to that man on the street, and he had come to Christ. So now, he thought, *I need to go to church. Well, there's a church, so I'll go in.* He walked in a few minutes late, and the church was full, with no place to sit in the back. He kept walking down the middle aisle, looking for a seat, but he couldn't find one. As he searched from side to side, everyone watched. He arrived at the front of the sanctuary, and then he did what no one else in that church had ever done before. He just sat right down in front on the floor.

A few of the people who found that a bit culturally unconventional quietly made sounds of disapproval. Then, from about three-fourths of the way back, an old gentleman, an elder in the church, stood up. He was an elder's elder, with beautiful silver hair, a three-piece suit, and a watch fob. He walked down the aisle with everyone so silent that the only sound was the clink of his cane on the floor. Most were assuming that this elder was going to give a piece of his mind to that young man. But with great pain in his frail knees, he sat down on the floor next to that fellow so that he wouldn't be alone as he came to worship the Son of God.

We need to become beloved disciples just like John. Not only do we need to be effective and sensitive cultural communicators, but we also need to see ourselves as beloved disciples, disciples whom Jesus loves. Let us never separate truth and love. They don't separate. You are a beloved disciple if you are a disciple at all. We need to be amazed that we are so loved.

Like the woman I was talking to that day, we need to be willing to see that the only thing stronger than our pernicious attempts to prove to Jesus how worthy we are of Him is the effectiveness of His grace— which cuts to our heart, convicts us of sin, shows us our failure, shows us the phoniness of our own righteousness, and then picks us up and says, "You are loved."

If you are beginning the journey of faith with Jesus Christ, not even sure you've crossed that starting line, the Gospel of John is for you. And for those of us who are down the road a way, the Gospel of John is for us. For both groups, the wonder is that Jesus is truth and love, the Christ, the Son of God and that He quite simply overpowers us and overwhelms us by His love.

2

THE WORD

In the beginning was the Word, and the Word was with God, and the Word
was God. He was in the beginning with God. All things came into being by
Him, and apart from Him nothing came into being that has come into being.
In Him was life, and the life was the light of men. And the light shines in the
darkness, and the darkness did not comprehend it. There came a man, sent
from God, whose name was John. He came for a witness, that he might bear
witness of the light, that all might believe through him. He was not the light,
but came that he might bear witness of the light (John 1:1-8).

WHEN WE FIRST MOVED to Dallas, Barbara and I bought a house that
had a beautiful foyer. The people from whom we bought this house, who
had also built it, had a wonderful sense of proportion. The area was just
the right size and the right height, and the doors and stairs were in just
the right places. It was a pleasant place to welcome people into our
home.

John's prologue, 1:1-18, has been called the "foyer" to his Gospel.
It is the "entrance hall" to the whole book. All of the book's themes are
introduced in this beautiful foyer, then they are expanded upon throughout the rest of the Gospel: light, life, witness, truth, grace, the world. We
could say that the whole of the Gospel is packed into these verses.

The key idea of the prologue is that the Son of God came to be the
man, Jesus, so that God's glory, grace, and truth might not be abstractions. *Glory, grace, truth* seem to be abstract words, but not when they
are made real, visible, and tangible in the person of God's Son. The prologue is about the Incarnation, the "infleshness" of the second person
of the Trinity. It is God's "foyer" into this world. It is God's coming into
the entrance hall of this needy world in order to bring light and life and
hope and peace and joy and all that we say Christ is.

Let's look closely at verses 1-8, then we'll look at verses 9-18 in the next two chapters. This passage is clearly one of the high-water marks of Scripture. It is hard to say that some parts of Scripture are higher or better than other parts, and yet this is clearly a part of God's Word that has been used again and again in the lives of God's people—everyday, ordinary Christians like you and me. It has also been a key passage for understanding deep, important truths that have marked and guided the history of Christ's church.

JESUS IS THE ETERNAL WORD

Look at John 1:1: "In the beginning was the Word, and the Word was with God, and the Word was God." What does the word *Word* mean? John chose this word *Word* because it would have a certain ring to the people to whom he was primarily writing. Remember, the people to whom John was writing were Jews scattered throughout a Greek culture. The word *Word* had resonance to it for people in a Greek cultural setting, and many Greek philosophers had their own ideas about the meaning of this word.

More important in John's mind than any of those philosophers, however, is what the Old Testament meant by the word *Word*. In the Old Testament we read that by His Word, God creates (e.g., Gen. 1:3, 6, 9, etc.; Ps. 33:6). By His Word, God makes Himself known (Ps. 19:1). By His Word, God heals and delivers His people (Ps. 107:20). By His Word, God judges (Isa. 11:4). By His Word, God displays His wisdom (e.g., Prov. 8:1, 8). Though he doesn't say it explicitly until verse 14, we already know that John says Jesus Christ is the Word, the unique self-expression of the Trinity, the God who is three-in-one. The question that John raises right from the very first verse is, How does the triune God choose to express Himself? God expresses Himself by and through His Word. He creates, He makes Himself known, He redeems, He judges, and He gives wisdom by His Word. The first thing that we need to see in this passage is that Jesus Christ is God.

This prologue is striking. In the Gospels of Matthew and Luke we have genealogies at or near the beginning, tracing Jesus' human ancestors in the nation of Israel; but not in John. John is not ignoring Jesus' human family tree, but he wants to emphasize the eternal existence of the second person of the Trinity.

"In the beginning," he says, "was the Word." That is a deliberate, obvious reference to Genesis, to the creation itself. From eternity past, before creation ever took place, there was One called the Word. And the Word was God.

D. A. Carson says, "Stretch our imagination backward as we will, we can find no point in time where, 'There was once when he was not.'"[1] Carson was quoting a statement made many hundreds of years ago by a man named Arius. Arius sought to be a genuine Christian, but he was sadly mistaken in his understanding of Christ's eternal existence. After many councils and deliberations, the ancient church made a difficult but strong decision about Arius: he was a heretic because he said, in essence, that there was a time when the Word did not exist and a time when God created the Word. Over and against that view, Christians have said for two thousand years, "No, there was never a time when the Word, the second person of the Trinity, did not exist." There was never a moment when He was actually created by the Father. He has always been with the Father and has always been equal to Him.

I love the country of Japan, and have traveled there many times to participate in ministry. It is an intriguing country, with fascinating layers of culture including the art of greeting and bowing. When Japanese people bow, the one seeking to express that the other person has more dignity than himself bows the deepest. When Japanese people first meet, they are sizing one another up, trying to discern who has more dignity. They look at each other as they bow, trying to see which of them should bow the deepest, perhaps repeating bows deeper and deeper if it is not clear who is more dignified.

In eternity past, God the Father and God the Son faced each other and both bowed, but neither of them bowed more deeply than the other. Forever they have been equal in power and in dignity. In the very same breath John tells us that the Word not only *was* God but was *with* God. This is remarkable, because he just said that the Word *was* God, and now he says the Word was *with* God, which means that He is to be distinguished from God. He is not to be identified precisely as God the Father; He is a distinct person from God the Father. The word here for "with" is generally used in the New Testament to mean "with a person." John is stating that the Word who was with God and the One who is God Himself are real persons. From eternity past there has been "with-ness." The Father and the Son have forever been in a relationship of love and communion. This relationship—an eternal conversation, if you will—is really the mystery of the Trinity. The Trinity means that God is personal.

For those who have grown up in the Christian church, it is customary to say, "I have a personal relationship with God." Don't let this truth slide by you without pondering it for a while. It is deeply worth your most honest, soul-searching reflection. God is personal, not a cosmic force, not a primal principle. Make no mistake: no other existing world religion says that God is personal.

In the Trinity we cling to a God who is personal in Himself, because He is one God and yet He consists of more than one person. We cannot figure that out and never will. The implications of the Trinity are absolutely extraordinary. The very existence of all human relationships between people has its meaning in the triune relationship of the Father and the Son and the Spirit. The concept of there being "me-ness" and "you-ness" is an idea that comes from the me-ness and you-ness in God's own person. The standards of what human relationships are to be are established by God Himself. We look ultimately to God's relationship among Himself, with Himself, the persons of the Trinity, as the standard for all of our human relationships.

JESUS IS THE CREATOR OF ALL THINGS

John 1:3 states, "All things came into being by Him, and apart from Him nothing came into being that has come into being." It is emphatic. Nothing was created in any other way except through Him, the Word of God. The best expansion of this truth in the New Testament comes from Colossians 1:16, where Paul says, "For by Him all things were created," and then he lists, "both in the heavens and on earth, visible and invisible, whether thrones or dominions or rulers or authorities—all things have been created by Him and for Him." And Hebrews 1:2 says, "In these last days [God] has spoken to us in His Son, whom He appointed heir of all things, through whom also He made the world." God spoke the worlds into being. God speaks His Word and it happens.

God said, "Let there be light," and there was light (Gen. 1:3). God didn't say, "I'm going to establish a process whereby light will be created." No, He said, "Let there be," and there was.

God's Word was able to produce the reality of what He said. That is not true of my word. My word does not affect the reality of which I speak. I wish it did.

My wife, Barbara, says, "Dinner is ready."

I go to the stairs and say, "Carey, come down for dinner."

She cheerfully replies, "I'll be down in a minute, Dad."

Well, she may come down in a minute, she may come down in ten, and she may come down in thirty minutes. (Not in my house!) My word does not have within itself an intrinsic power to affect the reality of which it speaks. God's Word does.

We often speak of God the Creator, and that is true. But it is also correct to speak of Jesus, the Son, as the Creator. This, too, is part of the mystery of the Trinity. Though there are distinct persons in the Trinity and each one has His particular role, their roles overlap in such a way that you can speak of each one doing what the other does. You can say, for example, that the Father creates and redeems, and you can say the same of the Son.

JESUS IS THE SUSTAINER OF ALL THINGS

Jesus not only created all things; He sustains all things as well. John 1:4 says, "In Him was life." He is the Lord, the Giver, the Source of life, and He sustains life at every moment. At this very moment as you read this book, Jesus Christ, the eternal Word, is the life-support system who is keeping you breathing. Hebrews 1:3 says, "[He] upholds all things by the Word of His power." Dallas Willard, an author and professor at the University of Southern California, describes Christ as, "The Master of the molecule."[2] Jesus knows how molecules work and holds the molecules of the world together.

Isn't it absolutely amazing that at the very moment the incarnate baby Jesus was being held as a helpless infant in His mother's arms, needing to have His diaper changed, or hungry and wanting to nurse, He was holding the world together by the Word of His power!

Jesus Is the Revelation of God

Look again at John 1:4: "In Him was life, and the life was the light of men." Verses 6-7 tell us that John the Baptist came to point to that light: "There came a man, sent from God, whose name was John. He came for a witness, that he might bear witness of the light, that all might believe through him." If the Word is the light, then John the Baptist is like the rheostat. You may have a rheostat in your dining room, though you probably call it a "dimmer switch." You don't pay much attention to the rheostat as long as it is working properly. People don't come into your dining room and say, "Oh, what a lovely rheostat." No, what they notice is the effect of the rheostat. They see the intensity of the lights just the way you want it, shining perfectly on your china and crystal. John the Baptist's role was to turn up the intensity, the beauty, the revelation of the One, the Word, who was and is the Light.

What does *light* mean? It is a key word in the Gospel of John. If you scanned the Bible noting every time the word *light* was used, you would have to conclude that light means "knowledge," particularly knowledge that is revealed by God. We often see phrases such as "light of knowledge" in Scripture (e.g., 2 Cor. 4:6; Acts 26:18). We can say, in fact, that what we are to know about God is revealed fully in Christ. The knowledge of God has come to us through the Light, who is Christ. Jesus called Himself the "light of the world" (John 8:12; 9:5), and Paul says that, "God, who said, 'Light shall shine out of darkness,' is the One who has shone in our hearts to give the light of the knowledge of the glory of God in the face of Christ" (2 Cor. 4:6).

But right away, the opposite of light is introduced in this passage: "And the light shines in the darkness, and the darkness did not comprehend it" (John 1:5). Darkness means "no light." Darkness is the opposite of light. It means we cannot see what is right before us. Have you ever been in such darkness that you literally could not see your hand in front of your face? One summer I spent three days alone on a mile-wide island off the coast of Maine. Every night I had to get to my sleeping bag before the sun went down because once the sun set it was so dark that I would not have been able to find my sleeping bag.

In the Bible, darkness is a metaphor for sin. Because Adam and Eve's hearts were plunged into darkness, the hearts of all people since then have been in darkness as well. The Bible says that this darkness is so overwhelming, so complete, that we cannot see what should be clear in nature. As Paul says in Romans 1, the truth about God can be clearly seen in nature, but men's hearts are darkened and we cannot see what we have no right to miss (see vv. 20-21).

"And the light shines in the darkness, and the darkness did not comprehend it." The darkness keeps us from understanding what is clear, until the light of Christ dawns on us. Unfortunately, this darkness is not just a passive condition. When the Scripture speaks about darkness stealing across our hearts, it is talking about willful darkness. We turn down the rheostat, plunging our own hearts into darkness. We are born into darkness by virtue of Adam's sin, yet continually go around in the houses of our lives turning off the lights and stumbling in the darkness, acting as if we can see perfectly.

We cannot and will not see the very things that we must see in order to have life. In fact, according to John, we love darkness. You say, "Wait a minute, I don't love darkness; I like the light." But in 3:19, John says the opposite: "And this is the judgment, that the light is come into the world, and men loved the darkness rather than the light; for their deeds were evil."

Light has come into the world and we are like roaches scurrying for cover when the kitchen light is flipped on. They head for the darkness as quickly as possible, trying to hide from the light. That is God's diagnosis on our hearts. It is hard to hear. We do not eagerly run to Jesus and say, "Here is all my sin, all the bad stuff in my life." *Darkness* is John's word for that complex of thoughts, attitudes, and deeds which characterizes our hearts and blinds us to our true condition and to God.

So light means "knowledge." But more than just "knowledge of a body of ideas," it means "knowledge of God." It is not an abstraction. No, the light is the presence of the Lord in our lives. Biblical commentator F. F. Bruce put it this way: "When he [John] speaks of the true light, he is not thinking in abstractions; he is not primarily thinking of a body of teaching . . . ; to him the true light is identical with Jesus Christ, the Word made flesh."[3]

This is the same light that the prophet Isaiah was talking about in chapter 60 when he said, "Arise, shine; for your light has come, and the glory of the LORD has risen upon you. For behold, darkness will cover the earth, and deep darkness the peoples; but the LORD will rise upon you, and His glory will appear upon you. And nations will come to your light, and kings to the brightness of your rising" (Isa. 60:1-3).

Both Isaiah and John are using the image of dawn—light rising to dispel the darkness—allowing us to see what we have missed all night long. That is why we can speak so readily of the gospel dawning upon our hearts. One of the most thrilling things for me as a pastor is to look into the faces of people in church on a given Sunday morning and see the light of the gospel dawning upon them. There are people sitting there who have been in good evangelical Christian churches all their lives, yet the light switch of the gospel may be turning on for them for the first time. The truth of the light begins to make sense.

That verb "shines" is present tense. It is the only time that the present tense is used in these first eight verses of John 1. In verse 4 John says, "In Him was life, and the life was the light of men," referring to the appearance of Christ. There was a specific moment in time and history when Jesus came onto the scene. But in verse 5 John says, "The light shines in the darkness." The present tense means that the light keeps on shining. But the darkness will not comprehend this light. It does not comprehend this light to this day.

The New American Standard Version gives "overpower" as an alternative translation for "comprehend," and this alternative translation yields its own unique perspective on John's words here. The darkness will seek to overpower the light, but Jesus calls us to follow Him, the true, ever-shining Light.

The whole work of Christ, beginning before the dawn of creation, but specifically in time and space up to and especially including the Cross, was a conflict between the light that He brings and the darkness of sin that is constantly seeking to overpower it. Verse 5 begins in the present tense—"The light shines in the darkness"—but it ends in the past tense—"and the darkness did not overpower it." That past tense is a specific past tense, meaning it happened on a single occasion in history, a specific moment of time when the darkness, for all of its effort and ugliness, sought but failed to overpower the light. That was at the Cross. Certainly it must have been between the sixth and ninth hours, when a deep darkness fell over the face of all the earth, and Jesus Christ, the eternal Word of God, who was ever alive with the Father, died. The Ever-living One was overpowered with darkness.

But wait a minute. Didn't we just say that the darkness was overpowered by the light? At that very moment when the darkness was so thick and so real, it appeared as if the darkness had won. Jesus, the Everliving One, is hanging dead on a cross. How can that be victory? It is precisely the wonder of our redemption that the cross is not defeat. It is victory. For in the darkness that overcame Christ on that cross, in this moment of eternal separation from the Father, wonder of wonders, the light and the darkness actually came into bitter and decisive conflict and the darkness could not prevail.

Jesus Is the Light of Our Lives

The conflict between darkness and light has been decided once and for all. The eternal Son of God has punched His way through time and space, into history. By virtue of being the Light of life, He has come into the foyer of the lives of those He has redeemed. He then turns around and defends us from the powers of darkness which seek to overpower us. Jesus, the Eternal One, in time and space, bleeds and dies for us. But by the accomplishment of His death and resurrection, He has overpowered the darkness, and the darkness can no longer pervade our hearts and lives. The Light can shine not only in the foyer of our lives, but in every room—the living room, the TV room, the closet where the golf clubs are stored, the cabinet where the liquor is kept, the computer room, the bedroom.

The light and life of Christ can pervade our lives and overpower all the darkness and sin to which we cling so eagerly, so insanely, so irrationally. Jesus took all of it into His own soul. The darkness smote Him, and He is dead but is also raised to new life and to new light. "Arise, shine; for your light has come, and the glory of the LORD has risen upon you" (Isa. 60:1). Jesus Christ, the light of the world, blazes into every dark place and every dark corner of our hearts.

Like John the Baptist, will you be a rheostat in every crevice, corner, and room of your heart? Will you turn the dimmer switch all the way up to better display the brightest of light?

3

THE TRUE LIGHT

There was the true light which, coming into the world, enlightens every man. He was in the world, and the world was made through Him, and the world did not know Him. He came to His own, and those who were His own did not receive Him. But as many as received Him, to them He gave the right to become children of God, even to those who believe in His name, who were born not of blood, nor of the will of the flesh, nor of the will of man, but of God (John 1:9-13).

IMAGINE THAT YOUR LONG-LOST cousin suddenly appears at your house on Christmas Eve. He has been making his fortune in foreign lands, so you haven't seen him since you were both children. Now he has come to spend the holidays with you and, of course, you welcome him into your home. The next morning, after everyone has unwrapped their presents, he says, "I have one more present." He takes you outside and points to a brand-new BMW, fully equipped, sitting in the driveway. He gives you the keys and says it is yours.

Now stretch your imagination even further and see yourself responding with a yawn. "Time for some breakfast. I really need some coffee," you say, as you turn and go back into the house. Your cousin follows you and says, "No, I really mean it. I intend to give you this car. It's all yours!" But you are busy with the remote, looking for the first football game of the day. Everyone else in the family gets excited, and they take the car for a spin, but you are totally apathetic. In fact, by the end of the day you are so tired of hearing about the BMW that you take a sledgehammer to it.

That is a silly illustration; but unfortunately, it is exactly what we have done to the true light that God sent into the world.

This passage teaches us the truly astonishing notion that the true light of God has been sent into the world. God's Son came in flesh, in the fullness of humanity. It also shows us the equally if not more astonishing truth that when He did so, we would have nothing to do with Him. Even worse, we sought to destroy Him. These verses report the tragic indifference and destructive rebellion of men and women against God precisely at the point at which He shines His brightest in our lives. The most remarkable thing that could ever happen in the history of the universe is that God has given to us the most precious thing He could possibly give us, and we have taken a sledgehammer to it . . . to Him.

John speaks of Jesus Christ as the true light that comes into the world to enlighten us. Other lights are mere flickers or glimpses of the truth. C. S. Lewis said that before he was a Christian he had to deny any value in other religions, but after he became a Christian he was free to think that all religions—"even the queerest," as he put it—contain at least some hint of the truth. Why? Because all religions in some way point us to the need for the true light. But these other philosophies and creeds are like holding a candle to the sun, Lewis says; they offer light, but after the dawn of the gospel, the candle is really quite useless.[1]

THE LIGHT IS TRUE

Let's look closely at the phrase in John 1:9, "the true light which . . . enlightens every man." This light is true as opposed to false. Christians make a fantastic claim—there is objective, factual truth to the gospel. A generation ago, Francis Schaeffer called it "true truth," meaning it is true whether or not I believe it.

I first heard Dr. Schaeffer speak when I was a junior at Harvard in 1968, and I could not believe what he said. It was so simple that it was obvious. He said, "God is there." I thought, *Dr. Schaeffer, you're at Harvard. You've really got to do better than that.* Schaeffer continued to reiterate, "God is there." That was the basis of his whole epistemology, his understanding of how we know God at all. *The God Who Is There* became the title of his first book. Someone specific, with an absolute, objective identity and character exists who has nothing to do with either our preference or our perception.

We could prefer a god who is different altogether. I might prefer a god who was a cute little green man on the farthest planet just outside the range of the sharpest telescopes. You would really like him. He has pointed, smoking ears, and he loves people who like grilled cheese sandwiches. Would you believe in my little green man? Why is that ridiculous? It is my preference, so who can say it is ridiculous? It is ridiculous because I cannot objectively show you that that little green man exists. Objectively, he has no "is-ness."

The Christian claim is that God's character is an objective reality that is true beyond our perception of Him and beyond any preference we might have. All true morality is built on that truth—true morality is built on true theology. Our view of God is central to our having a true morality, because we cannot say something is right or wrong based merely on our own preference or our own perception. If God is not there as the One who is absolutely saying, "True is true, and this is wrong, and this is right," then there is no basis for morality. Today we see people either making up their own morality or denying any morality at all, because they are wise enough to know that if God is not objectively there, there can be no such thing as true morality.

John says the true light, Jesus Christ, coming into the world enlightens every man. That word *enlighten* has an interesting etymology. It is the Greek word *photizei*. It is where we get the word *photography*. It means that Jesus, as the true light, is the exact photograph of God. Hebrews 1:3 says, "He is the radiance of [God's] glory and the exact representation of His nature." Jesus is not anyone's perception or preference of truth; He is the true light that enlightens, that photographs God for every man. He is the true and perfect image of God.

THE LIGHT IS GENUINE AND ULTIMATE TRUTH

The gospel is true but the gospel is also genuine, and there is a subtle difference between those two adjectives. God's gospel is true because it is God's. It is tied to His character as one who cannot lie. A person speaks truth because he is a truthful person, and John uses the word *true* in this double meaning all through his Gospel. The gospel is factually true; but it is also genuinely true—because of the One who speaks it.

In 4:23, John speaks of "true worshipers." Is he speaking of people who truly worship the one who is objective truth? Yes. But they are also those who genuinely worship. In 6:32 John speaks of the "true bread" from heaven. It is bread that is real bread, but it is also *truthful* bread; it is bread that really feeds us. In 15:1 he speaks of the "true vine," which is not only the one true vine but also the vine that truly nourishes us. Even God Himself is spoken of as the "true God" in 17:3 (cf. 7:28). "True" is not only real; it is the opposite of phony. There is a uniqueness and authenticity to God's existence as He portrays Himself through the true light, Jesus Christ—an authenticity we cannot find anywhere else.

John goes one more step in describing the truth of this true light. "True" also means "ultimate." While the manna in the wilderness was temporary, Jesus is the true bread, meaning the "ultimate bread," the bread that really feeds us like no other. While Israel was the vine (Ps. 80:8; Jer. 2:21; etc.), Jesus is the "true vine" (John 15:1), the ultimate vine that sustains our lives. And while there were the lights of the prophets in the Old Testament, now Jesus is the true light because He brings that light to us and *is* Himself the ultimate Light.

THE WORLD'S LIGHT

Isaiah speaks of the true light in chapter 60 of his prophecy. In verse 3 he says, "Nations will come to your light, and kings to the brightness of your rising." All people benefit from the coming of Christ, the true light, into the world. This is a wonderful statement about "common grace." The term *common grace* means that God's grace through Christ extends in some way to every human being, whether or not that human being happens to believe in Him. Let me give you an example. Say you live in a tiny village in Saskatchewan and there is no teacher for the children of your little village. You send for one, and finally a teacher comes. The students in the classroom will be the ones who will most immediately benefit from the teacher's presence. But the whole town will eventually become enlightened because of the education the children receive. That is common grace. The true light that comes into the world enlightens every man. Yes, primarily the students, those who are followers of Christ, are benefited; but from them the benefit extends to all the world.

THE WORLD'S MISSED OPPORTUNITY

Now look at John 1:10: "He was in the world, and the world was made through Him, and the world did not know Him." Christ is for the world, and the very availability of His light underscores the tragedy of this verse. The word *world* is repeated three times. Each time, in the original Greek, it appears first and thus is emphasized. The first phrase is literally, "In the world, He was." The verb expresses continuity, meaning that Jesus was in the world over an extended period of time. We know from the Old Testament that the light of Christ shone upon the world through all the working of the Old Testament prophets, priests, and kings. Of course, most fully and completely, the light of Christ was in the world through His Incarnation. The Incarnation is the focal point of Christ's presence, but His presence outlasts His physical appearance on earth. Before ascending back to His Father, Jesus promised that He would not leave us alone (14:16-18).

The second use of *world* in 1:10 is "the world was made through Him." The world owes its very existence to Christ, who is the upholding principle of all creation. All things were made "by Him and for Him" (Col. 1:16). We have already pondered the mystery that, as the little baby Jesus lay helpless in His mother's arms, He was holding together the molecules of the world.

The third use of the word *world* in John 1:10 has a heightened sense of drama to it: "He was in the world, and the world was made through Him . . ." We would expect the third part of this trilogy to say, "And the world received Him as its splendid Lord of light and glory." Irony of ironies, tragedy of tragedies, it says that the world did not know Him, did not acknowledge Him. The word *ironic* is best to describe that. It would be funny if it were not so sad. The world rejects its owner and maker.

One of the great Christian apologists of our age, Cornelius Van Til, taught this truth with a simple little word picture. He said it is like holding your baby in your lap. Your child slaps you in the face with his little hand. The baby can reach your face because you are holding him up, and so God is holding us up, holding our very existence together so that we can slap Him. In thus rejecting Jesus, the world is missing a huge opportunity, something incredibly valuable.

I wear contact lenses, and sometimes I lose one. They are not the throwaway kind, so when I lose one it needs to be found. It usually happens in the bathroom as I am standing there half dressed with the water running down the drain. The contact is gone. It is either on my clothes or the counter or floor or down the drain or in the sink, and I can't find it because I can't see! But I am afraid to move because I might step on it. So I stand there and do the only sane and rational thing I can do. I yell, "Barbara!" She has learned to recognize that call. It happens about once every other month. She comes with the flashlight, and, sure enough, in about ninety seconds she finds my contact. When I lose a contact, it is inconvenient, but it is not tragic. But when the world lost the One who came into the world as the true light that enlightens everyone, it wasn't just inconvenient; it was tragic.

The "world" in verse 10 means the majority of humanity. It is more specific than the "all things that came into being" of verse 3. It means the "all things that are all people"; and even more specifically, it refers to those who oppose God and His Son. The "world" is humankind gone wrong, a world shattered by human rebellion. This world stands under God's judgment as His opponent; and yet, amazing, it is also the object of God's love. That is so ironic, so unbelievable. Why should God love this lost, forsaken group of people who have turned away from Him? *God's love is so great not because the world is so big, but because the world is so bad.* That is what makes His love so significant. Christ comes into the world to save it, not to judge it.

A GREATER TRAGEDY

Here is the tragedy far greater than the rejection of a BMW. The world did not know Jesus. We didn't just fail to recognize Him as we might fail to recognize an acquaintance whom we hadn't seen for many years. We failed to acknowledge Him. We know who He is, yet we fail to acknowledge Him for who He is.

Not too long after college, when a good friend announced his engagement, I expected to be asked to be his best man at the wedding. He didn't ask me to be in the wedding at all! What a blow! Yet we do not even invite Christ to the wedding! What if a college student came home for the Christmas holidays and no one welcomed him or even acknowledged his presence? That is what we have done to Christ.

It is as though you had a really strange brother, and you were a little embarrassed by him. When you go out in public with him, you act as if you don't know him. That is what we do with Jesus. The world is a little embarrassed about Jesus.

The content of verse 11 heightens this tragedy: "He came to His own, and those who were His own did not receive Him." This is not just our passive failure to acknowledge Jesus, but our willful rejection of God's revelation. We have deliberately rejected the true light from God. He came to His own. He came *home*. He came home for Christmas vacation, and we did not acknowledge Him in His own home. His own people rejected Him. Yes, that is primarily a reference to Israel; but in the context here, which is talking about the whole world, all of us—the entire world—represent Christ's home.

Many years ago, I went to my tenth high school class reunion. I happened to be in my hometown in Connecticut the summer of the reunion. I would never have even considered going to my high school reunion had I not been in the area already. But there I was. I had no excuse. I would have been ashamed of myself if I hadn't gone, faced the music, faced my old friends. As I walked in the door of this reunion, I was afraid that no one would recognize me. (It is the stuff that nightmares are made of.) As it turned out, I was recognized and immediately fell into familiar patterns of banter with old friends. But Jesus came to His homefolk for a reunion and there was no familiar banter. He was not only not recognized, He was kicked out.

WE ARE THE WORLD

Let's be honest: it is abundantly obvious that "the world" in John 1:10-11 is none other than us. It will do no good to say that the world is that other guy or gal, the pagan in Micronesia or the person down the street who lives a terrible life. No, we miss the truth and the beauty of the gospel if we do not first see that we are the world. We have rejected the Lord of glory in spite of all our Christmas carols and pageants and cards. We want light, but we don't want the true light.

"But the next verse covers us," we want to say. "Yes, John 1:12 is our verse." "But as many as received Him, to them He gave the right to become children of God, even to those who believe in His name, . . ." Yes, that verse covers us, but only if we are not presumptuous about it.

Our eternal lives hang in the balance of the verb tenses in verse 12. Having "received" Jesus refers to an act that took place at a definite point in time. It happened, it's over; it's in the past. There was a time when those of us who are true believers received Him. To those people, God "gave" the right to become sons or daughters. In a moment in time, He gave us the privilege of our status. But the third verb is, "those who believe in His name." That verb is in the present continuous tense—it is an ongoing belief. Who are those who received Jesus? Who are those to whom He gave eternal life, the right to become children of God? They are those who believe in Him *today*.

It is no good to say, "When I was sixteen, I went to Christian camp and accepted Jesus." Or, "I responded to the altar call in my Baptist church when I was twenty." No, the proof of whether or not you are walking in the true light is your belief in Him today, amid the real and practical issues of your daily life. A child who is sick, a serious diagnosis from your doctor, a financial catastrophe, a wayward teenager, a trial that is harder than you ever believed you could bear—in all of the issues of real life, is Jesus real? Is He the light of your life in those things? If He is, then you are walking in the true light. It is the best possible proof that you have received Jesus and that you have been given the privilege of being a son or daughter of God.

Verse 13 is critical for our understanding of what it means to keep on believing: " . . . who were born not of blood, nor of the will of the flesh, nor of the will of man, but of God." The thing that has brought you to salvation is not your ancestors, nor your blood relatives, nor your ethnicity. For John's early readers, it was not that they were Jewish. For us, it is not the fact that we are cultural Christians. In fact, the irony of the gospel is that God is pleased to save those who seem most unsuited to becoming His sons and daughters.

It is thrilling to hear the accounts from lively gospel-centered churches especially in urban centers where drug addicts, prostitutes, and others who do not seem to fit in the kingdom of God come by the hundreds and thousands when God does a great miracle of His grace in their hearts. When you hear of their stories, it is important to ask yourself, Has God done that miracle of grace in my own heart? Do I believe in Him today? Do I need the Light today?

An Explosion of Light

More than 1,800 years after John said that Jesus is the true light, the true image, the true photograph of God, the camera was invented. I am no expert on photography, but I do know that a picture is made when an explosion of light appears on film in certain conditions.

Last year our family had its picture taken for a new photo directory at our church. Following the photo session, we went into a little room and met with people from the company producing the directory. Their job was to sell us as many poses as they could. They showed me an individual picture of me taken for the church staff page and said, "Now, Pastor Ryan, for a little bit extra we can touch it up." I replied, "Have at it!" Unlike my photographs, however, Jesus Christ is the *exact* photograph of God—no touching up done, no touching up needed. He is the real thing: true, genuine, ultimate.

I love pictures. If you come into my office, you will see nearly a hundred of them of my family, staff members, elders, and deacons of our church, and other friends. One of my favorite photographs is of my son in his football uniform. He gave it to me for Christmas and signed it, "For my #1 fan. Love, Chris." Imagine I invite you into my office and say, "Here is a picture of my son, my only son. Isn't that a beautiful portrait?" Then you take that portrait of my magnificent son and smash the frame and rip the picture. That is what the world has done to God's portrait of His Son.

The true light came into the world to explode onto the lives of those who receive Him, who believe in His name. That Light exploded into your heart and life in a moment of time when the Son of God hung on a cross and died for your sin and poured out His lifeblood for you. Has that picture been emblazoned on your heart? That portrait is God's great gift to you.

4

THE WORD MADE FLESH

And the Word became flesh, and dwelt among us, and we beheld His glory, glory as of the only begotten from the Father, full of grace and truth. John bore witness of Him, and cried out, saying, "This was He of whom I said, 'He who comes after me has a higher rank than I, for He existed before me.'" For of His fulness we have all received, and grace upon grace. For the Law was given through Moses; grace and truth were realized through Jesus Christ. No man has seen God at any time; the only begotten God, who is in the bosom of the Father, He has explained Him (John 1:14-18).

QUESTION: WHAT DOES GOD LOOK LIKE? *Answer:* We don't know. John 1:18 says that no one has seen God at any time. God is invisible or "incorporeal" to us. He doesn't have a *corpus,* a body.

A mother was watching her little daughter draw a picture and asked, "What are you drawing?" Her daughter said, "A picture of God." This mother, knowing something of John 1 and other scriptures about God's appearance, said, "But no one knows what God looks like." The little girl said, "Well, they will when I get through!"

Verse 18 says that if you want to know what God looks like, look at Jesus. If you want to know what God thinks, see what Jesus thinks. If you want to know what God says, see what Jesus says. If you want to know God's plan, it has been fully revealed to us in Christ. All that we need to know of God is in His Word, the Son. We can look at Jesus and understand God.

Verse 18 says that Jesus is the One who "explains" who God is. To "explain," in the Greek, means to "unpack," to "see all the parts separately," to "see the thing unfold like a flower." "Exegete" is actually the formal term. Jesus exegetes God, explaining who He is. In Colossians 1:15, Paul says that Jesus is "the visible image of the invisible God"

(NLT). And in Hebrews 1:3 Jesus is called "the exact representation of [God's] nature." The claim of the New Testament is broad and deep. Jesus says He is the truth and the life and that no one comes to the Father or to know the Father apart from Him (John 14:6).

But how do we know what Jesus looks like? We do not have pictures of Jesus in the sanctuary of the church I serve, for a good reason: it would be a violation of the second commandment. Jesus does not come to us visually, appealing to our eyes. He comes by a Word. God intends for His revelation to unfold in the Scripture in the primacy of the ear over the eye. This is not to say that visual beauty is not important; it is simply to say that, in God's way of revealing Himself, the ear is more important than the eye; God reveals Himself by a Word, a person, His Son.

To see Jesus, we must hear God speak. God's Word is the most accurate expression of Himself—in Scripture and, mostly and fully, in the person of His Son. We hear to see; or, to put it another way, we see by hearing. Even when you read the Bible, using your eyes, you are actually "hearing" it. This was certainly true until the printing press was invented, before which God's people would listen, often for long periods of time, to God's Word being read to them.

WORDS ARE NOT CHEAP

Language, however, has fallen on hard times. The modern person, especially the "postmodern" person, will immediately ask, "Can language adequately convey meaning to me? You tell me that the 'Word' is the form in which God reveals Himself, and that it is supremely in the Word that I come to know God; but words are cheap." There are more words in the Sunday morning newspaper of most large cities than there are in the Bible. In the post-Gutenberg era, to say nothing of the electronic information age in which we live, words do seem to have little value.

There is a crisis in the meaning of language today. Words are being degraded, their value for communication deteriorating, and we are all part of the problem. A certain deodorizer is described as the "breath of springtime." What in the world does that mean? A cough drop claims that it is the "most advanced formula." Really? We live in an era of language inflation. We know the danger of overstatement in a fight with a spouse or a teenager: "You always do that," or, "You are always guilty of that." That discussion will rapidly deteriorate! But advertisers do that to us all the time.

There is also a crisis of clarity in language. Words are used to create a mood rather than to define reality. We might overhear two women speaking: "Oh, darling, you look so beautiful today. Why, your hair is fabulous. Your makeup . . . blah, blah, blah."

Guys have their own version of that: "Hey, man, how's it going? How's your golf game today? Hey, did you see that game Saturday on TV? . . . chatter, chatter, chatter."

Our social chatter gives rise to a lack of clarity about language, to a devaluation of the meaning of words.

An elder and dear friend in the church I served in Virginia uses words very carefully. He is a professor at the University of Virginia, and he knows the value of language. I could ask him, "David, what do you think about this?" He might not say a word for what seemed to be a long time. Finally, he would speak some carefully chosen and wise words. While it frustrated me at times, I actually came to admire it because, by using them sparingly, he was saying how important words are. Words aren't used just to create a feeling. Words are used to convey content, reality, and truth.

There is a branch of philosophy called language analysis which says that there can be no clear meaning to words because all language is subjective and, in the end, relative. This philosophy asks, If we interpret the meaning of words, how can we use them to explain something that is ultimately and objectively true? Language analysis has seeped into the way we think today, causing us to devalue words. Many people no longer believe language is a useful or significant vehicle for the communication of truth.

WORDS AS AGENTS OF ACTION

Quite a different approach to language is given to us in Scripture. In the Bible, the spoken and then written (inscripturated) word is seen as the effective agent for accomplishing God's will. It not only can communicate truth, it can "actually actualize" the truth it communicates. So in

Psalm 33:6 we read, "By the word of the LORD the heavens were made." God's Word is God's action in God's world.

In Greek thought, with which John is consciously doing dialogue in John 1:18, the word is detached from the world. It is a divine rational principle, the *logos* that is a respectable bridge between an unknowable God and the material world.

But in Scripture the Word is not passively detached but passionately involved. John says that the Word is not a principle but a person, not just a personification of divine truth but a person who is the Truth, the Word speaking with meaning and clarity in the Son. In fact, John says that the Word is so involved with the world that He became flesh. There could be no greater way in which God could say that He was utterly committed to all that this world is, than by saying that the Word, who was the eternal Son of God, became flesh. The Bible doesn't say that Christ became a *man* or a *body,* though those things are true; it says that He became *flesh* (v. 14), because that is the most graphic way it can be said.

THREE SCANDALS

There are three scandals in the New Testament. One is that God speaks in words, that He values language even when we don't. The second scandal is that God dies on a cross in the person of His Son. And the third scandal is that God becomes flesh. The precise words are important here in John 1:14. It doesn't say that the Word *changed into* flesh but that the Word *became* flesh. God, without ceasing to be God, became man. There was no diminishing of His deity but an acquiring of manhood. Jesus is one hundred percent God and one hundred percent man. Now, how one hundred percent plus one hundred percent can equal one hundred percent, I don't know and cannot understand.

It is the stuff of poets, isn't it? G. K. Chesterton, writing at the beginning of the twentieth century, made his own effort to understand. As he thought of God becoming flesh and lying in a barn or cave with farm animals, he said,

> The child that was ere worlds begun, . . .
> The child that played with moon and sun,
> Is playing with a little hay.[1]

The Christmas card on which I saw that quotation from Chesterton said inside, "May He who flung the moon and the stars in their place and then plunged into our humanity, bewilder us once again, each and all."

When the eternal Word, who was God, became the man Jesus, He did not stop being the eternal Word. He was and is that eternal Word, the only begotten of the Father. When He became man, He acquired additional properties without changing His original nature.

This is tough stuff. No wonder the church took four hundred and fifty years to hammer out this concept. The Chalcedon Definition says, "The distinction of [His] natures [is] by no means taken away by the union, but rather the property of each nature being preserved."[2] The second person of the Trinity is distinctly God, distinctly man, united in one person, the man, the Lord, the God, Jesus. The Son of God remains the infinite and unchangeable Word of God, and yet the infinite enters the finite. The Word *became* flesh; He did not take on a human body, throwing on flesh like a coat over His essential self. His whole nature became that of a human being.

THE ERROR THAT PERSISTS

One reason John emphasizes the flesh of Jesus Christ, and why the early Christians spent a lot of time discussing this truth, is that in the first centuries of the church the heretical teaching of docetism was gaining ground. Docetism claimed that Christ was God but not man; He only appeared to be human. This teaching is as misleading as the teaching that Christ was man but not God. Docetism has been taught in history in some form or another right up to our new twenty-first century.

Salvador Dalí, who painted melting clocks hanging over ledges, also often painted Christ. His famous painting *The Crucifixion* has Jesus hanging on the cross, but He is not really hanging on the cross. He is actually about three feet from the cross, suspended in air. Dalí is saying that Jesus wasn't a real man who really died on a real cross with real nails, real wood, real flesh. No, He just seemed to be. Dalí's painting *The Last Supper* is the traditional scene of the apostles gathered around the table, and there is Jesus in the middle as usual. But look closely and you will see that Jesus is transparent. Dalí has painted Him as if He were a ghost, a vapor or spirit, but not a man.

For many, the idea that God would become a man is too dirty, too low, too base. Docetics of all varieties throughout history cannot accept the fact that God can tolerate human flesh even if we cannot—that He is able to sympathize with our weaknesses because He is flesh; that He is able to come to our aid in the midst of our temptations because He is flesh.

TABERNACLED AMONG US

When a person makes his home among people, he moves in with them. He identifies with them. The Incarnation is the moving in of the eternal Word so that He utterly identifies with us in every way. He took the whole nature of a human being, fully and totally identifying with all that it means for us to be human, including that which psychologists tell us is the most traumatic event of human life—birth. A well-loved Christmas carol contains the line, "He abhors not the virgin's womb."[3] This should cause a bit of wonder and awe. The eternal God of all the universe did not abhor a virgin's womb. How messy! I assisted with the delivery of two of our children. A few minutes before Christopher, our first child, was born, Barbara's obstetrician asked, "Do you want to do this?"

I said, "Sure."

He said, "Wash up." And I did. I delivered Christopher, and two years later I delivered Carey. I thought I might drop her, she was so slippery. Birth is messy! What a wonder that the eternal Word of God did not shun being born.

It had to happen this way. Only in the complete identification with our flesh could Christ be the Second Adam, the perfect man that Adam was not. Adam sinned and died as a man; only as a man could Jesus do what Adam failed to do and be the mediator between God and man. Why? Because only flesh can die.

THE GLORY OF THE TABERNACLE

The same truth is amplified in the next phrase of John 1:14, "the Word dwelt among us," literally, "tabernacled among us," which means, "He pitched a tent among us." The Old Testament tabernacle is where God moved in and lived with His people. This tabernacle had no meaning apart from Jesus Christ. Its whole purpose in the wilderness was to point people forward to the true Tabernacle who was to come, the Son of God. "For in Him all the fulness of Deity dwells in bodily form" (Col. 2:9).

Think about Jesus as the Tabernacle:

The tabernacle was for use in the wilderness: "Jesus was led up by the Spirit into the wilderness" (Matt. 4:1).

The tabernacle was outwardly humble and unattractive: "He has no stately form or majesty that we should look upon Him, nor appearance that we should be attracted to Him" (Isa. 53:2).

The tabernacle was where God met with men: "I am the way, and the truth, and the life; no one comes to the Father, but through me" (John 14:6).

The tabernacle was the center of Israel's camp, a gathering place for God's people: "And I, if I be lifted up from the earth, will draw all men to Myself" (John 12:32).

The tabernacle was where the priests and their families came to be fed: "I am the bread of life" (John 6:35).

The tabernacle was where sacrifices for the sins of God's people were made: "But He, having offered one sacrifice for sins for all time, sat down at the right hand of God" (Heb. 10:12).

The tabernacle was a place of worship: "My Lord, and My God" (John 20:28).

We do not understand the teaching of the Old Testament in all of its fullness unless we read it through Jesus Christ—His incarnation, life, death, and resurrection. The tabernacle has absolutely no meaning apart from Jesus.

"BEHOLD HIS GLORY"

Thousands of years before Jesus, God purposed that there be a tabernacle in order that there would be One who would fulfill the meaning of that tabernacle, who would be the true Tabernacle for us. Just as the tabernacle in the wilderness contained and displayed God's glory (Ex. 40:34-35), even more do we behold "the glory of God in the face of Christ" (2 Cor. 4:6).

Moses sought to look upon the glory of God and he was warned by God Himself not to look (Ex. 33:18-20); but we have the privilege of looking upon the face of the Word of God, upon Jesus, by faith through

His Word. Later, one day, by sight we will see the face of Jesus, who will be the full revelation of God and manifestation of His glory.

Glory means *weight* in the literal Hebrew. Many Christians today are into what we could call "Christian lite," like a "lite" beer. "Give me a little Jesus, just enough to make me happy." God thunders into our lives in His flesh and says that we behold in Him the glory of God, full of grace and truth.

Grace? What is grace? Is it a sprinkling of fairy dust; a warm, happy feeling? No. Grace is a power that lifts you out of the domain of darkness and transfers you to the domain of light. Grace is God's magnificent power erupting in your heart and soul by His own intervention so that you move from death to life, from darkness to light, from hell to heaven. Grace is power that is embodied in a person.

What is truth? Twenty-five times in the Gospel of John we read about truth. Does truth mean "factual truth?" Yes, it does. "Objective truth?" Yes. But it means more than that; it also means truth that is embodied, infleshed. It means truth that is in the character of an individual. We find in Jesus Christ the One whose glory is displayed by the grace and the truth that He powerfully delivers to people.

Glory in the Gospel of John is used to describe the death of Christ. That is amazing. In John 12:23-24, for example, we read, "And Jesus answered them, saying, 'The hour has come for the Son of Man to be glorified. Truly, truly, I say to you, unless a grain of wheat falls into the earth and dies, it remains by itself alone; but if it dies, it bears much fruit.'" John Donne, in *The Book of Uncommon Prayers,* says, "The whole of Christ's life was a continual passion; others die martyrs, but Christ was born a martyr. He found a Golgotha, where he was crucified, even in Bethlehem, where he was born; for to his tenderness then the straws were almost as sharp as the thorns after, and the manger as uneasy at first as the cross at last. His birth and his death were but one continual act, and his Christmas Day and his Good Friday are but the evening and the morning of one and the same day. From the crèche to the cross is an inseparable line. Christmas only points forward to Good Friday and Easter. It can have no meaning apart from that, where the Son of God displayed his glory by his death."[4] Grace and truth are a person.

Last year Barbara and I received a Christmas letter from an old friend. She had recently discovered that the breast cancer she thought she had beaten seven years ago had returned and metastasized. She wrote, "Our lives have pretty much been turned upside down since then. I can't drive or pick up anything heavy, including my sweet children. And I am fatigued much of the time, due to the treatments. I have been receiving radiation five days a week. I also can't tell you how many big and little miracles the Lord has done through this whole process. I have literally felt buoyed by the prayers of hundreds of people who have faithfully prayed for me through this time. In some strange way it is the best and worst of times. I have not felt so close and carried by the Lord in years or so deeply connected to my dear friends as I have in this season of life. One major truth that shouts to me at this time is the goodness of God. As awful as this cancer is and the accompanying treatments can be, our home has literally been flooded by the goodness of God, often carried by the human hands of friends and family. The poignant letters, the sweet musical gifts, the delicious food treats, toys for the children, and tender hugs and foot rubs have been ever-present reminders to us of God's ultimate goodness."

How can a woman in this extreme difficulty say that God is good? She answers that question at the end of her letter. She does so by quoting from Julian of Norwich, a saint of the fourteenth century. She says, "He has written words that sustain me through multiple trips to the M.R.I., tubes, and late-night ponderings all alone." And then she quotes Julian: "Whatever we may suffer, God has already suffered. The worst has already happened and has been repaired. All shall be well. All shall be well. And all manner of things shall be well."

Only a person who understands that the Son of God has utterly and completely identified with her amid the most serious crisis of her life can say that God is good. Only someone who understands that God is for her, so much for her that He took upon Himself the flesh of her own trial, can rejoice in her suffering. God's Son was not spared, so that He could die for all of our trials and weaknesses and diseases. He died for everything that would threaten us and keep us from heaven, especially the sin that so deeply embeds itself in our hearts. Only bleeding flesh could die for all of that. And die He did, that He might be raised to new life and to the glory which He shared in the Father's presence from all eternity. He lives and makes intercession for you in your hurt, your disease, and your loss right now. Grace is a person; Truth is a person—Jesus, come to you in the flesh.

Part II

The Witness of the Son of God in Word and Works

5

THE VOICE OF WITNESS

And this is the witness of John, when the Jews sent to him priests and Levites from Jerusalem to ask him, "Who are you?" And he confessed, and did not deny, and he confessed, "I am not the Christ." And they asked him, "What then? Are you Elijah?" And he said, "I am not." "Are you the Prophet?" And he answered, "No." They said then to him, "Who are you, so that we may give an answer to those who sent us? What do you say about yourself?" He said, "I am a voice of one crying in the wilderness, 'Make straight the way of the Lord,' as Isaiah the prophet said." Now they had been sent from the Pharisees. And they asked him, and said to him, "Why then are you baptizing, if you are not the Christ, nor Elijah, nor the Prophet?" John answered them saying, "I baptize in water, but among you stands One whom you do not know. It is He who comes after me, the thong of whose sandal I am not worthy to untie." These things took place in Bethany beyond the Jordan, where John was baptizing.

The next day he saw Jesus coming to him, and said, "Behold, the Lamb of God who takes away the sin of the world! This is He on behalf of whom I said, 'After me comes a Man who has a higher rank than I, for He existed before me.' And I did not recognize Him, but in order that He might be manifested to Israel, I came baptizing in water." And John bore witness saying, "I have beheld the Spirit descending as a dove out of heaven, and He remained upon Him. And I did not recognize Him, but He who sent me to baptize in water said to me, 'He upon whom you see the Spirit descending and remaining upon Him, this is the one who baptizes in the Holy Spirit.' And I have seen, and have borne witness that this is the Son of God" (John 1:19-34).

No man has seen God at any time; the only begotten God, who is in the bosom of the Father, He has explained Him (1:18).

SOMETIMES THE MOST STIRRING moment in a Christian meeting is during someone's testimony. That word *testimony* is fairly commonplace in the vocabulary of many Christians. In fact, the word can be overused. We talk about "giving our testimony" or "speaking our testimony about what Jesus has done for us." The word comes a bit too glibly to our lips, a bit too loosely in our conversation sometimes. But it is nevertheless a good word because it is a Bible word. The word that *testimony* comes from is the Bible word *witness*. This word is at the center not only of this middle part of John 1 but really of the first four chapters of the Gospel. Here we find a number of different people bearing witness to the Son of God and to His words and works.

The whole shape of this Gospel of John is a testimony, a witness. The atmosphere reminds us of depositions being taken in a courtroom, a succession of witnesses coming forward and bearing witness, giving testimony to who the Son of God is.

As we saw, the witnessing actually begins in the very first verses of the Gospel, in the famous prologue. Right at the end of that prologue, in verse 18, we are told that Jesus Himself "explains" God. As we have seen, the literal rendering of the Greek is that He "exegetes" God. He makes God known. He interprets God. He narrates God, you might say. Jesus tells us the story of God.

How does Jesus explain God, exegete Him, interpret Him? John says that Jesus explains God by being Himself the living incarnate Son of God. "Because we long to know who God is," John says, "we look to the Son of God." When we want to know what God thinks, we ask what the Son of God thinks. When we want to know what is on God's heart, we look to see what is on the heart of the Son of God as He is portrayed to us in this Gospel. When we want to know what concerns God has about His world, we look to see what concerns the Son of God expresses, for He is the fullest expression, the exact representation of God (Heb. 1:2-3).

So we find in the opening chapters of John a number of witnesses coming forward to say, "Jesus—He is the Son of God. This is how I know that this is true. This is what it means to me that He is the Son of God." In this Gospel, the Father Himself bears witness to Jesus as the Son of God. The Scriptures, we are told, bear witness to Jesus as the Son of God. John, the Gospel writer, himself bears such witness. Jesus bears witness to Himself. And in the first chapter of this Gospel, John the Baptist bears witness to Jesus as the Son of God. John the Baptist is first mentioned as a witness in the prologue: "There came a man, sent from God, whose name was John. He came for a witness, that he might bear witness of the light, that all might believe through him" (John 1:6-7). Then in verse 19 we read: "This is the witness of John [the Baptist]."

John the Baptist gives his testimony: "If you want to know who God is, look at Jesus. God has explained His ways, His truth, His love, His grace, His power, His judgment, His empathy, His joy, and His sorrows in the Son, so look at Him." John comes forward, swears the oath, takes the box, sits down, and begins his testimony. As is often the case in a court of law, the lawyer will begin by asking the person something about himself. There is no lawyer here asking John the Baptist questions, but John begins by bearing witness about himself, and then he bears witness to Jesus Christ.

JOHN THE BAPTIST'S WITNESS ABOUT HIMSELF

We know from this Gospel and other places that John the Baptist was born into a priestly family. He belonged to the tribe of Levi and was, in fact, a cousin to the Lord Jesus Himself. He began his work when he was twenty-nine or thirty years old. As this scene begins, he is baptizing people in the Jordan River, a baptism called in other New Testament passages a "baptism of repentance" (Luke 3:3; Acts 19:4).

In his reply to the Jewish leaders sent from Jerusalem to question him about his identity, we learn a lot about who John the Baptist is *not*. The religious establishment, particularly the priests and the Levites, are most interested in the purification rites of baptism, and here is this strange fellow way out in the countryside, seventeen miles from Jerusalem, not at the temple at all, but in the river, who is baptizing. Given what John the Baptist is doing, it would be irresponsible for the priests and Levites not to check him out.

The Levites mentioned here are not the sons of Aaron, so they really are not priests in the Old Testament sense. In Jesus' day these Levites were primarily musicians, but they served also as the temple police.

"Who are you?" they ask John the Baptist. They really mean, "What is the significance of what you are doing here? After all, you are *baptizing* people!"

John the Baptist is emphatic in his answer: "He confessed, and did not deny, and he confessed, 'I am not the Christ'" (John 1:20). *Confess* and *deny* are legal words, courtroom language. They are appropriate for John, as he gives his testimony. He says it clearly; he does not hedge about who he is not: he is not Christ. Remember, the word *Christ* is the Greek word for *Messiah*. John the Baptist is saying, "I am not the one the Jews are expecting. I'm not the Messiah of Old Testament expectation."

Secondly, he says he is not Elijah. Malachi 4:5 tells us that the prophet Elijah will return before the Messiah comes; and, in fact, an angel at the time of John the Baptist's birth says that he, John the Baptist, would go before Jesus "in the spirit and power of Elijah" (Luke 1:17). God sent John, who was like Elijah, one who had the same type of ministry and personality. But John rightly denies that he is Elijah himself.

Furthermore, John says, "I am not the Prophet" (see John 1:21, 25). This is a reference to Deuteronomy 18, where it is prophesied that, at the time of the Lord's coming, a great prophet like Moses would rise up. But John says that he is not that prophet, and the New Testament says that the "prophet like Moses" is Jesus Himself (Acts 3:18-22).

So who *is* John the Baptist? He has started out by telling us who he is not, but who is he? He says, first of all, "I am a voice of one crying in the wilderness, 'Make straight the way of the Lord'" (John 1:23). This quotation comes from Isaiah 40:3, and John the Baptist applies it to himself. Isaiah was talking about an improvement of the "interstate highway system" through the Babylonian desert, leveling off the hills, straightening the curves, so that God's people could return from exile in Babylon to the Promised Land. It is an Old Testament picture, drawn ahead of time, of the people of God returning from the exile of sin and darkness by the road that is provided by the Messiah.

John's wilderness voice is a lonely voice. He says, "Who am I? Well, I'm not Elijah, I'm not the prophet. I'm not the Christ."

"Well, then, who *are* you?" we all want to know.

"I'm a voice," John says. We can hear in John's own words that it is a lonely voice, not always listened to by the people. It is a lonely road forsaking sin, repenting, and returning to the Lord, John is saying. In humility, John the Baptist compares himself to a nameless voice, not even to a person. "I am just a voice," he says, "so don't focus on me." John the Baptist wants to be known only as a voice pointing to the Son of God.

On the radio, some voices call attention to themselves and some voices do not. You may or may not like Dr. Laura, but there is no mistaking her personality. She is very clear in what she believes, very clear in who she is. Other radio personalities are in the background, and all you hear is their voice. I like to listen to the radio late at night. It drives my wife crazy. We get in bed, and I can't get to sleep, so I flick on the radio. Predictably, about forty seconds later, I hear, "Please turn the radio off now." So I turn the volume down low enough so that only I can hear it. A particular voice that I like to listen to, maybe because it is so soothing that it helps me go to sleep, is the voice of the BBC announcer doing the news on National Public Radio at midnight. It is a voice with absolutely no personality. It is so unremarkable that it puts me to sleep.

Some voices have punch and personality, and some voices deliberately point away from themselves. Some are like Dr. Laura and some are like the BBC newscaster. John the Baptist is a voice who points away from himself. Each time he has an opportunity to focus on himself, he shifts the focus to Christ. His answer to the question, Who am I? is always, Who is *He?* For example, look at 1:27: "It is He who comes after me, the thong of whose sandal I am not worthy to untie." In that day, the lowest slave in a household would remove the shoes at the door. John the Baptist says that, when it comes to Christ, he isn't even worthy to do that.

Verse 30: "This is He on behalf of whom I said, 'After me comes a Man who has a higher rank than I, for He existed before me.'" This person is greater than John because He exists eternally.

In verse 31, John the Baptist says that he did not even recognize Jesus, which means he does not belong to that group of disciples and friends that Jesus is gathering about Him. He is only a voice, pointing away from himself.

John is also a baptizer. He is baptizing people in the Jordan River. "I baptize with water," he says (v. 26, note). Water baptism has its roots in the Old Testament rites of cleansing. In the inter-Testamental period, the 400-year period between the end of the Old Testament and the beginning of the New, a lot of people wanted to become Jewish. In order do to that, they had to go through a rite of cleansing with water that symbolized the washing away of sin. But John the Baptist is getting the Jewish leaders ready for a better baptism than his. He is saying in effect, "There is more going on here than you know."

JOHN THE BAPTIST'S WITNESS ABOUT JESUS CHRIST

As John deliberately shifts attention from himself to Jesus, he bears witness to Him in three crucial ways. First, he announces Him as the Lamb of God: "The next day he saw Jesus coming to him, and he said, 'Behold, the Lamb of God who takes away the sin of the world!'" (John 1:29). We are so used to that phrase. It has become perhaps overly familiar: "Behold, the Lamb of God."

What does John the Baptist mean by "Lamb of God." The exact rendering should probably be a bit more down to earth: "Look! God's Lamb!" That is really what he is saying. The use of the term *lamb* would have been familiar in at least three ways to Jews who knew their Old Testament: the lamb that was used for the sacrifice during the Passover season; the lamb that was led to the slaughter in Isaiah's prophecies; and the lamb that was offered daily as a sacrifice in the temple.

We in modern Western culture have no idea what this means. Imagine that every day at noon a lamb was slaughtered on a table at the front of your church sanctuary. Do you know what that would do to your sanctuary? The stench would be horrible for Sunday worship. The presence of the daily slaughtering of a lamb would fill your eyes, fill your nostrils, and blood would be everywhere. This is what the Lamb of God means to these Jews.

John the Baptist is saying that Jesus takes the place of and fulfills this continual, daily sacrifice in the temple. Now, he is saying, God has *once and for all* provided the true and final lamb that takes away by one definite act the sin of the world. "Jesus Himself," John is saying, "is the meaning of all of the rituals and all of the festivals that go on in the temple up there, seventeen miles away in Jerusalem." "Jesus the Lamb accomplishes salvation not just for the temple worshipers in Jerusalem," John says, "but for people from all over the world who receive Christ by believing in Him."

In John the Baptist's mind, the Lamb is not only humbled and sacrificed; He is exalted (1:30). Jesus Christ is of a higher rank than John the Baptist, and His taking away the sin of the people from all over the world is an act of power, not of weakness. When we think of a lamb, we often think of something weak and frail. But in the Bible, the Lamb of God is presented as having great strength, vitality, and power to do what only God's Son can do. The taking away of sin is an act of great power. The word *take away* actually means "to take up" or "bear up." Jesus took away our sin by taking it upon Himself and bearing it. The sin of the world—which means the totality of all that is sin among all those from the whole world who will follow Jesus—this huge weight of sin is too much for anyone to bear.

I was admiring a friend's jeep not long ago, so he let me drive it. (Driving a jeep is one of these middle-age things.) He was telling me that some Jeep Wranglers have a hard top that comes off.

I said, "Oh, that's pretty cool. You mean you just lift it off?"

He said, "Oh, no. One person could never lift off that top. In fact, it is so heavy that if you own one of those hard tops, you have a mechanical gizmo in the ceiling of your garage that comes down and clamps onto the hard top and pulls it off. It is too heavy for you to lift off yourself."

So it is with sin. Its weight is much too heavy for you to lift off by yourself.

Twenty years ago, a friend of mine was doing something that twenty years ago some of us used to do: a household construction project. He was hanging plasterboard in his basement. (I would no more consider plasterboarding a room in my house now than flying to the moon. But twenty years ago we tried these things.) Something terrible happened, and a dozen huge sheets of plasterboard fell on his one-year-old daughter. They were crushing her. My friend did all he could to lift this terrible weight off of his baby, but he couldn't do it. It was too heavy. He heard her whimpering and crying, and the cries got softer and quieter. But he was screaming at the top of his lungs for someone to come and help him lift the weight off of his daughter. He barely managed to hold the plasterboard up off of her so she could breathe until, finally, a neighbor heard and brought a second neighbor and the three of them were able to lift the plasterboard off and pull the little girl to safety. He couldn't do it himself. And you can't do it yourself. You can't lift the plasterboard of sin off of your own life. You can't bear it up. It is too great. It is too heavy.

Jesus was "crushed for our iniquities; the chastening for our well-being fell upon Him" (Isa. 53:5). "All of us like sheep have gone astray, each of us has turned to his own way; but the LORD has caused the iniquity of us all to fall on Him" (v. 6). "He Himself bore the sin of many" (v. 12). "He himself bore our sins in his body on the tree" (1 Pet. 2:24, ESV). That weight that you cannot bear, Jesus couldn't bear either. It crushed Him. But in His strength as the Son of God, He has the power to lift that weight off of you, as it were, and place it on Himself, even as it crushes Him.

That is what John the Baptist means when he calls Jesus the Mighty Baptizer. John promises that the One who comes after him will baptize with the Spirit. He says, "I baptize with water" (John 1:26, note). Water baptism is a remedial action; it washes away sin. But the mighty baptism of Jesus does so much more. It endows us with the Spirit of God who takes away sin, renews to new life, and brings the abundant life which Jesus Himself has promised that He will give. "I came that they might have life, and might have it abundantly" (10:10).

At Jesus' baptism, the Spirit remains on Him (1:32), not like in the Old Testament where the Spirit would come and go on the prophets. It remains forever on Jesus so that He is forevermore able to baptize you with the Holy Spirit. And lest you be confused, let me state it directly: That is precisely what happens to every one of us at the moment of our regeneration, at the moment when God, by His grace, renews us by His Spirit and makes us new people and causes us to begin the process of realizing how much weight the Son of God, the Lamb of God, has borne for us.

THE WORK OF THE LAMB

The Lamb of God is, in fact, the Son of God. "I have seen and have borne witness that this One who is the Lamb of God, who is the Mighty Baptizer, is the Son of God," says John (see John 1:29-34). He is the glorified Lamb of God, the Mighty Baptizer, the Son of God. He is strong to save you. He is able to save your soul from sin, hell, and destruction, and to keep you safe for the Father.

If He is not a weak lamb but the powerful Lamb of God who baptizes you in the Holy Spirit, cleansing you, renewing you, and giving you new life; if He can do all that for you, then here is my question: What can He *not* do for you? Right now in the circumstances of your life, where you live, with physical pain, with emotional heartache, with financial troubles, with a marriage in severe stress, with children who do not love or respect you, with a future that is uncertain—what can the Mighty Baptizer, the Lamb of God, do for you?

A little boy about ten years old was sitting on a park bench with his

Bible open, and he was just singing and praising God. "God is great! Hallelujah!" he yelled, not caring who heard him. Along came a man who had recently completed a college-level Bible course and felt very enlightened. He saw that this young fellow had an opened Bible on his lap, so he went up to him and said, "What are you so happy about?"

The boy said, "Do you have any idea what God is able to do? I just read that God was able to open up the water of the Red Sea and that the whole nation of Israel was able to just walk right through the middle."

The enlightened man laughed a little to himself and sat down next to the boy, feeling that he needed to advise him of the realities of the Bible. "Well, that story is easily explained this way," he said. "Modern scholarship has shown that the Red Sea in that location was actually only ten inches deep at the time, so it was no problem for the Israelites to wade across."

The boy's face fell, and he was stumped. Then his eyes wandered from the man, back to his opened Bible. The man, content that he had enlightened a poor, naïve young person to the finer points of biblical scholarship, turned to go. But scarcely had he begun to leave when he heard the little fellow just crying out all the more, exclaiming, "God is so great! God is so wonderful! Hallelujah!"

He turned back to find out the cause of the boy's renewed jubilation.

"Wow!" exclaimed the boy happily, "God is greater than I thought. Not only did He lead the whole nation of Israel through the Red Sea, He topped it off by drowning the whole Egyptian army in ten inches of water!"

If Jesus is the Lamb of God, what can He do for you? If He is the Mighty Baptizer who gives you new life, who bears away your sin, then what can He do for you amid your daily circumstances? Or, what can He *not* do? What can He not do *for you?*

Some time ago, a friend asked me about some jaw surgery I had endured several weeks earlier. I was trying to explain the odd sensations that I had in my mouth, and said, "The funny thing is that it was all numb on the surface. It's kind of like when you go to the dentist and you have Novocain. It was all numb like that, but underneath, in the bones, it was really painful at times."

My friend got this little twinkle in her eyes and said, "Oh, that's just like a lot of us most of the time: numb on the surface, in great pain underneath; and by looking at us, you can't tell any difference."

Is that you? Are you numb on the surface? Is there pain underneath? Then go to the Lamb of God who by one, mighty, definite act has taken away the sin of the world and your sin. If He can do that mighty, huge thing, then can He not be the Mighty Baptizer who moves in on your life with life and power and joy and hope?

Do you know Him as the One who has taken away your sin? In whom you are baptized with new life? And who is forever and ever the Son of God?

6

"COME AND SEE"

Again the next day John was standing with two of his disciples, and he looked upon Jesus as He walked, and said, "Behold, the Lamb of God!" And the two disciples heard him speak, and they followed Jesus. And Jesus turned, and beheld them following, and said to them, "What do you seek?" And they said to Him, "Rabbi (which translated means Teacher), where are You staying?" He said to them, "Come, and you will see." They came therefore and saw where He was staying; and they stayed with Him that day, for it was about the tenth hour. One of the two who heard John speak, and followed Him, was Andrew, Simon Peter's brother. He found first his own brother Simon, and said to him, "We have found the Messiah" (which translated means Christ). He brought him to Jesus. Jesus looked at him, and said, "You are Simon the son of John; you shall be called Cephas" (which is translated Peter). The next day He purposed to go forth into Galilee, and He found Philip. And Jesus said to him, "Follow Me." Now Philip was from Bethsaida, of the city of Andrew and Peter. Philip found Nathanael and said to him, "We have found Him of whom Moses in the Law and also the Prophets wrote, Jesus of Nazareth, the son of Joseph." And Nathanael said to him, "Can any good thing come out of Nazareth?" Philip said to him, "Come and see." Jesus saw Nathanael coming to Him, and said of him, "Behold, an Israelite indeed, in whom is no guile!" Nathanael said to Him, "How do You know me?" Jesus answered and said to him, "Before Philip called you, when you were under the fig tree, I saw you." Nathanael answered Him, "Rabbi, you are the Son of God; you are the King of Israel." Jesus answered and said to him, "Because I said to you that I saw you under the fig tree, do you believe? You shall see greater things than these." And He said to him, "Truly, truly, I say to you, you shall see the heavens opened, and the angels of God ascending and descending on the Son of Man" (John 1:35-51).

THE PATTERN OF WITNESS

Right from the beginning of the book of John, a pattern of witness emerges. The notion of witness is at the heart of John's Gospel. It is all about witness to Christ.

In this passage, John the Baptist leads Andrew and another unnamed disciple, who we have every reason to believe is John the Gospel writer, to Jesus. Then Andrew brings Peter, his brother, to Jesus. Probably it is Andrew who then brings Philip to Jesus, and then Philip finds another man, named Nathanael, and tells him about Christ. This is the pattern of witness in the Gospel of John, and it has been the foundational pattern for witness in the expansion of the church for two thousand years: new followers of Jesus become witnesses about Him to others, who in turn themselves become new witnesses, and they repeat the process. As this passage indicates, new believers are often the most excited about becoming themselves, promptly and cheerfully, witnesses to what they have seen and heard about the Lord Jesus Christ.

John Calvin says about this passage, "Andrew has scarcely one spark, yet, through it, he enlightens his brother."[1] Andrew has just been introduced to Jesus, yet he is thrilled about it and immediately wants to share this new spark with those to whom he is the closest. So Andrew brings his brother, Simon. Jesus speaks to Simon. Philip brings Nathanael, and Jesus speaks to Nathanael. There is the pattern of witness: we bring, Jesus speaks. We bring people to Christ, and Jesus speaks His Word to them. He even calls them by name, identifies them, defines their lives, highlights the magnitude of their need, convicts them of their sin, and immediately or eventually converts them.

We often talk about witnessing as if it were something we do on a street corner or in a shopping mall. While I would not deny that that is indeed something that can and should happen, the real witness goes on in church—in all the rooms of a biblically faithful church on Sunday and through the week. You may not think of witnessing as something that involves bringing people to church, but, actually, that is the most biblical kind of witnessing. It is bringing people to come and see Jesus as He is lifted up in the teaching of His Word, Sunday by Sunday, weekday by weekday, among God's people in the Lord's house. That does not mean witness does not happen outside, but it does mean that the goal of our witnessing is to bring people into contact with the words of Jesus.

Personal evangelism is more than bringing friends to church, but it is not less. Witnessing is getting people to hear the Word of Jesus whether it is in a Sunday sermon or Sunday school class or Bible study or wherever His Word is being lifted up. Providing abundant ways in which God's people come in contact with the Word of Jesus should be the church's goal in evangelism.

Our goal in witnessing is not to tell everyone everything they need to know the first time we meet them. That is not what happens in this passage. No, our goal in witnessing is to bring people to the Word of Jesus and trust that the Word of Jesus is going to do all that is necessary in them.

TWO STYLES OF WITNESS

There is a striking contrast between two different styles of witness in this passage. One is John the Baptist's witness to Christ, and the other is Jesus' witness to Himself. John the Baptist is blunt. He sees Jesus coming to him and says, "Look! God's Lamb" (see John 1:29). Later he says, "He is the Mighty Baptizer," and, "He is the Son of God." Those are very direct descriptions, stunning to his listeners.

But Jesus, witnessing to Himself in this passage, is much more subtle. We see Jesus' indirect approach in three rapid-fire exchanges between Him and His new disciples, each of which can be understood on two different levels. The first is in 1:37: "The two disciples heard Him speak, and they followed Jesus." What does following Jesus mean? Literally it means the physical act, "to walk after Him," but there is more than that to the word *follow*. It is to follow as a disciple, as Jesus describes it in 8:12: "I am the light of the world; he who follows Me shall not walk in darkness, but shall have the light of life."

Which level does Jesus mean here? Is "following" merely walking after Him, or is it a deeper sense of patterning your life after Him, pursuing Him? Jesus means both, speaking intentionally on two levels. The obvious level is for those who are just beginning to follow Him. He will develop the deeper level of coming after Him later on with these very disciples.

We find the second exchange between Jesus and His disciples in 1:38: "And Jesus turned, and beheld them following, and said to them, 'What do you seek?'" Is Jesus asking Andrew and John, "Are you looking for something? Excuse Me, I saw you following Me, what do you want?" Or is He saying, "What do you really want in life? What are you deeply seeking?" Which is it? It may well be both.

The third exchange is in verse 38 as well: "And they said to Him, 'Rabbi, . . . where are You staying?'" Does that mean that they want to know where Jesus is sleeping that night? It is about four o'clock in the afternoon. Do they want to go with Him to supper and then spend a quiet evening around the fire talking? Maybe, but there is a more subtle truth being broached here. The word *stay* is the same word that is used as *abide* later in the Gospel of John. In John 15:4 Jesus says, "Abide in Me [Stay in Me], and I in you. As the branch cannot bear fruit of itself, unless it abides in the vine, so neither can you, unless you abide in Me." Jesus is speaking about a much deeper inner reality of knowing Him.

Which is it? Is Jesus saying to them, "Come see where I am staying," or is He saying, "Do you want to abide with Me?" Unlike John the Baptist, Jesus leaves things open to interpretation, inviting further inquiry.

HOW GRACE WORKS

Jesus' subtle approach reveals how the grace of Christ actually works in our hearts.

Grace in Stages

First, this passage shows how grace works in stages. Compare John's Gospel account of the disciples' first coming to Jesus to the encounters in Matthew, Mark, and Luke. In those Gospels Jesus says, "Follow Me," and the disciples stand up from their fishing nets or their tax booths and follow Jesus immediately. In John's account, Jesus' approach is much more textured and complex.

John's Gospel depicts the first time that Jesus encounters these would-be disciples—their introduction to discipleship. He invites them for the first time to come and see. Later on, all four Gospels relate decisive calls to discipleship with Jesus. At first, grace arouses our interest; it raises more questions than it answers. Then it stirs our hearts and makes us think, *Who am I? Where am I abiding? Who am I following? What am I doing with my life?* Grace brings questions to the surface; and then later there comes, in most of our lives, decisive moments of all-or-nothing discipleship.

Personal Grace

The second way grace works is personally. It brings us into contact with a person. Grace does not bring us into contact with truth apart from the reality of the embodied, incarnate Son of God. *Truth is a person,* and to know the truth is to know the person. The grace of the gospel does not turn on just enough light to lead one to say, "Oh, I see. I understand that bit of theology." No, grace spotlights the path to a relationship with a person you grow to love.

The personal aspect of grace is found in John 1:39, for example: "He said to them, 'Come, and you will see.' They came therefore and saw where He was staying; and they stayed with Him that day, for it was about the tenth hour." Jesus invites them personally to come with Him for supper and to spend the evening with Him.

Another example is in verse 42: "He brought him to Jesus. Jesus looked at him, and said, 'You are Simon the son of John; you shall be called Cephas.'" What a personal response from Jesus! He seems to say, "I know you, Peter, and I want you to know Me." He calls him by name; in fact, He gives him a new name.

Then in verse 48 we read, "Nathanael said to Him, 'How do You know me?' Jesus answered and said to him, 'Before Philip called you, when you were under the fig tree, I saw you.'" Jesus is not talking so much about His physical sight, but about His seeing *into* Nathanael in a personal way.

Irresistible Grace

Grace not only works in stages and personally, but most significantly in this passage, grace works irresistibly in attracting us to Christ. Because of the irresistible beauty of Christ, you cannot say no. He is so beautiful when you get to know Him personally. He is so magnificent in what He does for us in the gospel that you are drawn in a compelling way to Him. He allows further inquiry and leaves room for our questions as we grow in our developing views and understanding of who He is. But the tug is sure, and He will not let us go.

Scripture reveals two types of calls issued by God to the one who does not know Christ. One is described as the general, or external, call of the gospel. It goes out to everyone indiscriminately, without distinction, and it can be and often is rejected. But there is also what is rightly called the particular, or inward, call which the Holy Spirit extends that inevitably brings to faith those it is intended to bring to faith. The inward call cannot be rejected. It always results in conversion. This inward call enlightens our minds spiritually and savingly so that we understand God and His purposes. It allows the lights to go on in our heads and hearts so that we see who Christ is and what the gospel is, and by means of this particular call the Spirit irresistibly draws sinners to Christ.

Paul says in Romans 8:30, "Those whom he called he also justified" (ESV). If you are called, you will surely be justified. There is an inevitable and compelling link between the two. If He calls you, He will bring you to be saved. He is not limited in His work of applying salvation by man's will, nor is He dependent upon man's cooperation, for He takes our will and He molds it by grace. John 1:12-13 says, "But as many as received Him, to them He gave the right to become children of God, even to those who believe in His name, who were born not of blood, nor of the will of the flesh, nor of the will of man, but of God."

To be born of God is to be born of the call of God. It is what happens inwardly when the call of God comes to us. The Spirit graciously brings us to spiritual life from our natural spiritual state—death. This is a difficult thing for us to hear, but God's pronouncement upon us is that in our guilt and sin, we are not just helpless or sick, we are dead. If you were in your bedroom lying dead on a bed, you would not answer the doorbell when it rang. That may offend us, because we do not want to admit that we are dead. "Wait a minute, Lord. I'm not completely dead. There is still some part of me that can respond . . ." No, the Scripture tells us that we are utterly and completely dead, and only the wakeup call of Christ will bring us to life.

The Spirit gives us the ability to cooperate with the Lord—to believe, to repent, and to come willingly to Christ. While God's grace effectually draws us to Jesus Christ, we have freely chosen to come. God's grace gives us this new willingness. When the Spirit makes us alive with Christ, we have this new desire to go to the door and see who is there.

In Acts 16 we read that the Lord gave Lydia the ability to respond to His Word. Verse 14 states that "the Lord opened her heart to respond to the things spoken by Paul." We do not have the ability to respond to the Word or His call until the Lord gives us that ability. God's grace is invincible. It never fails to result in the salvation of those for whom it is intended. As one writer put it, this is "no powerless, merely human calling [that] is in view. This calling is rather a kind of 'summons' from the King of the universe and it has such power that it brings about the response that it asks for in people's hearts."[2]

A CASE STUDY: GRACE FOR PETER

Look how the calling of grace works in Peter's first encounter with the Lord, drawing him irresistibly. Jesus' calling to Peter (John 1:42) is specific and concrete. Immediately Peter is given a new name, a new identity. No wiggle room. He is not invited but called.

Grace calls Peter irresistibly, and it also equips him irresistibly. Jesus' call to Peter is not just a name change but a signal about how Peter would be used in the founding of the church. Peter means "rock," and Peter is part of the foundation that God is using to establish His church through His Son. Calling *to* Christ leads to calling *for* Christ. There is a deep interconnection between the effectual calling that saves us and the calling that uses our gifts in service to the Lord.

Grace *provokes* Peter irresistibly as well. Jesus is almost teasing Peter with the deeper questions. Knowing Peter will later deny Him, Jesus is provoking him by asking, "Will you really follow Me, Peter?" He asks, in effect, "What are you seeking, Peter? What do you really want out of life? Do you want to see what is in My heart?"

EXPECTANT GRACE

In John 1:39, there is the final beckoning to these first disciples and to us: "Come, and you will see." It is not a beautifully engraved invitation that says, "You are cordially invited to attend . . ." but a compelling command that is beautiful because it is embossed with the very blood of Christ. It says, "You are cordially expected to appear before the Throne of Grace."

At whatever stage you are in your life with Christ, *come and see.* Are you being drawn by His grace to the first steps of recognition of who Jesus is? Come and see. Are you at an all-or-nothing decisive moment of discipleship in your life? Come and see. Don't stop right at the beginning. As Calvin says, "There are many who merely sniff at the gospel from a distance and thus let Christ suddenly disappear, and all they have learned about him slips away."[3]

If you are beginning with Christ, don't just sniff at Him. No, come and see that the Lord is good. Come if you are just being beckoned for the first time by that inner call of God's Holy Spirit. If you are at a moment of decisive discipleship, it is also a moment for you to come confessing what is in your heart that is a barrier to your discipleship in the Lord. The grace of Christ provides for you forgiveness of sins, a cleansing for your soul's pollution, vigor for the battle of living, and hope of heaven. Come and see that in Christ, who is calling you to follow Him, you have joy for the journey. Come and see that Jesus is calling you to follow Him personally and irresistibly. Come and see.

7

THE NEW WINE

And on the third day there was a wedding in Cana of Galilee, and the mother of Jesus was there; and Jesus also was invited, and His disciples, to the wedding. And when the wine gave out, the mother of Jesus said to Him, "They have no wine." And Jesus said to her, "Woman, what do I have to do with you? My hour has not yet come." His mother said to the servants, "Whatever He says to you, do it." Now there were six stone waterpots set there for the Jewish custom of purification, containing twenty or thirty gallons each. Jesus said to them, "Fill the waterpots with water." And they filled them up to the brim. And He said to them, "Draw some out now, and take it to the headwaiter." And they took it to him. And when the headwaiter tasted the water which had become wine, and did not know where it came from (but the servants who had drawn the water knew), the headwaiter called the bridegroom, and said to him, "Every man serves the good wine first, and when men have drunk freely, then that which is poorer; you have kept the good wine until now." This beginning of His signs Jesus did in Cana of Galilee, and manifested His glory, and His disciples believed in Him (John 2:1-11).

IF YOU ARE THE FATHER OF a daughter who has not yet married, then you probably think ahead to her wedding day, when you and your daughter will stand arm in arm at the back of the church, ready to walk down the aisle. At a certain moment your daughter will give your arm a squeeze and say, "Here we go, Daddy," and down that long aisle you will go.

Sooner or later most of us dads who have daughters are just like Steve Martin in *Father of the Bride*: we have a difficult time believing that our five-year-old little girl is actually going to get married, and we cannot quite figure out how we got to that particular day.

Of course, there is a moment after most weddings that assures you that it really has happened: when the bills start coming in. I am told by fathers of the bride who are a little ahead of me on the circuit that they frequently hear these words: "Actually, Daddy, that's a very good price." Dad immediately wonders what a bad price would be!

I don't know how expensive the wedding in Cana of Galilee was, but this passage is about the wedding reception that was part of the celebration, and particularly about new and unexpectedly good wine that became available at a critical moment at this wedding party.

THE SETTING: THE NEW HAS COME

A key idea of these first chapters of the Gospel of John is *newness*. In chapters 2–4 we find many new things being discussed; here, new wine; later in chapter 2, the new temple; in chapter 3, the new birth; in chapter 4, the new temple. These chapters could be summarized by what Paul says in 2 Corinthians 5 about what happens to us when the gospel comes to our lives: "The old has gone, the new has come" (v. 17, NIV). The gospel is always marked by newness, by freshness, by a new approach to thinking about our lives.

The new wine provided at the wedding in Cana has actually been a cause for much speculation over two thousand years of biblical interpretation. Some liberal scholars believe that Jesus is a kind of reincarnated Dionysus, the Greek god of wine, who supplies much of it for His people and is anxious that everyone has a good time.

Some people go to the other extreme. Their interpretation of this passage centers around one all-important enterprise: to prove that it is really grape juice, and not wine at all. However, John 2:10 literally says that when the men became drunk, they ran out of wine, and the poorer wine was then be served.

Certainly, neither John nor Jesus is condoning drunkenness, but it is clear that it was wine that was served. In the ancient world, however, wine was usually diluted to between one-third and one-tenth of its original fermented strength, not as strong as today's American beer.

The key verse is, of course, verse 11: "This beginning of His signs Jesus did in Cana of Galilee, and manifested His glory, and His disciples believed in Him." That verse ties the story of the wedding feast to the point and purpose of the whole Gospel of John as stated in 20:31: "But these [signs] have been written that you may believe that Jesus is the Christ, the Son of God; and that believing you may have life in His name." The Cana wedding passage has something to do with the purpose of the signs that Jesus begins to perform here. But the two obvious questions are: 1) What is a sign? and 2) What is the "glory" of Jesus? In the answers to these two questions we find the meaning of this passage and also the way to apply it to our own lives.

THE STORY: THE WEDDING RECEPTION

Let's get at that deeper meaning by first looking at the story. The first interesting thing to see is that Jesus and His five new disciples go to a wedding. Jesus attending a wedding demonstrates, among other things, that He enjoyed a good time, a happy celebration, and that He was not an ascetic or a "wet blanket." Throughout Christian history, Jesus' presence at the wedding in Cana at Galilee has been seen as an indication of His particular blessing on weddings. The Anglican *Book of Common Prayer* says in the wedding service, "Christ adorned and beautified [all wedding services] with His presence and first miracle that He wrought in Cana of Galilee."[1]

Jesus, His mother, and His friends are all invited to this wedding. Perhaps it was a family wedding or that of a dear friend. Like many such weddings, members of the family are probably responsible for the catering, so Mary feels a particular obligation when the wine is running out. But the financial burden for such an event would always belong to the groom, unlike our situation today where it usually belongs to the bride's family. It would be very embarrassing to run out of wine. In fact, in the ancient world, such a faux pas could actually be the cause of a lawsuit by the bride's family against the groom's family.

When Mary says to Jesus, "They have no wine," she is actually doing more than just passing along bad news. She is expecting something from Jesus; in fact, she tells the servants in John 2:5, "Whatever He says to you, do it." She knows Jesus can, and hopes that He will, do something about this situation. But for the last two thousand years, Jesus' response to His own mother has given many people a great deal of trouble. In verse 4 Jesus says to her, "Woman, what do I have to do with you? My hour has not yet come." Jesus separates Himself from His mother, creating a tension that has been the cause of much questioning over the years. What did Jesus mean? Why would He speak to His mother this way?

The form of address itself separates Jesus from His mother.

"Woman" is not a very endearing way to speak of one's own mother! The English word *woman* is, in fact, too distant, too impersonal. Some translations, therefore, go for something more palatable. They say, "Dear woman." But that makes it too sentimental. Some reverse the order of those two words and say, "Woman, dear." But that is too condescending. Some translations have "Lady," making it sound like something a New York City cabdriver would say. "Where you want to go, lady?" A Southern translator might render it "Ma'am."

The question itself separates Jesus from His mother. It seems abrupt. Literally, the text reads, "What to you and to me?" In the common speech of Jesus' day, it conveyed a tone of reproach that would distance the two parties involved. It would mean, "What do you and I have in common concerning this particular matter?"

We can't avoid the fact that Jesus is distancing Himself from His mother. He is stating at the very outset of His ministry His freedom from all human advice or agendas. For Jesus, His "true north" would have to be His Father's will. This must have been hard for Mary. D. A. Carson says, "She had borne him, nursed him, taught his baby fingers elementary skills, watched him fall over as he learned to walk."[2] Presumably a widow by now, Mary may have come to rely upon her firstborn son, and He may have provided for her by carrying on the family carpentry business.

But now Jesus is beginning His true calling, and Mary can no longer view Him in the same way. He is no less her son, but all of His ties, even His family loyalties, must be subordinated to His deepest mission. It is poignant that everywhere Mary is spoken of in the Gospels, Jesus is putting distance between them. It is not a show of lack of respect or lack of love. Indeed, as we will see, the Lord cares for His own mother from the cross when He indicates that John will provide for her. But she, like everyone else, must come to Him as the Christ, as the Son of God. Mary does not have an inside track. Maybe this is what Luke means when, at the time of Jesus' birth, he speaks of the "sword" that would pierce Mary's heart (Luke 2:35). D. A. Carson says, "For this we should honour her the more."[3] Mary had to bear an unusual burden as the mother of the Son of God, and that unusual burden was indeed a sword that would come to hurt her.

The mission, which must separate Jesus from all other loyalties, even loyalty to His mother, is His "hour." *Hour* is one of John's code words. We will see it again and again in this Gospel. It refers to the hour when Christ's mission will come to a climax, to the time of His death and resurrection. But by speaking of "My hour" here, Jesus is whetting our appetites, catching our attention. We want to ask, "What hour?" He wants to arouse our curiosity; but for Mary, Jesus' announcement of His hour must surely mean an hour of separation and, probably, heartache.

THE SIGNPOST: THIS WAY TO THE REAL WEDDING

What does this narrative mean? What does it really say beyond the story, underneath it, and through it? The narrative gives us a sign, or you might say a signpost, that reads, "This way to the real wedding."

Imagine yourself in a strong wind, hanging onto a signpost. The wind is blowing so hard in one direction that you are being lifted up and pulled horizontal to the ground. You are pointing one way, but the wind is blowing you the opposite way. Do you often feel that way, like you are hanging onto the very signpost that is telling you that you need to go *that* way, but all the wind in your life is pushing you the other way? The wedding in Cana story says, "This Way to the Real Wedding."

This was the first of Jesus' miraculous signs. Depending upon how you count them, there are seven such signs in the Gospel of John: the water to wine, the healing of the nobleman's son, the healing at the pool of Bethesda, the feeding of the five thousand, walking on water, healing the man born blind, and raising Lazarus. We will come to each of these in turn. For John, a "sign" (John 2:11) was an attesting miracle, a witnessing miracle, one that bears witness to who Jesus is.

Many miraculous things happen in this world; they are good, and point to the Lord Himself. But there are many apparently miraculous but crazy things that happen. Turn on your television on any given night and you can find all kinds of wild and crazy "miracles" happening. You can find people who have the ability to just hold up their hand and knock people down. Frankly, I do not think that that is a sign pointing in any direction except to the unusual power of mass psychology.

The issue, you see, is that a true sign points beyond itself. A true sign points to the *source* of the power, the wonder, and the truth that lies

behind the sign. The miracle at Cana is a signpost that points to the glory
of the best wedding—a wedding that is yet to come.

Right at the very beginning of His earthly ministry, Jesus goes to a
wedding. This is not coincidental. Jesus does not just say to Philip and
Andrew, on the spur of the moment, "Oh, well, I hear there's a wedding
in Cana. Let's go." No, it is part of His plan, because right at the *beginning* of His ministry He wants to show how His ministry will *end*—at
that great wedding that takes place between Him, the Bridegroom, and
His bride, the church. Every wedding is a sign of that greater wedding
when Jesus, the Bridegroom, takes His bride, the church, and promises
in covenant love and fidelity with vows that cannot and will not ever be
broken, that He will be loyal to His bride for all eternity.

I love weddings. I have performed more than three hundred of them.
Every one is different, and I always love the unexpected things that happen. During one wedding, at a certain point in the service the bride and
groom, the best man and the maid of honor, and I were to mount stairs
up to a platform. I was facing the congregation and had to turn around.
As I turned, I tripped over my robe. It got under my feet and thoroughly
tangled in them as I tried to climb the steps. I was struggling, and a
bridesmaid standing nearby started to giggle and couldn't stop. She and
the entire bridal party were nervous, so everyone started giggling. We
almost lost it at that particular wedding.

Weddings are one of the few places in our culture where we honor
the older people among us by giving them special seats and special places
and times to be seated in the service. It is a time when we all come dressed
up. It is a time when there is a formal procession. In cities like Dallas,
where I live, stately churches with center aisles are sought after as wedding sites. Why? Because a wedding is the one time in your life when you
want to be in a real church building with beauty and formality.

The groom comes out with the best man. He is "spiffed up." He's
got a little row of beaded sweat across his brow. Everyone enters in a
stately way. The bridesmaids are beautiful as they walk down the aisle;
a little flower girl throws her petals every which way. There is a pause,
the music swells, I nod to the bride's mother, she stands on her cue, and
everyone stands and turns toward the aisle, and down the aisle comes
the bride on her father's arm, resplendent in her white gown.

John is giving us a signpost to the greatest wedding of all, and telling us that the Bridegroom, Jesus Christ, will have His bride, the church, presented to Him spotless, because she will be wearing His righteousness. Why does a bride wear white? It is a direct indication that, in the plan and economy of God, He intends His church to be white and spotless. That is the historical background to the white dress a bride wears. It is the purity given to the bride of Christ by the Bridegroom, who gives to her His own perfect righteousness.

ABUNDANT WINE, ABUNDANT GRACE

Here is what the story is all about: the abundance of what Christ gives, shown first in the abundance of the wine itself. The amount and quality of the wine that Jesus will supply is great indeed, as promised in the prophets. Isaiah says, "And the LORD of hosts will prepare a lavish banquet for all peoples on this mountain; a banquet of aged wine, choice pieces with marrow, and refined, aged wine" (Isa. 25:6). Jeremiah 31:12 promises new wine: "And they shall come and shout for joy on the height of Zion, and they shall be radiant over the bounty of the LORD— over the grain, and the new wine . . ."

Jesus changed a great deal of water into a great deal of wine— approximately one hundred and fifty gallons of water become one hundred and fifty gallons of wine. These pots were used for the purification, perhaps for the guests to wash before and after their meal, but John's emphasis is that even that much water will never cleanse the stain of sin. Perhaps the water of purification symbolizes the *inability* of the old Law with all of its purification rights to cleanse, and the contrast, this sign, is pointing us to what only Jesus as the Bridegroom can do.

This wedding spotlights the glory of Jesus not only in the abundance of wine but in the abundant wine of Jesus' blood. We cannot cleanse ourselves from sin. It must be the blood of the Bridegroom who cleanses us. Jesus, the Bridegroom, has a passion for the purity of His bride, not just in our once-and-for-all purity that His blood achieved but also in our day-to-day living. All of us are stained, and only sacrificially shed blood has the ability to wash those stains of sin out. Jesus drank the cup of the bitter wine of the wrath of God, the cup that His Father takes to all the nations, demanding that they drink it down to the dregs (Jer. 25:15-16). It is the Son who drinks the wine of God's wrath for us.

This miracle is an expression of the superabundant grace of the New Covenant. In love, Jesus was in agony. In love, Jesus was abandoned. In love, Jesus was made derelict before the wrath of God. The grace of the new cup of the covenant in His blood is given to us so that, even as Jesus drinks the cup of God's wrath that we should drink, we are invited to come to the new feast where the new and better abundant wine is given, the wine of the new life of Jesus.

Andrew, John, Peter, Nathanael, and Philip were invited as disciples to this first wedding. But now, all of us who are disciples are invited to the wedding of the Bridegroom so that we may join the feast. Isaiah says, "Every one who thirsts, come to the waters; and you who have no money come, buy and eat. Come, buy wine and milk without money and without cost. . . . Delight yourself in abundance" (Isa. 55:1-2). There seems to be a contradiction here; he says, "Buy it," and then he says, "You can't buy it." It is too precious; there is no amount of money that can buy one tiny sip of the blood of Christ's wine poured out for you. The best wine is saved until last and it is given freely, without charge, out of the abundance of grace.

"This is the beginning of Jesus' signs which He did in Cana of Galilee, and He manifested His glory and His disciples believed in Him" (John 2:11). We could read this as, "This is just the beginning!" It is the opening act of a much larger drama and the foundation for everything that follows in Jesus' earthly ministry. The signpost of this best and superabundant wine points forward to the best possible cleansing— complete, thorough, absolute, and superabundant—by the blood of the Lamb shed for you.

THE FUTURE BANQUET

We look forward to that greatest wedding day, greater than any day when our daughters will marry, but what about now? In this passage Jesus says to Mary, "My hour has not yet come" (John 2:4), but then He says a moment later, to the master of ceremonies at the wedding feast, "Draw some [wine] out *now*" (v. 8, italics mine). Do you sense the tension? His hour is not yet come, but *now* is the time to draw some new wine out and begin to taste it. *Now* is the time to start living in the light of the abundant supply of the cleansing blood of Jesus Christ and His grace. The banquet is in the future, to be sure. But the celebration begins now. The blood of the new wine of Jesus, shed out of His grace and love, is available to you now.

The wine of the New Covenant can change your life. It should not be taken by the dropper. Get drunk on that wine! You must take it all, for the Savior gives it all, liberally pouring it out for you. He pours it out, out of love, gives it to you because you are His own, infinitely precious to Him. You must take it and drink it, and you must not stop drinking it.

George Herbert, an English poet of the seventeenth century, said it this way (I've taken the liberty to slightly update Herbert's English in the first stanza):

> He who knows not love,
> Let him take and taste that juice
> Which on the cross a nail against a beam did loose.
>
> Then let him say, if he did ever taste the like,
> Love is that liqueur, sweet and so divine,
> Which my God tastes as blood, and I as wine.[4]

As is promised in the Lord's Supper, you may by faith take and drink this cup of the New Covenant. But don't ask for just a drop; take it all and drink it all.

8

THE NEW TEMPLE

After this He went down to Capernaum, He and His mother, and His brothers, and His disciples; and there they stayed a few days. And the Passover of the Jews was at hand, and Jesus went up to Jerusalem. And He found in the temple those who were selling oxen and sheep and doves, and the moneychangers seated. And He made a scourge of cords, and drove them all out of the temple, with the sheep and the oxen; and He poured out the coins of the moneychangers, and overturned their tables; and to those who were selling the doves He said, "Take these things away; stop making My Father's house a house of merchandise." His disciples remembered that it was written, "Zeal for Thy house will consume me." The Jews therefore answered and said to Him, "What sign do You show to us, seeing that You do these things?" Jesus answered and said to them, "Destroy this temple, and in three days I will raise it up." The Jews therefore said, "It took forty-six years to build this temple, and will You raise it up in three days?" But He was speaking of the temple of His body. When therefore He was raised from the dead, His disciples remembered that He said this; and they believed the Scripture, and the word which Jesus had spoken (John 2:12-22).

IN SEPTEMBER THE JEWISH religion celebrates four holidays, beginning with Rosh Hashana, the Jewish New Year. Following Rosh Hashana is Yom Kippur, the Day of Atonement, the highest and holiest day in the Hebrew calendar. Five days after Yom Kippur begins an eight-day celebration called the Feast of Tabernacles, which begins and ends with a high holiday.

In New York City, where our family lived briefly just before moving to Dallas, the school year begins immediately after Labor Day. Then, promptly, in all of the public and private schools of New York City, there are four school holidays (six days total, because Yom Kippur and Rosh Hashana involve two days each out from school). Our kids immediately thought that New York City was a very cool place to go to school! I observed these holidays with more than casual interest, perhaps because my maternal grandmother was Jewish, for which I am deeply thankful and proud. As I watched the Jewish people in New York City celebrating these high holidays, going to and from their synagogues, I was struck again with a stark reality: there was no temple in New York, and more importantly, there is no temple in Jerusalem.

That there is no temple in Jerusalem is the single most important fact that shapes all of modern Judaism. Since the temple's destruction in A.D. 70, the Jewish people have been homeless. Even the formation of the nation of Israel fifty years ago does not change the fact that Jewish people are still roaming the earth looking for a home, because the truest home for a Jew is not Israel; it is the temple in Jerusalem. No wonder many conservative and orthodox Jewish people look forward to the day when they (mistakenly) believe the temple will be rebuilt in Jerusalem.

Many modern evangelical Christians also think that there will be a temple rebuilt in Jerusalem. But on the basis of this passage in John, there will *never* be a temple rebuilt in Jerusalem. If there is, it will have a name: "The Abomination of Desolation." A brick and stone temple in Jerusalem no longer serves any purpose, because of what this passage teaches us: the true temple is a temple of flesh, the body of our Lord Jesus Christ.

In Sunday school, many of us learned the "cute" story of Jesus overturning the tables and throwing out the animal sellers, but perhaps we have missed the massive hunks of gospel truth that, if we grasp them, will change our thinking, our lives, and our worship.

WHO OWNS THE TEMPLE?

In Jesus' day, during Passover visitors from all over the Roman Empire came to Jerusalem. It was not possible for them to bring animals for sacrifice, so the merchants in Jerusalem saw an opportunity for profit and sold animals in the outer court of the temple. Visitors also needed to pay a temple tax in order to worship there, but because Roman coins had an image of a Roman emperor on them, they could not be used for worship or for paying the tax. They had to be exchanged for Jewish coinage, for a shekel or a half-shekel piece, so moneychangers saw an opportunity to change money for profit, much as happens in any international airport in the world today.

Jesus did not object to the selling of animals or the changing of money; both were necessary in order for the people to come to worship. Rather, He objected to *where* it took place. In earlier times, sellers and exchangers had set up their tables and booths on the Mount of Olives, outside the Golden Gate, across the Kidron Valley a respectable distance from the temple. But gradually they had moved closer and closer into the outer court of the temple, called the Court of the Gentiles. These businesses, necessary as they may have been, prevented the Gentiles from coming to pray. The implication was, "Gentiles don't matter," and, "Gentile prayers don't count and aren't important." It turned the temple into a nationalistic stronghold, a symbol of the Jewish nationalistic fervor. Merchants, taxmen, and pilgrims all accepted as natural this combination of worship and merchandising, much like what you would see in modern Jerusalem today along the Via Dolorosa. D. A. Carson comments: "Instead of solemn dignity and the murmur of prayer, there is a bellowing of cattle and the bleating of sheep. Instead of brokenness and contrition, holy adoration, and prolonged petition, there is noisy commerce."[1]

When Jesus goes up to Jerusalem for the first of the three Passovers mentioned by John, He speaks and acts as the Son who comes to His Father's house. He takes charge in His Father's house because He understands it is His unqualified right to do so; and as He enters it, His zeal is ignited by what the people have done to that place of worship.

No sticks or weapons were allowed in the temple precinct, so Jesus made a whip from reeds, perhaps from the bedding used to house the animals at night. The text says that He drove them all out, and the "all" probably refers not just to the animals but to the men who were doing the selling. One colorful paraphrased translation puts it this way: "So he made a rough whip out of rope and drove the whole pack of them, sheep and cattle as well, out of the Temple" (PHILLIPS). His actions were strong and direct, but they were not overly provocative, because apparently they did not arouse any curiosity or complaints from the Roman soldiers, who would have been very sensitive to any possibility of rioting.

Jesus is purifying the temple for worship. He explains why by quoting Psalm 69:9 (as quoted in John 2:17): "Zeal for Thy house will consume me." King David wrote Psalm 69 while he was being hounded and persecuted because of his defense of God's honor. In verses 1-2, he says, "Save me, O God, for the waters have threatened my life. I have sunk in deep mire, and there is no foothold; I have come into deep waters, and a flood overflows me." Verse 4 says, "Those who hate me without a cause are more than the hairs of my head."

DRIVEN TO WORSHIP

The question for us is, Will difficult circumstances in our lives drive us to worship or away from it? Closer to the Lord or farther from Him? This is David's issue in Psalm 69, the background of Jesus' own thinking as He fashions the cord. Does hardship drive us to the Lord and increase our zeal in worship because we know how much we need Him?

David continues, in Psalm 69:5-6: "O God, it is Thou who dost know my folly, and my wrongs are not hidden from Thee. May those who wait for Thee not be ashamed through me, . . . May those who seek Thee not be dishonored through me." Do you see what concerns David and should concern us as well? When difficulties come upon us, when the mire is deep, when the waters are overflowing, when people are against us, will our reaction dishonor the Lord and cause people to move away from worshiping Him? Or will we react to the difficult circumstances and people in our lives with a holy, aroused zeal for worshiping the Lord, with the recognition that we need the Lord as never before?

God will use anything to make us zealous for worship: those who hate us, deep mire, and overwhelming waters. God wants our hearts, hearts cleansed by repentance, and He will not rest until we give to Him that holy worship that can come only after repentance.

Have you thought about the difficulties of your life this way? It is not just that God by His sovereign grace allows into our lives difficult circumstances and people in order to refine our *character*. Perhaps more importantly from the Lord's point of view, He allows difficult people and difficult circumstances into our lives to refine our *worship*. God wants our character to be honed and shaped; but even more, He wants our worship to be honed and shaped.

A couple of years ago, a family in our church had a child born with many serious physical problems. One Saturday shortly after the child was born, the dad said to me, "Skip, I need to come to worship in church tomorrow. I can't wait to get to church." The difficulties in his life were arousing his zeal for the worship of God.

WORSHIP PURIFIED

Malachi the prophet wrote the script for what Jesus does in John 2. Malachi 3:1 says, "Behold, I am going to send my messenger, and he will clear the way before Me. And the Lord, whom you seek, will suddenly come to His temple." Jesus is the Prophet, the One who is coming. The Lord will come to the place He owns, His temple in Jerusalem. "But who," Malachi asks in verse 2, "can endure the day of His coming? And who can stand when He appears? For He is like a refiner's fire and like fullers' soap. And He will sit as a smelter and purifier of silver, and He will purify the sons of Levi, and refine them like gold and silver, so they may present to the LORD offerings in righteousness." Jesus wants offerings in righteousness—offerings made to the Lord out of a heart made righteous by the work that goes on in that temple. He wants offerings given in worship. He wants zeal for worship.

Jesus' purpose in purifying the temple is to purify the worship there. The Lord is calling for *our* purity in worship. How do we worship the Lord? If we are honest, do we not sometimes come to worship to be emotionally moved? "I hope the songs are lively this morning, and I hope I know them."

"I hope the pastor is on his game and not boring."

We often think of worship as something for us. Yes, worship is for us. But it is for the glory of the Lord first, and when we get that part right, then our joy flows out of the glory of the Lord and we have excruciating joy in the presence of His glory. No true joy comes when the focus is wrong. If we put our satisfaction ahead of God's satisfaction, then neither of us will be satisfied. If we put God's satisfaction ahead of our own, then we are both satisfied.

WORSHIP IS NOT . . .

If we think of worship as something just for *us*, then we can easily fall into one of the following four conclusions:

First, it is easy to say, "I can go to worship when I want to, when it is convenient, when I'm not traveling, when I'm not up too late on Saturday night." No, worship is commanded. It is not optional.

Second, some people say, "I'll worship by myself this morning. I think I'll go to Bedside Baptist." But *corporate* worship is commanded.

Hebrews 10:24-25 says, "And let us consider how to stimulate one another to love and good deeds, not forsaking our own assembling together, as is the habit of some, but encouraging one another; and all the more, as you see the day drawing near." Yes, personal worship is commanded as well, but it can never be a substitute for the experience and joy of assembling together.

Third, many might say, "Worship is meant to meet my needs." But that approach will inevitably diminish the meeting of needs in worship. Whoever looks to worship primarily to have needs met will lose in the end.

Fourth, some people say, "We can do anything we want in worship as long as it is 'meaningful.'" But the Lord's Word, not anyone's idea, has defined how we are to worship Him. The Lord has given us the elements of worship He considers glorifying to Him. We have no right to take it upon ourselves to determine or invent any other elements. The congregation I serve will never see me coming down from the balcony on a high wire with balloons in my hand; nor will they see dancing bears in our church's sanctuary on Sunday morning. Some might think, *Well, there is no reason why God's people can't do that in worship if it is meaningful.* The criterion is not our definition of meaningful; the criterion is what the Lord says in His Word is meaningful to Him. Only then do we find joy in worship.

PROBLEMS REVEALED

The Jewish leaders react strongly to what Jesus does, one asking, "What sign do You show to us, seeing that You do these things?" (John 2:18). The question reveals three problems:

First, it demonstrates that they do not take what Jesus does as the cue to examine their own hearts for worship. Instead, they are offended by what happens and miss the entire meaning of the cleansing of the temple. They are not concerned with worshiping God or with having a clean heart but with institutional procedure. For them, procedure is more important than reality in worship.

True worship is less concerned with procedure than with the reality that lies behind the procedure. Many churches have order, but no ardor, in worship and ministry. Other churches have ardor but no order. In God's way of thinking, there must be both order and ardor, for the

Lord has ordered the way His church is to worship and to function. The order becomes the tracks along which the engine of ardor speeds to the hearts of God's people.

The *second* problem that this question demonstrates is disbelief. They want a display of power on demand and on their own terms. They want to control Jesus and His signs. As Carson says, they want to domesticate God,[2] put Him under control, put Him on a leash.

The *third* problem that this question reveals is that Jesus' real conflict is not with merchants or moneychangers but with the Jewish authorities. The issue is, Who has authority over the temple? Jesus is declaring that He, as the Son of His Father, has full authority over His Father's house. Little can be more sacred than a person's authority over his or her own property. We would feel violated if someone came into our home and stole something. Very little is more important to us than our right to our own property. This temple is the property of Jesus, the Son of God, and He has absolute authority over what happens there. The Jewish leaders miss this reality completely.

THE OBSOLETE TEMPLE

Jesus' response to the authorities is a cryptic statement that conceals His meaning to those who do not believe: "Destroy this temple, and in three days I will raise it up" (John 2:19). It appears that Jesus is inviting them to tear down the temple in Jerusalem, which took forty-six years to build. "Tear it down," He says, "as you are already doing by your mismanagement of this place."

They protest, "It took us forty-six years to build this temple!"

However, we are told, He was talking about the temple of His body (2:21). Now we are getting to the heart of the matter.

When Jesus died and rose in His body, temple worship ended. It was not coincidental that, at the very moment of Christ's death, the veil separating the outer court from the Holy of Holies was torn in two. The temple was in the process of being destroyed by the death and resurrection of Christ, and in A.D. 70 the Romans finished the job. It has never been and can never be rebuilt—for Jews, for Christians, for anyone—because it can never be the center point of worship again. The focal point of worship is the new temple, the body of Jesus.

"[I]t is the human body of Jesus," Carson says, "that uniquely manifests the Father, and becomes the focal point of the manifestation of God to man, the living abode of God on earth, the fulfillment of all the temple meant, and the centre of all true worship. . . . In this 'temple' the ultimate sacrifice would take place."[3] That "ultimate sacrifice" is a sacrifice not made of the animals purchased in the Court of the Gentiles but of the body and blood of the Lord Jesus Christ. It is the sacrifice of Jesus in the temple of His own body that makes sense of our life, that gives us hope, that gives us the blood necessary to avail for sin, the blood that does better than the blood of sheep and goats (Heb. 9:11-14). The blood of Christ makes all other blood obsolete. The blood of Christ was shed in the temple of His own body and raised to new life by the power of God. The center of all human worship for all eternity is the resurrected body of the Lord.

The Gospel writer John says in the book of Revelation, about his vision of the new heavens, "I saw no temple in it, for the Lord God, the Almighty, and the Lamb, are its temple" (Rev. 21:22). Jesus is the true Lamb of God, His true temple; and the Lamb in the temple is sacrificed once and for all for the sins of His people. There can be no more sacrificing, no more animals bought in any Court of the Gentiles, no more knives raised in any place of worship anywhere in the world. Never! It has happened once and for all and can never be repeated. To do so would be an atrocity, an abomination, and a lie.

By replacing the temple, Jesus says He is the house of prayer for all nations. Jews and Gentiles alike are welcome to come to Him. When Jesus replaces the temple, there is no longer room for merchants and moneychangers, because the Gentile nations are crowding in for worship from all over the world.

A NEW PLACE OF WORSHIP

Believers worship at this new temple, and this is a deep reality that expresses the heart of worship. We do not worship in a temple or in any special place. The only special place is where the resurrected body of Jesus Christ is, risen and sitting at God's right hand. I resist calling the room where we worship at our church a sanctuary. We do not come to the sanctuary. We come to worship. There is a big difference. Worship itself creates a sanctuary, not the building where worshipers are. It is the model on earth of that heavenly sanctuary where Jesus is right now. It is heavenly worship in which we participate. On Sundays we go to worship with all of our doubts and weaknesses and sins, yet we enter into heavenly worship. Sometimes we say, "Isn't it wonderful that angels worship with us on Sunday morning?" It is much more accurate to say, "We worship with the angels." We are somehow in the heavenlies at God's right hand as we worship; we are with the Lord Jesus Christ, and we are worshiping in the temple created by the presence of His own body.

In Revelation 1, John wrote of his vision on the isle of Patmos: "I was in the Spirit on the Lord's day, and I heard behind me a loud voice like the sound of a trumpet. . . . [I saw] . . . one like a son of man, clothed in a robe reaching to the feet, and girded across His breast with a golden girdle. And His head and His hair were white like white wool, like snow; and His eyes were like a flame of fire; and His feet were like burnished bronze, when it has been caused to glow in a furnace, and His voice was like the sound of many waters. And in His right hand He held seven stars; and out of His mouth came a sharp two-edged sword; and His face was like the sun shining in its strength. And when I saw Him, I fell at His feet as a dead man" (Rev. 1:10; 13-17a).

It is no surprise that John fell at the feet of the Lord Jesus Christ when he saw Him filled with glory. When we see the Son of God in all of His splendid glory, we too may fall at His feet as dead people. Like John, we need the Lord to put His hand on us and to say, "Do not be afraid. I have overcome death and hell and destruction. Stand up. Stand up and worship."

We are not left to guess what heavenly worship is like. Later in Revelation, we are told:

And the four living creatures, each one of them having six wings, are full of eyes around and within; and day and night they do not cease to say, "Holy, holy, holy, is the Lord God, the Almighty, who was and who is and who is to come. . . . Worthy art Thou, our Lord and our God, to receive glory and honor and power; for Thou didst create all things, and because of Thy will they existed, and were created. . . . And I saw between the throne (with the four living creatures) and the elders a Lamb standing, as if slain, having seven horns and seven eyes, which are the seven Spirits of God, sent out into all the earth. . . . And they sang a new song, saying, 'Worthy art Thou to take the book, and to break its seals; for Thou wast slain, and didst purchase for God with Thy blood men from every tribe and tongue and people and nation. And Thou hast made them to be a kingdom and priests to our God; and they will reign upon the earth." And I looked, and I heard the voice of many angels around the throne and the living creatures and the elders; and the number of them was myriads of myriads, and thousands of thousands, saying with a loud voice, "Worthy is the Lamb that was slain to receive power and riches and wisdom and might and honor and glory and blessing." And every created thing which is in heaven and on the earth and under the earth and on the sea, and all things in them, I heard saying, "To Him who sits on the throne, and to the Lamb, be blessing and honor and glory and dominion forever and ever." And the four living creatures kept saying, "Amen." And the elders fell down and worshiped (Rev. 4:8, 11; 5:6, 9-14).

OUR BODY A TEMPLE

Our worship is something far more important, far bigger than we ever dreamed. Our worship is heavenly worship. But, most amazing, it is also bodily worship. Our worship is not so "spiritual" that our bodies are not involved. Worship does not separate our spirit from our body in any platonic way. Paul says, "I urge you therefore, brethren, by the mercies of God, to present your bodies a living and holy sacrifice, acceptable to God, which is your spiritual service of worship" (Rom. 12:1). The amazing truth of God's Word is that our bodies are the temples of the Holy Spirit. Our bodies are where Christ chooses to dwell by His Spirit. Yes, Jesus is in heaven at the right hand of God the Father. He has created there the new tabernacle, the new Holy of Holies, and we are caught up in that heavenly worship. But also, in the mystery of God's grace, He has chosen to dwell in our midst, among us and in us, by His Holy Spirit.

By His incarnation and resurrection, Jesus has changed these sinful bodies into temples of worship. In 1 Corinthians 3:16 we read, "Do you not know that you are a temple of God, and that the Spirit of God dwells in you?" And 2 Corinthians 6:16 says, "We are the temple of the living God; just as God said, 'I will dwell in them.'"

All of our living is shaped by the reality that our bodies are designed primarily as instruments of worship for the Lord. Everything is measured by how it affects, detracts from, or adds to the wonder that God intends us to worship Him in these temples called our bodies. He says in 1 Corinthians 6:11-12, speaking of a whole catalog of sins listed there, "Such were some of you; but you were washed, but you were sanctified, but you were justified in the name of the Lord Jesus Christ, and in the Spirit of our God. All things are lawful for me, but not all things are profitable. All things are lawful for me, but I will not be mastered by anything." Paul says we are free in Christ, free to do almost anything as long as it is not a direct sin against the Lord. But not everything we are free to do is wise for us!

Paul continues: "Food is for the stomach, and the stomach is for food; but God will do away with both of them. Yet the body is not for immorality, but for the Lord; and the Lord is for the body. Now God has not only raised the Lord, but will also raise us up through His power. Do you not know that your bodies are members of Christ? Shall I then take away the members of Christ and make them members of a harlot? May it never be!" (1 Cor. 6:13-15).

Paul then begins to discuss sexual sin, that most pervasive of all sins of the body, and he is very frank about it: "Or do you not know that the one who joins himself to a harlot is one body with her? For He says, 'The two will become one flesh.' But the one who joins himself to the Lord is one spirit with Him. Flee immorality. Every other sin that a man commits is outside the body, but the immoral man sins against his own body. Or do you not know that your body is a temple of the Holy Spirit who is in you, whom you have from God, and that you are not your own? For you have been bought with a price: therefore glorify God in your body" (1 Cor. 6:16-20). Our bodies have been bought by the body broken on the Cross, by the blood that was shed by Jesus on that cross. Therefore, our bodies belong to Him.

I am all for physical fitness and eating right, but the real sins of the body are not lack of exercise or a poor diet. The real sins of the body are those things we do that the Lord Himself calls immoral in light of the fact that with these bodies we are to worship in the true temple. Our bodies are to be used for heavenly worship before they are used for anything else. Avail yourself of the sacrifice to end all sacrifices in the temple to end all temples, and let the blood of Christ cleanse and renew your body and make it a fit temple for the Holy Spirit's worship.

Confess to Him. Confess that you are full of infirmities, wants, and sin, and that your powers of body and soul are defiled. Admit that you love the world, and that the pride of life comes naturally to you. But praise God that He is full of grace and desires to have mercy on you. Ask Him to save you from everything that is natural to fallen man and to let Christ's nature be seen in you day by day. And then be fit to worship in the heavenlies, in your body.

9

THE NEW BIRTH

Now when He was in Jerusalem at the Passover, during the feast, many believed in His name, beholding His signs which He was doing. But Jesus, on His part, was not entrusting Himself to them, for He knew all men, and because He did not need anyone to bear witness concerning man for He Himself knew what was in man. Now there was a man of the Pharisees, named Nicodemus, a ruler of the Jews; this man came to Him by night, and said to Him, "Rabbi, we know that You have come from God as a teacher; for no one can do these signs that You do unless God is with him." Jesus answered and said to him, "Truly, truly, I say to you, unless one is born again, he cannot see the kingdom of God." Nicodemus said to Him, "How can a man be born when he is old? He cannot enter a second time into his mother's womb and be born, can he?" Jesus answered, "Truly, truly, I say to you, unless one is born of water and the Spirit, he cannot enter into the kingdom of God. That which is born of the flesh is flesh, and that which is born of the Spirit is spirit. Do not marvel that I said to you, 'You must be born again.' The wind blows where it wishes and you hear the sound of it, but do not know where it comes from and where it is going; so is everyone who is born of the Spirit." Nicodemus answered and said to Him, "How can these things be?" Jesus answered and said to him, "Are you the teacher of Israel, and do not understand these things? Truly, truly, I say to you, we speak that which we know, and bear witness of that which we have seen; and you do not receive our witness. If I told you earthly things and you do not believe, how shall you believe if I tell you heavenly things? And no one has ascended into heaven, but He who descended from heaven, even the Son of Man. And as Moses lifted up the serpent in the wilderness, even so must the Son of Man be lifted up; that whoever believes may in Him have eternal life.

"For God so loved the world, that He gave His only begotten Son, that whoever believes in Him should not perish, but have eternal life. For God did not send the Son into the world to judge the world, but that the world should be saved through Him. He who believes in Him is not judged; he who does not believe has been judged already, because he has not believed in the name of the only begotten Son of God. And this is the judgment, that the light is come into the world, and men loved the darkness rather than the light; for their deeds were evil. For everyone who does evil hates the light, and does not come to the light, lest his deeds should be exposed. But he who practices the truth comes to the light, that his deeds may be manifested as having been wrought in God" (John 2:23–3:21).

I CAME ACROSS AN OLD Jewish commentary on the book of Exodus not long ago. The author, a rabbi, lists seven things that are hidden from

96 THAT YOU MAY BELIEVE

a man: the day of his death, the day of consolation, the depths of judgment, one's reward, the time of the restoration of the kingdom of David, the time when the guilty will be destroyed, and what is within the heart of another human being.

What is in the heart of another human being is difficult to discern, not just for a Jewish rabbi but also for us. Yet John tells us that Jesus knew all of these seven things, especially what was within the heart of another person. According to John 2:24-25, that is why Jesus did not entrust Himself to the people of Jerusalem. There is a play on words in those two verses. It says many *believed* in Jesus, but Jesus did not *believe* in them. It is the same word. It is translated in the New American Standard Version, "Many believed in His name. . . . But Jesus, on His part, was not entrusting Himself to them," and most other English versions translate it in a similar way. But what John actually said was that Jesus didn't *believe them*. He knew what was in their hearts and souls.

The distinction between chapters 2 and 3 of John, an artificial separation added later, is quite immaterial. The first word of chapter 3 in the Greek is not "now," as most translations put it; rather, it is "and," or maybe "but." So it should read, "And there was a man of the Pharisees named Nicodemus . . ."

"[T]he idea," as D. A. Carson puts it, "is that Nicodemus exemplified those who in some sense believed in Jesus [like those other Jewish people in Jerusalem], but with a faith so inadequate that Jesus did not entrust himself to them."[1] Right away, the challenge to you and me from this passage is, "How about my faith? Is it adequate? Do I have the faith that Jesus says saves people?"

I am not trying to upset your sense of assurance, but I am trying to do what I think our Lord does here with Nicodemus, who seemed fairly confident at first in his understanding of the Scripture. Jesus executes a difficult yet straightforward plan as He totally undermines Nicodemus's confidence in understanding what the truth is.

Nicodemus, a man of the Pharisees, calls Jesus "Rabbi." It is very collegial and friendly of him to do so. He recognizes Jesus as a teacher come from God who does the kinds of signs a man could not do unless God were with him.

Nicodemus has not asked Jesus anything yet, but John 3:3 begins,

"Jesus answered and said to him . . ." Nicodemus's opening remarks had a question implied in them. He was saying to Jesus, "You must come from God, You do such miraculous signs, like at the wedding at Cana. So who *are* You?" The question is implied.

Nicodemus is a man in the midst of the most severe crisis of his life, trying to decide who he is personally and professionally. Everything about his life is being undermined in this conversation as he comes to grips with the fact that someone who has no business teaching him the Bible is suddenly showing him things that he, a scholar of the Old Testament, should know. "Where in the world did *You* come from?" is what Nicodemus is asking.

But Jesus turns the tables on Nicodemus by calling into question his ability to see and understand anything spiritually: "Truly, truly, I say to you, unless one is born again, he cannot see the kingdom of God" (v. 3). Jesus immediately introduces tension into this dialogue as He insists that Nicodemus grapple with his spiritual blindness and inability. Nicodemus must come to understand three things about himself: *one,* the need to be born again; *two,* the supernatural nature of this rebirth; and *three,* the results of being born again.

THE NECESSITY OF A NEW BIRTH

Jesus first shows Nicodemus that he does not understand an absolutely fundamental principle of spiritual life. In John 3:7 Jesus says, "Do not marvel that I said to you, 'You must be born again.'" Jesus is implying, "Why have I caught you off guard, Nicodemus? Why don't you understand this?"

Nicodemus should not be surprised, but he is. Why does Nicodemus need to be born again? Because he is a Presbyterian who was baptized as an infant and never really had some emotional conversion experience? Because he never stumbled into a Baptist revival service? Of course not. He needs to be born again because he is a human being. Otherwise, the kingdom of God is barred to him. There are no exceptions.

Jesus repeats, "Truly, truly," three times in His dialogue with Nicodemus. It means, "I really mean what I am about to say." Note this carefully: whether you have been brought up inside the faith, going to church every Sunday with Sunday school pins filling a wall at home, or whether this is the first time in your life you have read this, there is no distinction—*you must be born again.*

Jesus presses this home in verse 3, saying, "Unless one is born again, he cannot see the kingdom of God." Those not born again are blind—they cannot see the kingdom of God. When Nicodemus wonders how that can be (v. 9), Jesus responds, "Are you the teacher of Israel, and do not understand these things?" Unless the Spirit of God comes upon us and gives us sight, we cannot see the truth of the kingdom, no matter our position, education, or religious background.

Perhaps more than any chapter in the New Testament, Romans 1 has profoundly shaped my understanding of the truth. The blindness of mankind is pointed out in verses 19-21: "That which is known about God is evident within them; for God made it evident to them. For since the creation of the world His invisible attributes, His eternal power and divine nature, have been clearly seen, being understood through what has been made, so that they are without excuse. For even though they knew God, they did not honor Him as God, or give thanks; but they became futile in their speculations, and their foolish heart was darkened." It is like someone walking around with soda bottle bottoms riveted to his eyes for glasses, thinking, *Oh, I see very well, thank you.* He may think he knows what it means to be born again, but his vision is distorted. The Lord must remove the soda bottle bottoms from his eyes.

Echoing Isaiah 59:10 ("We grope for the wall like the blind; . . . we stumble at noon as in the twilight" [ESV]), John Calvin says, "Man is blind at noonday."[2] He does not see what he has no right to miss. When my lovely wife and I have discussions about issues in which we see things slightly differently, we know we're getting to the bottom of our argument when one of us says to the other, "Sweetie, you're blind at noonday." All of us, really, not just in the little discussions of life but in the most essential things of our hearts, are blind at noonday. Until we see our blindness, we will never have sight. Until the Lord gives sight, no one can see the kingdom of God.

And even if the unregenerate person could see the kingdom of God, he would have no power to enter it. As I watch my son and his teammates play football, I can see the play developing. I can see the wide receiver get free. I can see that the quarterback ought to throw the ball to him. But my ability to see it doesn't give me any power to execute the play. I can't make it happen. When my son was in high school, I watched his football games with Jim Eidson, a former Dallas Cowboy from the 1970s and a member of our church. When Jim comments on a football game, it makes the scales fall from my eyes. He sees things I would never see, like what the quarterback needs to do, the play that needs to be executed; but neither Jim nor I have any power to make it happen from the stands.

Flesh gives birth to flesh and Spirit gives birth to spirit. If we are to enter the kingdom of God, we must understand the seriousness of the human condition. It is not a little medicine that we need. We are in no better shape than Lazarus was in his tomb. Jesus did not roll away the stone and give him an antibiotic. Lazarus was dead. It was not until Jesus said to Lazarus, "Come forth," that regeneration happened.

THE SUPERNATURAL NATURE OF THE NEW BIRTH

A curious thing happens in this dialogue with the term "born again," because it also means "born from above." After Jesus states the necessity of being born again, Nicodemus responds, literally, "How can a man be reborn? Can he enter a second time into his mother's womb?" (see John 3:4). Jesus ignores his question and explains being born again in terms of being born from above. The rebirth is spiritual, not natural. It is from the top down, from heaven to earth, from the Holy Spirit to man. Jesus drives this home by comparing spiritual rebirth to the wind: "The wind blows where it wishes and you hear the sound of it, but do not know where it comes from and where it is going; so is everyone who is born of the Spirit" (v. 8). The sound of the wind as it moves through the trees and the feel of it on our face lets us know it is there.

When I was growing up, hurricanes hitting the East Coast of the United States would sometimes get all the way up to Connecticut, where I lived. Usually by the time they get there they have dissipated quite a bit, but occasionally they can still be blowing hard. When that happened, my friends and I would take sheets to the roof of our house, hold tightly to the corners, stretch them out behind us, and try to get lifted off the roof by the wind. Sometimes we could, but only when the wind "decided" to blow hard enough and in the right direction! (I can't believe we did this—*don't try this at home, kids!*)

You cannot control the wind, nor can you control your natural birth. What did you contribute to your natural birth? Absolutely nothing. *Being born again is not a decision you make.* Whoever you are, however you came to Christ, you have been the object of God's supernatural work on your heart. No matter whether it was dramatic or quiet, there was no less power exerted in your becoming a believer than there was exerted on the apostle Paul on the road to Damascus when he was knocked off his horse and made blind.

You may long for a dramatic experience to "authenticate" your being born again. Take comfort. It does not matter whether you had a dramatic experience or whether you have been in the church all of your life; *what matters is not the drama of coming but the drama of continuing in the wonder of being born again.*

We receive this new birth as an act of God's re-creative power. When Jesus described to Nicodemus the blowing of the wind, He compared it to the Spirit's moving. As an Old Testament scholar, Nicodemus quite naturally heard the reference to Genesis. Jesus is using the same word for *moving* as was used in Genesis 1:2, where it says that the earth was formless and void and the Spirit of God was *moving* across the face of the waters. Jesus declares that there is no less need for God's same amazing re-creative power to save us. Genesis 2:7 says that God formed man from the dust of the ground and breathed into his nostrils the breath of life. The breath of God is His life-giving Spirit who generates man from the dust.

Because of the Fall, we are born dead. Paul says in Ephesians 2:1, "And you were dead in your trespasses and sins." If a man has drowned and is lying dead on the bottom of the lake, do you throw him a life preserver and say, "Hey, hang onto the life preserver and you'll be okay?" That is what many of us do when we appeal to our friends and neighbors and say, "Decide to be born again. Make a decision for Christ today." Before regeneration, they are as dead as the person at the bottom of the lake. Someone named Jesus must jump into the water and swim to the bottom, breathe the breath of life into them, pull them up, and take them to the safety of the boat.

Until we are made alive by the Spirit of God, our death nature even accumulates sin as life goes on. This is evident in the tragedies that occur in our country and world, which demonstrate the ongoing unraveling of a world no longer what it was made and meant to be. Only the Lord and the Giver of life can break this cycle of death and sin as He uses His resurrection power to cause new spiritual birth.

WHAT DO WE DO?

God causes us to be reborn. This is called "regeneration." Then, by His grace, we respond in repentance and faith. This is often called "conversion." Conversion is our "yes" response to the marvelous awakening grace of God in our hearts in our new birth.

But in John 3, Jesus is clearly and primarily teaching about regeneration. That distinction is very important. Maybe you are reading "conversion" when I discuss regeneration and wondering when I will get to the part about what we do, when *we* repent and believe. The story of Nicodemus is about doing nothing at all. It is about what God does as the absolute, primary necessity for us being able to do anything. *We don't come to Christ to be born again.* Reverse the order: we are born again in order to come to Christ.

Regeneration and conversion are not two parts of the same operation, God's part and my part. They are two separate things. To repeat: God causes us to be reborn and then, by His grace, we respond in repentance and faith—and that is conversion. Some mistakenly teach that, in John 3, Jesus is asking for a decision. But thinking about regeneration should leave us feeling helpless, and then we cry out for help—*and our crying out for help is the very mark that we have been born again.* Then we come in repentance and faith and conversion—our will says yes to Christ, and we receive Christ and all of the benefits He gives us. A preacher or teacher cannot tell a dead man to get up out of the grave. There is only one Man who can tell us to do that, and He does it in our hearts.

Rebirth is like an iceberg. Above the surface of the ocean we see, feel, and touch our work of repentance and faith in responding to the gospel; but that part of the iceberg could not exist were it not for its massive underside. That underside is God's work of regeneration, about which, concerning which, and contributing to which we do absolutely nothing.

TRANSFORMING EFFECTS OF THE NEW BIRTH

In 2 Corinthians 5:17 we learn that if we are in Christ we are a new creation, or, literally, "There is a new creation." By God's grace alone we are born into an altogether new order which the Lord Himself has brought about. Now I am going to play the salesman and sell you on the beauty and the wonder of regeneration—its transforming effects on the new believer.

Transformation One: Sight to the Blind

The first transforming effect of the new birth is spiritual sight, or the renewal of the mind. In John 3:3 Jesus says, "Unless one is born again, he cannot see the kingdom of God." Unless one has God's Holy Spirit at work in his or her heart, he is not able to exercise faith, which is virtually synonymous with the language of *seeing* in John's Gospel.

Have you ever seen one of those photographs that was taken of, say, shadows of trees or clouds, and it is supposed to be a picture of something that you are supposed to see, but you can't see it? You stare and stare and you look at it from all different angles and then, all of a sudden it comes together. That is a picture of what happens in regeneration. Sometimes it happens gradually, and sometimes it happens all at once. Either way, there is a sense of, "Now I see. I was blind but now at last I see." What you see is Jesus Christ. Once you saw Him as the founder of a religion or as a good moral leader. But now the camera lens has become crystal clear and you can see Him as Life-giver.

Transformation Two: Freedom of the Will

The second transforming effect of the new birth is the liberation of the will. Both before and after we become Christians, our freedom is defined and confined by our nature. Is man's will free? Yes. Man is free to act—but only to act according to his nature. Was the Gadarene demoniac a free man? Yes, he was free to cut himself, to run around naked, to scare people. Was he free, however, to sit quietly at the feet of Jesus and hear the Lord speak words of life and truth to him? No, not until God changed his nature. Not until Jesus touched him.

Let me tell you about a woman I called "the Ladybug," who

appeared at our church in Virginia in its early days as a new church just getting started. We were meeting at the time in a chapel small enough that I could see everyone. She would come in Sunday after Sunday and sit in the back row with arms folded across her body in an antagonistic pose and a scowl on her face. Her hair went in every direction. She was well known around town, the wife of a philosophy professor at the University of Virginia. She drove an old VW "bug" that she had repainted red with black spots, hence the name "Ladybug." She sat there for many Sundays listening to me, and she let me know she didn't like a word of it. Finally, one Sunday, as the service went on, I saw her composure change. She was literally melting into a different kind of person in the back of the church. At the end of the service I went up to her and asked, "What has happened?"

And she said, "The light has come on. I understand. The Lord has worked in my heart."

"Why don't you come to my office in a couple of days and we'll talk a little bit more about it," I said. She came in a couple of days later. She was still soft but was a little bit more her old, grumpy self. Trying to get the conversation going, I made a strategic mistake when I said, "Well, tell me what happened to you the other day when you decided to follow Jesus."

Her eyes got big and she readied her lecture: "Young man, the only thing I had decided to do was how I was going to run you over in my Volkswagen. *Jesus* decided that I was going to be His follower."

Did she decide? Yes, she turned her heart to the Lord in repentance and faith. But underneath her decision was the massive undergirding of the iceberg—regeneration. "For God so loved the world, that He gave His only begotten Son, that whoever believes in Him should not perish, but have eternal life." Put this famous and wonderful verse into the context of Jesus' dialogue with Nicodemus. "Whoever believes in" Jesus must be the one who has been born again. He can now "see" the kingdom of God (John 3:3), he can now "enter" the kingdom of God (v. 5), and therefore he does believe. John 3:16 is saying that *anyone can repent and believe who has been given eyes to believe and has been raised from the dead.* Blind people don't see, dead people don't believe, but those who have been given new birth see, believe, and enter the kingdom of God.

Sometimes we think there are three votes as to whether I am saved:

God gets one; the devil gets one; and I get to break the tie. But this is not a helpful way to think. Rebirth is not a democratic process, though there is an election: it is God's sovereign election, to which I respond in repentance and faith.

Transformation Three: Freedom from the Fear of Judgment

As Jesus concludes this discourse, He takes an interesting tack, seeking to assure Nicodemus that being born again removes the fear of judgment. He says in John 3:19 that, by nature, people turn away from the light because they love the darkness—until their nature gets changed. We are like worms a man hunts for fishing. He turns over a rock, and all the worms scurry away from the light.

The unregenerate human heart does not seek the light that shows the truth about the heart. It is like those bright lights in the doctor or dentist's office that get in our eyes and reveal every imperfection on our face or in our mouth. I hate those lights! I like the lights in the restrooms on airplanes. They are soft lights, purposefully designed to make me look good. But look at verse 20: "For everyone who does evil hates the light, and does not come to the light, lest his deeds should be exposed."

Scripture teaches us deep human psychology here. Hide it though we try, we live under the fear of judgment. It is not always a conscious thought, but every human being actually lives under what Hebrews calls a certain and terrifying expectation of judgment. We see this in many small ways in our lives. Because we do evil, we avoid the light, lest our deeds be exposed. And what we do out of the fear of being found out by others in countless small ways, God says we do in the largest ways: we run from *Him*. But when we are born again, we see that He who would be our Judge has now become our Savior. Verse 17 says, "For God did not send the Son into the world to judge the world, but that the world should be saved through Him." John says that the man or woman who has been born again is spared the judgment of separation from God.

Transformation Four: Freedom from Pride

The fourth transforming effect of regeneration is humility. Regeneration is very humbling. Nicodemus had to endure much bruising of his ego. He had to come at night under the cloak of darkness. He had to ask

questions of an itinerant preacher who didn't graduate from the best theological seminary. He had to admit that he simply didn't understand the
spiritual meaning of Jesus' words.

We see this in our own lives as well. It is hard for us Nike-types who
"just do it" to see that we cannot make happen what needs to happen.
Like Nicodemus, all of our education, prestige, social status, or wealth
cannot give us new birth. In fact, they are often roadblocks, getting in
the way as they provide a false sense of security—footholds that will
crumble.

But it wasn't just intellectual humbling or social humbling that
Nicodemus had to endure. It wasn't just his biblical ignorance or his failure as a member of the Sanhedrin and teacher of Israel that had to be
brought into the light. Jesus spotlighted a need for *heart* humility, identifying the core of Nicodemus's pride as a human being. What could
Nicodemus contribute to his own rebirth? Nothing.

Man does not like this process of being humbled, Spurgeon says:
"The 'gate of heaven' is not quite high enough for the head, and he does
not like stooping."[3] The human condition is prone by nature and by
practice to secure a foothold for its own standing.

The summer before my freshman year in college, I went to a school
in Maine called Outward Bound. It is a rugged, month-long outdoor
"boot camp." When we were rock climbing and rappelling, we would
always look for footholds for some sense of security. But the ultimate
security wasn't in having a place to put your foot, but in the fact that
you were being belayed by someone else at the top of the cliff.

In our small group of twelve guys, there was a tough kid from the
meanest streets of the Bronx. He had been sent to Outward Bound by a
juvenile judge as the last stop before prison. He didn't like a lot of us.
He would pull knives on us and was always in trouble. Guess what this
guy from the Bronx thought of a lily-white kid from the suburbs who
wore buttoned-down shirts? And guess who, when we were rappelling
and rock climbing, was belaying me at the top!

Imagine you are climbing a mountain and lose your foothold. You
search, but there is no place to put your foot. Spiritually, on your own
there is no place to put your foot. You are in danger of falling and per-
ishing, as Jesus says in verse 16. But you look up and see that you are
being belayed by your strong Best Friend. Do you feel more secure? The

humility of regeneration means that there are no footholds. We are totally dependent upon Jesus Christ, who has the ropes in His hands, and He has sworn an oath in blood to keep us from falling. That is what it means not to perish but to have everlasting life.

Transformation Five: Love for New Things

Changed affections are another transforming effect of the new birth. Look again at John 3:5: "Jesus answered, 'Truly, truly, I say to you, unless one is born of water and the Spirit, he cannot enter into the kingdom of God.'" A lot of theological ink has been spilled over this verse. We know what "the Spirit" means here, but what does "water" mean? I think it is best to connect it with Ezekiel 36:25-26, where the prophet, speaking for the Lord, says, "I will sprinkle clean water on you, and you will be clean; I will cleanse you from all your filthiness and from all your idols. Moreover, I will give you a new heart and put a new spirit in you; I will remove the heart of stone from your flesh and give you a heart of flesh."

People really change!

I love an illustration from author and professor Sinclair Ferguson. A young man begins coming to church, and eventually becomes a Christian. He then says to the leaders of the church, "I can't believe how much this church has changed within the last few weeks. The hymns are so lively now. The worship is so wonderfully meaningful. Why, even the preacher is better!"

Think about it in your own life. Have your affections changed with new life? Aren't the things you love different? Don't you begin to have a love for the things that are wholesome and true and right, and a distaste for other things? That is a mark of being born again.

Transformation Six: Childlike Trust

The final effect of the new birth discussed in this passage is childlike trust in a crucified Savior. John 3:14-16 says, "And as Moses lifted up the serpent in the wilderness, even so must the Son of Man be lifted up; that whoever believes may in Him have eternal life. For God so loved the world, that He gave His only begotten Son, that whoever believes in Him should not perish, but have eternal life." Maybe the deepest humiliation Nicodemus had to endure was that he had to become a child again. Because regeneration precedes faith, one of the results of the new birth is genuine faith—child-like trust in the Son of God. Nicodemus looked up and he simply believed, which means he put his trust in the Son of God. Just as Moses lifted up the serpent in the wilderness so that when the Israelites looked up at it they were healed, so, too, was Jesus lifted up before Nicodemus, and he believed and was saved.

But when was Jesus lifted up before Nicodemus? On the cross. His witnessing of the Crucifixion so changed Nicodemus that, in child-like faith, he helped take the body of Jesus down from the cross and arranged for a proper burial (19:39-42). Nicodemus tenderly took the body of Jesus to the tomb, trusting that God would raise Him up. As an old man, Nicodemus had become a baby again, this time in the womb of spiritual dependence. To be born again we, too, must stoop low, down to the helplessness of a newborn infant needing life and nurture from our heavenly Father—a life and nurture that is available through His Son's death and resurrection, by the regenerating power of the Holy Spirit. We must be people who say, "Thanks be to God who raised me from the dead and gave me new life, and to that great work I contributed absolutely nothing."

10

THE (REAL) NEW AGE

After these things Jesus and His disciples came into the land of Judea, and there He was spending time with them and baptizing. And John also was baptizing in Aenon near Salim, because there was much water there; and they were coming and were being baptized. For John had not yet been thrown into prison. There arose therefore a discussion on the part of John's disciples with a Jew about purification. And they came to John and said to him, "Rabbi, He who was with you beyond the Jordan, to whom you have borne witness, behold, He is baptizing, and all are coming to Him." John answered and said, "A man can receive nothing, unless it has been given him from heaven. You yourselves bear me witness, that I said, 'I am not the Christ,' but, 'I have been sent before Him.' He who has the bride is the bridegroom; but the friend of the bridegroom, who stands and hears him, rejoices greatly because of the bridegroom's voice. And so this joy of mine has been made full. He must increase, but I must decrease. He who comes from above is above all, he who is of the earth is from the earth and speaks of the earth. He who comes from heaven is above all. What He has seen and heard, of that He bears witness; and no man receives His witness. He who has received His witness has set his seal to this, that God is true. For He whom God has sent speaks the words of God; for He gives the Spirit without measure. The Father loves the Son, and has given all things into His hand. He who believes in the Son has eternal life; but he who does not obey the Son shall not see life, but the wrath of God abides on him" (John 3:22-36).

ONE EVENING I SAW ON "The News Hour with Jim Lehrer" a fascinating discussion with Edmund Morris about his book *Dutch: A Memoir of Ronald Reagan*.[1] Morris, a distinguished political biographer who also wrote the authoritative biography of Teddy Roosevelt, was interviewed by Lehrer and then by a panel of other political biographers. At issue was Morris's literary device of creating a character who does not exist. The character is really Morris himself, who is injected fictitiously back into the real life of Ronald Reagan. Morris defended this unusual approach by saying how difficult it is to know another person. He had lots of reasons for claiming President Reagan was a particularly difficult person to get to know. He interviewed President Reagan for two full years off and on in the last years of his presidency and had known him for fourteen years. But he struggled to know who Reagan was as a man and as president.

I thought about this difficulty in relation to this particular passage in John's Gospel, and I was struck by how amazing it is that we have these historical and biographical memoirs of our Lord in the Gospels written not by fictitious characters but by real men: John, the apostle, who wrote this Gospel; and, in this case, John the Baptist, who relates his final testimony about Jesus. No literary device had to be created to present to us the truth about Christ. These men were real, contemporaneous figures who gave witness to Jesus, their friend and their Lord; and in doing so they have given us some of the most accurate history of any event or any person in the ancient world.

This narration from chapter 3 is a presentation from John the Baptist through John the apostle about how the old ways of purification are surpassed by Jesus, who opens to us a new and living way and an altogether new era in history—not a new age of crystals, gurus, chants, and meditations, but the real new age of God's dealing with His people in a new and complete way, a way that addresses the heart of the human problem and human condition.

THE OLD AGE

The "old age" is shown in this story about John the Baptist. Jesus had spent the Passover in Jerusalem, where He had cleansed the temple and had His secret meeting with Nicodemus. But now He goes out into the rocky barrenness of the rural areas of Judea. John 3:22 says that Jesus was baptizing there, but this is amplified in 4:2, where we read specifically that it really wasn't Jesus who was doing the baptizing but His disciples.

(By the way, verse 24, which says, "John [the Baptist] had not yet been thrown in prison," reveals an interesting assumption on the part of John the Gospel's author: he expects that you have already read Matthew, Mark, and Luke. Why? Because in John's Gospel there is no mention of John the Baptist being thrown into prison. He is assuming you already know that from your reading of the other Gospels.)

Verse 25 tells us, "There arose therefore a discussion on the part of

John's disciples with a Jew about purification." "Discussion" literally means "a dispute, a controversial question" about purification. Verse 25 is the key to this passage, the key to unlocking what is going on in this last testimony of John the Baptist. It is a discussion with an unnamed Jew about how you become pure, how you become clean.

It may seem at first that the concern of John the Baptist's disciples' about the competition from Jesus' disciples in the baptism market is the central issue. So many are flocking to Jesus and beginning to follow Him. But the real discussion is about the relationship of baptism to purification. Discussions about baptism are still common. What does it mean? Why do some denominations, including mine, baptize infants, and others do not? Is there any difference between infant baptism and baby dedication? (Yes, there is a great difference!)

What is the relationship of water baptism to purification? The core issue is this: how does one get rid of sin? That word *purification* is synonymous with cleansing the heart. I admit this is not a hot topic in our everyday lives. You know what is a hotter topic for me? What do I do when I get a spot on my beautiful new tie? I anguish. That is why we guys do these silly things with our ties at lunchtime. We throw them over our shoulders or tuck them into our shirts—anything to avoid getting spots on our ties. We care about the purity of our ties.

LAST VOICE OF THE OLD AGE, FIRST VOICE OF THE NEW

John the Baptist wants us to care about the purity of our hearts. He is explaining the relationship between water baptism and the real purification that needs to go on in a person's heart. He says that Jesus is providing an altogether new age of purification, much more effective than anything he, John the Baptist, can do. He tells his disciples not to worry if Jesus' disciples are baptizing more people. John reminds them that his role is that of herald, running ahead to announce Jesus' coming. He is the best man at the wedding, pointing attention to the groom.

REARRANGING THE STAGE

A familiar term from the theater is when one actor "upstages" another. Technically, that is when all the other actors on the stage turn their backs to the audience when an actor comes onto the stage, to force all the attention on the newcomer. Now, more commonly, to upstage someone simply means to become the center of attention. John the Baptist is saying that it is time for Jesus to step into the spotlight to upstage John, and the timing is according to the precise stage directions of the Playwright.

"He must increase, but I must decrease" (John 3:30). And as D. A. Carson puts it, "The 'must' [in that statement] is nothing less than the determined will of God."[2] God has said that it is time for John the Baptist to move off the stage and for Jesus to take center stage. John finds his joy in this, the joy of the best man who is thrilled for his friend, the Groom, and who sees that it is God who has sovereignly put them into their respective positions.

So John's stepping back, his decreasing, is the transition from the old age to the new age. Remember that the key question of the passage is how you become pure. The old age represented by John the Baptist is the ministry of purification in the temple, limited to the temple, with the continuous daily offering of the lambs performed by priests. It was inadequate cleansing.

What is to come is the ending of temple sacrifice by the once-and-for-all sacrifice of the Lamb of God, which gives abundant purification for God's people. This is what we have been studying in all the Gospel of John. That is what all those big waterpots mean at the wedding in Cana. The cleansing water, a hundred and fifty gallons, Jesus turns into wine, symbolizing that His blood is far better cleansing than that water could ever be. He not only cleanses the temple in chapter 2, He replaces it and calls us to move into an altogether new age where worship, sacrifice, and purification are not tied to what goes on in that temple. John the Baptist was the last voice of the old world and the first voice of the new.

Jesus said elsewhere that John the Baptist was greater than all the Old Testament prophets, yet he was the least among all of his own disciples. John's greatest day was his last day. Like Moses, who brought the people of Israel to the very edge of the Promised Land, John the Baptist brought history to a new boundary that he himself would not cross. But for disciples from all over the world, John the Baptist's last day is the first day of the rest of our lives, and he gives a humble but purposeful voice to the mighty power of the Lamb of God to cleanse hearts. He says he is the announcer, one not to be seen, just heard, with a voice that is fading more and more. He is a friend of the Bridegroom who stands and hears the Bridegroom proclaim His love for His bride, and he rejoices at the loud voice of the Bridegroom compared to his own diminishing voice.

In weddings that I perform, the groom, the best man, and I are usually standing alone at the front of the aisle for a few moments before the rest of the procession comes in. I like to hear the encouragement a best man will often voice to the groom. He may say something like, "It's okay; you'll make it through this." (I always wonder whether he means the wedding or the marriage!)

FINDING YOUR VOICE

John the Baptist calls himself a voice crying in the wilderness (John 1:23), and says that he has found his voice by listening to the voice of his friend, the Bridegroom (3:29). You know the expression, "She has found her voice." When we say that, we usually don't mean, "She had a cold and then got her voice back." No, we mean that she has found her identity, her role, and her voice in life.

The challenge of John the Baptist's life to us is not just that we would be humble before the Lord like he was. The deeper challenge is that we would know who we are before the Lord, that we would find our own voice. A clear mark of finding our voice is joy—the joy of the best man who is thrilled for the Groom. John the Baptist says, "This joy of mine has been made full" (3:29). Jesus repeats that concept three times in various ways in the Gospel of John: "These things I have spoken to you, that My joy may be in you, and that your joy may be made full" (15:11); "Until now you have asked for nothing in My name," Jesus says, so, "ask, and you will receive, that your joy may be made full" (16:24); and then in chapter 17 Jesus is praying to the Father for us and says, "But now I come to Thee; and these things I speak in the world, that they may have My joy made full in themselves" (v. 13). Joy made full—that is what we are supposed to have.

The words "made full" come from the Greek word *plērōma*. It is the same word that Paul uses when he describes Jesus as the *plērōma* of God, the fullness of God (Col. 2:9). There is nothing more full of God than Jesus. This is the last time that John the Baptist is mentioned in this

Gospel; he is out and Jesus is in—but he is full of joy. That is not the way we usually work. I don't like it when the other guy is in the spotlight. I don't like it when the other guy gets the promotion. I don't like it when the other kid gets to play first string. Women don't like it when the other woman gets her picture in the society paper. But for John the Baptist there is fullness of joy in decreasing, in knowing his place before the Lord.

It is a major obstacle to our joy that we Christians do not know our place in the Lord's kingdom, that we have not found our voices. We either take on too much in the Lord's service or avoid responsibilities by being over-invested in other things. Some of us need to be reminded of what Barbara once wrote to me on a Post-it note on the bathroom mirror during a particularly hectic time: "For peace of mind, resign as general manager of the universe." Some of us need to be reminded of that in the Lord's work. To find my voice, my place is to realize that God is sovereign and I am not. He can do His work without me. For me to find my place is for me to find joy, the *plērōma* of joy in doing significant but small things in the Lord's kingdom.

Some other people, frankly, need to do a little more for the Lord to find their place. They need to watch a little less television or take one less vacation in order to free up time for the new age.

LORD OF THE NEW AGE

What is that new age like? How do we give voice to Jesus as the Lord of the new age? First, we recognize that Jesus is *from above*, not from earth, and that we must therefore be born from above (John 3:31). Remember Jesus' conversation with Nicodemus? The word *earth* there in verse 31 is not the word *kosmos*, which means "the sinful world," as in "God so loved the world." The word for "earth" in verse 31 means, "the finite, limited planet earth." John the Baptist is saying that he is from earth, but Jesus is from above.

Second, in the new age Jesus gives *firsthand* witness because He got it from the Father (v. 32). He had been with the Father in a way that no other prophet has ever been before or since.

Third, although this witness is rejected by mankind, in the new age Jesus' witness is *confirmed* by God (v. 33).

Fourth, in the new age Jesus speaks God's words *by the Spirit's full power* (v. 34). Throughout history, God has spoken through His messengers the prophets. To each one He gave the Spirit in proportion to the assigned task—some more, some less. But now in the new age the Spirit is given without measure to the Son.

And, fifth, in the new age Jesus *receives all things* from the Father because of the love the Father has for the Son (v. 35). *The new age is characterized by the authority of the Son of God to purify hearts.* No one else ever before was able to do it. No matter how much Spirit power was given to prophets of old, no matter how much gold dust may fall on some man's preaching, there is no power to purify hearts unless that authority is given from above, and the Father has chosen to give that authority to His Son.

PROMISES OF THE NEW AGE

The promise of the new age is that we shall enter into it. John 3:36: "He who believes in the Son has eternal life." That is present tense. We *have* eternal life. We enter into it *now*. Literally, "eternal life" is to be translated "the age of the life to come." It is a *new* age, an altogether *eternal* age into which we enter *now* by virtue of the authority of the Son cleansing our hearts.

But with the promise comes a warning. The second part of verse 36 says, "He who does not obey the Son shall not see life, but the wrath of God abides on him." That is strong language. To disregard the word of the Son about His purification from sin is to reject the Son Himself. It is to miss the age of the life to come. One who disregards the voice of Jesus on purification will not see life, just as Nicodemus could not see the kingdom of God until he repented and believed. *Failure to trust in the Son is disobedience as much as it is disbelief.* Such a person will see wrath, and wrath is not a popular subject.

J. I. Packer has given us a beautiful definition of wrath in his book *Knowing God:* "God's wrath in the Bible is never the capricious, self-indulgent, irritable, morally ignoble thing that human anger is. It is, instead, a right and necessary reaction to objective moral evil." Packer then asks a question: "Would a God who did not react adversely to evil in His world be morally perfect?"[3] The answer must be no.

"He who believes in the Son has eternal life; but he who does not obey the Son shall not see life, but the wrath of God abides on him." Verse 36 is John the Baptist's last sentence recorded in this Gospel. After this, he disappears from the scene. He "decreases" completely. His strong last words are a warning against disregarding the Son, the only way of purification. We will not become pure on our own, by trying to be good people, by trying to prove to God that we are somehow worthy of what Jesus did for us.

John the Baptist echoes John the Gospel writer, who later says, "He who has the Son has the life; he who does not have the Son of God does not have the life" (1 John 5:12). It is a promise and a warning. To have faith in the Son is to believe that He alone has the authority to purify our hearts for the age to come. If you call upon Him, He will purify you.

THE COSTLY WEDDING FEAST

Imagine this picture: a bride arrives at the church and steps out of the car in her beautiful white dress. A second later, an eighteen-wheeler goes by, hits a big puddle, and splatters mud, grease, and road tar all over her beautiful white dress. A horrified bridesmaid immediately runs up and says, "Oh, let me help!" She takes out a sponge and tries to dab the dress clean. What happens? The dirt just spreads around in a big, blurry blob. The bride needs an altogether new dress.

In the new age, we need some new clothes. We need an altogether new "dress" that only Christ our Bridegroom can give us. We need the dress that is the righteousness of the Groom Himself, that He gives to His bride out of love. That is the only way that we will be pure. This purification He gives without limit. There is no limit to the Son's ability and authority to purify. You or I can turn over a new leaf, but the leaf will still be dirty. We can try harder, but it doesn't get us anywhere. Only the Son can cleanse our hearts to their very depths.

The new age is the age of a new, cleansed life that is a foretaste of the great wedding banquet to come. The new life into which we enter now, the joy of the forgiveness of sins, of purity of heart, gives *plērōma*. There is fullness of joy but it is just the appetizer of the greater meal to come. This meal is very good and expensive. Do you ever get invitations to big fundraising banquets? The tickets may cost a thousand dollars or ten thousand dollars to sponsor a table. Is that expensive? No, it is cheap, compared to the price paid by the Son for *His* wedding banquet.

Isaiah said it beautifully in Isaiah 55:1: "You who have no money come, buy and eat. Come, buy wine and milk without money and without cost." The contradiction of buying without money is intentional. We can't buy because we can't afford it. We can't pay because the price has already been paid by One whose suffering and death bought our redemption. He purged our stains by giving up His life, and now He invites us into this new age of purity. We can only acknowledge that the price has been paid by acknowledging the Son as the One with the complete authority to pay it for us. All authority and power, every status and domain now belong to Jesus Christ, who, unlike the fictional character created by author Edmund Morris, is real and is reigning as Lord of the new age.

11

WATER, WORSHIP, WITNESS

And He had to pass through Samaria. So He came to a city of Samaria, called Sychar, near the parcel of ground that Jacob gave to his son Joseph; and Jacob's well was there. Jesus therefore, being wearied from His journey, was sitting thus by the well. It was about the sixth hour. There came a woman of Samaria to draw water. Jesus said to her, "Give Me a drink." For His disciples had gone away into the city to buy food. The Samaritan woman therefore said to Him, "How is it that You, being a Jew, ask me for a drink since I am a Samaritan woman?" (For Jews have no dealings with Samaritans.) Jesus answered and said to her, "If you knew the gift of God, and who it is who says to you, 'Give Me a drink,' you would have asked Him, and He would have given you living water." She said to Him, "Sir, You have nothing to draw with and the well is deep; where then do You get that living water? You are not greater than our father Jacob, are You, who gave us the well, and drank of it himself and his sons and his cattle?" Jesus answered and said to her, "Everyone who drinks of this water shall thirst again; but whoever drinks of the water that I shall give him shall never thirst; but the water that I shall give him shall become in him a well of water springing up to eternal life." The woman said to Him, "Sir, give me this water, so I will not be thirsty, nor come all the way here to draw." He said to her, "Go, call your husband, and come here." The woman answered and said, "I have no husband." Jesus said to her, "You have correctly said, 'I have no husband'; for you have had five husbands, and the one whom you now have is not your husband; this you have said truly." The woman said to Him, "Sir, I perceive that You are a prophet. Our fathers worshiped in this mountain, and you people say that in Jerusalem is the place where men ought to worship." Jesus said to her, "Woman, believe Me, an hour is coming when neither in this mountain, nor in Jerusalem, shall you worship the Father. You worship what you do not know; we worship what we know, for salvation is from the Jews. But an hour is coming, and now is, when the true worshipers shall worship the Father in spirit and truth; for such people the Father seeks to be His worshipers. God is spirit, and those who worship Him must worship in spirit and truth." The woman said to Him, "I know that Messiah is coming (He who is called Christ); when that One comes, He will declare all things to us." Jesus said to her, "I who speak to you am He." And at this point His disciples came, and they marveled that He had been speaking with a woman; yet no one said, "What do You seek?" or, "Why do You speak with her?" So the woman left her waterpot, and went into the city, and said to the men, "Come, see a man who told me all the things that I have done; this is not the Christ, is it?" They went out of the city, and were coming to Him. In the meanwhile the disciples were requesting Him, saying, "Rabbi, eat." But

He said to them, "I have food to eat that you do not know about." The disciples therefore were saying to one another, "No one brought Him anything to eat, did he?" Jesus said to them, "My food is to do the will of Him who sent Me, and to accomplish His work. Do you not say, 'There are yet four months, and then comes the harvest'? Behold, I say to you, lift up your eyes, and look on the fields, that they are white for harvest. Already he who reaps is receiving wages, and is gathering fruit for life eternal; that he who sows and he who reaps may rejoice together. For in this case the saying is true, 'One sows, and another reaps.' I sent you to reap that for which you have not labored; others have labored, and you have entered into their labor." And from that city many of the Samaritans believed in Him because of the word of the woman who testified, "He told me all the things that I have done." So when the Samaritans came to Him, they were asking Him to stay with them; and He stayed there two days. And many more believed because of His word; and they were saying to the woman, "It is no longer because of what you said that we believe, for we have heard for ourselves and know that this One is indeed the Savior of the world" (John 4:4-42).

EAST RIVER DRIVE in Philadelphia is a park-like road that winds along the Schuylkill River. It passes by Boathouse Row, where rowing sculls are kept, and nearby there is a statue of a pilgrim with an open Bible in his hands. If you stop and explore a little, you can see a stream running by the statue to the river, and if you follow the stream up the hill to its source you will find an aqueduct that the city built many years ago to direct the waters of the stream into the river. On the aqueduct the city fathers chose to write, "Everyone who drinks of this water shall thirst again." In the well-known couplet of John 4:13-14, where Jesus tells the woman the same truth about her well water, the key word is *whoever* in verse 14, and it harkens back to John 3:16 and the *whoever* in that famous verse. "Whoever drinks the water I give him will never thirst" (NIV).

The story of the Samaritan woman is a commentary on John 3:16. The issue is the "world," which does not mean every single human created, but the whole world under the reign of sin. It is every person taken as one, and it is the cosmos run amuck. The *whoever* is a hypothetical *anyone*. The message of the gospel goes out to everyone and anyone. The only prerequisite is that the "anyone" who hears and believes recognizes that he or she is a part of this cosmos and needs the living water. John

3:16 is more than an invitation to come; it is a prescription for coming. It is how *anyone* can come.

With that in mind, put yourself into the mindset of Christ's disciples. What would they have heard when they heard Jesus say that *anyone* can come (3:16)? They would have agreed, but they would have understood "anyone" in terms of a "Jewish," "male," "morally upright" anyone. The amazing thing is that the *anyone* here, in chapter 4, is *not* Jewish, *not* male, and *not* moral. And worse, she is a Samaritan, the lowest of the low to the Jews. Samaritans and Jews were total enemies. Jews saw Samaritans as socially inferior religious heretics who had been greatly influenced by the Babylonians during the captivity and had developed a syncretistic mix of Judaism and paganism. They had even built their own temple for worship, which was anathema to Jews.

Not only is she a member of a despised race, she is a woman, and this alone would have relegated her to low status in all ancient cultures. Men rarely talked to women in public. So startling is Jesus' behavior that both the woman herself and the disciples remark about it.

And not only is she Samaritan and a woman, she is an outcast. Why is she alone? Why is she there at the well *at that particular time of day?* Traditionally, women in Jesus' day had to carry several pots of water to the well, enough for that day's bathing, cleaning, washing, and cooking. The pots would be impossibly heavy for one person to carry on the return trip home, so they would not come alone. Furthermore, women never went to the well at the sixth hour, which is high noon, the hottest part of the day. Rather, they would come in the morning or the evening when it was cooler. But this woman comes alone, at the worst part of the day, because she is a moral outcast. She has had a lot of men in her life, and the man she is living with now is not her husband.

VIOLATING THE SOCIAL TABOOS

An amazing thing that must strike us upon the first reading of this passage is the incredible diversity of people to whom Jesus spoke. The woman herself is amazed that He would talk to her. The disciples are amazed when they return.

John intends us to see the contrast between this woman and Nicodemus, to whom Jesus has just been speaking in the previous chapter. Nicodemus is educated, powerful, respected, upright, moral, theologically trained—a pillar of the community. This woman is uneducated, without social influence, immoral, poor, and has a simple, false folk religion. Nicodemus is a Jew, a man and a ruler. She is a Samaritan, a woman, and a social no-count who has made a thorough mess of her life. Jesus gives His time, His talk, His grace to anyone, and He is happy to violate all of the social taboos to do it. The amazing thing about the gospel's grace is that it is for anyone, and anyone includes people who are not like you and me.

Charles Spurgeon, the great Baptist preacher, said, "Many have found room in 'whosoever' who would have felt themselves shut out by a narrower word."[1] This is not a narrow word. It is a *whoever*. Whoever will come, can come.

The surest sign of someone understanding grace is that he doesn't expect or even want to have a church with people just like himself. My friend Tim Keller, pastor of the thriving Redeemer Presbyterian Church in New York City, says, "If Christianity is a matter of grace, then when you come to church, you need to leave something at the door. Out there what matters is class, race, gender, moral performance. Leave all that at the door."[2]

The church is a supernatural community! It is made supernatural by the intervention of God's grace. Come, undeserved; come, anyone. We did not ask for this grace. We cannot demand it on the basis of anything we say or do. It comes to us, it comes to anyone, and therefore the community of the church is a supernatural community. It is a community on the terms that God defines, and He says that *anyone* can be in this community.

If things like class, race, gender, or moral performance that mean so much in the world are brought into the church, then the church does not understand grace at all. Diversity is a sure sign of the grace of the gospel having free run among the people of God. It is a sign that the community of the church is supernatural, because grace goes to anyone.

RUNNING WATER AND LIVING WATER

The only common denominator in the community of the church is that anyone who wants to know the grace of God in the gospel must thirst.

I actually have a difficult time understanding thirst. I almost never get thirsty. I can go two and three days and survive on a couple of Diet Pepsis, but my wife is a different story altogether. She doesn't go anywhere without her bottle of water. Barbara won't go to the curb to get the newspaper in the morning without carrying her bottle of water along. In the hot, sun-baked, Middle Eastern climate, Jesus and this woman both knew about what happens to a human body deprived of water.

Jesus uses this physical reality to relate to the woman in her urgent need for water. He uses the expression "living water" because it has two levels of meaning. First, it means "fresh running water from springs." The word in John 4:6 for Jacob's "well" is actually the word *spring*, and despite all the social barriers of talking with a Jewish man, this woman is interested because she would like very much to have such a supply of living, running water nearby. In verse 15 she says, "Sir, give me this water, so I will not be thirsty, nor come all the way here to draw." This woman, unlike Nicodemus, comes not for talk but for water; but Jesus takes her from that need into something she needs even more.

The second meaning of "living water" is the soul-satisfying grace of God, or that which only God can give to satisfy a soul. It is synonymous with terms such as the "eternal life" of 3:16 or 3:36: "He who believes in the Son has eternal life." Jesus told Nicodemus about the kingdom of God, and now gives the same good news to the Samaritan woman, using the metaphor of *living* water. The living water is the transforming life and power that God alone gives in and through the gospel of His Son, that leads to eternal life, and that satisfies as nothing else can.

Clearly in the background of Jesus' mind is Jeremiah 2:13, where God says, "For My people have committed two evils: they have forsaken Me, the fountain of living waters, to hew for themselves cisterns, broken cisterns, that can hold no water." The people reject the springs of God's grace and instead they make leaky pots that can hold no water, hoping to create their own satisfaction.

"GO, CALL YOUR HUSBAND"

Many commentators suggest that John 4:16 is an abrupt change of subject when Jesus says, "Go, call your husband." He seems to switch the subject suddenly from living water to the woman's husband. Actually, it is not abrupt at all; Jesus is simply showing the woman what her "broken cistern" is. He doesn't condemn her; rather, He convicts her by the implied question, "What have you been seeking for your satisfaction?" In this woman's case it is men. She has had serial common-law marriages, a series of "live-in boyfriends." As the song goes, she was "looking for love in all the wrong places."

But let's be careful here not to condemn this woman. The intent of this text is not for us to condemn her but rather to be convicted ourselves about the broken cisterns in our own lives. Do you seek meaning and purpose in your career, your appearance, your social status, your bigger house, your acceptance, getting into the inner circle, the right college, the right team? All of these are cracked and broken cisterns; they cannot hold the living water. They cannot ultimately satisfy.

Jesus says, "Go, call your husband," to get the woman to identify what her broken cistern is, what her idol is; and He does the same to us. He says to you and to me, "Go, get your [fill in the blank], whatever it is, and bring it here right now. Go get what you worship, what you hope will satisfy you and give you meaning." When Jesus makes us think about our idols, particularly about how they fail us in the end, He is creating in us a thirst for living water. The question is, Into what well have you dipped the bucket of your soul?

Jesus is talking about the nature of real spiritual worship. I think the woman understands what Jesus is asking her to do when He says, "Go, get your husband." She knows that He is moving into her heart, into what she worships.

Most commentators say that at this point the woman tries a diversionary tactic. "Sir," she says, "I perceive that You are a prophet" (John 4:19). Most commentators say that the woman is feeling the heat; Jesus is getting too personal, too close to pay dirt, and she wants to retreat to a nice, safe, theological discussion. In verse 20 she says, "Our fathers worshiped in this mountain, and you people say that in Jerusalem is the place where men ought to worship."

The key to understanding this whole passage is recognizing that the woman is *not* changing the subject. It is not that Jesus is getting so close that now she must distract Him. She is realizing that her broken cistern can't hold the living water. She is beginning to realize that Jesus is talking about what is in her heart and about worship. He has created a thirst for living water in her and has shown her that she is drinking from broken cisterns. "What you are worshiping isn't working," He says to her and to us. "It doesn't really satisfy you, does it?"

Her question about the right place to worship is not out of the blue either. She is beginning to want to know, "Where do I go to worship? Where can I find the water that really does satisfy?" It is crucial that we understand the meaning of His answer in verse 23: "true worshipers shall worship the Father in spirit and truth; for such people the Father seeks to be His worshipers."

THE HOUR, NOT THE PLACE

The word *spirit* in John 4:24 does not have a capital *S*. It is generally understood not to be a reference of the Holy Spirit or, at least not primarily; it is a reference to *our* spirits. We must worship *internally,* without reference to Jerusalem or Mount Gerizim, or to a temple or sanctuary. Real worship bubbles up from within, from a heart deeply satisfied with living water that has become a well springing up into eternal life.

Jesus is saying that if worship is internal we do not need to go to a particular place to worship. He is also saying much, much more. Look at verse 23 again: "But an hour is coming, and now is, when the true worshipers shall worship the Father in spirit and truth." The critical information is not the place; it is the hour.

Remember, *hour* is one of John's key words, a trigger he uses again and again as a reference to the hour of Jesus' death. We saw earlier that Jesus says we need a new temple, the temple that is His body. He is saying, "I am the place of sacrifice where sin is paid for." The hour of His death is the hour that makes Jesus the place of mankind's eternal, central, universal worship.

THE GREATEST THIRST

It is interesting that Jesus never gets a drink from this well. He is weary and thirsty, but He never gets any water. Why? It is a preview of the "hour" that was to come. When Jesus said on the cross, "I am thirsty," the searing heat of God's justice burned within Him. As the prophet

Nahum put it, "His wrath is poured out like fire" (Nah. 1:6). On the cross, there was no well of life springing up for Jesus. He was cut off. Dehydration, even an awful thirsting to death is nothing compared to what happened to Jesus when the wrath of God burned in Him. Jesus died of thirst—a thirst for God, the quenching of which He was denied.

On the cross, Jesus quoted from Psalm 22:1: "My God, my God, why hast Thou forsaken Me?" Other words from Psalms were undoubtedly on His mind as well: "My strength is dried up like a potsherd; and my tongue cleaves to my jaws; and Thou dost lay me in the dust of death" (Ps. 22:15). That is the description of a man dying of thirst.

The hour of Jesus' thirst is the hour of real worship, because real worship takes place because of and around the cross of Christ. It is the cross of Christ and the hour of His death that provide for us a new and living way, a source of living water that is the only thing that can ultimately satisfy our souls.

Everyone drinks polluted water: non-churchgoers, Mormons, Jehovah's Witnesses, Roman Catholics, Presbyterians, the socially in or out, the black, brown, or white, the rich or poor. Jesus went thirsty and died to give living water to such as these. Anyone can know the soul-satisfying grace that seeks us even when we are looking for satisfaction from broken cisterns. The nature of grace is that it finds us when we aren't looking for it. The woman wasn't looking for living water; she was looking for running water. Maybe, when we go to church or read our Bible, we are looking for a little running water because we are emotionally thirsty. Be ready for grace to turn the heart so that you thirst for more than just a sip of water—so that you may drink deeply and be satisfied.

If you are a Christian, I have a hard question for you: Do you keep going back to all those old cisterns, those old things that can't hold the water you once tasted? Take a page from this woman's life. She leaves her waterpot behind. Oh, she'll probably come back and get it again sometime. But something else, *someone* else is far more important to her, someone much better. Someone is giving her water that has become a well that springs up to eternal life.

So whether you have been in church all of your life and have heard this story dozens of times, or whether you have never heard it before in your life, the impact is really the same. We are all, Christian and non-

Christian alike, prone to return to these broken old cisterns that we hew out ourselves. We must turn from them, from anything we count on more than Christ, and find in Him the only source of soul-satisfying water. Jesus says, "An hour is coming, and now is . . ." Is this the hour for you to lay down your broken cisterns? The gospel of grace is for anyone. Are you one who will never taste this water, never have this life, never have your soul satisfied for eternity; or are you one who asks, "Where can I find this water? I want to come and drink, and I want to do it right now"? This is the hour—for us, and for anyone. If we put up any barriers to any type of person, anyone in the world coming to drink this water, we are denying the gospel of grace and truth. We are taking the living water for which Jesus thirsted and died and we are pouring it out on the ground.

FRUITFUL WITNESSING

Many people talk about the Lord's conversation with this woman as a model of evangelism. I have some problems with that because the Lord offers so many models of evangelism. There is no one pattern. Every time we put the Lord Jesus in a box, He surprises us. Always look for the surprises in the Gospels, because that is where you find great kernels of truth. Interestingly, as a method of evangelism, there is no similarity between the Lord's encounter with this woman and any other such incident recorded in Scripture.

Nevertheless a wonderful pattern does emerge in this dialogue. We see this both in Jesus' witness to the woman and in the woman's witness to others. Jesus starts with a woman who is completely disinterested in Him. She doesn't come with a little interest; she has *no* interest. She is not seeking. She does not come to the well to talk about spiritual things; she comes to get some water, and she has timed her visit to the well to avoid hassle or embarrassment. (Nicodemus, on the other hand, represents the kind of person who comes with an interest, albeit at night and under the cloak of darkness.)

Grace finds the woman when she doesn't care and isn't searching at all. But note the particular way that grace moves in on her life. Note how the Lord deals with her in steps and in stages, each one drawing her in a bit closer. Look at four ways in which the Lord does this:

First, Jesus is alone with her at the well. If she had come with a group of women, the usual way, He would never have had this conversation. How did He get her alone? She was *already* alone, because of being a social outcast.

When you are doing well, you usually don't feel alone. When things are going well in business, or on the playing field, or in the home, you always have lots of folks around you. At such times, you don't analyze things very much or think about your life. You don't ask the big questions. But when things get tough, that is when the Lord gets you alone. Is Jesus getting you alone?

Second, Jesus makes her think. He stimulates her intellectually. He gives her conundrums and questions to make her think about her life. Faith is more than intellectual, but it is not less than intellectual. One of the travesties of American Christianity is that we no longer think about our faith. We want to experience our faith. We want to be washed over in a sea of emotion, but we don't really know how to think very hard. Jesus is saying, "You can't have all the wonderful experience of the living water if you leave the thinking out."

I love to see people think about their faith. Sometimes we treat our faith like a football game; we're excited when our team wins, we're disappointed when it loses, but we don't know why either happened. During a football game, however, the players and coaches are thinking about the game all the time, and a good football game or a bad football game actually depends on how well and how much the players and the coaches are thinking. Whether new to the faith or mature in the faith, Christians beginning to think about their faith may say, "Wait a minute, I never thought about it that way before. Wow! Is that what you really believe? I can't believe that." "Is that what Christianity is all about? I never thought about that. Can I have something to read?" It is so exciting to see people beginning to use their minds to grapple with the deep truths of God's Word. Christianity is more than intellectual, but it is not less.

Third, Jesus makes her honest. In John 4:15, the woman is still saying, in essence, "This living water—you mean running water, right? You mean water I can have right there in my house so I don't have to come here every day at high noon?" But Jesus tells her to go call her husband, which forces her to look at the well from which she is currently drawing water. This is part of Jesus' strategy to make her, and us, honest. He is asking us the same thing: "What is your leaky cistern? Into what well are you dipping the bucket of your soul today?"

Fourth, Jesus focuses on her worship. Verse 24 says that those who worship God must worship in spirit and in truth. In response to her question in verse 26, when she asks who is this One who deserves this kind of worship, Jesus answers, "I who speak to you am he." "I am the truth," He says, "who replaces the idols, the broken cisterns. I am the truth who gives you the water that will take away your thirst. I am the truth who will be for you a well of water, springing up to eternal life."

Do you know that every human being is innately religious? Paul says in Romans 1 that every human being knows God (v. 21) and has an internal gyroscope that is moving in toward God all the time. It is just that we find the *wrong* god and latch onto him, her, it, or them. Jesus says, "I am the One you are looking for. And you must worship in spirit and truth. Worship must spring from the living water that I give you in the gospel."

Now look at the woman's witness to others. Obviously something happens in this woman's life, and she begins to share her witness with others.

First, she speaks personally. She says, "Come, see a man who told me all the things that I have done" (John 4:29). Not a lot of sophisticated argumentation there. She doesn't give them a book or tell them to sign up for a seminar. She speaks very personally about a person. She doesn't say, "Come, and see the new code of conduct that has changed my life." She says, "Come, and see a man who told me everything I ever did." She has met a man who, for the first time in her life, treats her with dignity.

Second, she repents happily. "Come, meet the man who has told me all the things I've ever done." My guess is that when she started talking about her sin there were some men in the town who decided it was time to take a quick business trip. She is willing, even happy to tell you how Jesus changed her. Have you ever noticed how new Christians do this? Newer Christians often put us older Christians to shame in this regard. With refreshing simplicity they say, "Do you know what the Lord did for me?" They begin to talk about all the things that God did for them and all the kinds of things that they used to be and do. And we say, "Wait a minute, don't say that. Don't go there, please."

So many of us are more like moralists than like Christians. We don't like hearing about the wrong stuff, perhaps because it reminds us of our own wrong stuff. We have long ago forgotten how to drink from the living water, and we don't know what to do about the wrong stuff that is in our life. Sometimes it takes a new Christian to remind us.

Third, she loves boldly. She goes to the people who don't like her. No one wants to be seen with her, at least publicly, and yet she loves them. True witness is made bold by love, because love compels you to go right into the heart of darkness with the light. The first time, she comes alone to the well; but the second time, she comes with a whole group (vv. 28-30).

A WHITE HARVEST

After the woman returns from the city with the people to whom she has witnessed, Jesus says some amazing things about the "harvest." Rendered in the Aramaic language, His words are, "It takes four months for the harvest to come" (John 4:35). It was an expression which meant, "Be patient about your life. You can't plant and reap on the same day. Don't rush things." But Jesus is saying, "You've heard that expression, but let me tell you that when the grace of the living water begins to be poured out, watch out, because the time between sowing and reaping will be greatly condensed." Massive change is going to happen in villages and cities and individual hearts.

Jesus tells us that we should look around the world today and look for those places where that kind of harvest is about to be reaped. We should invest our time, resources, and energy in those kinds of places, because those are the places where the Lord is about to reap a great harvest. They are "white for harvest" (v. 35).

Many years ago I was preaching a series of sermons at a Bible conference in Yazoo City, Mississippi, a Delta town. On my free afternoon I went to a cotton gin because I had never seen one before. It was fascinating to see the way cotton is processed. On a huge wall there was an absolutely enormous map of the world. It was like a missions map, except this was a cotton map, and it showed the cotton belt which wraps all the way around the world. It goes right through our Deep South, of course, and around the world at a certain latitude that includes Egypt and Israel.

After I visited the cotton gin, I took a walk. It was the time of year when the cotton was full and ripe on the plants. It was hanging off the branches, begging for someone to come along and remove it. Looking up, I saw acres and acres of white.

I went back to my hosts and said, "I think it is time for cotton harvesting." They looked at me and said very kindly to this Yankee, "Sir, we do not call it cotton harvesting; we call it cotton picking." Today, it is cotton picking time in specific places around the world. It is cotton picking time in Asia, for example, perhaps especially in China. The crop is smaller in North America now, though there is still a crop to be had. But the cotton belt is moving west over the Pacific Ocean, and the fields are white for harvest.

There is only one way that you and I are ever going to care about picking cotton in China or Mongolia or Russia. It is if we drink the living water that Jesus provides, if we take the grace that He gives and each of us says, "I see that my heart is full of sin. *Today* I need Jesus and His living water." When the Lord quenches that thirst, He also gives you a thirst to help other people have their thirst quenched. But keep drinking deeply from the well that bubbles up to eternal life in your own heart, so that you are continually strengthened from the well of grace to go pick the cotton ripe for harvest all over the world.

12

A SIGNPOST TO HOME

And after the two days He went forth from there into Galilee. For Jesus Himself testified that a prophet has no honor in his own country. So when He came to Galilee, the Galileans received Him, having seen all the things that He did in Jerusalem at the feast; for they themselves also went to the feast. He came therefore again to Cana of Galilee where He had made the water wine. And there was a certain royal official, whose son was sick at Capernaum. When he heard that Jesus had come out of Judea into Galilee, he went to Him, and was requesting Him to come down and heal his son; for he was at the point of death. Jesus therefore said to him, "Unless you people see signs and wonders, you simply will not believe." The royal official said to Him, "Sir, come down before my child dies." Jesus said to him, "Go your way; your son lives." The man believed the word that Jesus spoke to him, and he started off. And as he was now going down, his slaves met him, saying that his son was living. So he inquired of them the hour when he began to get better. They said therefore to him, "Yesterday at the seventh hour the fever left him." So the father knew that it was at that hour in which Jesus said to him, "Your son lives"; and he himself believed, and his whole household. This is again a second sign that Jesus performed, when He had come out of Judea into Galilee (John 4:43-54).

A NUMBER OF YEARS AGO I was returning to the United States from East Africa. On the flight home the plane made a stop at the Lagos, Nigeria, airport, and the passengers were allowed to get off for a few minutes to stretch while the plane was refueled. It was a difficult time of political unrest in Nigeria. Armed guards lined the tarmac, and we could walk only where guards were present. They were everywhere, and there was an intense feeling of hostility in this military presence. It was very uncomfortable, and all of us Americans who were on that flight were extremely uneasy. We reboarded the plane, took off, and flew across the Atlantic Ocean.

Early the next morning, in the rising dawn, we approached John F. Kennedy Airport. The sun cast a beautiful red glow against the skyline of New York City and across the face of the Stature of Liberty herself, and the pilot banked the plane so we could see the inspiring scene before us. It was one of those quiet times during a long flight after everyone has woken up, has had breakfast, and is waiting to land. With the stunning red glow of the city and the Stature of Liberty out our windows, someone began to sing softly, "O beautiful, for spacious skies . . ." and everyone on the plane joined in and sang the song. After the ugly and difficult situation we had experienced in Nigeria, there was such relief that we were safely home. We had come to the place where we belonged. This was our homeland and we were thrilled to be home.

AN IRONIC HOMETOWN WELCOME

It wasn't the same for Jesus when He came to His homeland, according to this passage from John 4. The Lord had just spent two days in Samaria, then He left for Galilee, a trip that He first began back in verse 3. What did Jesus mean when He said that a prophet "has no honor in his own country" (v. 44)? What is "his own country?" Literally, the word for "country" is *patris* or "homeland." We get the word *paternal* from it. Some say it refers to Judea or Jerusalem, which is south of Samaria and from where Jesus had just come. This would make His hometown Jerusalem, which makes sense, except that four times in the Gospel of John it is noted that Jesus' hometown was Nazareth, which is not in Judea to the south but in Galilee, north of Samaria. What actually makes the most sense is that Jesus means both: Jerusalem in the south as His spiritual hometown; and Galilee or Nazareth in the north as His physical hometown.

The context of Christ's remarks is that He has just been well-received in Samaria. Those who received Jesus were not the hometown crowd. We can say that His home is Galilee or His home is Judea, but we cannot say that it is Samaria; and yet, that is where He was received.

But if the Jews in Judea and in Galilee rejected Jesus (v. 44), then what does verse 45 mean: "when He came to Galilee, the Galileans received Him, having seen all the things that He did in Jerusalem at the feast; for they themselves also went to the feast"? It must mean that, although they did not receive Him as the Samaritans did—with true faith—they did receive Him as someone who had done some notewor-thy things. They had heard about all the commotion Jesus had caused, overturning the moneychangers' tables and expelling the animal sellers. They had heard about how many of John the Baptist's disciples were now following Jesus. According to verse 46, these Galileans already knew that Jesus had become a kind of one-man distillery in the town of Cana, where He had turned the water into wine. They were impressed with His signs and miracles. They liked the show, these Galileans, and they wanted more of it, so they received Him not as the Savior of the world but as the entertainer of the world.

We already know what Jesus thinks of such a reception. Back in 2:23-24 we read, "Now when He was in Jerusalem at the Passover, dur-ing the feast, many believed in His name, beholding His signs which He was doing. But Jesus, on His part, was not entrusting Himself to them, for He knew all men." When John now says that the Galileans received Him (4:45), his writing is dripping with irony. There is a reception, but it is a reception for what Jesus gives them, for the show He might put on, for the miracles He might perform, not for who He is.

DESPERATE FOR A SIGN

Now a nobleman appears on the scene, looking for a sign from Jesus—a cure for his son. He is called a "royal official"; the Greek is *basilikos,* which is a derivative of *basileus,* meaning "king." It means he is a noble-man in the service of the king's court. So he is probably a servant of Herod, who was virtually the king of Galilee from 4 B.C. to A.D. 39.

John intends that this nobleman be an illustration of the kind of wel-come the hometown crowd gives Jesus. The nobleman is desperate, but his desperation doesn't move him to real faith—not at first. Instead he is an example of how the Galileans received Jesus. He wants the mira-cle cure but not the Man who gives the miracle. He heard what Jesus can do and wants some of it without caring who Jesus really is.

Are there not times in your life when you become desperate as this nobleman was desperate? No one needs to tell a mom and a dad to pray for their sick child. I can safely tell you that in my twenty-seven years as a pastor, I have *never* met a parent in a children's hospital who was an atheist. We know how God can get our attention: a child or a grandchild is in trouble, or there is an unwelcome test result from a doctor's office, or the financial bottom drops out of our lives.

Why does Jesus respond sternly to this man? "Jesus therefore said to him, 'Unless you people see signs and wonders, you simply will not believe'" (John 4:48). There is a strong tone of rebuke in these words. Throughout John's Gospel we see repeatedly that too much focus on the sign itself is actually a distraction from the One who performs the sign. The sign is meant to point to Jesus, not to itself. For example, in 6:26, after Jesus feeds the five thousand, He says to them, "Truly I say to you, 'You seek me not because you saw signs, but because you ate the loaves and were filled.'" In other words, "You don't really understand what the sign means. You just want more of what the sign is. You don't really come to have faith in Me."

We might be thinking that Jesus still seems a bit insensitive to the understandable desperation of this man who is begging Jesus to come before his child dies. But Jesus knows that the miraculous sign is miraculous only if it is understood as pointing to something—to *someone*— beyond itself.

LETTING THE SIGN BE THE SIGNPOST

The place of miracles in John's Gospel is subtle but very important; they don't necessarily compel real faith. Some people want the miracle but not the Man, but miracles are intended to be signposts. For those who understand them directly and correctly, they point in the right direction.

For example, if you are driving south on I-35 from Dallas to Austin, and you see a sign that says, "Austin, 50 miles," you don't stop at that sign, take out your suitcases, sit down under the sign, and say, "Here we are, we have arrived." Of course not. It is just a sign. It is intended to point you in the right direction. We need to let the sign be the signpost, not the destination.

The royal official of John 4 is actually not like most Galileans. He accepts Jesus' word, believes in Him, and then encounters his servants, who confirm the fact that the healing took place at the precise moment when Jesus had spoken the word. The sign does its real work in this man; he believes in Jesus, together with all his household. The sign is working; it is compelling belief in Christ, the One to whom it is pointing. Faith in Jesus causes the nobleman to see the sign differently, not as an end in itself but as an arrow pointing to Christ.

CAN YOU GO HOME AGAIN?

You know the old expression, "You can't go home again." That is certainly one conclusion we can draw from this passage. In Samaria, where Jesus should not have been accepted, He is seen as the Messiah, the Savior of the world. But when He comes to His own people, they are opposed to Him, sometimes aggressively and actively so.

In the preface to John's Gospel we read, "He came to His own, and those who were His own did not receive Him. But as many as received Him, to them He gave the right to become children of God, even to those who believe in His name" (John 1:11-12). Beginning here at the end of chapter 4, and running all the way to chapter 12, we see a growing intensity of opposition to Jesus. As D. A. Carson puts it: "[Jesus] may have been popular in Samaria, but he presses on to his own *patris* where public sentiment will finally take him to Calvary."[1]

The real question that this passage raises is, Have we found our way home, or are we still just looking for the signs? Do we love Jesus, or what Jesus does for us?

I think one of the reasons people spend a lot of time making their homes beautiful is that in most of us there is a deep, innate desire for a place that is really home. It is one of the reasons many of us love to travel. Somewhere in the back of our minds we are looking for the perfect place on earth. We think if we could ever find the perfect place on earth, we would go vacation there all the time. Earlier in my life, I did my best to actually find such a place. I would study *Travel and Leisure* magazine, looking for the perfect "home."

In John 4, Jesus wants us to see our own desperation for a true home in the mirror of this man's desperation for his son. Understandable though his desperation is, the deeper desperation in all of our hearts is for our true homeland, the place where our sins can be forgiven—the Cross, which is the most important signpost of our lives. Jesus came to His own in order to save not the righteous but the desperate sinner.

When the doctor comes into the emergency room and sees the desperate condition of a person brought in on a stretcher, does he turn away and say, "Oh, no, I can't help that guy, so I'll just move on to something else"? No. The very critical condition of the person is what compels a good physician to apply all of his skill and effort to the end of healing that person. It is the severity of our situation that compels the magnitude of the response. Our utter lostness in sin compels the magnitude of the outpouring of God's grace on us.

No one could say it better than Jonathan Edwards two hundred years ago when he wrote, "The greatness of divine grace appears very much in this, that God by Christ saves the greatest offenders. The greater the guilt of any sinner is, the more glorious and wonderful is the grace manifested in his pardon. . . . Therefore, no doubt, Christ will be willing to save the greatest sinners, if they come to him. . . . for he will not be backward to glorify himself, and to commend the value and virtue of his own blood."[2]

Is the value and virtue of Christ's blood displayed when we minimize our sin, thinking we're not "that bad" and just need a little saving grace? No, the value and virtue of the blood of our Savior is affirmed when we agree with Him that we are great sinners. The magnitude of our sin is only met by the even greater magnitude of the grace of our dear Savior's cross.

We do ourselves no favors and are not looking in the mirror of God's true Law when we minimize our sin. Our sin is not a small thing; it is a huge thing, and for such a huge thing we need a huge Savior who can accomplish much for His people. We need One who can come and die to the uttermost, One whose blood can be shed and avail for all of our sin.

I must ask myself, "How desperate are you, Skip? How desperate are you for Christ? How much do you really need Him? Do you think so lightly of your sin that you want a lightweight Savior? Or do you understand that your sins are so heavy and so weighty that if God does not pick you up and rescue you from your sins, you could easily fall into the abyss for eternity? Do you refuse to make light of that over which the Lord would compel you by His grace to be desperate, and instead, in your desperation, turn to Him?"

There is one sign that we should camp under, unpacking all our bags and staying forever. It is the sign of the Cross. As the wonderful hymn by Elizabeth Clephane says,

Beneath the cross of Jesus I fain would take my stand,
The shadow of a mighty Rock within a weary land;
A home within the wilderness, a rest upon the way,
From the burning of the noontide heat and the burden of the day.[3]

Are you looking for home? Are you looking for the true home? To be a Christian is to appreciate and care for the world but in some ways to be uncomfortable in it. We are outsiders, called to follow Him outside the camp (Heb. 13:13), to our true home. The Cross is the sign to that place, and it is the place itself. The Father of our true fatherland receives you there, and there He pours out for you infinite grace for infinite wickedness. When we are willing to say that our wickedness is infinite, we are enabled to start for home and to receive the infinite grace of Christ.

PART III

*The Opposition to Jesus as
the Son of God*

13

THE CONFLICT

Now there is in Jerusalem by the sheep gate a pool, which is called in Hebrew Bethesda, having five porticoes. In these lay a multitude of those who were sick, blind, lame, and withered [waiting for the moving of the waters]. . . . And a certain man was there, who had been thirty-eight years in his sickness. When Jesus saw him lying there, and knew that he had already been a long time in that condition, He said to him, "Do you wish to get well?" The sick man answered Him, "Sir, I have no man to put me into the pool when the water is stirred up, but while I am coming, another steps down before me." Jesus said to him, "Arise, take up your pallet, and walk." And immediately the man became well, and took up his pallet and began to walk. Now it was the Sabbath on that day. . . . Afterward Jesus found him in the temple, and said to him, "Behold, you have become well; do not sin anymore, so that nothing worse may befall you." The man went away, and told the Jews that it was Jesus who had made him well. And for this reason the Jews were persecuting Jesus, because He was doing these things on the Sabbath. But He answered them, "My Father is working until now, and I Myself am working." For this cause therefore the Jews were seeking all the more to kill Him, because He not only was breaking the Sabbath, but also was calling God His own Father, making Himself equal with God. Jesus therefore answered and was saying to them, "Truly, truly, I say to you, the Son can do nothing of Himself, unless it is something He sees the Father doing; for whatever the Father does, these things the Son also does in like manner. For the Father loves the Son, and shows Him all things that He Himself is doing; and greater works than these will He show Him, that you may marvel. For just as the Father raises the dead and gives them life, even so the Son also gives life to whom He wishes. For not even the Father judges anyone, but He has given all judgment to the Son, in order that all may honor the Son, even as they honor the Father. He who does not honor the Son does not honor the Father who sent Him. Truly, truly, I say to you, he who hears My word, and believes Him who sent Me, has eternal life, and does not come into judgment, but has passed out of death into life. . . . and He gave Him authority to execute judgment, because He is the Son of Man. . . . I can do nothing on My own initiative. As I hear, I judge; and My judgment is just, because I do not seek My own will, but the will of Him who sent Me. . . . How can you believe, when you receive glory from one another, and you do not seek the glory that is from the one and only God?" (John 5:2-3, 5-9, 14-24, 27, 30, 44).

THERE ARE VARIOUS STYLES OF conflict management. One is the "bring it on" personality. These are the aggressive sorts who are not at all afraid of conflict; they sort of enjoy it. You get the feeling that they are up and ready for it almost anytime. They are the "in-your-face" people.

Then there are the opposites of the hardball type. One is the "deny everything" personality. This is the one who says, "Conflict can't exist. There is no such thing. I don't like it, and I'm not even going to admit it is there."

Another version of that is the "reconcile-at-all-costs" person who is psychologically incapable of dealing with conflict. The psychological phrase for this response is "avoidance." Such types will do anything to avoid conflict and to be reconcilers.

When my daughter was in middle school, she told me about a style of conflict management that she had observed among her peers. It is the "silent treatment." The person is basically not pleased with you, and the way you know it is that she just shuts down when she is with you—no talk, not even a look at you.

Then there is the "smile and kill" approach, subtitled "if looks could kill." I received an e-mail not long ago describing this type of conflict management: "Picture yourself near a stream. You can hear the birds chirping in the cool mountain air. Nothing can bother you here. No one knows about this secret place. Here there is total seclusion from the world. There is the soothing sound of a gentle waterfall, the cascades of serenity. The water is cold and clear. You can just make out the face of the person whose head you are holding under water." And it ends, "There now, feel better?"

Another version of that is the "kiss and tell" person who deals with conflict very nicely with you; in fact, he may behave as if there is no conflict at all, but then he proceeds to go tell everyone else about his problem with you.

ESCALATION OF OPPOSITION

This passage from John 5 is all about the conflict between Jesus and the religious leaders. It is a conflict that cannot be avoided. An important shift takes place. Mild reservations about Jesus, which we have seen in previous chapters, now emerge and focus as furious opposition.

In chapter 5 we see a strong reaction to the healing of the man at

Bethesda. By the end of chapter 6, even some of Christ's disciples will abandon Him. At the end of chapter 7, He will be charged with demon possession, and the religious leaders will try to arrest Him. And things will get nothing but worse from there.

What is so significant is that, not only does Jesus allow this conflict to happen, but one gets the feeling that He is actually encouraging it, endorsing it, and managing it. He does so in the context of delivering in chapter 5 the single longest recorded address about His own identity, and He does so before the most important religious supreme court of His time and His land, the Jewish Sanhedrin. It is the most complete and formal defense of His deity and of His work that we have in any of the Gospels.

THE CONFLICT PROVOKED

A silly myth and a miracle first provoked the conflict. There was an opening near the northeast corner of the city wall of Jerusalem that was used as a gate for sheep to come in and go out, and just inside this gate was a pool perhaps three or four times the size of an average backyard swimming pool. It was surrounded by five porticoes or colonnades. This pool had become a place where many disabled people would linger.

There is a verse inserted into many old manuscripts of the Gospel of John which is printed in the margin of some translations. It tells of the myth that, when the angel of the Lord stirred up the waters, the first person who got down to the water at the edge of the pool and dipped his hand or foot in the water would be healed of his particular ailment. The verse doesn't belong in the original manuscripts of John, but the myth was no doubt present in the minds of the people at the time. Perhaps John or even later editors purposely inserted this idea as a contrast to the living water of chapter 4, where Jesus says that only the living water which He gives can bring healing. Stirred-up water in a pond cannot heal.

One particular man has been at the pool for thirty-eight years, and Jesus asks him if he wants to get well. At first blush that seems an odd question. He has been there for *thirty-eight years* waiting for his opportunity to get well. What does Jesus mean by asking him if he *wants* to get well?

When I was working in youth ministry many years ago, I would give a talk based on this passage. I made the point that perhaps Jesus asks the man this question because, after thirty-eight years, there might be reason to wonder whether he really does want to get well. Maybe by this time he was seeing himself as the-sick-man-by-the-pool-of-Bethesda-who-had-been-waiting-thirty-eight-years-for-someone-to-come-along-and-put-him-in-the-water. That was the only identity he knew.

Maybe there is something to that interpretation, but after thirty-eight years of reading this passage, I now have a better idea. Just as the water in the jugs at the wedding at Cana or in the jugs of the Samaritan woman could not purify hearts, so a silly myth cannot help this man. Jesus wants the man to focus on his own identity in a way that forces him to ask himself, "In what do I really hope? Is it something that will endure? Have I built my life on something that can withstand the weight and pressures of real-life existence, or have I built my life on something that is ultimately not going to be able to hold the weight of human existence?" D. A. Carson puts it this way: " . . . so the promises of merely superstitious religion have no power to transform the truly needy."[1]

Real hope has died in this man. I don't think he thought every day, "*This* is the day. I am going to get healed today." No, belief in a silly myth has replaced real hope.

There are a lot of people who, down deep, ask, "Can there be any hope for me? I don't know how to resolve this old issue in my life. Life is a bit overwhelming, and I'm not sure I know how to deal with it. I'm not sure that the structure of my belief can sustain the weight of what's going on in my life."

Hope in the midst of life's pressure—what does it look like? Read the words of this remarkable letter that Barbara and I received from old friends, a husband and wife. I am changing a few of the words in order to protect the identity of the writers, but I am not changing the meaning of what they said:

> This year has marked a decade of hard work and perseverance which has culminated in the fulfillment of dreams and lifelong goals. However, it has also marked our individual struggles over issues of health, mortality, heartache, and loss. We have reflected on the past, not with exuberance but with an all-encompassing weariness from

the seemingly voracious, chronic problems of life which daily eat away at the heart and soul. At the very depth, we woke up one day and said, "Too much heartache, too much sadness; we have to make a change." . . . As we found our way back to church, we were captured and provoked by the gospel. Its depth and passion rang deep and true and struck at the soul of our beliefs, awakening new hope. The gospel can counter both cynicism and numbness which has resulted from life's assaults. It does not avoid the hard questions, and thereby fights the unspoken presumption that what God offers is inadequate to deal with harsh reality, unanswered questions, tragedy, and the messy battlefield of trying to live well. In and by the gospel of Christ, we feel respected and incredibly encouraged to keep on.

What a fine expression of the power of the gospel to unravel the hardness of the cynicism that so easily overtakes us. Those of us who have been Christians for many years are not scot-free from that kind of cynicism, that sense that life's burdens are too much and the gospel, God Himself, may not be big enough to handle our problems.

The Clueless Man

Is the gospel big enough for our problems? The answer in this passage is yes, it is. *He* is. But in order to get to the answer, one must first face the reality of looking down the barrel of a life with no hope. That is what happens to this man who is healed. This man has no real hope. He is clueless. He doesn't even know Jesus' name. When the Jewish authorities confront him about carrying his pallet on the Sabbath, he tries to get out from under their scrutiny by shifting the blame to the man who had healed him. He takes their side and remains in his old patterns of thought, under his old burdens where he has been for thirty-eight years, and he does not allow himself to be led out of it.

The Sabbath Breaker

The crisis of this conflict is provoked because Jesus heals the man on the Sabbath. He tells him to pick up his pallet, a portable straw mat, and be on his way. But he does this on the Sabbath, so there is tremendous irony in verse 10 where we read, "Therefore the Jews were saying to him who was cured, 'It is the Sabbath, and it is not permissible for you to carry your pallet.'" Here is the man healed after thirty-eight years of suffer-ing from a debilitating physical disease, as well as all the emotional pain underneath it, and all the Jewish authorities can think to say is, "Oh, this was done on the Sabbath day, and that's not right."

The Old Testament Law did forbid work on the Sabbath, but the Jewish rabbis and Pharisees had developed a code that went way beyond the Scriptures in listing what was considered as work on the Sabbath. For instance, on the Sabbath a man was permitted to borrow something that belonged to his neighbor, but not if he asked for it by saying, "Please, lend it to me." Using that terminology made it a form of a con-tractual obligation; and they were not allowed to enter into contracts on the Sabbath. Or, a man could put out a lamp on the Sabbath day if he did so because he wanted to hide from robbers, or perhaps from an evil spirit or even from Gentiles. But if he put out the lamp with the intent to save the oil or the wick, that was a violation of the Sabbath.

Here is the funniest one of all: a man was not permitted to put vine-gar on his teeth for medicinal purposes if he had a toothache on the Sabbath. But if some vinegar was put into his food on the Sabbath and he ate it and his tooth got better inadvertently, then the Jewish rabbis said, "If he is healed, he is healed." You certainly could not heal a man on the Sabbath, and you certainly could not pick up your pallet and walk away with it on the Sabbath.[2]

The Sin Breaker

The real issue isn't that Jesus breaks the Sabbath; it is that He claims to break the power of the cycle of helplessness and sin that has been grip-ping this man's life for thirty-eight years.

Later Jesus finds the man in the temple and tells him not to sin any-more, lest anything worse happen to him. It is the connection with sin that tips this clueless man off as to who Jesus really is. In this man's case, there was a connection between his sickness and his sin. This does not mean that all sickness is related to sin. Sickness, suffering, and all the difficulties that diminish hope in our lives, including those that just involve getting older and weaker, are the natural consequences of living in a world that is not what God intended it to be. In that sense, all sick-ness is related to sin but not necessarily to specific sin.

But for this man and for us, we are not off the hook. *We* may be waiting at the pool, having false hopes for what we trust to make life work. What do you say will make life okay? What myth do you believe about your own life? What do you cling to as the hope that will make sense out of the hurts and struggles? Whatever that myth is, whatever that idol is, whatever has been gripping your life for thirty-eight years, whatever those patterns are, Jesus exposes them as false hopes and false idols. To this man and to us, Jesus says, "Do not sin anymore." Do not put your trust in these things. Do not persist in your patterns of sin. Renounce them as the demonstration that you are a new person and that these old things cannot satisfy you.

What about the relationship between psychology and faith? I do not claim any expertise in psychology. But pastors get around, and I have seen the way in which psychological explanations can be given for things that, at their root, must be understood in terms of idolatry. Yes, there are psychological manifestations that I would never deny, but at the core of the human personality is the inveterate tendency to grip on to some idolatry, some myth around which we center our lives to make them meaningful. An identity that defines itself as I'm-the-guy-who's-got-these-problems becomes the false idol itself. Only Christ and the gospel can break the power of idols, whatever they are.

THE CONFLICT PRESSED

Jesus presses the conflict out of love for us. He does not want us to hold onto that which cannot give us meaning in life. The authorities challenge Jesus. In fact, according to John 5:16, they begin some form of systematic persecution: "And for this reason the Jews were persecuting Jesus, because He was doing these things on the Sabbath." They realize that more is going on, though, than just Sabbath breaking: "For this cause therefore the Jews were seeking all the more to kill Him, because He not only was breaking the Sabbath, but also was calling God His own Father, making Himself equal with God" (v. 18). That's the real issue here. Jesus claims that He has the ability that only God would have to deal with this man's problems, or with your problems and mine.

After many years of dealing with conflict, we develop ways to handle it. Maybe we just bite our tongue or walk away. But in this remarkable speech, Jesus wades right in. Not belligerently, but out of love He marches right into our hearts and says, "Where have you been for thirty-eight years? What have you been trusting in? What do you cling to for meaning and purpose?"

One could argue that Jesus had been thinking about that question for a few billion years. But the point is that when Jesus is pursued and presented with this challenge by the authorities, He does not hesitate to say that which He knows will make the opposition angrier. He goes to the jugular, and He does it out of love.

In his wonderful paraphrase of the English New Testament, J. B. Phillips inserts a subheading in this section of John 5: "Jesus Makes His Tremendous Claim." Jesus makes His claim with five bold statements, all of which press the conflict by claiming that He is equal with His Father.

William Barclay calls this "an act of the most extraordinary and unique courage. . . . He must have known that to speak like this was to court death. . . . He knew well that the man who listened to words like this had only two alternatives: the listener must either accept Jesus as the Son of God, or he must hate Him as a blasphemer and seek to destroy Him."[3]

Jesus wades into the conflict because He knows that out of the conflict will come your soul. He is the Warrior-God, the Warrior-King. Why is there so much warfare in the Old Testament? It is a picture of Jesus as the warrior who is willing to step onto the field and fight for your life and your freedom from thirty-eight years of whatever has gripped you. But He will only do it as the Son of God. That is why He claims that He is equal with God.

Equal in Essence

By calling God "Father," Jesus was making Himself equal to God. He plays into an actual argument the rabbis were having about whether or not God Himself rested on the Sabbath day. The question was: If God did rest, who was sustaining the universe on the Sabbath day? It is a fairly decent question. If God stops being God, takes a complete rest, and stops sustaining the universe, it would immediately fly apart. Jesus sides with those who say that if God were not working to uphold the universe, its molecules would splinter apart (John 5:17a). By going on to say that He, too, is still working (v. 17b), He makes Himself equal to the Father; and by calling God "My Father" (v. 17a), He does something Jews would never do. Jews would say, "Our Father" occasionally, but they would never say, "*My* Father."

Equal in Works

Jesus doesn't let up. In John 5:19 He says, "The Son can do nothing of Himself, unless it is something He sees the Father doing." Perhaps He is thinking of the many sons in the ancient world who were apprenticed to their fathers to learn a trade from them. This is perhaps how Jesus learned carpentry from His human father. But more importantly, Jesus learned His trade as the Son of God from His heavenly Father.

Jesus is saying that He responds to the Father's initiative. "The Father," Carson says, "initiates, sends, commands, commissions, grants; the Son responds, obeys, performs his Father's will, receives authority."[4] The claim Jesus makes here is to equality, but it is not equality on His own accord; it is equality in submission, under authority to His Father. That isn't an expression of modesty; but it is an expression of His willing apprenticeship. So the Son receives authority equal to His Father as He submits to His Father: perfect submission, and perfect authority granted to the Son of God.

The love of the Father for the Son is shown in the Father's revealing all He does to the Son, and the love of the Son is shown in His perfect obedience to the Father. This obedience points us forward to that one work of perfect obedience above all others, Christ's death on the cross.

One commentator says this: "On the human level, what Jesus did that day [in this dialogue with the Jewish rabbis in John chapter 5] cost Him His life. They never forgave Him."[5]

Equal in Life

Jesus claims that He can bestow life just as the Father can (John 5:21). There is an old rabbinical saying that God does three things that no human being can do: give rain, cause the wind to blow, and raise the dead. Here is Jesus coming along raising the dead. Here is Jesus coming along giving life, as He will do with Lazarus later on, as He will do when He Himself rises from the dead.

Equal in Rendering Judgment

John 5:22 says that God "has given all judgment to His Son." That is a powerful way of putting it. When the hour of judgment comes, there will be a huge divide between two groups of people: those who hear God's Word and believe that the Father did indeed send the Son; and those whose evil deeds (v. 29) demonstrate that they have not heard the Son's Word in the gospel. The first group hears and believes and does not come into judgment, but passes from death to life (v. 24). The second group will come to a resurrection of judgment (v. 29).

Jesus continues to press this conflict because the issues are critical. He is saying, "The way you deal with this conflict will determine whether you experience life or judgment. The stakes could not be higher." Out of love He will not let up. He pushes us to see the conflict that He creates not just in the man who was healed, not just in the Jewish Sanhedrin, but in you and me.

THE CONFLICT DEFENDED

Jesus defends His identity as the Son of God, equal to His Father in essence, works, life-giving power, and authority to render judgment, by calling upon four sets of witnesses to verify His own identity: John the Baptist (John 5:33-35), His own works (v. 36), the Father (vv. 37-38), and the Scriptures (vv. 39-47). All of these are witnesses to the identity of Jesus, but He presses the question not to leave it with John the Baptist or with the works or even with the Father or the Scripture, but to press the question to you.

Jesus ratchets up the meaning of His identity so that just when we start to feel comfortable and think we are beginning to understand this Christian faith, Pow!—He comes and challenges us at perhaps some very personal point in our lives and says, "Do you really know who I am? Do you really trust Me in this area of idolatry, in this area that you have not yet given over to Me?"

"The one who utters such things," Carson says, "is to be dismissed with pity or scorn, or worshipped as Lord."[6] The point of conflict is, which is He?

THE CONFLICT PRESSED AGAIN

The chapter ends with a question that could not be more pointed: "If you do not believe his [Moses'] writings, how will you believe My words?" (John 5:47).

How will you believe that Jesus is God's Son? Do you believe that Jesus is God's Son because He died for your sins?

You say, "Yes, and that should get me to heaven"?

No, that response is not good enough.

It is not good enough, because the way Jesus presses His own case to be the Savior of your soul is that He insists on being Lord over all of the idolatries of your heart. He insists that no matter what grips you, He can deal with it. He is not satisfied just to win your soul for eternity, as great as that is. Instead, He wants you to ask hard questions about whether, if you are locked into a pattern of idolatry to which Jesus has no access, you really understand the gospel.

How will you believe? There are some like the Jewish authorities who don't believe that Jesus is the Son of God. They will know judgment. Then there are some of us who claim to be Christians but who are like the sick man. We are sick Christians at best. We believe in the healing, but we don't really believe in Jesus. We like being around the Christian community, we like being in the church, but we never deal with the heart issues that Jesus wants to uncover in our lives—the idolatries that grip us. We are then people who toy around with spiritual things but don't know the power of them.

You must be willing to come before God and say, "Here is the thirty-eight-year-old pattern in my life. Oh, Lord, I can't do anything with it. Please, please, help me." You cannot profess that Jesus is God's Son without a thorough renunciation of the particular idols that grip your heart. You cannot have life in *His* name without giving up life in the name of whatever it is other than the Lord that grips your heart.

All of these questions push the conflict that Jesus, out of love, presses upon us. He will not back away; He loves us too much. All of His claims to equality with God are intended to push us to this summary

question: Who is in charge? To whom or to what do we give the absolute sovereignty in our lives? The gospel is an offer of life, but it is also
a demand to acknowledge the authority of the Life-giver.

This points to the hardest question of all: From whom do you
receive glory? It is the question Jesus raises as He brings this conflict to
an almost unbearably personal crescendo in verse 44: "How can you
believe, when you receive glory from one another, and you do not seek
the glory that is from the one and only God?" The religious leaders could
not believe because they were too preoccupied with their own standing,
their own glory. If we seek the applause of other people and get it, then
we have our reward and should seek no other.

In light of all that Jesus claims for Himself here, how will you
believe? If Jesus is equal to God, if He is to receive from you the glory
and honor that is due to God, then you must honor the Son or you cannot honor the Father. You must not seek glory for yourself but the glory
that comes from the one and only true God.

If we believers don't do this, then we are swimming upstream spiritually. We are moving counterintuitively to the way in which the Lord
has set up the universe. He has intended that the Son of God save us not
only *for* heaven but *from* ourselves. He wants us to be free, experiencing the joy and liberty of the sons and daughters of God. When we are
free of those old ways, then the wonderful truth is this: God gets the
glory and we get the hope, the real hope that we don't need to sit by the
pool waiting for someone to come and do something for us. We have in
the gospel what we need, because we are giving glory in the gospel to
the one true God and to His Son, Jesus Christ.

14

A SIGN OF PROVISION

After these things Jesus went away to the other side of the Sea of Galilee (or Tiberias). And a great multitude was following Him, because they were seeing the signs which He was performing on those who were sick. And Jesus went up on the mountain, and there He sat with His disciples. Now the Passover, the feast of the Jews, was at hand. Jesus therefore lifting up His eyes, and seeing that a great multitude was coming to Him, said to Philip, "Where are we to buy bread, that these may eat?" And this He was saying to test him; for He Himself knew what He was intending to do. Philip answered Him, "Two hundred denarii's worth of bread is not sufficient for them, for everyone to receive a little." One of His disciples, Andrew, Simon Peter's brother, said to Him, "There is a lad here who has five barley loaves and two fish, but what are these for so many people?" Jesus said, "Have the people sit down." Now there was much grass in the place. So the men sat down, in number about five thousand. Jesus therefore took the loaves; and having given thanks, He distributed to those who were seated; likewise also of the fish as much as they wanted. And when they were filled, He said to His disciples, "Gather up the leftover fragments that nothing may be lost." And so they gathered them up, and filled twelve baskets with fragments from the five barley loaves, which were left over by those who had eaten. When therefore the people saw the sign which He had performed, they said, "This is of a truth the Prophet who is to come into the world." Jesus therefore perceiving that they were intending to come and take Him by force, to make Him king, withdrew again to the mountain by Himself alone (John 6:1-15).

THE FEEDING OF THE multitude is the only miracle other than the Resurrection that is repeated in all four Gospels. Maybe that is one reason it is so well-known. Like many familiar passages, it has an interesting and checkered history of interpretation in the church over the ages.

For example, some people say that this miracle really takes place in the hearts of the people when they share. Just as the little boy shares his lunch, so a spirit of generosity pervades the crowd, maybe by his example, maybe by the Lord's teaching, and then everyone shares. So the miracle really is that people become less selfish. That is a nice thought, and there may be some elements of truth to it, but it is not what the text teaches.

Another interpretation has been that this is a kind of sacramental meal like Communion, where everyone receives just a little wafer, just a little piece of bread. But actually, the text says that everyone eats as much as he or she wants.

Some say that, just as Jesus has compassion on the crowd and feeds them, so must we. Jesus intends to teach us that we are to feed the hungry around the world in whatever way we can.

None of these historical interpretations is central to what this text teaches, yet each no doubt contains a bit of truth. Certainly God does want us to be less selfish and give up our meager lunches or whatever else we might have so that He can multiply it for others. That is undoubtedly true, but it is not the main point of this passage.

And there is an overtone of the Lord's Supper in this passage, particularly as it connects with later verses in John 6, where Jesus teaches that He is the Bread of life, giving His flesh for the life of the world. The sacrament is the outward, visible sign and seal of the inward feeding on the Bread of life which the Lord is symbolically providing here in this miracle.

Yes, we are to feed people in Jesus' name. This is also true. The problem comes, however, when we separate our feeding and loving our neighbor from the Lord's feeding and loving of us in the gospel. That is really what some interpreters have sought to do—make this simply a moralistic truth: Jesus fed people, now go and do likewise. But when Scripture is reduced to moralisms, we are disconnected from the gospel power that underlies any application of the truth. This approach renders Jesus, in the end, as our example at best. Jesus did it, now we do it. The problem is that the passage actually exists to teach us precisely the opposite—that Jesus is *not* our example! For the main point of this passage is that He is *unique*. He does what only Jesus can do. He is the unique Son of God infleshed in the man Jesus. While we may indeed feebly imitate Him in the living out of our Christian lives, the point of this passage is that He provides what you and I cannot provide. It is the uniqueness of Jesus that is the key to understanding this miracle as a sign.

THE CONDITION OF THE CROWD

How can we describe this throng of people who received this miraculous feeding? Evidently they wanted a miracle. John 6:2 says, "And a great multitude was following Him, because they were seeing the signs which He was performing." The verb tense indicates that they were continually following Him. They were always on His heels. We see this throughout the Gospel accounts. John said they kept after Jesus because of His healing miracles.

We have already been told that Jesus knows what is in man and does not trust his motivations (2:24). Later in chapter 6, He says to the crowd, "Truly, truly I say to you, you seek Me, not because you saw signs, but because you ate the loaves and were filled" (v. 26). Jesus separates the miracle from the sign. They want the miracle for itself, but not for what the miracle signifies. That is a huge difference. They don't want Jesus as much as they want what Jesus will give them.

We see that in the church today as well. Some Christians focus a bit much on what the Lord will do for them, on the blessings the Lord gives, or on the miracles that the Lord has performed, or on the prophecies that are coming true. The focus is all on something Jesus does for the individual, rather than on Jesus Himself.

This is certainly not the first time in church history that this has happened. In the fifth century, St. Augustine wondered about those who see God only in the unusual or miraculous: "For certainly the government of the whole world is a greater miracle than the satisfying of five thousand men with five loaves; and yet no man wonders at the former; but the latter men wonder at, not because it is greater, but because it is rare, for who even now feeds the whole world but He who creates the cornfield from a few grains?"[1] The Lord creates fields of food from a few grains, and yet we don't wonder at that. We are drawn to the sensational, to the miraculous—not as often to the Lord Himself.

There is an Old Testament story that is interesting background to this account. We read in 2 Kings, "When Elisha returned to Gilgal, there was a famine in the land. . . . Now a man came from Baal-shalishah, and brought the man of God bread of the first fruits, twenty loaves of barley and fresh ears of grain in his sack. And he said, 'Give them to the people that they may eat.' And his attendant said, 'What, shall I set this before a hundred men?' But he said, 'Give them to the people that they may eat, for thus says the LORD, "They shall eat and have some left over."' So he set it before them, and they ate and had some left over, according to the word of the LORD" (2 Kings 4:38a, 42-44).

In John's Gospel there is also an attendant, a young boy who was probably a servant to one of the disciples. John seems to call particular attention to the diminutive size of this boy. He uses what is called a double diminutive in the Greek language. Other languages have such a tool, like *niñeto,* which means a "little boy" or "small boy" in Spanish. The boy brings his lunch of barley bread, like the story in 2 Kings.

Barley bread was the most common form of bread in the ancient world. It was a poor man's bread, very coarse, not very tasty. It would grow stale quickly. It was inexpensive. So we can gather that the people in both accounts are very poor. The two fishes are more like little minnows, certainly not big fish. The minnows were mere seasoning on the dry and tasteless bread. In fact, John Calvin said, "Christ did not supply great delicacies for the people, but . . . [they] had to be satisfied with barley-bread and fish without any sauce."[2] What a meager lunch for one, let alone for many thousands.

The servant's question in 2 Kings is, "What, shall I set this before a hundred men?" It was much like Andrew's question John 6: "What are these for so many?" The real issue in both passages is that poverty and famine are predominant. The people in both passages are poor, hungry, and too numerous for the resources available. The problem is beyond the scope of anyone to really help.

THE MOTIVE OF THE LORD

The Lord's deepest motive in performing this miracle is to impress the people with their helplessness. John 6:3 tells us Jesus leaves the crowd with His disciples and goes up onto the mountain, more accurately translated as "the hill country." Jesus often retreats to the hill country. He goes there for the same reason that you and I would—to get some rest.

Jesus frequently leaves crowds precisely at the "wrong" moment, not at diplomatic, polite, or seemingly appropriate times. But He always does it for a purpose—to get them to realize how helpless they are. As long as Jesus is there doing something wonderful, they keep their focus on Him. But when He leaves, they have nothing to do but look inward, which is necessary for seeing their helpless condition.

When the crowd goes after Jesus and finds Him, Jesus asks a key question: "Where are we to buy bread, that these may eat?" (v. 5). Jesus asks that rhetorically; He already knows the answer (v. 6). Philip is the natural person to have a go at an answer, because he is from that area. He probably knows the "restaurant scene" throughout the region, and he can do the mental arithmetic of counting nickels and noses. There is no McDonald's in the whole area that could take care of this crowd. In fact, he says that two hundred denarii would not be enough. That sum would be about eight months of wages for the typical laborer of that day.

Leon Morris says, "Philip does not point to a solution, but to an impossibility."[3] There is no solution. The situation is impossible, and the Lord is seeking to impress these people with the impossibility of their situation, with their helplessness.

We know from the other Gospel accounts that Jesus is also seeking to express His compassion to the people. Mark 6:34 says, "He saw a great multitude, and He felt compassion for them because they were like sheep without a shepherd; and He began to teach them many things." It doesn't say that Jesus had "pity," but that He had "compassion." What do you feel when you see someone in dire straits? When you see a beggar on a street corner holding a sign, do you feel pity? Sometimes, if we are honest, we feel scorn. "Oh, it's his own fault. He could work if he wanted to . . ." Our passage says that when Jesus sees the crowd in a destitute, helpless situation, He feels not scorn, not even pity, but compassion.

In Luke 15, when the prodigal son starts for home from a far-off land, he begins rehearsing his religious speech. He is trying to get his act together in hopes of making an impression on his father. At the same time, his father is watching for him at home. He is standing on the porch of the house when he sees his son coming a long way off, and he is stirred with compassion. He runs out and greets his son and throws his arms around him. He doesn't even listen to his silly speech.

Compassion always takes the initiative, and God is the Great Initiator. The initiation of compassion means that God moves towards us in our helpless condition, that God is the One who sees our destitute state and is stirred up about it. We never catch the God of all the universe by surprise. He is stirred up by our helpless condition and moves toward us by providing the bread—yes, the physical bread to this crowd, but also the living bread of His own flesh.

THE PROVISION OF THE GOSPEL

In the Old Testament, eating and drinking were always the demonstrations of God's abundant provision. God was a God of blessing, and where He blessed there was plenty to eat. Conversely, lack of food and drink in the Old Testament was always a sign of despair or lack of blessing.

There is a note in John 6:4 that this miracle takes place at the Passover time. There are three Passovers in the Gospel of John: chapter 2, here in chapter 6, and in chapters 13 and following, during the last week of Jesus' earthly life. The Passover would remind this crowd of what their forefathers experienced in the wilderness: God's blessing. The manna and the Passover are symbols that God can abundantly provide, even when the situation is helpless, even when there is no human recourse.

Jesus tells the disciples to get the folks seated—five thousand men plus women and children, perhaps up to twenty thousand people. John includes an interesting detail—that there is much grass there. It is springtime, Passover time, so the grass is coming up. There are places to sit. Jesus gives thanks, and then His disciples distribute the meal.

They are all filled. There is an abundance. Everyone gets as much as he or she wants, and there is some left over—twelve basketfuls—twelve more than there was at the beginning—one for every disciple, perhaps?

"Lord, I can't believe You love me so much," would have been John's response.

Peter is trying to organize the picking up of the fragments. "You get that bunch, Bartholomew. Thomas, over there, that's your area."

Imagine Judas with his basket, probably looking over his shoulder, wondering if the guy behind him got more in his basket than he has in his.

Yes, the Lord meets physical needs. Yes, we ask Him for our daily bread, and He meets our needs day by day. That is what, "Give us this day our daily bread" means. He is the Lord of the earth and of the harvest, as we acknowledge in our nation on Thanksgiving. But if you confine this miracle to only the physical, you truncate its meaning. The provision is demonstrated by the physical, but the sign points to the kingdom of God. The Jews understand, and that is why they seek to take Jesus and make Him king (6:15). Many Jews were probably sincerely impressed with Jesus' leadership. "He is a good leader, we need a good leader," they would say. Jesus knows they want to make Him king by force. John Calvin calls this "reckless audacity."

The Passover season was like the Fourth of July for Americans. It was a time for a lot of national patriotism among the Jews, so it was a natural time for them to again want a leader who would throw the Romans out and establish the kingdom of Israel in Jerusalem. But Jesus wants no part of such a kingship. Jesus simply leaves, retreating back to the hill country.

One commentator notes the irony in the passage: "He who is already king has come to open His kingdom to men; but in their blindness men try to force Him to be the kind of king they want; thus they fail to get the king they want, and also lose the kingdom He offers."[4]

Calvin summarizes it excellently, as he often does: "We are aware of how Christ's detractors attempted to smother his glory. . . . If Christ had allowed them to make him king then, his spiritual kingdom would have been ruined."[5]

We should not be surprised that when *we* seek to make Jesus King according to *our* terms, fitting in to *our* plans and programs and visions, He retreats and obscures Himself from us. No, the kingdom over which Jesus is King is not of our making; it is one He establishes on His own terms. His kingdom goes to the core of human helplessness and need; it is a kingdom of grace. Jesus does care for the physical needs of people, and so must we. In doing so we reflect the reality that the rule and reign of King Jesus has come to our hearts. But, as Paul says, "the kingdom of God is not eating and drinking, but righteousness and peace and joy in the Holy Spirit" (Rom. 14:17). The kingdom of God is the place where Jesus makes things right in the righteousness He gives us in the gospel. It is where He reigns with peace. It is where there is joy in our lives. Evangelicals are fond of saying, "Jesus lives in my heart." True enough; but if Jesus lives in the heart, then there in the heart should be the righteousness, peace, and joy that come from the Holy Spirit's presence. That is the mark that the kingdom is ruling in a person's heart.

Jesus has compassion on the crowd, yet He does not immediately feed them. Rather, He teaches them about the kingdom of God. In the wilderness form of God's kingdom, back in the Old Testament, the Israelites " . . . all ate the same spiritual food; and all drank the same spiritual drink, for they were drinking from a spiritual rock which followed them; and the rock was Christ" (1 Cor. 10:3-4). Later in John 6, Jesus will explain Himself as the One who provides for His people living bread, which He contrasts with the manna in the wilderness which cannot truly give life (vv. 30-33). Jesus gives the true bread that comes out of heaven, the bread of God. By this simple and abundant meal for the multitude, Jesus makes visible the promise of that great wedding banquet yet to come and the consummation of all things when Jesus establishes His reign and rule in the new heavens and the new earth.

OUR CONDITION, OUR HOPE

How does this passage apply to us? Our issue is really the same as the crowd's. We need physical food, but even more this passage teaches us that we need grace. We are like the multitudes—poor and famished, without hope, and helpless. Our sin has left us in spiritual poverty, and if we are striving to feed ourselves, we are missing the real thing of the grace that only God can give. We desperately need what only God will give us. Why do we not see that in ourselves? We don't see it because we are materially rich. If you don't think you are wealthy in things, then you can disqualify yourself, but most Americans are materially wealthy compared to the rest of the world.

Material riches obscure spiritual poverty. That is a consistent truism in the Scripture. Jesus says that a sign that the genuine gospel is going out is that the materially poor are hearing it. He is not saying that rich people cannot come to faith; but He is saying that in order to come to faith, they must put aside all of the false security that their riches give them. Unless they do so, they cannot see the reality of their helpless situation, their inward poverty, their spiritual starvation. Whatever obscures that realization of spiritual poverty and starvation must go.

The Lord's motive is to show us our helplessness. That is why Jesus sometimes retreats from us. He wants us to see the famine in our hearts, our lack of resources in the midst of life's problems. That is why fasting so demonstrates our need. Not having physical bread sometimes shows us significantly our need for the spiritual bread that only God can give.

Someone may think in his heart, *Well, I have been in the church all of my life. I know God. I know Christ. I've been on the Sunday school committee, and I've given my money, and I've done that mission project.* Jesus says that no activity can be the basis of our identity. It is not even growing up in good churches where we have heard the right things. No, the basis of our identity as Christians is recognition of our spiritual poverty. Unless we live on the edge of the reality that we need the Lord *today and every day,* we fool ourselves.

All we can do is ask for the food of the gospel. "Man shall not live on bread alone, but on every word that proceeds out of the mouth of God" (Matt. 4:4). That word is a word of compassion in the midst of helplessness, a word of grace in the midst of all of our failures and sin. It is a word of life in the midst of loss and death.

Jesus says later in John 6, "I am the bread of life; he who comes to Me shall not hunger, and he who believes in Me shall never thirst" (v. 35). That sounds a bit preposterous. We shall not hunger? We shall never thirst? The sheer abundance of grace is preposterous. When you can say, "This is ridiculous. I can't believe that I'm invited to this meal"—that is a sign that you are really getting at the truth. If you say, "Oh, I kind of deserve to be here," you don't get it.

The only thing greater than our sin is the greatness of grace. Paul put it this way: "Where sin increased, grace abounded all the more" (Rom. 5:20). Martin Luther said, " . . . sin boldly, but believe and rejoice in Christ even more boldly."[6] He wasn't saying, "Go out and sin all you want." He was saying that there is something far greater than our sin. We don't need to force an artificial morality on ourselves or others, because when the greatness of grace comes, we will be motivated to all the goodness we will ever need.

The grace of the gospel is all out of proportion to our deserving. The grace of the gospel is all out of proportion even to our need. We get so much more than we need.

A soldier was returning from the Vietnam War to his home in East

Texas. The young man had been badly wounded in the war. He lost a limb or two and his face was marred and disfigured. He wasn't very handsome anymore. He wrote home to his parents ahead of time, saying, "Mom and Dad, I'm coming home, but I have been badly injured and don't look very good. I would understand if you don't want to see me. I will understand if it is just too much for you to handle. Let's work it this way. I am going to take the train into town. You know that old oak tree there as you come into the station? If I see a yellow ribbon in the oak tree, then I'll know it is okay with you for me to get off the train. But if the ribbon isn't there, that's okay. I'll understand. I'll just stay on the train and go on."

You can imagine what he thought when the train pulled in to his hometown, and he looked out the window, and all he could see everywhere were yellow ribbons, all over the tree, all over the station. Even the conductor was wearing yellow ribbons from head to foot.

We have been marred, broken, wounded by sin. All that has happened to us and all that we have done ourselves has wrecked our lives. God, out of compassion, hangs ribbons in our hometown. But the ribbons are not yellow: they are red with the blood of His Son.

The grace of the gospel is all out of proportion to our deserving, even to our need. The satisfaction of grace is overwhelming. The crowd ate as much as it wanted. Do you have as much grace as you want? Do you have as much of God as you want? Do you have as much of the gospel as you want? Probably not. The train is pulling into the station. What color are the ribbons you see? How marvelous and wonderful is His grace that is greater than all our sin, that restores us and renews us and makes us new people. Take and receive that grace, and then keep your basket, because there is a lot left over that you don't even need.

15

"THE WILL OF HIM
WHO SENT ME"

"For I have come down from heaven, not to do My own will, but the will of Him who sent Me. And this is the will of Him who sent Me, that of all that He has given Me I lose nothing, but raise it up on the last day. For this is the will of My Father, that everyone who beholds the Son and believes in Him, may have eternal life; and I Myself will raise him up on the last day" (John 6:38-40).

DURING THE WEEKS BEFORE CHRISTMAS, as the wonder of the Incarnation becomes the focus at the church I pastor, many in the congregation are also busy shopping, going to parties, delivering gifts, and sending and receiving Christmas cards. These cards may contain pictures of the family, little written messages, poignant words from Scripture, lovely poetry, or beautiful artwork. Some of them will have a message something like this: "May the spirit of the Christmas season be yours throughout the New Year." That's not a bad sentiment, I suppose. I just wonder what it means.

What does this one mean: "May the buoyant holiday spirit be with you through the New Year"? Perhaps it means, "May that attitude which marked the birth and the life of Christ be your attitude"; or, "May the attitude of Christ Himself, who came to earth in the flesh, be yours"; or, "May the attitude of God when He sent His own Son be yours."

That is a pretty good thought and a fairly deep one, worth a little pondering and unfolding. What does it mean to suggest that the attitude of Christ be in us? Jesus' attitude was nothing less than the absolute, sure, complete, and deepest submission to the Father's will. The

Incarnation is perhaps the highest and grandest indication, short of the Cross itself, of the preparedness of the Son of God to do what was His Father's will, out of perfect submission and perfect obedience.

Jesus says, "For I have come down from heaven." That is the Incarnation right there. He came from heaven to earth, was born an infant, grew up as a man, and lived sinlessly among us with all the trials, temptations, and difficulties that define our humanity.

HEAVEN: THE PERFECT COMMUNITY

Whatever kind of place heaven is, it is a real place, surely, and it is a place where the Father, the Son, and the Holy Spirit have lived together forever in perfect love and community. There was a certain time when God, the incarnate Son, came down from heaven. But until that time and up until that moment, from eternity past, all three persons of the Godhead had been in heaven together in perfect unity, perfect love, and perfect fellowship. In that perfect eternity together they talked.

The conversation went something like this: The Son and the Spirit said to the Father, "You create the heavens and earth." The Father and the Spirit said to the Son, "You go and redeem a people." The Father and the Son said to the Spirit, "You take Our words and apply them with power to the hearts of Our people." God the Father, God the Son, and God the Holy Spirit purposed and planned in eternity past that you would be saved, that you would come to be a part of those whom the Son would not lose.

Jesus came to do the will of the Father that was planned and purposed in eternity past. What is that will for Christ? John 6:39-40 says that the will of the Father for the Son is that He would lose nothing that was given to Him, but that He would raise it up on the last day. God purposed from all eternity, together with the Son, that no one who was intended to be with the Lord forever would be lost, and that means you and me—if you have put your trust in Him.

In eternity past the three persons of the Godhead planned that God would have a people, that those people would indeed come to Him, and that those people would be preserved forever with the Lord. That is the burden of what the Lord says in verse 39. If any should fail to be raised up with Christ, then it would indicate the failure of the Son. Either He was not able to do what the Father sent Him to do, or He was some-how disobedient to the Father's will, and therefore His work of redeeming us was incomplete and imperfect.

God is absolutely sovereign in the conversation that He and the Son and the Spirit had in all eternity. That is what verse 39 teaches us: in their sovereign conversation, they decided in eternity past that there would be a people, and that the Son would raise them up and, on the last day, bring them with Him safely to heaven. Out of their eternal communion came an eternal love affair that involves you.

Verse 40 says it another way. By giving eternal life to those who believe in Him, the Son is fulfilling the promise that also was designed in eternity past, namely, that the instrumentality of our coming to be a part of God's people is our faith. As we behold the Son and see the beauty of who Christ is and believe in Him, we will be saved.

THE ETERNAL MYSTERY

Verses 39 and 40 of John 6 make a complete package, one that I do not understand. On the one hand God is sovereign, and in the eternal conversation held forever in eternity between the Father, the Son, and the Spirit, they purposed to raise us up and to bring us to themselves. Yet we are told that it is our responsibility to behold the Son and to believe Him, and to believe that He is the One by whom we have salvation. D. A. Carson said it this way: "John is not embarrassed by this theme [of God's sovereignty in salvation], because unlike many contemporary philosophers and theologians, he does not think that human responsibility [to believe in Christ] is thereby mitigated."[1]

How do you hold both of these truths simultaneously—that God is sovereign and that man is completely significant in his choices? Do you go to seminary to find out how it works? No. Does anyone understand how God could be absolutely sovereign in determining from all eternity to raise up a group of people who are His, so that no one or nothing can ever snatch them away from Him, and yet put the burden of responsibility upon us to repent and believe? No, no one understands. But in the faith that is ours, we hold these seemingly contradictory truths together, and we refuse to give up one for the other. Both are there, both are needed, both are part of the gospel story.

COSTLY, PAINFUL OBEDIENCE

If God's will for the Son is that none of His people are lost, it is accomplished by the obedience of the Son. In Philippians 2:5-8 we read that the Son, although God, did not regard equality with God a thing to be grasped. He emptied Himself, not of His nature but of all the prerogatives and perks and privileges of being the Son of God. He humbled Himself by being obedient to the point of death, even death on a cross.

The obedient, deepest possible humbling of Jesus Christ, the incarnate Son of God, was required for you and me to be saved. There was no other way. Romans 5:19 puts it this way: "For as through the one man's disobedience the many were made sinners, even so through the obedience of the One the many will be made righteous." The disobedience of Adam led to the downfall of the human race; the many were lost. But the obedience of the One true Man, perfectly God and perfectly Man, results in life. Out of obedience comes the power to give life.

That is Jesus' theme in John 6. He has the power to be the Bread of life. He has the power to give life because He is obedient to the Father in a way that no one else ever was or ever will be again. Only by the costly obedience of Christ in the Incarnation and the Cross will we be made righteous. It is an obedience that led to the Garden of Gethsemane, where Jesus fell on His face and cried out, "My Father, if it is possible, let this cup pass from Me; yet not as I will but as Thou wilt" (Matt. 26:39).

Jesus agonized over the Cross. He agonized over it even more than you and I would because He understood the implications of His separation from God—that it would be worse than the death itself. They had been together eternally in love and communion, and that was about to be broken.

Luke's version of that same garden story says, "Being in agony He was praying very fervently; and His sweat became like drops of blood, falling down upon the ground" (Luke 22:44). Medical professionals have told me that when a person is highly anxious an actual physiological process can take place where blood vessels surface on the forehead, and by osmosis blood comes through the vessels to the skin to mix with sweat, appearing as great drops of blood on the brow.

Hebrews 5:7 describes Jesus' state of mind in the garden: "In the days of His flesh, He offered up both prayers and supplications with loud crying and tears." He wanted some other way to be found. Although He was the Son, He learned obedience from the things that He suffered (see v. 8).

How can the Son "learn" obedience? Wasn't He perfectly obedient in all of eternity past? How could the Son learn any obedience He did not already perfectly perform? The answer is the Incarnation. In His humanity He took upon Himself flesh, and flesh is the category of our existence which disobeys God. In His flesh, Jesus took upon Himself all of that which rebels against God. In the mystery of His person, He, in His humanity, had to learn obedience in order that He might be made perfect, and thereby to be made a source of salvation for those who believe in Him.

Why did it have to happen this way? In the perfection of His divinity, Jesus could provide the perfect sacrifice. All the other sacrifices that had been provided were inadequate. They had to be repeated day after day. Only the perfect Son of God could die a perfect death for His people, but He had to be a man to do it. He had to be in flesh, because only flesh can die. A spirit cannot die. Jesus in His eternal state as the eternal Son of God could not die.

HIS CALLING BECOMES OURS

When Jesus died, perfect flesh died because of the eternal conversation in eternity where they planned it for you and for me. Jesus said, "I have come down from heaven, not to do My own will, but the will of Him who sent Me" (John 6:38). If Jesus was sent, then surely we who are, like Him, in the flesh are to understand that we are sent as well. This is the calling for everyone who is a follower of Jesus Christ. We are to understand our lives in terms of Christ's obedience. The obedience of the Son of God is the mirror that each of us holds up to our lives and says, "How am I doing? Am I being obedient?" God intends to work through obedient people. That is the promise of His Word. You and I will not be perfect in our obedience. That is why we need the Savior and His grace. The amazing thing is that we have the audacity to pray, in the Lord's Prayer, "Thy will be done." That prayer has been called "The awful petition," because it is a petition for the active obedience of God's people.

The accomplishment of God's will is not dependent on our obedience. He doesn't need our obedience, but in His grace He determines to work through obedient people as the instruments of accomplishing His will on earth. He doesn't need us, but He uses us. God wills to use an obedient life because God intends to use an obedient person as the evidence of the triumph of grace.

Your obedience says that you know and understand that the conversation among the Trinity in eternity past was about you. It also says that you, at a specific time or maybe over time, have come to behold the Son and to believe in Him. You are therefore a trophy of God's grace, the grace planned from eternity past and executed in time and space when Jesus died and when you subsequently believed in Him. Jesus says, "I do not seek My own will, but the will of Him who sent Me" (John 5:30; cf. 6:38). The challenge is, are you willing to seek and do God's will?

WILLING TO BE WILLING

There was a time in my life many years ago when I was struggling with whether or not I was called to Christ. Oh, I believed in Jesus. I had trusted Him for salvation, but I was really struggling with whether or not I was going to follow Him. Was I going to do what I wanted or what He wanted with my life? One cold, rainy spring day in my hometown in Connecticut, I took a walk. I got drenched. I was in physical discomfort and spiritual agony. It was an admittedly cheap and minor imitation of the agony of our Lord in Gethsemane, but I was in agony nonetheless. I wondered if I could pray, "Lord, I will to do Your will." I answered, "No, I cannot will to do Your will. I don't want to do it." (If we are honest, a majority of believers will say that.) So I backed up a step and said, "If I can't pray, 'Lord, I will to do Your will,' maybe I can pray, 'Lord, I am willing to be made willing to do Your will.'" Can you pray that? Or if you can't pray that, can you pray the one that goes before that: "I am willing to be made willing to be made willing to do Your will"? Take it back as far as you need to!

What is at stake is whether or not you are a trophy of grace, because obedience is a sign that grace is operative in your life. If grace is operative in your life, you will understand yourself as one who is the object of that eternal conversation, and one who beholds the Savior. You will become one who grows in your willingness to be obedient to the Lord. It is not the way you become saved; it is the evidence of your salvation.

Why are you here? Why are you alive? The ultimate answer must be that it is to do the will of Him who sent you, to be a trophy of grace thereby, and to know that the Father and the Son and the Spirit have been talking about you forever out of love, and that at a specific moment in time you beheld and still behold the Son of God and that you therefore gladly, willingly, eagerly give your life to Him.

16

THE PAST, PRESENT, AND FUTURE WITH JESUS

They said therefore to Him, "What shall we do, that we may work the works of God?" Jesus answered and said to them, "This is the work of God, that you believe in Him whom He has sent." They said therefore to Him, "What then do You do for a sign, so that we may see, and believe You? What work do You perform? Our fathers ate the manna in the wilderness; as it is written, 'He gave them bread out of heaven to eat.'" Jesus therefore said to them, "Truly, truly, I say to you, it is not Moses who has given you the bread out of heaven, but it is My Father who gives you the true bread out of heaven. For the bread of God is that which comes down out of heaven, and gives life to the world." They said therefore to Him, "Lord, evermore give us this bread." Jesus said to them, "I am the bread of life; he who comes to Me shall not hunger, and he who believes in Me shall never thirst. . . .

"I am the living bread that came down out of heaven; if anyone eats of this bread, he will live forever; and the bread also which I shall give for the life of the world is My flesh." The Jews therefore began to argue with one another, saying, "How can this man give us His flesh to eat?" Jesus therefore said to them, "Truly, truly, I say to you, unless you eat the flesh of the Son of Man and drink His blood, you have no life in yourselves. He who eats My flesh and drinks My blood has eternal life, and I will raise him up on the last day. For My flesh is true food, and My blood is true drink. He who eats My flesh and drinks My blood abides in Me, and I in him. As the living Father sent Me, and I live because of the Father, so he who eats Me, he also shall live because of Me. This is the bread which came down out of heaven; not as the fathers ate, and died, he who eats this bread shall live forever." These things He said in the synagogue, as He taught in Capernaum (John 6:28-35, 51-59).

I AM A NEWSHOUND. I like events and listening to the news about them. When I can't sleep at night, I turn on the radio and disturb my wife. Sometimes I even go downstairs and turn on CNN in the middle of the night. The turn of the century weekend was an absolute feast for a guy like me. I was up at 4:00 A.M. watching the New Year come to

Auckland, New Zealand. I didn't intend to get up, but some inner clock said, "This is big, Skip." So I got up and watched the New Year come in Auckland, then Sydney, and then I tracked it around the world. It was tremendous fun. Early the next morning, when everyone else was sleeping, I snuck out in my pajama top and a pair of jeans, got in my car, and stole down to the nearest 7-Eleven to buy the keepsake version of *The New York Times.*

THE CENTER OF HISTORY

Some of us believe that *The New York Times* is the be-all and end-all of news sources. Old prejudices die hard, so you will excuse me for my old East Coast bias, namely, it really hasn't happened until *The New York Times* has commented on it. For the hundred and fifty years of its existence, the *Times* has printed a little box up in the corner that says, "All the news that's fit to print." Some of us take great comfort in that fact. We enjoy the idea that it's all there, even if we don't read it all—and *The New York Times* does claim to have it all there!

Most biases and prejudices, as you know, are not very logical, and I confess that mine about *The New York Times* is not very logical. When I read the editorial pages, I most often think differently than the editors of the *Times.*

My life is rooted in a revealed religion, that is, a belief system that underscores the frailty of the human condition and the necessity of redemption from outside humanity. So I have to say that *The New York Times* does not get it right most of the time, with its unwavering belief in the ability of man to solve most of the world's problems.

Of course the *Times* says it so beautifully. It is wrong, but it says it well! There is no better example of that than the editorial that appeared there on New Year's Day, 2000. It is a masterfully written testimony to the liberal idea of humankind at the turn of the millennium. Here are a couple of quotations from the editorial, which was titled "The Shape of an Age to Come":

> So now at last begins the year 2000, a juncture in time so long antic-
> ipated it is hard to believe it has arrived, disguised as a mere
> Saturday. . . . What remained undone on Friday will still need doing
> on Monday. Yet there is no denying that we have arrived at the gate-

way to another epic, and the moment commands respect and reflection about the world to come. In a thousand years, when people look back at what has preceded them, they will see that the chronicle of this new millennium began with us. . . . None of this, however, relieves us of the obligation to do what is within our power. That is to help form the future by bequeathing the best of what we have learned about constructing and sustaining an enlightened civilization.

After a survey of world events and issues at the turn of the millennium, the editorial ends this way:

Something about the sound of 2000 draws past and future near in a way that we have never quite known before. So here we are now, all of us, just next door to yesterday and yet somehow in a different world. This day's firstborn are already with us, and the first of us to die in this new calendar have already gone. Soon we will have slept a full night in this strange-sounding year, and then another. We cannot know how the new millennium will end, but we do have the power to determine how it begins and, perhaps, what it will remember of us.

There probably could be no more beautiful statement of the liberal ideal than that. We are the new millennium; what we make of it and what history will make of us is all important.

Christians do not diminish what history will make of us; we just put it under a larger and more important heading, the heading of a sovereign Lord. Human history and human endeavor are very important but secondary to God's will determining whatsoever comes to pass. Christians care about the past, the present, and the future. Our faith is rooted in the real history of the past, and it does give purpose and joy to the present, and it also makes certain the most important parts of an uncertain future. The liberal secularism of *The New York Times* would incorrectly put mankind in control of history—past, present, and future.

The editorial calls us progenitors of a new millennium. The Christian view is that Jesus Christ is not only the progenitor of the new millennium. He is the center of all history. Only that fact makes lasting sense out of our past, our present, and our future. The Christian's rootedness in his past, his motivation in the present, and his hope for the future nowhere come into better focus than when he stands, sits, or kneels before the Communion table and takes the ancient meal that the Lord has commanded believers to take.

We hear past, present, and future come together, even in the familiar words, "'Do this . . . in remembrance of Me' [the past]. . . . For as often as you eat this bread and drink the cup [the present], you proclaim the Lord's death until He comes" [the future] (1 Cor. 11:25-26). The table of the Lord spreads a banquet of historical meaning before partakers. John Calvin said he would rather experience the Lord's table than explain it. (But, of course, then he went on and tried to explain it for almost a hundred pages in his *Institutes of the Christian Religion!*)

When Christians meditate on the Lord's Supper and reflect on their own past, present, and future in light of it, we often fall off the horse on either one side or the other. We make either too much of it or too little of it. Sometimes we view it as just a memorial meal, something we do in remembrance of Christ's death, like a reenactment of a historical event like the Alamo or Appomattox. Sometimes it is too exaggerated in meaning, as when some say that the presence of the Lord is *in* the bread or *in* the wine, and that the bread actually *becomes* the body of the Lord and the wine actually *becomes* His blood. But Jesus Himself said to His disciples at that first Lord's Supper, "This is My body," and He held out His hand with bread in it. Obviously, in some measure, Jesus was speaking symbolically, because His body was right there.

Localizing the physical presence of Christ to the bread actually diminishes rather than enlarges its spiritual meaning. It confines His body just to those elements. But the Bible neither plays down nor exaggerates the significance of the Lord's Supper. The metaphor of eating is the common way that Jesus talked about taking something into our innermost being. John Calvin said, "The soul must truly and deeply become partaker of Christ, that it may be quickened to spiritual life by his power."[1] The spiritual presence of the Lord is at the Communion table.

There is importance in the breaking of the bread. During the Lord's Supper at our church, I hold the bread aloft and break it in two before the congregation, saying, "This is the body of Christ, broken for you." Then partakers repeat those words to one another as the bread is distributed. The promise of our Lord is that He is spiritually present in the Lord's Supper in a way that He is not otherwise present. It means that He ministers to us individually, according to our needs of the moment.

What needs about the past, the present, and the future do you take to the Communion table?

THE PAST WITH JESUS

The Jews expected that when Messiah came, He would redo the miracle of manna in the wilderness. Here they ask Him, "What then do You do for a sign, so that we may see, and believe You? What work do You perform? Our fathers ate the manna in the wilderness; as it is written, 'He gave them bread out of heaven to eat'" (John 6:30-31). Just prior to this, Jesus had fed the five thousand. Now there was an expectation on the part of the Jewish people that He was going to provide a permanent supply of food. But Jesus did not say He had come to give them bread from heaven; He said He *was* the Bread from heaven.

It is hard to understand Christ's claim to be the Bread from heaven. In the Greek it is the strongest possible way of saying that He was in heaven, then, at a specific moment, He left heaven to come here in order to be the Bread of heaven for us. The emphasis is on His specific coming in time and space in the past—on the Incarnation itself.

Christ really gave His flesh, for a worldwide group of people—from Auckland, New Zealand, to Sydney, Australia, and all the rest of the way around the world, just like on New Year's Day, 2000. The real meaning of our faith is attached to the "realness" of Christ's flesh. The Incarnation took place in history. The saving events of Christ's life and death actually happened! They are neither abstractions nor stories over which we warm our heads and hearts to give our lives some meaning. Any form of spirituality apart from history is a fairy tale. And not all fairy tales are good for you.

Paul says in 1 Corinthians 10 that the bread we break is the participation in the body of Christ, and the cup is the participation in His blood. Because Christ came down from heaven in history and in His flesh actually died, we participate in the benefits of His accomplishment by eating and drinking the bread and the cup. By believing in Him, we participate in all that history meant when He came. What we believe is not just that Christ will be our friend and help us out a little today with our problems, but that He has actually accomplished salvation in history by His broken body and His shed blood. That is our past with Jesus.

THE PRESENT WITH JESUS

Jesus upset the Jews' expectations by not providing the bread they wanted. Instead, He said He *is* the Bread. They were hoping for the kind of bread that makes a turkey sandwich. John 6:41 tells us the Jews were grumbling. Some Christians grumble because Jesus doesn't give them what they want. But He is the real food, He is the food that fills the hunger that no other food can satisfy.

In the present of your life, what fulfills you? What do you take for the meaning of your soul?

When we first moved to Dallas, my son, who was eight years old at the time, began playing on a baseball team. Chris was a pretty good player, and he hated to lose. One time that spring his team lost, and they lost badly, and I had to stay up talking to Chris until midnight because he was crushed. He just couldn't believe they played so poorly and that he had played so poorly. Finally, about midnight, I said, "Christopher [we still called him Christopher in those days], life is not baseball." He looked at me like I was nuts. His eyes grew large, and he exclaimed, "It's not?" But a couple of days later he said to me, "Dad, that was the best talk we ever had."

Anything in our lives that replaces the Bread of heaven is an idol. Anything. Any *good* thing, no matter how good, if it takes the place of the Bread of heaven, becomes an idol in our hearts. When we worship that idol, we are guilty of what some have called temporary insanity, like the starving man walking past a banquet to go out looking for food in the garbage.

For many, Communion is when you realize again the present communion that you have with the Lord of life and glory, and you realize that He is with you now—in trials, in the difficulties of this life. Communion becomes a time when you say again, "Lord, I will be obedient to You. Forgive me for how I failed You. Forgive me that I have put idols in the place of the Bread of heaven. And, Lord, feed me with the only Bread that truly satisfies."

THE FUTURE WITH JESUS

The Lord's Supper is a tremendous source of future hope. Jesus says, "I am the living bread that came down out of heaven; if anyone eats of this bread, he shall live forever" (John 6:51). In verse 54 He says, "He who eats My flesh and drinks My blood has eternal life." And in verse 58 He says, "Your forefathers ate manna and died, but he who feeds on this bread will live forever" (NIV).

Eternal life does not seem relevant to many modern people, especially if we are busy celebrating new centuries, new millennia, new marriages, new births, new homes, new cars, new this and new that. Our life is so full with new things that we forget the newness of eternal life. Yet those in Christ who are walking close to the shadow of death know the hope and the promise. They know that nothing or no one can ever replace the hope that we have for eternity because of Christ. And they know that we need to reorient our lives today according to the future.

Some scholars argue that the center of the New Testament is the future, not the past nor even the present; that we are living all of life in light of the great future, as we focus on the One who has come and promises that He will come again. Four times in John 6, Jesus says that He will raise us up with Him on the last day (vv. 39, 40, 44, 54).

Bonnie Prince Charlie of Scotland, the grandson of James II of England, was exiled to France by George II. But Charlie was very popular, especially in Scotland. All over Scotland, when there was a public toast at any meal or gathering, Scotsmen would lift the goblet and then silently pass it over a glass of water, by which they symbolically said, "To our king who is coming over the waters."

In the Lord's Supper we salute the future when we take the goblet and say, "To our King, who is coming over the waters of time." He is coming, and your past, your present, and your future are sealed in Him.

17

RIVERS OF LIVING WATER

But when His brothers had gone up to the feast, then He Himself also went up, not publicly, but as it were, in secret. The Jews therefore were seeking Him at the feast, and were saying, "Where is He?" And there was much grumbling among the multitudes concerning Him; some were saying, "He is a good man"; others were saying, "No, on the contrary, He leads the multitude astray." Yet no one was speaking openly of Him for fear of the Jews.

Now on the last day, the great day of the feast, Jesus stood and cried out, saying, "If any man is thirsty, let him come to Me and drink. He who believes in Me, as the Scripture said, 'From his innermost being shall flow rivers of living water.'" But this He spoke of the Spirit, whom those who believed in Him were to receive; for the Spirit was not yet given, because Jesus was not yet glorified (John 7:10-13, 37-39).

IF WE ARE TO UNDERSTAND the Lord's meaning in these chapters, we must focus on three remarkable verses, John 7:37-39, where the promise of the Spirit is clearly given, where Jesus attaches Himself to that promise, and where He shouts out His invitation on the last day of the feast.

Isn't it interesting that Jesus cries out loudly in the temple? Crying out loudly in church isn't usually well-received these days. Once a big sister and her little brother were sitting together in church, and the little brother was giggling and making a lot of noise. Finally his sister had had enough and said, "You are not supposed to be so loud in church." "Why not?" asked the boy, "who is going to stop me?" His sister pointed to the back of the sanctuary and said, "You see those guys in dark suits back there? They are called *hushers.*"

I'm not sure that story is true, but I know this one is: One Sunday morning as I entered the church building I overheard a dad seeking to prepare his young son for the worship service. He asked the boy, "Why do you think it is important that we be quiet in church?" Without any hesitation his son answered, "Because people are sleeping."

No, we shouldn't be sleeping, of course, and we really don't need ushers to be "hushers." But we really do need to shout out sometimes, maybe even in corporate worship, when the Lord moves in on our lives.

In the church I served in Virginia, there was a little boy with cerebral palsy who always sat on the front row, year after year, in a bigger and bigger wheelchair as he grew. Sometimes Martin would get so excited in church that he would just want to shout out. But because of his disability, he sometimes did it a little late. So after everyone else had reacted to something, maybe a special piece of music, Martin would put his hands in the air and yell, "Wow, God!" Sometimes all of us need to say, "Wow, God!"

One of my biggest challenges on Sunday morning is my own spiritual lethargy. Sometimes I arrive at church early Sunday morning and say to my colleague and friend Colin, who is our organist, "Play something loud," because I want my own heart to be quickened to the music that communicates something of the wonder of the Lord's presence. Do you ever feel that your life is in a rut? Oh, you believe the right things, I suppose, but the problem is those things you believe make so little difference in your life.

Sometimes life gets overwhelming, whether from fatigue or illness or the worries and complexities of life. We can get so preoccupied with the wrong things. It is like a weight, and we have to figure out how to unload it in order to liberate our hearts and get above the ceiling in the room where we worship.

God has promised to give us what we need. He has promised to bring Jesus to our hearts in and by His Holy Spirit, to make the gospel real in our hearts again. Then by God's grace the Spirit gives us power for living that overcomes the lethargy, even the despondency.

THE PROMISE OF THE SPIRIT

When Jesus speaks of the coming of the Holy Spirit (John 7:37-39), He is not referring to a specific Old Testament promise. Rather, He is referring to the whole tone and tenor of the Old Testament. The promise of the Bible is the Spirit of God. The promise of the Old Testament from beginning to end is the promise that God will come and be with His people in the power and presence of His Holy Spirit.

The Holy Spirit is not for the esoteric Christian. It is not for those who have some "higher life." It is not for those who have some second experience. It is not just for those who have some dramatic trial in their life and have a breakthrough of understanding. I do thank God for those breakthroughs in my own life when I hit a brick wall, cannot go any further, and cry out to Him and He says again to me, "I am here. I will help you. I will move in on your life." I thank God for times like that, but the promise of the Spirit is for *every* Christian, at *all* times.

THE PROMISE OF THE FEAST

The Feast of Tabernacles is an important context to this promise from our Lord. Why did Jesus choose this particular celebration to make this shouted declaration? This feast was an annual eight-day celebration in Jerusalem to commemorate God's provision of daily water for the Israelites as they wandered in the wilderness. During the feast, the people would carry leafy branches called *lulabs,* which probably symbolized the various stages of vegetation in the wilderness. They would carry these into the temple while chanting Psalm 118:25, which says, "O LORD, do save, we beseech Thee; O LORD, we beseech Thee, do send prosperity!" This was probably a prayer for rain and for a fruitful harvest season.

On each day of the feast, the priest would draw water from the pool of Siloam in Jerusalem, bring it in procession to the temple, and pour it out in a bowl near the altar. In the ancient Talmud, the "catechism" of the Old Testament, there is this question: "Why is the name of it [referring to the priest's action] called the drawing out of water?" The correct answer is, "Because of the pouring out of the Holy Spirit according to what is said, 'With joy you shall draw water out of the wells of salvation,'" which is a quotation from Isaiah 12:3.

The Spirit is clearly and consistently promised in Isaiah, first to Jesus Christ, and then, through Him, to believers.

THE PROMISE OF THE SPIRIT TO CHRIST

In Isaiah 11:1-4a we read, "Then a shoot will spring from the stem of Jesse, and a branch from his roots will bear fruit. And the Spirit of the LORD will rest on Him, the spirit of wisdom and understanding, the spirit of counsel and strength, the spirit of knowledge and the fear of the LORD. And He [Christ] will delight in the fear of the LORD. And He will not judge by what His eyes see nor make a decision by what His ears hear; but with righteousness He will judge the poor."

The promise is that the Messiah will receive the Spirit, and the Spirit will be the equipment that the Messiah needs in order to carry out His messianic role—to give counsel, to give wisdom, to correctly judge, to care for the poor.

In Isaiah 42:1 we read, "Behold, My Servant, whom I uphold; My chosen one in whom My soul delights. I have put My Spirit upon Him; He will bring forth justice to the nations." The Servant who is going to lay down His life for God's people needs the Spirit as His own equipment in order to do that; and then, as well, in order to bring forth justice to the nations. That is the main theme of what the Messiah is going to do: somehow all those who have been the objects of some injustice will find that the wrongs are righted. When the Messiah comes, especially at His second coming, there will be justice amply given out for all those who have missed it until then.

Isaiah 61:1-2 is one of the most famous passages in Isaiah concerning the coming of the Spirit to the Messiah Himself. These are the very words that Jesus makes the charter of His own ministry, as recorded in Luke 4:18-19: "The Spirit of the Lord is upon Me, because He anointed Me to preach the gospel to the poor. He has sent Me to proclaim release to the captives, and recovery of sight to the blind, to set free those who are downtrodden, to proclaim the favorable year of the Lord." Jesus takes these very words as His platform, as it were, for His messianic campaign.

You remember what happens. The Spirit of God comes upon Jesus like a dove at His baptism, and the Father's voice is heard saying, in essence, "This is My Son. Of Him I am very proud" (see Matt. 3:17).

In John's account of Christ's baptism (John 1:32-34), we read that when John the Baptist saw the Spirit descending as a dove on Jesus, he knew he was seeing the Son of God. John knew his Old Testament well enough to know that unless and until the Spirit of God came upon the Messiah and equipped Him for His messianic task, He could not be the Messiah. We don't shrink from saying it: The eternal Son of God could not do what God called Him to do without the Holy Spirit.

THE PROMISE OF THE SPIRIT TO CHRISTIANS

The Spirit is provided not only to Christ but also to God's people through Him. Look at a passage like Isaiah 44:3-4: "For I will pour out water on the thirsty land and streams on the dry ground." The Feast of Tabernacles image is provision of water in the wilderness, but note to what it is connected. The verse continues, "I will pour out My Spirit on your offspring, and My blessing on your descendants; and they will spring up among the grass like poplars by streams of water."

I don't know if poplars grow in your part of the country, but I had a poplar in Virginia. My wife gave me one for my fortieth birthday and we planted it in the yard behind our house. That tree grew so quickly it was unbelievable, and because it grew so quickly, it needed water all the time. I don't think it is by chance that Isaiah speaks about poplars needing water!

You will see this tremendous promise again and again in Scripture. In words echoed in Acts, the prophet Joel says, "It will come about after this that I will pour out My Spirit on all mankind; and your sons and daughters will prophesy, your old men will dream dreams, your young men will see visions. And even on the male and female servants I will pour out My Spirit in those days" (Joel 2:28-29; quoted in Acts 2:17-18). The Spirit of God comes as a great equalizer. When the Spirit of God shows up, all believers are equal before God. Whether a man, a woman, young, old, a servant, a slave, a landowner—no matter who we are, we all stand on the same level before the Lord by His Spirit.

The promise in Joel is echoed in John 3:34: "For He gives the Spirit without measure." The Spirit of God is not given by the Lord with an eyedropper. He doesn't say, "Well, just a little bit for you, Sarah." "Just a drop for Joe." "Jennie, you get a half-cup." No, He gives the Spirit without measure. It is the heart of God to give that which reveals Jesus in our hearts without measure.

The Lord is for you. In your fatigue, your lethargy, your weakness, your materialism, and your sin, the Lord is with you. The Lord wants to give Himself to you. That is what Isaiah and the Old Testament promise. John, in his Gospel, says it comes to pass in Jesus Christ. Jesus comes in the power of the Spirit, and He therefore gives new life by the power of the Spirit to His people.

POWER FOR A CHANGED LIFE

The provision of the Spirit that Jesus promises is the provision of life. The words *life* and *spirit* are frequently associated in this Gospel. The Spirit is He who bears the life of Christ home to our hearts. The Spirit does not, as it were, bring sheer, raw power to our lives. Some people think the Spirit is like an electric current; they say, "I just need to figure out how to plug into God and get the Spirit to zap through me." That is not the way the Spirit works. The Spirit is always the power of a person.

He is not so much an electric current as He is a magnetic personality. Who is the most magnetic person you know? A coach? A teacher? A father? A friend? When such people walk into the room, the atmosphere changes. There is just something about them. They are dynamic. Now multiply that by a billion and you have an idea of the power of Jesus Christ.

You see this in the effect that Jesus has on the people around Him. His presence changes the atmosphere in a life. His saving benefit put into hearts quickens them from death to life. We have looked at two such people already in the Gospel of John—Nicodemus and the woman at the well.

Nicodemus and the Spirit's Sovereignty

If you think again about Nicodemus, you see the absolute necessity of being changed by the power of Jesus. Jesus teaches that the kingdom of God is invisible until the Spirit of God works to open the eyes of the unbeliever. Nicodemus came by night, its darkness to be removed by the dawn. But the darkness of Nicodemus's interior life could be removed only by the Spirit bringing rebirth.

Some of my neighbors have automatic spotlights on their driveways or in their yards. Sometimes I'm taking a little walk after dark and, all of a sudden, their yard or driveway lights up as I walk past. In the darkness they can't see who is in their front yard, until those automatic lights come on. In the darkness of our hearts we cannot see Christ coming until the spotlight of the Holy Spirit shines on our hearts and reveals Jesus there. That is the Spirit's job description—to shine on Jesus and make us see the truth of what He brings to life in His gospel.

Jesus tells Nicodemus that he cannot control the Spirit, just as he cannot control the wind (John 3:8); he cannot modify, bottle, or contain the Spirit in any way. We do not know the power of a changed life until we realize that the power that changes our lives is given by God, who is absolutely sovereign to move in on our lives when, where, how, and under what circumstances He chooses.

A changed life requires humility. Only when we bow before the sovereignty of God, who has the absolute right to bring His gospel into our hearts as He chooses, do we begin to know the power of that gospel. When we insist that it depends on *our* decision to receive Jesus, we try to grab some of that sovereign power back from God. Yes, it depends on a decision. Yes, we need to exercise faith. But faith is the gift of God, and He sovereignly gives His grace and power to His people so that their hearts might be quickened to new life. Only when we rest in the wonder that He is sovereign and we are not, do we enjoy the benefits of changed lives.

The Samaritan Woman and the Spirit's Availability

Anyone can be changed by the Spirit's revealing Jesus. Anyone. She is a woman, a cultural outcast, and not a Jew. The gospel always surprises us by Jesus' indifference to social niceties. You don't have to be Jewish, male, upright, solid, religious, and going to Sunday school to receive the sovereignty of His Spirit. In fact, if we join John 4 with all the promises of the Spirit in the Old Testament, we see that it is better to be poor, not in the "in crowd," and the object of injustice or oppression in the world, because then we will find that the Holy Spirit is eager to search us out.

The Samaritan woman "gets it" better than Nicodemus does. Maybe by the end of the Gospel he gets it, too. But the woman understands right away. The Spirit gravitates toward the truly needy. One dear brother in our church put it this way: "The Spirit cannot resist weakness." Where are you weak? Rejoice! Where are you at risk? Rejoice! Where is your life falling apart? Rejoice, because the Spirit of God is eager to move into your life in those weak places—not in the places of your strength, where you don't feel the need for Jesus. It is in the place of your weakness that you need the gospel, so live in your weakness. Don't try to do those things that, humanly speaking, eliminate weakness from your life. I'm not saying to avoid the responsibility of dealing with problems in your life; but

I am saying that, where you are weak, there you are strong, because that is where the Spirit of God moves in your life.

The Spirit of life brings water to the thirsty soul. So as long as you are out there digging your own well, looking for your own water supply, looking for your own remedy to your problems, the Spirit of God will resist you and pass on to a needy, thirsty soul who is saying, "Only the water that Jesus gives can satisfy my thirst."

POWER FOR A HOLY LIFE

In John 7:37 we read, "If any man is thirsty, let him come to me and drink." The tense of that verb is "keep coming." We don't just come once; we come again and again and again. We should be thirsty every day. Yesterday's water doesn't quench my thirst today. Today I need more water. John 16:8 says that the Holy Spirit keeps on convicting me of my sin and that the righteousness of Christ is the only remedy for my sin; and He keeps on convicting me that, if I don't do anything about my sin problem, I am inevitably going to face the judgment seat of God. Thank God the Spirit acts continuously as well. Just when I think everything is going well, the Holy Spirit comes again and convicts me of more sin. I need to live in the reality of that conviction, because that is where again and again I find Jesus and the joy of the gospel.

There is always a prayer of confession at our church's midweek vespers service. Often we use prayers from *The Valley of Vision*, a beautiful book of old Puritan prayers. One of them includes this line: "Our Father, when You are angry toward us for our wrongs, we try to pacify you by abstaining from future sin."[1] I'm convicted. I know I've done wrong, and immediately I think, *Okay, Lord, here is my self-improvement program. Here is what I am going to do to avoid that sin in the future.* That is not a gospel response. Yes, He wants my behavior to be better, but first He wants my heart to be better. Behavior does not change the heart.

The prayer continues: "But teach us that we cannot satisfy Your law, that this effort is a resting in our righteousness; that only the righteousness of Christ, ready-made, already finished, is fit for that purpose." The Spirit of God will convince us that the only way to a holy life is receiving the righteousness of Christ. Holiness begins not with anything we do, including resolutions for the New Year or the new century or the new millennium. It begins with the recognition that we are entrapped in sin, and that only the gospel of a sovereign God can free us from it.

The prayer ends this way: "You are everything, and to possess You is to possess everything." The power of a holy life is the blessedness of not wanting anything more than we want Christ. That is what happened to the woman at the well. She began to want Jesus more than she wanted all those men in her life; and that is the work of the Spirit. He comes to our hearts and quickens in us a desire to have Jesus. Holiness isn't trying to do better, but loving Him above all else.

POWER FOR AN INSTRUCTED LIFE

Nehemiah 9:19b-20a says, "By day the pillar of cloud did not cease to guide them on their path, nor the pillar of fire by night to shine on the way they were to take. You gave your good Spirit to instruct them" (NIV). The Spirit of God is always provided in order that the people of God might be instructed. Jesus Himself promises that the Holy Spirit "will teach you all things, and bring to your remembrance all that I said to you" (John 14:26).

This e-mail message to some pastor friends came from John Piper on the first day of the year 2000: "Brothers, do whatever you have to do on the first day of the year to be in the Word daily all year long. Be ruthless with your schedule. Cut off your hand or pluck out your eye if you have to. Slash and burn, die if you must, to get the delight of knowing God through His Word. . . . Delight is a fight."

Delight is a fight. It is not natural to fallen people. The last time I checked, I didn't always want to read my Bible. It is hard. When I got up this morning and opened my Bible, much in me resisted it.

Only a life-long commitment to growing in delighting in the Word of God gives you an appetite and a hunger for it, and I'm not there yet. Sometimes I get glimpses of it. "Join me," Piper says, "in the fight to delight in the Word of God day and night. Plan it today, brothers. It won't happen without a plan. Without a rugged plan you will default to checking e-mail rather than reading the Bible. Plan a time. Plan a place. Plan what parts of the Bible you will read. . . . But wherever, whenever, however you do it, *do it!*"

Then Piper challenges the pastors he is addressing: "Our people's lives hang on our being Word-saturated leaders. They will smell the aroma of Christ when we have been with God, and they will smell the world when we lead out of the shallowness of our own mind. O, brothers, let us commune with Christ daily in the solitude of our chosen place. And let us bring this aroma of communion to our assemblies and lead the people to God. . . . Beat the path to God daily while you have light. . . . Make the path well worn. Then when you are weak and the darkness falls, your body, like a weary ox after a long day will find its way home through the evening mist to food and refreshment."

If anyone tells me that they can have the power of Jesus without the power of the Scripture, I do not believe them. It is just not possible, because the Lord has promised to conjoin His power to the power and truth of His Word.

POWER FOR A LIFE OF GIVING

The tense of the verbs in John 7:37-38 is "keep coming, keep drinking, keep believing, keep flowing." The Spirit's abundance is compared to a mighty overflowing river, an artesian wellspring.

The Qumran community was a group of people living near the Dead Sea during Jesus' time on earth. They had withdrawn into the wilderness about seventeen miles from Jerusalem in order to preserve their private piety and avoid contamination by the world. They made no effort to influence others or to bring blessing on them. Their community was "appropriately" located, overlooking the northern end of the Dead Sea, which receives the Jordan River but has no outlet. Nothing can live in the Dead Sea because nothing flows through it. The Qumran community received the promises of God, but nothing flowed through it. It gave life to no one; consequently, it bent the truth in important ways.

The Puritan John Bunyan called this "Piety of the Pond," or "the rule of the stagnant pool." Bunyan contrasts the One who gives with the one who keeps. He also wrote,

A man there was, though some did count him mad,
The more he cast away the more he had.[2]

The poet William Wordsworth wrote:

> . . . the good old rule
> Sufficeth them, the simple plan,
> That they should take, who have the power,
> And they should keep who can.[3]

Living waters, if they are only received, will dry up in your soul. They are meant to be shared. Pastor and missionary Jack Miller said that the abundance of the Spirit is for those who are believing now and who keep right on believing.[4] Believing is ongoing, moment-by-moment, coming, drinking, believing, flowing.

As a pastor, I have many opportunities to speak of Christ and His gospel as the only power for a changed life. When someone comes to my office wanting to talk about some problem, and I realize that he or she is not a believer, I confess that about 75 percent of the time a huge wave of lethargy comes over me. I don't want to go through the spiritual birth. I don't know why. Is it my sin? It may be. Is it the Evil One clouding my head and heart? It may be. But when I begin to speak of Jesus and the power of the gospel as the only power to save a soul, and when I do so by God's grace, there begins to move through my spirit and my soul a river of life. I am giving what I am receiving.

So many of us have stopped receiving because long ago we stopped giving. In the power of the Spirit, Jesus came to give His life away for us. In the power of the Spirit, we are to give our lives away to the thirsty, to the needy, to those who desperately need a drink of water even if they don't realize it. May God help us to live changed lives, holy lives, instructed lives—lives lived on the basis of the power of the gospel to change us.

18

"I Am"

Now when evening came, His disciples went down to the sea (John 6:16).

When therefore they had rowed about three or four miles, they beheld Jesus walking on the sea and drawing near to the boat; and they were frightened. But He said to them, "It is I; do not be afraid" (6:19-20).

Jesus said to them, "I am the bread of life; he who comes to Me shall not hunger, and he who believes in Me shall never thirst" (6:35).

The Jews therefore were grumbling about Him, because He said, "I am the bread that came down out of heaven" (6:41).

The Jews therefore began to argue with one another, saying, "How can this man give us His flesh to eat?" (6:52).

As a result of this many of His disciples withdrew, and were not walking with Him anymore. Jesus said therefore to the twelve, "You do not want to go away also, do you?" Simon Peter answered Him, "Lord, to whom shall we go? You have words of eternal life. And we have believed and have come to know that You are the Holy One of God" (6:66-69).

And there was much grumbling among the multitudes concerning Him; some were saying, "He is a good man"; others were saying, "No, on the contrary, He leads the multitude astray" (7:12).

Jesus therefore answered them, and said, "My teaching is not Mine, but His who sent Me" (7:16).

"I know Him; because I am from Him, and He sent Me" (7:29).

Jesus therefore said, "For a little while longer I am with you, then I go to Him who sent Me" (7:33).

So there arose a division in the multitude because of Him (7:43).

Again therefore Jesus spoke to them, saying, "I am the light of the world; he who follows Me shall not walk in the darkness, but shall have the light of life" (8:12).

Jesus answered and said to them, "Even if I bear witness of myself, My witness is true; for I know where I came from, and where I am going; but you do not know where I come from, or where I am going" (8:14).

"I said therefore to you, that you shall die in your sins; for unless you believe that I am He, you shall die in your sins." And so they were saying to Him, "Who are You?" (8:24-25a).

Jesus therefore said, "When you lift up the Son of Man, then you will know that I am He" (8:28a).

Jesus said to them, "Truly, truly, I say to you, before Abraham was born, I am" (8:58).

In John 6–8 a transition is taking place, a heightening of tension. Opposition to the Lord Jesus Christ is mounting, and it will continue to escalate through chapter 12.

The multitudes, the Jewish leaders, even the disciples question who Jesus is. They disagree over His identity, squabbling and grumbling among themselves, and Jesus does nothing to remove the sting of the offense that His presence seems to cause.

When someone misunderstands me, I am quick to want to explain myself. I want to end any anxiety about something I might have said or done. Not Jesus. He presses on, seemingly oblivious to the fact that again and again His own person is heightening the offense to these people.

A key verse for understanding our passages from John 6–8 is 8:25: "Who are You?" It is fitting that the question comes at the end of this section where there has been so much controversy about the Lord's identity. As we shall see, in both this chapter and the next, Jesus inflames the growing tension by the way in which He answers this question.

What do we acknowledge at Christmas? God becomes a baby. We think of manger scenes, a precious infant, and shepherds. These images are true and relevant and warm our hearts, but they cannot change our hearts. They can make us feel happy about the Christmas season, but there is no way that these truths alone can change who we are. There is no dynamic that can actually change our hearts. Not until we begin to see *who* became a little baby—the God-Man, Jesus Christ—will our hearts not only be warmed but also profoundly changed. What is really astounding is that the Lord of heaven and earth, a God of immeasurable dignity and power, a God of terrifying holiness has become a baby. That truth will change us, because in that truth is the gospel. In that truth is what theologians call the transcendence of God, the immensity of God, and also the immanence of God, the closeness of God. At the fulcrum of these two truths, the holy otherness of God and the proximity of God in the incarnate Son, is where there is torque to change our hearts.

If we do not see this first side of Jesus Christ, if we do not see the fearsome holiness of who He is, then He remains a pleasant, perhaps even a persuasive figure, a fine teacher of moral truths. But He cannot change us.

THE DIVINE NAME

Beginning with this section of the Gospel of John, Jesus is "in our faces" about His own identity. He so confronts us by using a particular phrase, two Greek words that are very important in the Gospel of John, *egō eimi.* Jesus takes these two words upon Himself as His deepest identity, as the expression of who He ultimately is.

For example, in John 6, during a storm on the lake, the disciples see Jesus walking across the water and they are fearful. Jesus tries to calm their fears by saying, "It is I; do not be afraid" (v. 20). Literally the words are not, "It is I," but "I am." Translators have a problem with that because in English it makes no sense. "Do not fear; I am."

Jesus repeats Himself in 8:24: "I said therefore to you, that you shall die in your sins unless you believe . . . that I am He." The English says, "I am He," but the exact words are "I am." So Jesus actually says, "You will die in your sins unless you believe . . . that I am."

Jesus is taking upon His own lips, in describing Himself, the most important name for God in the Old Testament. He is calling Himself by the most divine name of God, and is saying, "That is My name—I AM."

The origin of this name is in Exodus 3, where Moses sees a bush that is burning but is not consumed. Moses says, "I must turn aside and see this amazing sight." He is curious, a scientific inquirer at this point. The voice of God speaks to Moses from the bush and says, "Moses, Moses!" Only five times in the whole of the Bible does God repeat a name, and whenever He does, it always means, "Watch out, get ready." "Moses, Moses, the ground on which you are standing is holy ground. Take off your sandals." Moses the scientific inquirer becomes Moses the worshiper.

God tells Moses that he will lead God's people out of Egypt, and Moses cannot imagine why they will follow him. He inquires as to what he should say to them about who has given these instructions. God answers by taking upon His own lips this name of all names. He says to Moses, "I AM WHO I AM. And when you go to the people of Israel, that is what you are to say My name is" (see Ex. 3:14).

Notice that God does not say, "I was who I was." To do that would be to imply that God was something else in the past. God doesn't change. Notice that He doesn't say, "I will be who I will be." God is immutable. God, in all times and in every situation, says that the heart of His identity is I AM, the God who has no beginning, no end, who will never need to become something that He is not. "I AM just because I AM." No one else can say that. Everything else that exists, every person and every thing, has a primary cause behind it. Only God is His own cause, and, in fact, the cause for all existence. Everything that is, exists because of God's will. So when Jesus Christ comes and claims, "I am," He is saying that He is God in the most dramatic way possible.

Some might say Jesus is the "the spark of the divine," or a "life force" or the "power of good." But when Jesus claims to be I AM, He is using the most improbable, the most difficult, and the most incomprehensible name to describe Himself. He is using a name which can never be shared by any human being. He is saying that He is a personal God. He is a God who is an "I." God has a distinctive, personal existence. He is not a spark of the divine in you or in anyone else. He *is*. He is an existent person with a distinct identity.

Furthermore, God is not just a life force. Rather, He is the prime cause of all things. He is the force behind all existence. The apostle Paul says that, "In Him everything holds together. He is the One who created everything" (see Col. 1:16-17). The molecules and atoms of the universe hold together in Him.

And furthermore, Jesus is saying that He is not a vague power for good but the absolute standard of good for all time. Now the waters get deeper here, so hold your breath. Jesus Christ, man in flesh, God incarnate, comes and takes upon Himself the name that every Jew would recognize as meaning the eternally existent, one and only, utterly separate God who is not just a life force but is *the* power, *the* force, *the* cause of everything that exists, and who is not just *a* measure of good and evil but is *the* absolute standard of everything that is right or wrong in all of the universe. There is no possible way that Jesus could have more thoroughly stated His claim to be the eternal, self-sufficient, all-powerful, and all-good God of heaven and earth. And when He says, "I am," He is saying at least this: "I have authority over you." Those listening to Him may not believe it, and they don't like it, but it is clear that He claims absolute authority over them and over the created order. This section of John begins with Christ's word calming the storm. He is the authority over creation. He is the authority over your life, over my life.

In effect He is saying, "Other issues in your life are not primary—even being hungry, out of a job, or very ill." Of course He cares about these things. But He says that all the issues of life must be understood under the umbrella of allegiance to Him. His sovereign control and power over the universe is not suspended just because people have problems.

PUSHED TO EXTREMES

Jesus pushes everyone to extremes. He pushes people to the logic of what He is declaring about Himself. *We cannot accept anything Jesus says without accepting what He says about Himself.* We cannot maintain intellectual credibility and do that. If we reject His claim to be God, then we cannot accept anything else He says about the way we are to behave toward one another.

Perhaps you are objecting, "Wait a minute, Skip. You are overstating it. There are plenty of people in the world who say something about themselves that I disagree with. But I don't discount everything they say." The problem is Jesus isn't just anyone. He is the One who claimed to be I AM. He is the One who claimed to be God. If He is wrong on that point, then He cannot be right on any other point. You cannot say you like what He says and what He did and also say, "I do not accept it when He says He is God."

C. S. Lewis says this with humor and insight in these well-known comments in his book, *Mere Christianity:*

> I am trying here to prevent anyone from saying the really foolish thing that people often say about Him. "I am ready to accept Jesus as a great moral teacher, but I don't accept His claim to be God." That is the one thing we must not say. A man who was merely a man and said the sort of things Jesus said would not be a great moral teacher. He would either be a lunatic—on the level with a man who says he is a poached egg—or else he would be the Devil of Hell. . . . Either this man was, and is, the Son of God: or else a madman or something worse. You can shut Him up for a fool, you can spit at Him, and kill Him as a demon; or you can fall at His feet and call Him Lord and God. But let us not come with any patronizing nonsense about His being a great human teacher. He has not left that open to us. He did not intend to.[1]

Either you must discount everything Jesus says, or He is who He claims to be and you must count everything He says as absolutely true, including everything He says about Himself. To do anything else is to be intellectually dishonest.

Jesus is the most self-centered man in history because of what He said about Himself. *Egō eimi.* "I am." If you had Jewish ears, you would grab a stone and be ready to throw it at Him, as some of them were.

Everyone around Jesus is pushed to extremes. The Jews grumble and argue around Him. The disciples withdraw. Some of them leave Him when He is teaching about who He is—about His flesh and blood and what that means. They can't take it. The multitudes are divided. The leaders are divided. Everyone gets pushed around by the "I AM-ness" of Jesus Christ.

In Flannery O'Connor's short story "A Good Man Is Hard to Find," the main character is a misfit and a killer. When he is confronted and asked why he kills people, the misfit said it was because of Jesus. "He thrown everything off balance. If He did what He said, then it's nothing for you to do but throw away everything and follow Him, and if He didn't, then it's nothing for you to do but enjoy the last few minutes you got left the best way you can—by killing somebody or burning down his house or doing some other meanness to him. No pleasure but meanness."[2]

Why not kill? Why not rob? Why not plunder and rape? Why have any pretense of morality at all? It all boils down to one question: Is Jesus who He said He is? If He is who He said He is, then you must fall on your face, worship Him, and do what He says. If He is not who He said He is, then ultimately there is no basis for morality. There is no reason why you should obey any other civil command. You should just do as you please.

Jesus doesn't leave the way of moderation or balance open to us. When you begin to wrestle with the I AM-ness of Jesus Christ, you are really wrestling with how different He is from us. We like to portray Jesus as a man, and He is a man, the One who identifies with us in our weaknesses. That is the whole meaning of the Incarnation. But you must let the other shoe drop: He is not like us at all. He is holy. He comes from God in a way that we do not. His teaching is from God in a way that ours is not. He is different, above, beyond, *holy.*

About a hundred years ago, Rudolf Otto wrote a book called *The Idea of the Holy.*[3] Otto said that the idea of the "holy" exists in every religion, and when people confront the idea of the "holy," universally there is deep ambivalence. We are drawn to it, but we are repelled at the same time. Otto called this "numinous awe." He said we rightly fear the "holy." How can this Holy One bring us good news?

What I have been saying is not good news: there is a Holy One so different from you and me that were we to stand before Him in His presence, we would smoke up in a cinder and be gone. How can that be good news?

"I Am Your Savior"

Seven of the twenty-three times Jesus says, "I am," He conjoins a metaphor to His own name: "I am the bread of life," the "light of the world," the "door of the sheep," the "good shepherd," the "resurrection and the life," the "way, the truth, and the life," the "true vine." They are metaphors drawing God close to us, showing how He cares for us. He cares that we are hungry; He gives us bread. He wants to show us the way. He cares that we find the right door. He becomes our gentle shepherd.

Jesus takes the holy name I AM and conjoins it with His other name, *Savior*, lover of our souls. He says He is both holy *and* the little baby who grew up as a man to tell us that He cares about us in our sins and trials. "Do you need bread? I give it. Do you need a way? I give it. Do you need hope in life? I give you the Resurrection." We need not be terrified of this Holy One; we need not shrink in fear. Our Judge has become our Savior.

This is the great holy mystery of the Incarnation, that on the cross and in the flesh of Jesus Christ, the ambivalence between God's distance and His closeness is reconciled. God did not become less than God to love us.

In his sermons and writings Jonathan Edwards would ask, "How do you know you are a real Christian?" How would you answer that question? Edwards's reply, repeated in various forms, was, in effect: the holiness of God doesn't terrify you anymore. He meant that you begin to understand that the one who was and is and evermore will be the holy one of God has drawn close to you.

I like God's power because I know I am weak. I like God's mercy because I may mess up and need it. I like the wisdom of God because I have difficult decisions to make. But the holiness of God? I don't like that so much, because it tells me about my true condition. The Light of life shows me how much darkness is in my own heart. So how can the holiness of God comfort me?

Edwards calls our attention to a wonderful passage of Scripture: "If we confess our sins, he is faithful and just to forgive us our sins and to cleanse us from all unrighteousness" (1 John 1:9, ESV). Notice that John didn't say He is faithful and *merciful* to forgive us our sins. Is God merciful to forgive our sins? Yes. But mercy is not the primary category of God's character with regards to His forgiving our sins. The primary category is His justice. God sent the perfectly Holy One to live the life that we could not live and to die the death that we could not die for us. *I AM* died. It is fair to say that if God did not forgive the believer his sin, God would be unjust, because the justice of God has been perfectly displayed and satisfied in the justice He wrought in His own flesh on the cross.

Conversely, for the unbeliever, for God to forgive his sin would not be merciful; it would be a radical, tragic malfeasance of justice. A just and holy God won't do that. He won't wink at sin or close His eyes to this sin or that sin. He is the great I AM. God gave His only begotten Son, not just so that He could be merciful, but so that He could be just. God gave the Son of His love for the sons of His love, in order that we who are God's enemies might live as His sons and daughters.

I have a son. I am so proud of him sometimes that I could just burst. I know he is frail and a sinner and can even be unpleasant at times. But he is my son. I sometimes just can't believe how much I love him, and I would not give up this far-from-perfect object of my love for anyone. I am neither holy enough nor merciful enough to do so.

Do you see what a holy, righteous, infinitely loving, infinitely just, but infinitely merciful God has done? Do you see that in His Son justice and mercy come together? Do you see that in Him the great I AM became the "I am not"? *I AM* died for you. The One who had no beginning or end to His existence went to hell for you so that you might live forever with Him and with His Father. I beg you, receive Him, take Him, know Him, have Him; receive not only the mercy of God but also the justice of God.

19

Truth That Frees . . .
and Makes You Odd!

"I am He who bears witness of Myself, and the Father who sent Me bears witness of Me." And so they were saying to Him, "Where is Your Father?" Jesus answered, "You know neither Me, nor My Father; if you knew Me, you would know My Father also" (John 8:18-19).

Jesus therefore was saying to those Jews who had believed Him, "If you abide in My word, then you are truly disciples of Mine; and you shall know the truth, and the truth shall make you free." They answered Him, "We are Abraham's offspring, and have never yet been enslaved to anyone; how is it that You say, 'You shall become free'?" Jesus answered them, "Truly, truly, I say to you, everyone who commits sin is the slave of sin. And the slave does not remain in the house forever; the son does remain forever. If therefore the Son shall make you free, you shall be free indeed. . . . Why do you not understand what I am saying? It is because you cannot hear My word. You are of your father the devil, and you want to do the desires of your father. He was a murderer from the beginning, and does not stand in the truth, because there is no truth in him. Whenever he speaks a lie, he speaks from his own nature; for he is a liar, and the father of lies. But because I speak the truth, you do not believe Me. Which one of you convicts Me of sin? If I speak truth, why do you not believe Me? He who is of God hears the words of God; for this reason you do not hear them, because you are not of God" (John 8:31-36, 43-47).

SEVERAL YEARS AGO, when our children were youngsters, my family and I took the great American pilgrimage to Disney World, where every day is the Fourth of July. As usual, my wife organized this outing down to the last minute. She figured out exactly how we needed to traverse Disney World in order to avoid most of the lines. In fact, because she did such a good job, all day long we waited in line only once. She also decided that in such a large crowd at such a large place we would want to spot one another more easily, so she purchased lime-green outfits for us all. I'm not talking soft lime, either. It was the kind of lime that glows in the dark. We all had lime-green shirts, lime-green shorts, lime-green socks, and, yes, lime-green hats. We looked about as silly as one family could in Disney World.

As we waited in the only line of the day, I noticed right behind me a guy about my age wearing khaki shorts, a polo shirt, a webbed belt, and Nikes. He looked very nice, very normal. I felt so embarrassed that at one point I turned to him and said, "Most of the time, I look like you!"

There was one incredibly, unexpected, stunning moment for me in the midst of our day in Disney World, at the exhibit called "The Hall of Presidents." Every American president is standing on a stage in a mannequin-type form. As the show begins, each of the mannequins begins to move in lifelike gestures, in a way only Disney can orchestrate. They begin to move around the stage a little and talk to one another, and after a moment or two, Abraham Lincoln steps out to speak for them all. He looks like every photograph you've ever seen of Lincoln. He delivers a brief speech, talking about the American presidency. It is very moving, and I will not forget one particular line. In fact, I found a piece of paper in the pocket of my lime shorts, wrote the precise words down and looked in my edition of Carl Sandburg's *Lincoln*, as soon as I got home, to see if Lincoln had actually said these words. And he had. He said, "I am nothing; truth is everything. I will perish, but truth will endure."

I was transfixed. As an amateur student of history, who loves the American presidency and actually enjoys the politics of it, I found myself asking, "What modern American president would ever say those words today?"

Frankly, I cannot imagine any president since perhaps Woodrow Wilson saying those words. The reason is that modern man is not sure if truth is everything, and modern presidents, regardless of their personal convictions, reflect this modern view of truth in their public statements. Modern people don't believe in Truth anymore, because we are not sure that there is one truth that will endure. We want to say, "Well, at least Christians believe in a truth that will endure—in an absolute truth."

Sadly, even that is not true.

The results of a Barna Research Group poll taken just a few years ago show the proportion of adults who say there is no such thing as absolute truth is 67 percent. Among people who do not claim any Christian faith, 74 percent say that. Those two figures we can understand, but the third one is staggering. The proportion of "born-again Christians" who say there is no such thing as absolute truth is 52 percent.

The inscription, "Ye shall know the truth, and the truth shall make you free" appears on more college and university buildings in America than any other inscription. I wonder how many undergraduates today know who said those words, and how much our understanding of truth has changed since those words were inscribed on so many buildings at places of higher learning in earlier times. What is going on here?

THE CRACKED MIRROR

Modern presidents and, indeed, modern people would not say the things that Lincoln said about truth, because our perception of truth has changed far more than we know. One of the better commentators on this shift of perceptions is Peter Berger. He is a Christian and also a sociologist. He writes about what he calls the "plurality of social worlds." Berger says that the people who lived in the era of agriculture and even in the industrial era of our Western civilization lived in a unified, coherent worldview. A person was one and the same person whether involved in family, work, friendships, church, or leisure. That coherency centered around an individual's identity, seeing himself as the same person no matter where he was. But "microchip man," modern man, is many people in one. There are no "unified fields," as Berger calls it. There is no unified vision to our lives anymore. We play many different roles. I am a husband. I am a son. I am a father. I am a minister of the gospel. You are businesspeople, homemakers, parents, sons, daughters. These roles do not necessarily connect with each other anymore.

For example, an executive of a major television network who claimed to have had a religious experience was questioned by *The Washington Post* as to whether his conversion had changed his thinking about the kinds of programs his network ran. He responded, "All it does is give me peace of mind in my personal life. But whether it affects my programming, it doesn't. It just makes me think more clearly, more commercially than before."

There is no coherence in such a statement. I may be one sort of person at work, another sort of person when I am working out at the "Y," and yet another kind of person when I am at a party and a fourth kind of person when I am traveling. Berger says that, "Because of the plurality of social worlds in modern society, the structures of each particular world are experienced as relatively unstable and unreliable."[1] There is no stable identity for an individual because there are too many identities. We wear too many hats. It is as if we were looking at our lives through a cracked mirror.

Have you ever dropped a mirror you were trying to hang? In the old days, the glass would shatter into hundreds of pieces. But if you drop a newer mirror made of safety glass, ripples appear all through the mirror so that it is grossly distorted but not splintered. Berger says, in essence, that we are looking at ourselves in such mirrors, that distort everything they reflect.

Pablo Picasso was a man ahead of his time because he essentially painted cracked mirrors. In a Picasso painting, you might see a human form from three or four different angles at once. Picasso said the same thing Berger is saying, forty years earlier.

The cracked mirror means, for modern man, that "the institutional order undergoes a certain loss of reality. . . . the individual's experience of himself becomes more real to him than his experience of the objective social world."[2] In other words, more important than any way in which I see my role in the social order is the way I see myself, because the cracked mirror of the social order cannot give me accurate feedback. I must depend on some inner sense of who I am. Does that sound familiar? That is the way many of us live our lives. We will even say, "It is far more important what I think of myself than what you think of me." Agricultural man and industrial man would have said that there was coherence between the way you see me and the way I see myself. Now that coherence is not there. "Therefore," Berger says, "the individual seeks to find his 'foothold' in reality in himself rather than outside himself."[3]

THREE APPROACHES TO TRUTH

This is an important insight into our contemporary culture, and it helps to explain the radical subjectivism that characterizes our time. For most people in Western society today, truth is "what is true for me." Francis

Schaeffer's idea of absolutely true truth is anachronistic for the modern person. What is ultimately true is what a person finds to be true, and any claim to truth with authoritative backing, mediated from some spiritual or social order, is perceived as narrow and maybe even bigoted and dangerous.

That is why the discussion of abortion in America today has become such a yelling match. Those in support of abortion believe that they have every right to it. They are acting in good faith according to their own view of reality, believing that a woman has a right to determine what happens to an unborn baby within her. Don't make fun of their belief. They believe it, and they believe it precisely because they are modern.

For the modern person, truth is the degree to which he or she is "authentic"—authentic to himself or herself. "Authentic" is a good but abused word. I am "authentic" if I am faithful to my own opinions, regardless of how good or bad those opinions might be.

We could say there are three kinds of baseball umpires, and they each represent a different way of looking at truth.[4] The traditional umpire says, "There's balls and there's strikes, and I call 'em the way they are."

A modern umpire says, "There's balls and there's strikes, and I call 'em the way I see 'em." His view says that what is most important is not what *is* but what he sees. This view makes modern people reluctant to make moral judgments based on any external standard. The important result of truth being so completely subjective is that modern people are highly susceptible to the media's creation of an image. Instead of asking what is there or what is true, the media leads us to ask, What do we see?

This shift in the perception of truth is as old as Eden. When the woman *saw* that the tree was good for food, *saw* that it was a delight to the eyes, *saw* that it was desirable to make one wise, she ate it. She based her decision on her perception, rather than on what God had said, and chaos followed. The modern media reduces everything—values, beliefs, politics, events—to personal preferences, which emphasizes image and appearance rather than truth.

This modern view of truth and politics was clearly described a generation ago by Joe McGinniss in *The Selling of the President,* concerning the 1968 presidential campaign of Richard Nixon. He quotes from a memo by Ray Price, one of Nixon's speechwriters, which said, "We have to be very clear on this point: that the response is to the image, not to the man. . . . It's not what's there that counts; it's what's projected."[5] You will see precisely this philosophy working out in the political commentary of many if not most of the political candidates in any election year. Perception is everything. But that is a profound lie, is it not?

The motto of a Christian school in Dallas is *Esse Quam Videri* ("to be rather than to seem"). That is an excellent motto for a Christian school or for any of our lives. It is more important to *be* something than to *seem* to be something. The image is not as important as the reality. That is what Jesus points to when He says, "I speak the truth" (John 8:45). He is trying to say that truth is specific, knowable, hearable, and understandable, and that it is identified with words.

There is a third umpire, the postmodern one, who says, "There's balls and there's strikes, and they ain't nothing till I call 'em." For the postmodern person, reality and truth are what he wills them to be. Traditions, standards of excellence or beauty, and morality are all judged by the individual's own perceptions and desires. Postmoderns are radically relativistic.

WHAT *IS* TRUTH?

When Lincoln said that truth is everything, meaning that it is all-important, he was much closer to Jesus, who said, "The truth shall make you free" (John 8:32). Postmodern man is much closer to Pilate, who asked Jesus, "What is truth?" Pilate's sarcasm preshadows all of the subjectivism of our day. He was saying, "Look, Jesus, the only truth is truth that works, solves my problems, and gets the job done. Truth is what I invent."

When Jesus said, "You shall know the truth, and the truth shall make you free," He meant something very different by truth. He meant two things, the first being "correspondence." Truth corresponds to what is. When Jesus said, "You shall know the truth," He meant that there is a specific content to truth, something concrete that is rightly expressed in words and in statements.

A biblical view of truth believes in propositions. There are statements that are true, and there are statements that are false. The modern idea is that there is no such thing as a proposition; there are only ideas.

Your idea is as valuable as my idea, and my idea is as valuable as the next guy's idea. But Jesus said, "I speak the truth" (8:45); He will later acknowledge of His Father that "Thy word is truth" (17:17); and two dozen times in the Gospel of John He says, "Truly, truly," which is an Aramaic way of saying, "I tell you the truth, and what I am about to say to you is really true."

The words of Jesus accurately describe reality, whether He is talking about rocks or resurrections. In fact, the Gospel of John says that not only does Jesus speak the truth, He is Himself the accurate speech of God. "In the beginning was the Word" (1:1a). That was Jesus. "And the Word was with God and the Word was God" (1:1b). If we want to know what God's truth is on any subject, then we rightly listen, first and last, to what Jesus says. Jesus not only spoke the truth, He is the very embodiment of truth. Jesus speaks for God. Jesus speaks, and therefore there is truth—not merely true for you, not merely true if you make it so, not merely true if you wish it to be—but true.

TRUTH AT A GREAT PRICE

Nien Cheng was an aristocratic Chinese woman born in Peking (now Beijing) in about 1915. Her father was a vice minister in the Chinese navy. She met her husband in 1935 in London, when they were both studying at the London School of Economics. After the communists overthrew Chiang Kai-shek in 1949, Nien Cheng and her husband remained in Shanghai, where he worked as general manager of the Shell Oil Corporation for all of China. Shell was the only multinational oil company that stayed in China after Mao Tse-tung's triumph over Chiang Kai-shek. When her husband died in 1957, Shell admired Mrs. Cheng so much that it hired her as a consultant, and she worked with Shell until the company left China in 1966, the year that Mao started the great proletarian Cultural Revolution. In August 1966, Red Guards ransacked Mrs. Cheng's house. A month later she was arrested and then spent seven years in solitary confinement in a detention house in Shanghai, a miserable place. Every week or so they would take Mrs. Cheng to an interrogation room and say, "Mrs. Cheng, you may walk out of this prison today if you will say these words: 'My husband was an enemy of the Chinese people.'" She refused to say those words for seven years.

A little white lie would have freed her, but she believed in truth, a truth that corresponds to reality and cannot be violated. It was not only a matter of integrity for her and her family; it was a matter of what is true.

In her marvelous book, *Life and Death in Shanghai*, Nien Cheng talks about making friends with a spider in her cell. For two or three years this spider was her friend, the only friend she had. She used to talk with the spider. It was real, with a definable existence, like truth has. The spider became very important to her because it was a reminder that there is such a thing as truth, that existence really matters, that words really matter.

Truth matters. Take the issue of abortion on demand as a means of birth control. It is right to say that this kind of abortion is wrong—not wrong for you, not wrong for me, not wrong for her: it is wrong. Jesus spoke words, and His words are truth. His words in the Word are truth. So when this Word speaks truth about abortion or any other subject, we must not listen to it through the grid of our own assumptions, certainly not with the postmodern mentality that says, "Truth is what I make it." We must listen to the words themselves.

The opposite of truth, biblically speaking, is not just factual error; it is falsehood. Jesus calls the devil the father of lies because he leads people away from life-giving truth, away from *the* life-giving truth, the One who said, "I am the way, and the truth, and the life." The Man who speaks the truth is inseparable from the words He speaks.

THE TRUTH THAT MAKES YOU ODD

Remember Psalm 86:11: "Teach me your way, O LORD; I will walk in your truth; give me an undivided heart, that I may fear your name" (NIV). Modern man has a divided heart, a shattered heart, like a shattered mirror. In the face of a wicked world that denies that truth exists in any form, we must stand up at the risk of severe consequences and say, "There is truth. And there He is. He is my Savior and my Lord." Truth is a person, a person who accurately diagnoses who I am, a magnificent person who can look at the sin of abortion and condemn it with His words, but who will in the very same breath take the woman who has had an abortion into His forgiving arms, and by the truth heal the shattered mirror of her soul.

When students at colleges and universities see those words, "You shall know the truth, and the truth shall make you free," on a building, they probably do not think about truth the way Jesus did, even if they are Christians, because they have been so affected by the modern and postmodern views of truth. So in the face of modern man for whom the claim to truth is quaint, or in the face of the postmodern man for whom the claim to truth is dangerous, to say that there is an objective truth actually makes you a very unusual person.

Flannery O'Connor put it this way: "You shall know the truth, and the truth shall make you odd."[6] That is quite true today. If you believe that Scripture speaks to you true words, and that those true words define your life, and that Scripture's truth is identified with a person, and that this person is the One who is the actual embodiment of truth, you will be increasingly odd.

You will be odd for two reasons: 1) you are saying that truth corresponds to what is, and; 2) you are saying truth is trustworthy, and you are identifying yourself with a trustworthy person.

One of the most amazing things about modern philosophy is that it totally doubts the ability of words to convey truth. Modern philosophy tells us words are incapable vehicles for communicating truth. That view has permeated every university in this country, so when Jesus says, "I speak the truth" (8:45) and "Thy word is truth" (17:17), He is saying something very odd indeed.

Truth Is a Person

Truth makes you odd because it is not just a proposition to be believed but a person to be trusted. It is to be believed because of the truthfulness of the One who speaks it. When you think about that, it is very logical. Do you trust someone? If so, you generally believe that what he or she says is true. Truth has to do with trustworthiness and reliability. The opposite of truth is not just falsehood but untrustworthiness. Truth is worthy of personal commitment. The more truthful you know a person to be, the more reliable his or her character, the more you are inclined to trust that person. In John 8:26, Jesus says, "He who sent Me is true," but the NIV translates that more accurately as "He who sent me is reliable." Truth and reliability go together.

The reliability of Jesus has much to do with the Incarnation. Truth did not remain abstract. When God wanted to communicate truth, He communicated proposition through a person. Modern theology often attempts to separate the proposition from the person, as if to say, "Oh, I can love Jesus, but I don't need to believe every word that He said."

Such thinking makes little sense even in our human relationships. If you trust a person, you trust what he or she says. When the Word became flesh, God spoke Himself into humanity and lived among us. He showed us the truth in the marketplaces of our lives, in the town squares, at the bedsides of sick children, in the nursing homes with aged parents. So when Jesus said, "If you abide in My word, . . . you shall know the truth, and the truth shall make you free" (8:31-32), we learn that the teaching we hold to is not bare fact, it is not mere proposition, not only correspondence, not only objective reality, though it is all those things. It is more. It is not that if we attain to a high level of knowledge we will somehow lift ourselves up out of the worldly and the mundane, and we will find truth.

That thinking is at the cornerstone of every worldview and philosophy except Christianity. In every other worldview or philosophy, the object is to raise oneself up to attain a higher knowledge, an enlightenment that elevates one above the real. The Christian way of understanding the world is precisely the opposite. Truth, Himself, came down. Truth, Himself, utterly identified with us in our flesh. Our goal therefore is not to become something we are not. Our goal is to become who we are, fully human. For Jesus was fully human. In fact, Jesus was the one, true, perfect, infleshment of truth as a human being. Truth came down in the Incarnation.

So when Jesus says, "If you abide in My word, . . . you shall know the truth, and the truth shall make you free," you hold to Jesus Himself, and you find His teaching utterly reliable and worthy of your trust.

Truth therefore is relational. There are a lot of people who love the truth and the Bible who get a little nervous when a Christian starts talking like that, because many people with less than good motives have taken that line of thinking and divorced truth from proposition. We must never separate the truth of Jesus from the truth of His Word. We hold them together; and, therefore, I don't have any qualms about saying that truth is a person and truth is relational.

To prove this, Jesus Himself says, quite offensively to some, "Your reliability is dependent on who you are related to, on who your father is" (see 8:43-47). This whole section in John 8 actually has to do with who Jesus' Father is, who His listeners' father is, and, ultimately, who our father is. Have you ever heard someone say, "Oh, you can trust him—I knew his daddy"? They are saying, "Because I knew his father and the kind of man his father was, you can trust this fellow."

"IF YOU ARE TRUE, THEN WHO IS YOUR FATHER?"

The Pharisees said that Jesus' reliability was questionable because it wasn't clear to them who His father was. They had also accused Him in John 8:13 of bearing testimony to Himself: "The Pharisees therefore said to Him, 'You are bearing witness of Yourself; Your witness is not true.'" They go on to explain, as every good Jew would know, that there needed to be two witnesses to verify the reliability of anyone. So Jesus says in verses 17 and 18, "Even in your law it has been written, that the testimony of two men is true. I am He who bears witness of Myself, and the Father who sent Me bears witness of Me." There it is. Jesus is claiming that His reliability, His truthfulness is dependent upon who He is related to, and who He is related to is the Father in heaven.

The answer to the question posed to Jesus in 8:25, "Who are You?" is related to the answer to the question He is asked in 8:19, "Where is Your Father?" We cannot separate those questions. Is Jesus reliable? It depends on who His father is. In this section in John, we read of three possible "fathers" of Jesus, and the true identity of His father is absolutely critical to the reliability of Jesus. The entire structure that we call the Christian faith and the very essence of our lives are completely dependent on who Jesus says His father is. Let's look at the options.

Is Abraham the Father of Jesus?

Responding to Jesus, His Jewish listeners say, "We are Abraham's off-spring, and have never yet been enslaved to anyone; how is it that You say, 'You shall become free'?" (John 8:33). It was a deeply held Jewish conviction that if you were a child of Israel, a son or daughter of

Abraham, you were by definition free. No person or institution could ever enslave you.

The problem is one of presumption. They were saying, "If Abraham is our father, then we are okay." But Jesus says that being a son of Abraham or being Jewish does not ensure freedom. Freedom is not ultimately or even primarily a matter of national identity. We rightly cherish our political freedom in this country, but political freedom is not the ultimate freedom. Jesus is saying a very simple thing here: "If you think you are free because you are an American, or culturally literate, or educated, or a modern person, you are seriously misjudging what freedom is."

Is the Devil the Father of Jesus?

We have said that, for the postmodern, truth does not exist. But if truth does not exist, then what? If there is no ultimate truth, then what about right and wrong? It doesn't exist. Then what about the Bible's concept of sin? It doesn't exist. To a postmodern, sin is at best a transgression of some vague impulse to goodness that he or she feels. The ultimate sin is to be unauthentic to oneself, so there can be no external standard by which right, wrong, or sin itself is evaluated. This is the cornerstone of postmodern thought and, according to Jesus here in John 8, it comes from the father of lies. Believing such lies about oneself makes one a child of the father of lies. In verses 43 and 44, Jesus defines the father of lies as a murderer. By his lie he led Eve to her death. This is not "the devil made me do it" talk but a question of one's truest identity and ultimate family loyalty. The devil is the ultimate postmodern person. " . . . there is no truth in him," Jesus says (v. 44).

God the Father

The two options for fatherhood that we have seen so far aren't very good, are they? If Abraham is one's father, then truth is narrowly provincial, narrowly cultural, narrowly nationalistic. If the devil is one's father, truth does not exist. Abraham and the devil are both unreliable fathers. Both make one a slave rather than a son. There is only one Father who frees us from slavery and makes us His sons and daughters. If you are a slave, there is no permanent place in the family for you. Perhaps you have heard someone call a lifelong housekeeper "a part of our family." It is a sweet thing to say, but it is not really so. John 8:35 says, "And the slave does not remain in the house forever; the son does remain forever." Freedom is having a place in the family. Freedom is being free from all that is contrary to who God is.

TRUTH DEFINED AT THE CROSS

So how does God become our Father? How does the Son set us free from slavery to sin? In John 8:28 Jesus says, "When you lift up the Son of Man, then you will know that I am He." That is a reference to the Cross, of course. When the Son of Man is lifted up on the cross, the key crossroad of our lives has been reached. There we see how God becomes our Father as His holy anger at sin is diverted to Jesus. The Cross is the critical defining point of Jesus' reliability and truthfulness to do what He said He would do. Only by the Cross could He, would He, did He free us from our sin. The Cross is critical as the defining point of our identity. Are we slaves to sin or sons and daughters of God? The Cross is the oddest thing of all. On it Jesus became a slave to sin's punishment and to death in order that those who trust in Him would no longer be slaves to sin and death.

The only truth that frees is the Truth that was willing to go under the scalpel of the Cross, willing to bear the curse and the punishment for all that sin deserves. The critical issue of the Cross is whether or not you believe in it. Because whether or not you believe in it is determinative of whether you are a slave or a son or daughter. There is no freedom if your father is Abraham. There is no freedom if your father is the devil. There is freedom only if God is your Father. And the only way God will be your Father is if Jesus is your Savior.

And when you believe that, you will be odd. Flannery O'Connor was right. The truth will make you odd in at least ten ways, which are actually a summary of this whole passage. Let's call them the Ten Commandments of Oddness.

THE TEN COMMANDMENTS OF ODDNESS

1. You will not seek truth in your national, ethnic, or cultural identity. You won't rely on your school, or team, or profession, or wealth. You will see that they have failed to define you.

2. You will prize objective truth. You will resist the spirit of the age that says either that truth is what you perceive it to be or that there is no truth at all.

3. You will listen to the words of Jesus, who speaks the truth when He says, "I have many things to speak and to judge concerning you" (John 8:26). You will want to know what these things are.

4. You will prize Jesus above any treasure. He said, "If God were your Father, you would love Me" (8:42). One of the signs that you are odd is that you love Jesus more than anything else and that you really don't care who knows it.

A number of years ago a young man whom my friend and advisor Edmund Clowney was mentoring just walked away from it all one day—from his wife, his church, his friends, his job, and the Lord Himself. Ed went after him, pursuing him in love again and again, to no avail. Once Ed said whimsically and almost to himself, "You know, when it is all said and done, I can't believe he walked away from Jesus." Jesus is a person. If you love that person, it is a sign that God is your Father.

5. The truth will make you odd in that you will be more concerned about freedom from sin than about having personal freedom or having political freedom or having more stuff.

On a trip to China in 1999, the group I was traveling with met with some underground pastors. When we asked how we could pray for them, they answered, "Please don't pray that the persecution stops, because persecution has made us know who we really are in China as Christians." Don't prize political freedom. It won't last forever. Times change. Cultures change. There are seismic political shifts. Prize, instead, the One who makes you truly and eternally free.

6. You will never be content to see others ruled by the lies of sin. You will hunger and thirst for others' righteousness as well as for your own. Caring about the family's holiness is a wonderful sign that God is your Father. You will long for your Father's house to be full of maturing sons and daughters.

7. The truth will make you odd as you become an instrument of grace and truth in others' lives, even at great cost. Jesus paid a great price to bring grace and truth to us. He said very offensive things, though not out of malice, vindictiveness, or religious superiority; He did it out of love, because He wanted the scalpel of truth to dig down deep into the

cancer and to cut it all out. He knew that grace and truth are better for people than their own ideas of happiness.

8. You will be growing in holiness and righteousness. A slave of sin "does not remain in the [Father's] house forever" (8:35). Hear those words, and it is okay to tremble a little. If you are a slave to unremitting sin, you may in fact not be a son, despite the profession of your mouth. Believers are not perfect, but, progressively, they look more and more like Christ. Holding on to sin with tenacity proves that one is a slave, not a son.

9. You will be willing, even happy, to be lifted up with the Son of Man to misunderstanding, to ridicule, even to abuse, because it is better to be identified with the Son than with the pleasures of this world (see Heb. 11:24-26).

10. Finally, you will be free. Freedom from sin and freedom to Christ is unusual and very odd. But in the end you will be odd, and you will not care.

May God grant us the grace to hear and receive that truth who is a person who lived, died for us, and rose again so that truth would be triumphant, so that we would lean against everything in our world that denies the reality that words have meaning, that truth is truth, that Jesus Christ is who He said He was and is. That means that whatever our sin, whatever our background, whatever our past, if we call upon Him, His Word is true; and His Word says that He saves those who call upon His name (Acts 2:21).

20

BLINDING LIGHT

And as He passed by, He saw a man blind from birth. And His disciples asked Him, saying, "Rabbi, who sinned, this man or his parents, that he should be born blind?" Jesus answered, "It was neither that this man sinned, nor his parents; but it was in order that the works of God might be displayed in him. We must work the works of Him who sent Me, as long as it is day; night is coming, when no man can work. While I am in the world, I am the light of the world." When He had said this, He spat on the ground, and made clay of the spittle, and applied the clay to his eyes, and said to him, "Go, wash in the pool of Siloam" (which is translated, Sent). And so he went away and washed, and came back seeing. The neighbors therefore, and those who previously saw him as a beggar, were saying, "Is not this the one who used to sit and beg?" Others were saying, "This is he," still others were saying, "No, but he is like him." He kept saying, "I am the one." Therefore they were saying to him, "How then were your eyes opened?" He answered, "The man who is called Jesus made clay, and anointed my eyes, and said to me, 'Go to Siloam, and wash'; so I went away and washed, and I received sight." And they said to him, "Where is He?" He said, "I do not know."

They brought to the Pharisees him who was formerly blind. Now it was a Sabbath on the day when Jesus made the clay, and opened his eyes. Again, therefore, the Pharisees also were asking him how he received his sight. And he said to them, "He applied clay to my eyes, and I washed, and I see." Therefore some of the Pharisees were saying, "This man is not from God, because He does not keep the Sabbath." But others were saying, "How can a man who is a sinner perform such signs?" And there was a division among them. They said therefore to the blind man again, "What do you say about Him, since He opened your eyes?" And he said, "He is a prophet." The Jews therefore did not believe it of him, that he had been blind, and had received sight, until they called the parents of the very one who had received his sight, and questioned them, saying, "Is this your son, who you say was born blind? Then how does he now see?" His parents answered them and said, "We know that this is our son, and that he was born blind; but how he now sees, we do not know; or who opened his eyes, we do not know. Ask him; he is of age, he shall speak for himself." His parents said this because they were afraid of the Jews; for the Jews had already agreed, that if anyone should confess Him to be Christ, he should be put out of the synagogue. For this reason his parents said, "He is of age; ask him."

So a second time they called the man who had been blind, and said to him, "Give glory to God; we know that this man is a sinner." He therefore answered, "Whether He is a sinner, I do not know; one thing I do know, that, whereas I was blind, now I see." They said therefore to him, "What did He do to you? How did He open your eyes?" He answered them, "I told you already, and you did not listen; why do you want to hear it again? You do not want to become His disciples too, do you?" And they reviled him, and said, "You are His disciple, but we are disciples of Moses. We know that God has spoken to Moses; but as for this man, we do not know where He is from." The man answered and said to them, "Well, here is an amazing thing, that you do not know where He is from, and yet He opened my eyes. We know that God does not hear sinners; but if anyone is God-fearing, and does His will, He hears him. Since the beginning of time it has never been heard that anyone opened the eyes of a person born blind. If this man were not from God, He could do nothing." They answered and said to him, "You were born entirely in sins, and are you teaching us?" And they put him out.

Jesus heard that they had put him out; and finding him, He said, "Do you believe in the Son of Man?" He answered and said, "And who is He, Lord, that I may believe in Him?" Jesus said to him, "You have both seen Him, and He is the one who is talking with you." And he said, "Lord, I believe." And he worshiped Him. And Jesus said, "For judgment I came into this world, that those who do not see may see; and that those who see may become blind." Those of the Pharisees who were with Him heard these things, and said to Him, "We are not blind too, are we?" Jesus said to them, "If you were blind, you would have no sin; but since you say, 'We see,' your sin remains" (John 9:1-41).

WHEN YOU ARE SICK, how do you handle it? I handle it badly—just ask my wife. When I am sick, I immediately think I have every right to boss her around, tell her exactly what I need, and be perturbed when I don't get it exactly when I want it. When I ask for a Diet Pepsi, I don't want ginger ale, and when I say I want it, I want it *now*.

Does this passage on the healing of the blind man reflect in any way your thinking about how you handle sickness? Do you relate your illness to some specific sin in your life, or do you think the idea that your sickness could be related to your sin is preposterous? For some believers with overly scrupulous consciences, every time they are sick they immediately begin to think of a particular sin they committed and think, *God has found me out*. Others have never had any thought about the relation of their sickness to their sin. As is often the case, both extremes are wrong.

THE MEANING OF HIS BLINDNESS

The passage explicitly asks, Was the man's blindness caused by his own sin or by the sin of his parents or of someone else close to him? (John

9:2). The disciples assume, like most good Jews of their day, that the sin and the sickness are directly related. They think that the man's blindness therefore must be the direct result of his sin or his parents' sin.

It is true that all sickness is related to sin in the sense that all sickness is the working out of the catastrophe of the Fall. If mankind had never disobeyed God, there would be no sickness, no death, no blindness. However, it is quite another thing to say that each and every individual sickness is to be tightly connected to this or that very specific sin.

The issue that Jesus raises is not what sin caused this man's blindness, but what we do about it. During an elder retreat at our church, David Powlison of the Christian Counseling and Education Foundation talked about the relationship between sin and sickness and our reactions to being sick. He said that some men ignore illness. Some macho men absolutely deny they are sick—total cognitive dissonance. Some get angry and grumble against the providence of God, saying, "Why has God done this to me? I don't have time for this sickness. I've got too much to do!" They are really saying that God is not sovereign, and that His power is not perfected in their weakness.

The way we react to sickness can reveal certain dispositions of our heart that are ultimately sinful. Some of us get very discouraged, and while a certain discouragement when we are very ill is understandable, a pattern of deep discouragement is really a pattern of non-faith. It is not seeing our sickness in the light of God's overall purposes in our lives. If God is sovereign, is He not sovereign in our specific illnesses? What does He have for us in it? What are we supposed to learn? The Lord wants us to ask those kinds of questions.

Some are preoccupied with their sicknesses and their ailments. You know the type. A father told a story about his six-year-old daughter. They were sitting in a booth in a restaurant, and in the next booth were four people who were going on and on about every single sickness and pain they had ever had, every doctor they had seen, every joint that was stiff, and every medicine they took. The father whispered to his little daughter, "What do you think they are really saying by their conversation?" This very perceptive question from a father to a six-year-old was answered even more perceptively by the little girl when she said, "I think they are afraid of dying."

Scratch beneath the surface of such a conversation and you find hearts of unbelief. Christians, of all people, should be people for whom death is, in the end, not something we profoundly fear—even though we do not seek it.

Some respond to sickness with escapism. "Oh boy, I'm sick. I don't have to go to school today." Some kids know all about that. "Mom, I've got a little scratchy throat this morning. It's going to be a bad sore throat by ten o'clock, Mom. I'd better not go to school."

This passage tells us that sickness becomes an opportunity for sin, but it really should be an opportunity for reflection. How I thank God for so many in my congregation with whom I have walked through a time of illness and have seen how the Lord has worked to reveal the motives of their hearts, to make them more vulnerable, to make them more of the person that the Lord wants them to be.

Inner Blindness

Jesus leads the blind man, as well as a number of other people in the account, through this kind of reflection. He wants us to reflect on the meaning of blindness. He wants us to see that the man's outward physical blindness is actually a parable for the inward blindness of his soul. The meaning of his blindness is that he cannot see his true condition or need.

Note, I said *cannot* see. Do you remember your high school grammar? Have you ever had a conversation at the table with a child like this:

She asks, "Can I have the butter?"

You reply, "You *may* have the butter."

Can has to do with ability; *may* has to do with permission. This man *cannot* see. He is absolutely incapable of seeing his true condition.

One of the most interesting and tough goals in pastoral work is trying to help people see the reality of our blindness as humans. The Word of God in its entirety has strong and pungent things to say about the fact that we cannot see ourselves accurately, that we are "blind at noonday" to the true condition of our inward lives, and that we cannot see in ourselves what so often is pitifully obvious to those around us. That is one of the reasons that we need good fellowship in this Christian walk. It is why we need people who will hold up to us an accurate mirror, why we need trusted people to whom we can open our hearts, and who will give us the biblical feedback we need.

The issue in this passage is not the remedy for physical blindness as much as it is the remedy for spiritual blindness. Jesus says that the man's blindness happened "in order that the works of God might be displayed in him" (John 9:3). What is the work of God? Is the work of God simply to cause this blind man to see physically? It is, but certainly by the end of this chapter there is something far deeper going on than just physical vision. Only the work of God can make the spiritually blind man see.

The same message was given to Nicodemus: "Unless one is born again, he cannot see the kingdom of God" (3:3). One of the most difficult things for us proud human beings to reckon with is the reality of our spiritual blindness, that we cannot see that which we have no right to miss. The Lord says we have no right to miss the accurate description of our hearts' condition before Him. But we miss it until the Lord Himself opens our eyes and gives us the ability to see ourselves.

There is an urgency to it. "Night is coming," Jesus says (9:4), perhaps with a double meaning. The night of the Cross will come to Jesus when He will be taken away. But for us there will come a night when the days of opportunity for proclaiming the gospel are over, and some will be plunged into the eternal night of judgment.

When you step from a dark house into a bright, beautiful, sunlit day, your eyes react. Your pupils contract, your eyes may hurt, you squint and reach for your sunglasses or shade your eyes. We have parallel reactions to the light of Christ as it shines into the eyes of our hearts. There is a real irony in John 1, where the subject is introduced: "There was the true light which, coming into the world, enlightens every man. He was in the world, and the world was made through Him, and the world did not know Him" (John 1:9-10). The Light has come into the world and there is a reaction to that Light. In the story of the blind man in John 9, there are four clear reactions to the light of Christ.

FOUR RESPONSES TO THE LIGHT

The *neighbors* of this man who have known him all his life care most about how the miracle took place. They are interested in the mechanics of what happened. They want to know about the spittle and the kneading of the dirt. They are missing the real truth—not *how* it happened; but *that* it happened at all.

The *Pharisees,* too, are distracted, but they are distracted with *when* it happened. When did it happen? On the Sabbath. They care most about their Sabbath rules. The grid through which they see this miracle is the grid of their ideas about when such a miracle was permissible. Healing on the Sabbath was forbidden except when a life was in danger. Work such as that involved in Christ's kneading of the mud and spittle was also prohibited on the Sabbath. The Pharisees conclude that Jesus could not be from God because He does not follow their oral tradition of law.

One commentator says, "There were those so firmly in the grip of darkness that they saw only a technical breach of their law, and they could not discern a spectacular victory of light over darkness."[1] Have you ever seen anything like that? What is your reaction when someone walks into your church's worship service on a Sunday morning who doesn't look or dress in an acceptable way? Do you find rising in your heart the thought, *What is he doing here?* Be careful, because that is the rising of your oral tradition about who is acceptable and who is not, and about *how* the miracle of grace is to reach that person or not reach that person.

The man's *parents* have another reaction. Called on by the Pharisees, they were ready to testify that, 1) the man was their son, and, 2) he had been born blind. So far, so good. But on the question of *who* opened his eyes, they are conflicted. They are afraid of the Jewish leaders because they already know that whoever says that Jesus is the Christ will be put out of the synagogue. They are also fearful of what people might think of them if they go out on a limb for Christ.

Is that sometimes true of you? Do you find yourself shrinking back from saying things that may need to be said directly and boldly about the Lord Jesus when it just doesn't seem to be the right social setting to do it? If the Pharisees are straightforwardly opposed to the truth, the parents know the truth but are corralled into silence by social pressure. They dodge the bullet by saying, "He is of age," which means he is over thirteen and, therefore, a man who by Jewish custom can answer for himself.

The fourth kind of person in this story is the *blind man* himself. He has a colorful personality and a mind of his own. He shows more common sense and insight than anyone else in the account. With a twist of sarcasm and humor, the man responds to the second round of questioning of the authorities by saying, "Well, here is an amazing thing, that you do not know where He is from, and yet He opened my eyes" (John 9:30). He is saying that the Pharisees' unbelief in the face of his new sight is actually a greater marvel than the fact that he was healed.

His logic is pretty good for a man who had been blind and begging on the street all of his life. Look at the flow of his reasoning: "Since the beginning of time it has never been heard that anyone opened the eyes of a person born blind. If this man were not from God, He could do nothing" (vv. 32-33). He is saying, in essence, "I am the evidence that He did it. How can you deny that He is who He says He is? I am the living proof."

What the man's parents fear will happen to *them* actually happens to *him*. He is put out of the synagogue, excommunicated. It is a precise example of John 1:11: "He came to His own, and those who were His own did not receive Him." But Jesus knows who His own are, and He seeks them out. Look at 9:35: "Jesus heard that they had put him out; and finding him, He said, 'Do you believe in the Son of Man?'"

Don't glide over some seemingly insignificant words in the middle of that statement: "And finding him." Imagine this: the eternal Son of God, the One who had been in the bosom of the Father from before the dawn of time, this One who owned everything, who has under His sovereign dominion and control everything in heaven and earth—this God and Savior runs around Jerusalem looking for a formerly blind beggar!

WHICH RESPONSE TO THE LIGHT IS OURS?

For his part, the beggar then does two things. He believes in Jesus and worships Him. John is quite deliberately asking *us* the question, "With whom do *you* identify?" Are we like the neighbors, who are distracted from the real issue by the mechanics of the miracle? Are we like the Pharisees, whose hearts are closed in order to justify their stubborn unbelief? Are we like the parents, who are embarrassed and fearful of taking the side of Christ publicly? Or are we like the blind man, upon whom the light dawns and who believes and worships?

Three out of the four possible responses are evasive tactics. The neighbors evade the work of the Lord by focusing on something else.

The Pharisees evade the work of the Lord by focusing on their rules. The parents evade the work of the Lord by being socially intimidated. The Lord is asking if we are willing to squarely face the reality of our true inner condition. Are you prepared to cry out to the Lord and say, "O Lord, I need Your help even to face the truth about myself; O Lord, I am a blind beggar when I stand before You; and O Lord, I need You by the light of Your Word and Your Spirit to search out my heart and reveal all the ways in which I have been pretentious and proud before You, and all the ways in which I hold back this or that corner of my heart and keep it from You"?

The real issue in this passage is how easily we miss what is really going on in our hearts and lives. Whether it is an illness, a difficult marriage, a rebellious child, a job that is not working out, a financial situation that is not going well—whatever it is, do you see that a sovereign Lord who comes to our lives uses all of these circumstances to lift out of our hearts the things that need to be held up to His light?

THE SIGHT OF THE BLIND AND THE BLINDNESS OF THE SIGHTED

The Lord Himself is about the business of bringing sight to the blind and blindness to the sighted.[2] His highest agenda is to ask us to face the reality of where we have allowed sin to overpower our hearts, the darkness of all that we have clung to for hope and life and meaning in this world, and where we need the light of the Savior to free us from the chains of sin.

Jesus, the One in whom the man believes and the One he worships, is described in John 9:35 as the Son of Man. That title for Jesus is a bit unusual in John's Gospel. He uses it only about half as much as the other Gospel writers. Most of the time John calls Jesus the Son of God (or simply "the Son," with the "of God" implied), but here He is the Son of Man. That name almost invariably points to a certain characteristic of our Lord, that of His being our Judge.

Look at verse 39: "And Jesus said, 'For judgment I came into this world, that those who do not see may see; and that those who see may become blind.'" It might seem that what Jesus says here contradicts something He said earlier. For earlier He said that He did not come to judge the world but to save the world (3:17), and He will say it again in John 12. But think of it this way: "to save" inevitably means "to judge." Why? Because if some are saved from judgment, others are by definition exposed to that judgment.

In a sense it isn't Jesus who judges at all; it is the light that judges. This is what Jesus says back in John 3:19-20: "And this is the judgment, that the light is come into the world, and men loved the darkness rather than the light; for their deeds were evil. For everyone who does evil hates the light, and does not come to the light, lest his deeds should be exposed."

You say, "I am a Christian. I have seen the truth about myself." Yes, you have, but how much? Some of us as Christians are like people with eyes half open. We want the light but we want only the part we can "handle." We are afraid to open our eyes and see the light of Christ blaring down upon the reality of all that is in our hearts.

Jesus says He came into the world so that those who do not see may see, and those who see may become blind. When He refers to "those who see," He means "those who think they can see." Like the Pharisees in this passage, if we think we can see ourselves accurately on our own, knowing who we are with our few admitted faults and problems, then we do not see ourselves at all. We need to beg the Lord to do what only He can do: open our eyes to see ourselves the way He sees us. This is a lifelong process. It is not something that just happens to us once, at our conversion.

The light of Christ is not a flattering light. As I have noted elsewhere, it is not like the light in airplane lavatories, soft and smooth, hiding our spots and wrinkles. No, it is a harsh light, revealing what is truly in our hearts. We must look in the mirror and say, "I am blind. Lord, give me light to see myself so that I can offer myself to You." The same light that reveals who we are will purge away our sin, because the Light of life is the lover of our sinful souls. The gospel gives light that permits me to see my real condition.

The Christian life is all about light to see more light, repenting and believing, trusting the Light of life who is the lover of our souls. When we reveal openly to Him what is really in our hearts, He will not cast us out. He already knows what is there, and yet He has already loved us.

21

THE TRUE AND GOOD SHEPHERD

"Truly, truly, I say to you, he who does not enter by the door into the fold of the sheep, but climbs up some other way, he is a thief and a robber. But he who enters by the door is a shepherd of the sheep. To him the doorkeeper opens, and the sheep hear his voice, and he calls his own sheep by name, and leads them out. When he puts forth all his own, he goes before them, and the sheep follow him because they know his voice. And a stranger they simply will not follow, but will flee from him, because they do not know the voice of strangers." This figure of speech Jesus spoke to them, but they did not understand what those things were which He had been saying to them.

Jesus therefore said to them again, "Truly, truly, I say to you, I am the door of the sheep. All who came before Me are thieves and robbers, but the sheep did not hear them. I am the door; if anyone enters through Me, he shall be saved, and shall go in and out, and find pasture. The thief comes only to steal, and kill, and destroy; I came that they might have life, and might have it abundantly. I am the good shepherd; the good shepherd lays down His life for the sheep. He who is a hireling, and not a shepherd, who is not the owner of the sheep, beholds the wolf coming, and leaves the sheep, and flees, and the wolf snatches them, and scatters them. He flees because he is a hireling, and is not concerned about the sheep. I am the good shepherd; and I know My own, and My own know Me, even as the Father knows Me and I know the Father; and I lay down My life for the sheep. And I have other sheep, which are not of this fold; I must bring them also, and they shall hear My voice; and they shall become one flock with one shepherd. For this reason the Father loves Me, because I lay down My life that I may take it again. No one has taken it away from Me, but I lay it down on My own initiative. I have authority to lay it down, and I have authority to take it up again. This commandment I received from My Father" (John 10:1-18).

I KNOW VERY LITTLE ABOUT sheep and next to nothing about sheep farming, so I decided to "get educated" before studying this passage. I drove north toward Oklahoma, and was not going to stop until I found some sheep. Just north of McKinney, Texas, I finally found some sheep, pulled to the side of the road, and watched them for a while. They didn't care much that I was there. They weren't very polite at all. One thing I learned by way of observation is that sheep are not dogs.

Jesus did not say to us, "You are My doggies." Perhaps the reason is that dogs are generally affectionate. You give them affection, they respond in affection. And generally, you can train a dog, getting some response from discipline.

One evening we had a few people over to our house. Barbara prepared a large plate with cheese and crackers and put it on the dining room table. When she turned her back, Clyde, our golden retriever, decided the cheese was his. He jumped up on the table, scratching the table mercilessly, and ate about three-fourths of the cheese. The minute we walked in the dining room and looked at the cheese plate and looked at him, he knew he was guilty. He was in doggie exile for the rest of the evening. Sheep, however, just don't seem to connect with affection or guilt in the same way. There is one thing, though, that sheep can do. They can recognize a familiar voice.

There is a story about a grandfather who is attending a family reunion. Everyone is gathered, the television is on, and there is a lot of commotion. He is hard of hearing and doesn't hear anyone, even his grandchildren. Amid all the hubbub, however, there is one voice he hears. It is his wife. When she speaks to him, he hears it because his ear has been trained by fifty years of marriage.

Some of us need to have our ears trained to hear the Shepherd's voice, and some of us who are under-shepherds of the flock—pastors, elders, church leaders—need to learn how to speak the Shepherd's words so that people can hear His voice.

In some church circles today, shepherding is out and ranching is in. Shepherds are called upon to be ranchers, that is, to spend their time organizing the church rather than shepherding or pastoring the sheep. So there are quite a few cowboys, you might say, in the church these days.

Let's note in this passage two things that Jesus teaches us about Himself, and, by implication, about His under-shepherds and the sheep of His flock as well. First, Jesus is the true Shepherd because He comes to His own sheep. Second, He is the Good Shepherd because He knows His own sheep.

The True Shepherd Comes to His Own

The true Shepherd comes to His own as the rightful owner of the sheep. Back in the first century, sheep would live in a large pen in the village. Probably several families in that village would keep their sheep together in the same enclosure, with one shepherd to guard the sheep. There would be only one door by which the sheep could go in or out, allowing no one who was unauthorized to enter. If someone wasn't an owner of the sheep, they would have to go over the fence and break in.

Jesus says that He is the true Shepherd, the owner of the sheep. And "true" here means "legitimate, rightful." He is the rightful Shepherd, the authorized Shepherd who enters by the door. He comes in the right way.

How does Jesus as the true Shepherd enter? He comes according to the plan and purpose of the Father. He is legitimate because He comes in the Father's plan, obeying His Father. His Father, who owns the sheep, authorizes Jesus to be the true Shepherd. Don't miss that undercurrent in this whole passage: the authorization by the Father of Jesus as the one, true Shepherd who comes in the plan and purpose of the Father and legitimately claims His right to be the true Shepherd. The sheep belong to Jesus because the Father has given them to Him. "My Father, who has given them to Me, is greater than all; and no one is able to snatch them out of the Father's hand" (John 10:29). Jesus comes announced by the Scriptures. It is in the plan of the Father, announced in the Old Testament, that there would be a true Shepherd, and Jesus understands Himself rightfully to be that true One sent by God.

There are many passages in Isaiah and Ezekiel that portray the coming of this great, true Shepherd. Isaiah 40:11 says, "Like a shepherd He will tend His flock, in His arm He will gather the lambs, and carry them in His bosom; He will gently lead the nursing ewes."

Not only does Jesus enter by the right door as the rightful owner of the sheep, but He is also, as the true Shepherd, the Door to the sheepfold: "I am the door; if anyone enters through Me, he shall be saved, and shall go in and out, and find pasture" (John 10:9). Jesus is the *only* One who provides the legitimate entry into the sheepfold. Doesn't that sound like what Jesus says later in the Gospel of John? "I am the way, and the truth, and the life; no one comes to the Father, but through me" (14:6).

Others enter in over the fence, however. They are identified in this passage by two words which sound like they have similar meanings in our English usage: *thief* and *robber.* Actually, the word *robber* means something more akin to "terrorist." These thieves and robbers are victimizing the sheep and frightening them. Instead of dealing tenderly with them as the good and true Shepherd would, they frighten the sheep, undermining their security.

Who are these terrorist shepherds? In the context of this section of the Gospel of John, there is really only one answer: the Pharisees. The religious leaders of Jesus' day do not properly care for the flock of God, but instead use and misuse the flock for their own purposes. If the true Shepherd is announced by the Scriptures, then the false shepherds are denounced by the Scriptures. In sections of the Old Testament such as Ezekiel 34, the Lord condemns the false shepherds of Israel for failing to look after the flock. The false shepherds "clothe [themselves] with the wool and slaughter the choice animals" (Ezek. 34:3, NIV). They "have not strengthened the weak or healed the sick or bound up the injured." They "have not brought back the strays or searched for the lost," but "have ruled them harshly and brutally" (v. 4). Rather than caring for the flock, these shepherds were using them for their own purposes.

God is insisting that these sheep are His. Ultimately, they do not belong to anyone else but Him. The shepherds who go in His name must treat the sheep properly. For the shepherds to misuse the sheep for their own ends is not only a travesty of fairness to the sheep but a denial of everything a shepherd is supposed to be.

Some who are leaders of various branches of the church today are thieves and terrorists, because, as the Pharisees did, they mislead the sheep. They lead them to fields that are barren, with no grass to eat. They scatter and confuse them with poor teaching. They feed themselves yet don't feed the flock of God the one thing that the flock must have— God's Word.

If a shepherd feeds the sheep his own opinions, even if those opinions are reliable, but he does not feed them God's Word, he is a false shepherd. If a shepherd uses the pulpit to promote political candidates and causes, he is a false shepherd. If a shepherd does not labor to feed the flock from the Scripture, he is denying the sheep the *one* thing that God says they must have to live. Such false shepherds do not care about building up and protecting the flock. Even if they themselves believe in

Jesus, they do not rightly use His Word in ministry, and they come into the sheepfold by some other way. They are hirelings in the end, who care more for their own reputation or success, perhaps, than for the sheep.

I am painting a rather stark picture here, but I think you have only to look at a variety of churches around the world today to find what I am describing. If the Word of God is not central in the life of God's people, then the sheep are not being fed, no matter how many good things seem to be going on in that church.

THE GOOD SHEPHERD KNOWS HIS OWN

Jesus Christ knows His own, and His own know Him. So intimate is the Shepherd with His sheep that He even knows their names. "When he puts forth all his own, he goes before them, and the sheep follow him because they know his voice" (John 10:4).

Shepherds in Europe and in North America usually drive their sheep, often using a sheepdog. But in the Near East, both now and in Jesus' time, the shepherd is not behind the sheep driving them but out in front, leading them, beckoning them, calling to them, personally and intimately. He calls them individually, by name.

When I was working in youth ministry just out of college, it became evident that a young teen in one of the high schools where I was working had become a believer. I wanted to know how it had happened, so I asked him, "When did you become a follower of Christ?" He answered, "I believed in the Lord Jesus when you learned my name."

Consider the way Jesus calls Zaccheus by name out of the tree. "Zaccheus!" (Luke 19). Or consider the Gadarene demoniac. Jesus goes to this man filled with demons and says to him, "What is your name?" (Mark 5). What an amazing thing for Jesus to ask. Here is a deranged man, absolutely victimized by these demons, and Jesus asks him his name. The demons answer, "My name is Legion." The man could not even give his name until Jesus called him by name. You know you have real freedom when you are intimately known and loved by the true Shepherd who knows His sheep by name.

How well does Jesus know us? "I am the good shepherd; and I know My own, and My own know Me, even as the Father knows Me and I know the Father; and I lay down My life for the sheep" (John

10:14-15). The only measure of the degree to which the Good Shepherd knows us is the degree to which the Father has known the Son from all eternity. How well is that? How close have they been forever and ever? That is how close the Good Shepherd is to us. That is how close Jesus draws to us, how intimately He knows us.

He Calls His Sheep Effectively

Because Jesus knows His sheep, He effectively calls them to follow Him. Back in the first century there were several flocks in any one sheepfold, and the picture here is that the shepherd calls his own out of the larger sheepfold, and those who are his hear his voice and follow him. They are separated out of the larger group.

There are four characteristics of the Good Shepherd's effective call. *First,* this intimate calling is by the Word of the Shepherd. His Word applied in a saving way to our hearts by the Holy Spirit assures that His sheep will hear His voice. It is His own Word that they hear. His Word is compelling like no other word.

Has there ever been someone in your life whose voice made you jump when you heard it? When I was in high school, I had a drama coach named Miss Mifflin. She was as tough as nails, but she was very good. One day we students were moving around the stage being told where to go to get into position for the different parts of the play. (It's called "blocking.") Miss Mifflin was sitting back in the dark of the theater where we couldn't see her, but we could hear her. "No, Skip, you turned the wrong way again," she barked. And I jumped. I can still hear her very unusual voice.

An even better example is that of the late Tom Landry, for many years coach of the Dallas Cowboys. Following his death, many praised him as the fine gentleman and leader that he was. Especially we who live in Dallas heard stories about the way he spoke to his players and how his voice had presence, character, and command. When his players heard his voice, they responded without hesitation. His word had power. (My son, the football player, says that by his words a good coach evokes precisely the right combination of respect and fear.)

God's Word is *the* Word that defines us. God's Word, says Peter, is the word by which we are "born again" (1 Pet. 1:23). "And this is the word," he says, "which was preached to you" (v. 25b). "The grass withers, the flower falls off, but the word of the Lord abides forever" (vv. 24b-25a). The Word of God compels. It has the ability to move us from death to life. It is irresistible.

Second, this effective calling is a conscious calling—in our ears, in our minds, and in our hearts. It is not a mystical thing; it actually happens. We think. We interact with God's truth in His Word. We hear the Word preached. We hear the Word taught. We open the Bible and we read it. We think about what we read, and God works through our reasoning to persuade us that it is His voice that we hear. Then we follow.

Third, it is a calling that cannot be rescinded. It is irrevocable. It is "without repentance," says Paul (Rom. 11:29, KJV). When God calls a person, He does not change His mind. The Word of the Shepherd is never taken back. When He quickens you to new life by using His Word to call you to Himself, He will never go back on His Word.

All of this should be a great encouragement to any of us who seek to minister that Word to others. Every Sunday morning at our church, many dozens of adults minister the Word of God to about fifteen hundred young people from infancy to age eighteen. The Word they speak to those young people is powerful. The Word can change their hearts and lives. It is not the teachers' own words. It is not the drivel of their own ideas or their own nice thoughts about how to live a moral life. It is the Word of God, which never perishes, which endures forever. It is the voice of the Good Shepherd, and He promises to apply that Word faithfully to convict, to convince, to convert, and to comfort hearts.

How do you defend a lion? You let him out of his cage. How do you defend the Word of God? You start reading it. Start speaking it. The Word of God will defend itself, because the voice of the Shepherd is true and pure and pierces to the point of division between soul and spirit (Heb. 4:12) like no other word ever can.

Fourth, His Word, His voice, effects what it speaks. Its calling is made effective intrinsically. My word, by contrast, does not have intrinsic power to make happen what it says. An illustration I have already used bears repeating here: when it is time for dinner in my house, I go to the stairs and say, "Kids, come on down for dinner."

"Be down in a minute, Dad."

Well, they may come in a minute, they may come in five minutes, they may come in thirty minutes. My word does not have intrinsic power to make them come downstairs. I would like to think it does; but it doesn't. But the Word of the Good Shepherd has the very power in it to do what it says: change a heart, change a life.

He Provides for His Sheep Abundantly

When Jesus knows me, He gives me what I need most. I come in and go out, and I find pasture (John 10:9). He gives me abundant life, the whole of life, including my daily needs (v. 10); not just spiritual life, but everything I need. He is faithful as a Shepherd to provide that for me.

Invariably, if we are honest with ourselves, we are looking for life in the *if onlys*. *If only* I could get that house, or that job. *If only* I could buy that car. *If only* I could get on that team or in that college. *If only* I could be that sort of person. *If only* the economy lasts two more years. *If only* we elect this candidate. We live our lives in the *if onlys*.

John Calvin says quite rightly that the human heart is a perpetual idol factory. We keep grasping onto things as if those things will make us happy, when in reality it is only the presence of the Good Shepherd who makes us happy and safe and secure and who provides for us. The abundant life that He gives is pasture that is always green and waters that are always calm. Why do I say that, when I know your life isn't calm? Why, when I know my life isn't always calm? The reason our lives are so often not calm is that we are grasping onto this or that, seeking anchor and meaning and purpose. But we can go into any storm knowing that the Lord, the Good Shepherd, brings calm in the midst of chaos, quiet waters in the midst of our thirst.

As D. A. Carson put it, He gives us "life at its scarcely imagined best."[1] I love the line of C. S. Lewis: "Our Lord finds our desires not too strong, but too weak."[2] We want stuff, as if it will make us happy, when what we really should want is the presence of the Good Shepherd, who alone gives abundant life and purpose.

He Protects His Sheep Completely

I tend to think of a shepherd as a sentimental sort of fellow, his arms full of cuddly lambs. But when Jesus is called the Good Shepherd, the word *good* means more than "kind." It actually means "noble" and "worthy," and this is opposite to the ignoble self-interest of those hired to do the job. The idea is that the Good Shepherd is a strong defender, a warrior on behalf of the sheep. He is One who comes and promises, with His rod in hand. The shepherd's rod was a weapon, not a stage prop in a Christmas play, and it was used to defend the sheep from prey. The promise is that no one will ever snatch one of the Good Shepherd's sheep from His hand (John 10:28). He will defend and protect them from the wolves that seek to snatch the sheep away, so that the sheep can lie down in green pastures.

As I said, I don't know that much about sheep, at least not the woolly kind. But I do know this: they cannot lie down unless they are totally secure. Lying down without the shepherd guarding them would mean they are vulnerable to all attackers. Only in the safety of the sheepfold, or when guarded closely by the shepherd in the pasture, will a sheep lie down. In the Near East in Jesus' day, the door or gate to the sheepfold wasn't a swinging door with a latch on it. It was simply an opening in the fence. The only sure way to protect the sheep, particularly at night when they and the shepherd would want to sleep, was for the shepherd to lie down in the doorway so that any intruder—human or animal—would have to step over the shepherd, which would arouse him so that he could defend the sheep.

As the door of the sheepfold, the Good Shepherd risks His life for the sheep. The hired one runs away. He doesn't really care when the sheep are threatened. But the Good Shepherd risks everything for them. Jesus not only puts His life at risk, but chooses to lay down His life for the sheep (v. 15).

Jesus sees how much He is loved by His Father (v. 17), and He sees how much the Father, who loves Him, loves the sheep. So out of obedience and love He lays down His life for the sheep.

A good shepherd does not intend to lose his life. If he does, the sheep are exposed and made vulnerable. But Jesus intended to lose His life. His death is precisely what is intended as the ultimate way to protect the sheep. Paul says, "Christ also loved the church and gave Himself up for her" (Eph. 5:25). The great Shepherd says, "I lay down My life for the sheep" (John 10:15), not as an example, as if He throws Himself off a cliff and says, "I love you, therefore I kill myself." No. He is not an example, but a substitute, because the sheep are in mortal danger. His life is the only sacrifice that will save the sheep from the mortal terror that comes from the terrorist of all terrorists: sin. Sin leads to death, and the only way to protect the sheep is if the Shepherd becomes the victim of the terrorist.

Peter talks about sheep in his first epistle, saying, "For you were continually straying like sheep, but now you have returned to the Shepherd and Guardian of your souls" (1 Pet. 2:25).

How about you? Be honest with the Good Shepherd. Are you straying from Him? Do you know that even when you were wandering away from Him, with no thought in your heart or mind to turn to Him, dead in your sins and full of the wickedness that He should rightfully hate, even then He died for you (Rom. 5:8)? Let go of whatever you seek besides the green pastures and the still waters to which the Lord leads you. The abundant life you were made and meant for is yours. Return from your straying and come to the One who is the King of love, the Shepherd whose goodness never fails.

22

"LAZARUS, COME FORTH"

Now a certain man was sick, Lazarus of Bethany, the village of Mary and her sister Martha. And it was the Mary who anointed the Lord with ointment, and wiped His feet with her hair, whose brother Lazarus was sick. The sisters therefore sent to Him, saying, "Lord, behold, he whom You love is sick." But when Jesus heard it, He said, "This sickness is not unto death, but for the glory of God, that the Son of God may be glorified by it." Now Jesus loved Martha, and her sister, and Lazarus. When therefore He heard that he was sick, He stayed then two days longer in the place where He was. . . . So when Jesus came, He found that he had already been in the tomb four days. Now Bethany was near Jerusalem, about two miles off; and many of the Jews had come to Martha and Mary, to console them concerning their brother. Martha therefore, when she heard that Jesus was coming, went to meet Him, but Mary still sat in the house. Martha therefore said to Jesus, "Lord, if You had been here, my brother would not have died. Even now I know that whatever You ask of God, God will give You." Jesus said to her, "Your brother shall rise again." Martha said to Him, "I know that he will rise again in the resurrection on the last day." Jesus said to her, "I am the resurrection and the life; he who believes in Me shall live even if he dies, and everyone who lives and believes in Me shall never die. Do you believe this?" She said to Him, "Yes, Lord; I have believed that You are the Christ, the Son of God, even He who comes into the world." . . .
  Jesus therefore again being deeply moved within, came to the tomb. Now it was a cave, and a stone was lying against it. Jesus said, "Remove the stone." Martha, the sister of the deceased, said to Him, "Lord, by this time there will be a stench, for he has been dead four days." Jesus said to her, "Did I not say to you, if you believe, you will see the glory of God?" And so they removed the stone. And Jesus raised His eyes, and said, "Father, I thank Thee that Thou heardest Me. I knew that Thou hearest Me always; but because of the people standing around I said it, that they may believe that Thou didst send Me." And when He had said these things, He cried out with a loud voice, "Lazarus, come forth." He who had died came forth, bound hand and foot with wrappings; and his face was wrapped around with a cloth. Jesus said to them, "Unbind him, and let him go" (John 11:1-6, 17-27, 38-44).

WHEN OUR DAUGHTER BEKAH was born, we discovered within five days that she had some serious problems. Those problems have been both the crucible and the joy of our lives, molding Barbara and me as adult Christians perhaps more than any other life experience we have had.

Bekah seemed to be fine at first, although her birth was not completely normal. We took her home from the hospital only to get a call late the same day from the pediatrician, who said, "We have a problem." He had noticed something in Bekah's eye earlier that day, a twitch, which to his trained mind meant a seizure. Although older children may have seizures that are not serious, seizures in infants are problems. At ten o'clock at night we took our little Bekah back to the University of Virginia Hospital in Charlottesville. Inexplicably to me, over the next four hours, all twenty-five elders from our church showed up in the pediatric intensive care unit. I don't even know how they heard, but they came.

One of them, Dr. Ed Rose, a professor at the University of Virginia Medical School, stayed with us all night. Ed's field wasn't pediatrics or neurology, the issues that were most germane to Bekah at that time, but he knew the hospital—the byways, red tape, and who's who. And he knew I needed to talk to someone who knew how to make that hospital work.

Though Bekah is severely cognitively delayed, autistic, and "different" in many ways, she is, today, a much loved, matter-of-fact part of our lives and part of our church's life. Yet what I have never been able to take as matter-of-fact is the closeness of many of the members of the two congregations I have served in their concern for us and Bekah. Just like Dr. Rose, who stayed with us through the night, we measure friendship by closeness, even physical closeness by taking the trouble to go and be with someone.

THE SITUATION IN BETHANY

It is obvious from this passage that Jesus considered Mary, Martha, and Lazarus His friends, and their friendship had grown to the point that when Lazarus became ill, Mary and Martha sent the news to Jesus. In doing so, they describe the depth of the friendship: "Lord, behold, he whom You love is sick" (see John 11:3).

There are two words for "sick" in the New Testament Greek language. One means mildly sick, like having a cold. The other means very sick. Here they are saying, "Lord, he is sinking fast." Verse 5 says that Jesus loved Lazarus and his two sisters, but in spite of His love, He seems to violate the principle that love always means proximity, always means going, always means closeness. In spite of His love for them, He stays where He is for two more days. Doesn't that seem odd?

Poor Martha. Poor Mary. Jesus loves you. But what a strange way to show it. Actually, a careful reading of the text shows it is *because* of His love for Mary, Martha, and Lazarus that Jesus stays where He is for two more days. Verse 6 says, "When therefore He heard that he was sick, He stayed then two days longer in the place where He was."

Friendship with the Lord is measured in our trials. In the severity of our lives we find the Lord's care and compassion. But the principle therefore means, that to those whom the Lord loves, *really loves,* He sends trials. Our trials and illnesses and those of the ones we love become, as it were, a bouquet of flowers from the Lord. I know that sounds ridiculous. Maybe you are thinking, *Wait a minute, if the Lord loves me, He blesses me; and blessing means I am free from trials and difficulty.* No. Unhappy is the Christian disciple who does not have trials, because he does not know the Lord's closeness and love if everything is going beautifully. It is a principle of human conduct that we do not flourish in our life with the Lord when everything is going well. It is in our severe trials and in our needs that we cry out to Him.

It also appears that Jesus is moving by some internal time clock. His care for those He loves is not determined by *their* timetable. It is set for purposes that He knows and Mary and Martha do not know. This is not new in this Gospel. Remember in John 2, Jesus' mother urged Jesus to do something when the wine ran out at the wedding, but He did not immediately respond to her pressure. And later, in John 7, He went up to Jerusalem when *He* determined to go, not when the disciples told Him to go. There is an inner authority that directs Jesus' timing. He does not operate from the pressure from even dear friends or an angry mob—or from you or me.

My wife ministers to me when she reminds me, "Don't operate on the basis of what people say. Operate on the basis of what the Lord says." God's agenda is larger and more comprehensive than ours or others'. God's timing is not oriented to our desires; rather, according to this passage, His timing is oriented toward His love and His glory—His love toward us and His glory manifested in us.

When Jesus arrives in Bethany, Lazarus has already been dead for four days. This is significant because Jewish superstition said that the soul stayed near the grave for three days, hoping that it might be able to return to the body. But on the fourth day, the soul saw that the body was decomposing and it finally left. This specific note about four days is probably intended to dissuade us from over-spiritualizing this text, which is what some people try to do. "Lazarus is dead, Israel is spiritually dead, lost in their deadness," some say. Others say, "Lazarus is Everyman, dead in trespasses and sins." That might be true, but the most important thing to say here is that Lazarus is just plain dead, so dead that the decomposition of his physical remains has already begun.

Many of Lazarus's friends from Jerusalem, just two miles away from Bethany, have come to mourn. According to the *Talmud,* mourning in the Jewish tradition would involve three days of weeping, seven days of lamenting, and thirty days of refraining from cutting one's hair and ironing one's clothes. I don't know why, but those were the rules. Professional mourners were hired, including flute players and at least one professional wailing woman. In our day, we often see such mourners in news stories from the Middle East. In 11:33 we find that Mary, Lazarus's sister, is weeping. The word there does not mean "soft crying." It means the unrestrained, noisy weeping and wailing of mourning.

THE DIALOGUE WITH MARTHA

Martha is less "weepy" than Mary. Perhaps she feels a need to get away from all the wailing. This may explain why Martha goes out to meet Jesus when she hears He is coming. She says in John 11:21, "Lord, if You had been here, my brother would not have died." Some think that is a rebuke. But Martha knew that if Jesus had come sooner, something good would have happened. Her words are a statement of faith—and some understandable disappointment. Martha believed that Jesus could have healed Lazarus before he died. This is probably what Mary and Martha had been saying to one another during the previous two days.

In verse 23, Jesus turns Martha's thoughts not to what He could have done but to what He will do: "Your brother shall rise again."

Martha takes perfunctory comfort in this, considering it to be the sort
of thing that one Jewish person would say rather glibly to another—like
we might say to a person we are trying to comfort who has lost a loved
one—"She's in heaven." The Jews would say, "He will rise on the last
day." That phrase reflected their understanding of the Old Testament
teaching about the resurrection, which was just enough to suggest that
there should be a kind of national hope to which all Jews looked forward. (It is probably stated most clearly in Daniel 12:2 [KJV]: "Many of
them that sleep in the dust of the earth shall awake, some to everlasting
life, and some to shame and everlasting contempt.")

Jesus responds to Martha with a statement that is one of the absolute high-water marks of the New Testament: "I am the resurrection and
the life; he who believes in Me shall live even if he dies, and everyone
who lives and believes in Me shall never die. Do you believe this?" (John
11:25-26). Jesus meets Martha's "if" with His own "if." "If you will
only believe, if you will see what I am about, then you, Martha, will see
the glory of God in this situation and in your life."

THE PERSON OF THE RESURRECTION

Jesus has already revealed Himself in the Gospel of John as the Bread of
life, as the Water of life, and as the Light of life, and now He reveals
Himself as Life itself. The question Jesus poses to Martha in various
ways in this passage is the question He asks us: "What do you believe
about Me? Do you believe that My delay was nonchalant? Or purposeful?" Do you believe that the glory of God can be shown in even
the worst circumstances in your life? Do you believe that, even in the trials of your life, what is being manifested is the love of a Savior who has
committed Himself to you irrevocably? Or do you believe that God has
left the phone off the hook? What do you believe about the person of
the resurrection and about the promise of the resurrection?

Jesus tells Martha to lift up her eyes from her circumstances, from
the houseful of mourners, from her own plans and altered hopes and
dreams, even from the apparent finality of her brother's death, and to
put her eyes on Him. Jesus does not say that He will *give* resurrection
and life; He says that He *is* the resurrection and the life. The resurrection of Lazarus points forward to Christ's own resurrection as the place

where God confirms the final authority of Jesus as His Son and His authority over everything that could ever separate us from the love of God, even death itself.

By His resurrection, Jesus is given the authority to be the Son of God. Now that may seem rather obvious to you. Jesus was the Son of God, and God raised Him from the dead. But remember the big framework here in the Gospel of John: the point in the whole Gospel is to get us to believe like we have never believed before that Jesus, the Christ, is the Son of God, and that by believing, we will have life in His name (John 20:31). To those of us who say we've believed that all of our lives, He wants us to *really* believe it. He wants us to believe it layers and layers deeper than we ever have before, because He wants us to be quickened with the power of that new life that Jesus gives. Sometimes when we look square in the face of that which we think we know, we realize how little we understand it.

When the sisters sent word to Jesus, "Lord, behold, he whom You love is sick," Jesus responded, "This sickness is not unto death, but for the glory of God, so that the Son of God may be glorified by it" (11:3-4). The resurrection of Lazarus is going to reveal the Son's glory, His true identity, and His authority. Later on, after Jesus orders the stone removed and Martha warns of the odor, Jesus says, "Did I not say to you, if you believe, you will see the glory of God?" (v. 40).

This is a difficult situation, but the issue is not the difficulty of the situation for Martha or for us. The issue is whether or not the glory of God will be manifested in and through our trials and difficulties. The question is, Who is Jesus in the midst of this difficulty?

Jesus is not a miracle worker who does what we want when we want:

"Raise Lazarus."
"Okay, I'll do it."
"Fix my troubled finances."
"Okay, I'll do it."
"Fix my wayward child."
"Okay, I'll do it."

No, He is the Son of God who does this for His own glory. That is why Jesus says in verse 15 that He was glad He was not present when

Lazarus became sick. The agenda of the Son of God is far greater than our human agendas.

The resurrection of Jesus expresses the deepest core of His identity. Paul says that his letter to the Romans is all about Jesus, "who was born of a descendant of David according to the flesh, who was declared the Son of God with power by the resurrection from the dead" (Rom. 1:3-4). Jesus could not be God's Son if men triumphed over Him in His execution. The early church thundered out that message, that God would not allow the last view of His Son to be the humiliation of the Cross or the coldness of a dark tomb. In the Resurrection, God reveals that it is His intent to reverse the sentence of men. Men killed Jesus; God raised Him up. God brings glory out of even the wickedness of His creatures. The most wicked act in all history, putting the Son of God to death, is used to bring glory to God.

Peter says in his great speech in Acts 2, "It was impossible for death to keep its hold on him" (v. 24, NIV). Why? Because He was God's Son, and God could not and would not leave Him to death. The Resurrection is the proof of Jesus' identity and His authority. Every place in the Bible where the resurrection of Christ is proclaimed and discussed, even where it is met with disbelief, it is the affirmation that God made Jesus to be Lord and Christ. When men did their worst, God did His best. Philippians 2:8-9 affirms, "And being found in appearance as a man, He humbled Himself by becoming obedient to the point of death, even death on a cross. Therefore also God highly exalted Him, and bestowed on Him the name which is above every name."

In Ephesians 1, Paul talks about the power that was exerted by God in this great act of resurrection to raise the Son from the dead and seat Him at His right hand, even in the face of human hatred and sin. This power did not simply resuscitate Jesus; it exalted Him to the place of prime authority. Jesus' resurrection does not simply show His power over death; it shows His power over our lives. He is ruling right now from a heavenly place at the right hand of God. This is not trivial, pious chatter, but truth, more true than anything else that we will see, taste, touch, or feel this day. Jesus is manifesting His glory in our poor lives right now. By His resurrection, Jesus is given the authority of the Son of God over death and over life.

When Jesus saw Mary's grief and that of her friends, He was deeply "troubled" (John 11:33). "Jesus wept," says John in verse 35; and in verse 38 he tells us that Jesus, "being deeply moved within, came to the tomb." The word for "moved" is used in the Greek to refer to sheer, raw anger. Carson says that Jesus was "outraged" in spirit[1] as He stood before the tomb of Lazarus. Why was Jesus so deeply moved? Was He mourning like those around Him, even Martha and Mary? No, of course not. He knew what He was about to do. Jesus was outraged at death. He stood before the grave of Lazarus with a holy disgust and anger at all that would ever separate humanity from His Father. It was necessary that Jesus be outraged. Carson observes that grief without outrage is sentimentality, but "outrage without grief hardens into self-righteous arrogance."[2] Only Jesus could perfectly rage at death.

John Calvin says that Jesus "does not come to the tomb as an idle spectator, but like a wrestler preparing for the contest. . . . the violent tyranny of death which he had to overcome stands before his eyes."[3] B. B. Warfield says, "It is death that is the object of his wrath, and behind death him who has the power of death, and whom he has come into the world to destroy. . . . His soul is held by rage."[4] The mission of Jesus is to destroy that which is ultimately bent on destroying us. He dies on the cross for the sin that causes us to die, and He is raised from the tomb to display His authority over death itself.

In 1 Corinthians 15, Paul uses various images and metaphors to describe the nature of death. Death is declared a defeated enemy, the last and greatest enemy to be destroyed. Death is mocked as a loathsome insect which, because of Christ, no longer has the power to sting us with its venom. Death is conquered like a fallen gladiator. Jesus strides forth as a victor, as a conqueror of hell. The Welshman William Williams wrote in 1745 that Jesus' resurrection is the "Death of death, and hell's Destruction."[5] The Son of God is a warrior, and He went to war for you and me! He went to war that we might be raised from the dead, that sickness and death and sin itself would not be the end.

THE PROMISE OF THE RESURRECTION

"If a man dies, will he live again?" asked Job (Job 14:14). The answer is yes! Paul wrote in 1 Corinthians 6:14, "Now God has not only raised the Lord, but will also raise us up through His power."

The person of the resurrection makes a promise, that His glory in our lives will one day be perfectly displayed when we, in the dust we have become, are knit back together into glorious, new, life-filled bodies, like unto His glorious body (Rom. 8:11).

Jesus asks Martha pointedly, "Do you believe this?" Many don't believe, but not many are as honest about their disbelief as John Donne, who said, "Death is a bloody conflict and no victory at last; a tempestuous sea, and no harbor at last; a slippery height and no footing; a desperate fall and no bottom" (Donne eventually professed a strong Christian faith). Few are as honest as Aristotle: "Death is a dreadful thing, for it is the end." Or as Thomas Hobbes: "I am about to take my last voyage, a great leap in the dark." Or Rousseau: "He who pretends to face death without fear is a liar."

These philosophers and poets show us that there is a real difference between those who believe and those who don't believe. There will be a resurrection of all humanity, but Jesus speaks of the resurrection of life and also of the resurrection of judgment. It is clear in all of the teaching of the New Testament that one day all will rise, but those who have not believed in Jesus as the Son of God and the conqueror of death will find the resurrection to be what one commentator called "a serious matter indeed."

For the sake of your own eternal and temporal joy and welfare, note the content of Martha's belief in John 11:27: "Yes, Lord; I have believed that You are the Christ, the Son of God, even He who comes into the world." *One,* Jesus is the Christ, the Messiah, the Savior of Jewish expectation. He is the Savior of all who put their trust in Him. *Two,* He is the Son of God who bears all authority that has been given to Him by the Father. And *three,* Jesus brought eternal life to us, right here, in this world, beginning now. Like Martha, each of us must answer Jesus' question, "Do you believe this?"

Jesus' resurrection is announced to us as unique. He does not invite us to think of Him as the resurrection and the life. He does not say, "If you accept Me, I will be the resurrection and the life." He says He *is* the resurrection and the life. It is up to us, then, to believe it or not believe it.

I recall a game we played during recess in grade school. Kids would all get in a circle, take their shoes off, lie on their backs, and put their stockinged feet up into the air. One person would then stand in the middle and let himself go, falling onto the feet. He trusted that he would be held up by the feet of his friends. That is what faith is—leaning on Jesus and trusting that when we are dead in our grave, He will quicken us to new life.

"I tell you the truth," Jesus says, "whoever hears my word and believes him who sent me has eternal life and will not be condemned; he has crossed over from death to life. I tell you the truth, a time is coming and has now come when the dead will hear the voice of the Son of God and those who hear will live. For as the Father has life in himself, so he has granted the Son to have life in himself" (John 5:24-26, NIV). . . . "Lazarus, come forth" . . . "Brittany, come forth" . . . "John, come forth" . . . "Matt, come forth" . . .

23

THE ANOINTING

Many therefore of the Jews, who had come to Mary and beheld what He had done, believed in Him. But some of them went away to the Pharisees, and told them the things which Jesus had done. Therefore the chief priests and the Pharisees convened a council, and were saying, "What are we doing? For this man is performing many signs." . . . So from that day on they planned together to kill Him. . . . Jesus, therefore, six days before the Passover, came to Bethany where Lazarus was, whom Jesus had raised from the dead. So they made Him a supper there, and Martha was serving; but Lazarus was one of those reclining at the table with Him. Mary therefore took a pound of very costly perfume of pure nard, and anointed the feet of Jesus, and wiped His feet with her hair; and the house was filled with the fragrance of the perfume. But Judas Iscariot, one of His disciples, who was intending to betray Him, said, "Why was this perfume not sold for three hundred denarii, and given to poor people?" Now he said this, not because he was concerned about the poor, but because he was a thief, and as he had the money box, he used to pilfer what was put into it. Jesus therefore said, "Let her alone, in order that she may keep it for the day of My burial. For the poor you always have with you, but you do not always have Me" (John 11:45-47, 53; 12:1-8).

THE BEAUTIFUL ACT OF anointing Jesus' feet, performed by Mary out of a heart overflowing with love for her Lord, is a gem of the New Testament. And like a beautiful gem, let's hold it up to the sunlight and twist and turn it and see how the rays of the sun hit it from different angles.

The passage is about a banquet—actually a celebration—for Lazarus has been raised from the dead. Now, in the home of Mary, Martha, and Lazarus there is a dinner in Jesus' honor as they thank the Lord for His kindness in raising Lazarus. Imagine the setting: many friends and family, probably quite a crowd gathered in their home; Martha doing her practical thing, very concerned, of course, about people getting enough to eat, about the dinner being served hot and in a

timely fashion. Then in comes Mary, and she does an amazingly imprac-
tical thing.

THE CONDITIONS OF MARY'S LOVE FOR JESUS

At first, no one would have been surprised as Mary approached Jesus
with her perfume. In those days, when people gathered socially, it would
be normal to bring out the perfume. No one would have showered
before they came to this dinner party. There were no baths, no deodor-
ants, no aftershaves, so people would come in this particularly hot climate smelling bad! And, no, I don't think they got used to it then any
more than we would now.

So the fragrances would come out on special occasions, and the host
or hostess would put a little on the head or face of each guest to cloak
the odor. But what Mary does in this understandable social context is
unexpected and quite startling.

In Mark 14, a parallel passage, we read that the guests at the banquet rebuked Mary harshly for what she did, meaning literally that they
"bellowed or snorted with anger like an animal." It is the same word
used in John 11 when Jesus bellows in anger at death at Lazarus's tomb.
These people are outraged at what Mary did, and they are yelling at her.

Why such outrage? The *unconditionality* of Mary's devotion to
Jesus angers the people in the room. *First,* she pours out all of the perfume. In John 12:3 we read that it was a pound of very costly, genuine
spikenard ointment. Mark, in his account, adds that Mary has to break
the vial in which the ointment is contained to pour it all out. She doesn't
just put a little drop on Jesus. It isn't a matter of "a little dab'll do ya."
She pours out the whole thing on Him, and the house is filled with the
pungent—probably overly pungent—odor of this costly fragrance. The
people are angry that this very expensive perfume is being wasted.

The perfume would have cost three hundred denarii, Judas tells us,
which was almost a year's wages in that time. Mary and Martha and
Lazarus were probably well-off, probably better off than average, but
unless they were extraordinarily rich—private jets and homes on the
Riviera kind of rich—this perfume would have been the most valuable
thing they possessed.

Mark says the container is an alabaster jar, which is probably a family heirloom itself, passed down from generation to generation. The jar, plus the ointment in it, actually represents financial security to this family, particularly in the face of potential disaster. This is their savings account if an earthquake or famine hits, so when Mary first brings the vial out, they undoubtedly think, *Oh, what an honor, Mary is going to put a little drop on Jesus.* But then she breaks it and pours the *whole* thing out. Gasp!

Mary is saying, "I will not allow my following of Jesus to be conditioned by cost." She is not saying, "I will follow You as long as it doesn't cost me too much, Lord; as long as You don't expect too much of my checkbook. But if You start talking about tithing, I'll get nervous. Stay away from that thought, and I'll follow You." No, she is saying, "I am willing to give You anything . . . everything." She is not giving 10 percent but 80 or 90 percent of the family's net wealth. She is willing to follow Jesus without conditions, at all costs.

Secondly, she anoints Jesus' feet with the perfume. This was a time and a place in which dealing with the feet was considered demeaning. No Jewish person—not even a Jewish slave—dealt with anyone's feet except his or her own. That task was left to Gentile slaves.

Slavery in this particular day and place was different from the cruel institution we have known in the West. In ancient times in this part of the world, when Jewish people fell into debt and were unable to repay it, they could not go to bankruptcy court, so they would go into servitude to the person to whom they owed the debt—in order to work it off. In doing so, they would, of course, lose many of their rights. But the rabbis said that a Jewish servant or slave did have some rights. There were certain things they never had to do, and touching another's shoes or feet was one of them. That is why all of the disciples are so completely put off when Jesus starts to wash their feet (John 13). It was absolutely unheard of!

As she touches Jesus' feet, Mary is giving up her rights before the Lord. There is nothing He cannot ask of her. Touching His feet becomes a pledge of her unconditional service.

The *third* amazing thing that happens is that Mary takes down her hair and proceeds to wipe the excess perfume from the feet of Jesus. In ancient times, a woman would never let down her hair in public. If she did so, it was grounds for her husband to divorce her. If a single woman let down her hair in public, it could possibly be grounds for public ston-ing. In their culture (and to a lesser degree in our own culture) a woman's unbinding of her hair expressed openness, love, and intimacy. It was something that a woman would do only at home and only in the presence of her closest family members.

When Mary lets down her hair to wipe Jesus' feet, she removes all conditions to her devotion to Him. She erases any barriers that would keep her from being absolutely devoted to Him. The apostle Paul says in 1 Corinthians 13 that it is possible to give up everything, even all our possessions, and our bodies to be burned, but to not have love. To be honest, many of us say to Jesus, "I know I owe You my wealth. I know I owe You my service, and I will give You those things as a good soldier of Jesus. I'll write the check. I'll join the church committee, but do I have to give You my heart?" Mary says, "I am going to love giving my wealth to You. I am going to love giving my service to You."

What the Lord does not want is to hear us say, "I am going to give You my stuff, and I am going to give You my time, but I will put my deepest delights in my work, or in my athletic activities, or in my pro-fessional status, or in my social opportunities and advantages, or even in my family." The Lord says that every delight, as good and right as it might be, is severely and ultimately compromised if it is placed ahead of Him as our chief delight.

The guests bellow that this public display is unbecoming. They can't take it. They feel rebuked by her pouring out the perfume, by her touch-ing His feet. But most of all, they feel rebuked by her letting down her hair, because they know that act means she will withhold nothing. When Mary pours out the perfume, she is saying, "Take my silver and my gold; not a mite would I withhold." When she touches Jesus' feet, she is saying, "Take my will and make it thine; it shall be no longer mine." But when she lets down her hair, she says, "Take my love; my Lord, I pour at thy feet its treasure-store. Take my self, and I will be ever, only, all for thee."[1]

There is stark contrast in this passage between Mary and Judas. Mary delights in the Lord, and Judas delights in all of the murky ambi-guities of his false devotion to the Lord. The two extremes demonstrate that in the end there are only two options; either sell Jesus out, or be sold out to Jesus. We either use Jesus or make ourselves available to be used by Him.

Do we stick with the Lord as long as He does for us what we need, taking our problems away and blessing us? Do we "hang in there" with the Lord, or do we delight in the Lord for who He is? There is a huge difference. Do we use God or love Him? If we love God first, we will delight in everything else and use it properly; but if we love something else first, we will end up using God, making Him an instrument of some other goal—blessings, a problem-free life, whatever it is. *God is not a means to an end; God is the end of all means.*

Have you ever asked, "What good is it for me to believe in God when it causes me all these problems? Why do I believe in Him? It seems that the more I believe in Him, the more trouble comes my way"? Mary demonstrates that she not only will obey God but will work whatever He sends her way into her heart until the Lord becomes her delight again.

You may have had severe trials in your life: sickness, loss of loved ones, financial reversals, betrayals, or other tragedies. You begin to wonder, *What is God doing? Why me?* The Lord's answer is always the same. He wants you to let down your hair. He wants you to learn to delight in Him in the midst of life's difficulties. He wants those difficulties, whatever they are, to be so worked into your life that you no longer define your life in the Lord in terms of the blessings He showers upon you but in terms of the delight in Him that He grants you by His grace. Then you have given Him what Mary gave Him—your heart.

How does this work? How do we get beyond the pious rhetoric, to the devotion of a unique person like Mary?

THE CONFIDENCE IN MARY'S WORSHIP

To get at the answer to that question, we could ask another question: Who is so upset with Mary? It is the religious people. They thought she was too extreme, undignified, and presumptuous. Religious people can't figure Mary out. They can deal with the perfume and the feet, but when it comes to the hair, they can't handle it. Religious people don't let their hair down.

Letting her hair down shows that Mary is confident and secure. It is an act done only among intimate friends and family. To do this in the presence of Jesus means she is comfortable in His presence, aware of the fact that He has unconditionally accepted her. Such security gives her the freedom to express her delight in Him. Mary's devotion flows out of a heart that has been quickened by grace. She realizes how much she is loved, and now it is her joy and her delight to return that love in the form of lavish, luxurious, extravagant worship, which she pours out upon Jesus.

The psalmist says, "Delight yourself in the LORD" (Ps. 37:4), and then he explains what he means: you delight yourself in what the Lord has done for you, which is ultimately expressed in the gospel. That produces worship that is unfeigned, unaffected. Lavish worship is real, intense, and sometimes unbearably honest. It is an expression of the confidence that we may have before the Lord because He has lavished His grace-filled acceptance upon us.

Confidence Before Others

Mary apparently doesn't care what other people—even Martha—think of her. She doesn't care about what a woman should or shouldn't do in such a setting. Can you imagine how uptight Martha was?

"What are you doing, Mary?"

"Mary, that's our life savings!"

"Mary, His *feet?*"

"Mary, your *hair?*"

Religious people don't know how to let their hair down. They are more concerned about cultural mores, appearances, and tradition, about whether their tie is right or about what someone said to them as they came into the sanctuary. They care what others think, concerned with looking like they're doing it right. Not Mary. She is humble, yet bold and exuberant in her adoration.

Worship Leads to Mercy

A big section of this passage deals with the poor. You can't miss it. Judas objects. It is a feigned objection, we know. He is masquerading for his own selfishness, his own eagerness to have the wealth that might have been produced by this ointment. Nevertheless, he says, "Why wasn't this sold and given to the poor?" (see John 12:5).

Jesus' response sounds like He doesn't care about the poor at all:

"The poor you always have with you, but you do not always have Me" (v. 8). He is not saying that He does not care about the poor; in fact, He is saying just the opposite. He is saying that, before you can show mercy, you must worship.

Worship comes before mercy because that is where we realize how much mercy has been shown to us. Then we are ready and able to show mercy to others. The only way to have a heart for the poor is to have a heart for worship of the Lord; if you have no regard for the poor, you are demonstrating that you may not have a heart for the Lord.

MARY'S CONSCIOUSNESS OF THE GOSPEL

When Judas complains about Mary's lavishness, Jesus tells him to leave her alone, for He knows Mary is anticipating His burial (John 12:7). All the spices, perfumes, and ointments would be brought to a burial in those days. They did not have an embalming process, so those ointments and spices would be used to preserve and protect the body.

Apparently Mary actually understood that Jesus was going to die; the text of John makes it clear that she did. Every time you see Mary in the Gospel of John, she is at the feet of Jesus. She is listening to and learning from Him. She is a great disciple, and therefore she understands Jesus is teaching that inevitably He is going to die for the sins of His people.

Before Lazarus was raised, Martha said, "Lord, if You had been here, my brother would not have died" (11:21). Gently and lovingly, Jesus taught her in His response, "I am the resurrection and the life. If you believe in Me, you will never die" (see vv. 25-26). But when Mary said exactly the same thing, "Lord, if You had been here, my brother would not have died" (v. 32), He did not teach her but wept with her. Why? Because she already "got it." She already understood that Jesus would die. Mary also knew that the Pharisees were coming after Jesus to kill Him. That had been their response to the raising of Lazarus (11:45-46, 53).

Mary is conscious of the fact that Jesus' death would be the fullest expression of His love for her. That consciousness melts her heart. Very consciously she gives herself to the Lord. She gets it! She knows the gospel! She understands that Jesus would give His life, and that somehow it was for her. Such great love, displayed in His coming death, awakens love in Mary. That is what makes her love back to the Lord so unconditional, so humble yet bold. She is happy and eager to give her wealth and her service, but even more she is happy and eager to give her heart because He has given His heart to her.

Scholars have suggested that the particular spikenard used on this occasion was almost certainly so potent that the smell of it stayed on the body of Jesus all through His trials, all through His scourgings, His sufferings, and through His death; and when Joseph of Arimathea took the body of the Lord down off the cross, his nostrils would have been filled with this sweet odor of Mary's love.

Mary's devotion was quickened by her understanding of what the Lord had done for her. Is your devotion so quickened? Is mine? Do we see what the Lord has done for us? Do we respond with a mechanical, "Yes, I know all that," or does it begin to melt our hearts? Does it cause us to let our hair down? Do we begin to want to be honest about what is in our own hearts? As we, with God's help, start to be that honest with Him and with ourselves, we smell something sweet, and our hearts begin to delight in the smell of His body, crucified, dead, buried, and risen again for us.

24

"BEHOLD, YOUR KING COMES"

On the next day the great multitude who had come to the feast, when they heard that Jesus was coming to Jerusalem, took the branches of the palm trees, and went out to meet Him, and began to cry out, "Hosanna! Blessed is He who comes in the name of the Lord, even the King of Israel." And Jesus, finding a young donkey, sat on it; as it is written, "Fear not, daughter of Zion; behold, your King is coming, seated on a donkey's colt." These things His disciples did not understand at the first; but when Jesus was glorified, then they remembered that these things were written of Him, and that they had done these things to Him (John 12:12-16).

ALL OF US HAVE EXPECTATIONS of one kind or another, and we all have to deal with the reality that they may not be met or may be met differently than we expected them to be—like in my family's move to Texas. Our expectations of Texas had been formed by a lifetime of impressions, and we had never been in the state itself. I have found that my now much-loved home state is not at all what many people think it is who don't live here. (For example, you see more cowboy boots on the streets of Manhattan than you do in Dallas.) The image of any place or any experience often changes with exposure to reality. That is one of the issues we must deal with in this passage.

The Triumphal Entry is one of the most vivid passages in all of the Gospels, a familiar and wonderful word picture of waving palm branches and huge crowds. Many of the followers of Jesus who had seen Him in Galilee were now in Jerusalem for the Passover holiday—as well as all of those who had seen Him raise Lazarus from the dead.

The historian Josephus gives us a most remarkable detail. He says that 2.7 million people came to Jerusalem for this celebration. That sounds like a Charlton Heston movie in the making! Jesus does make a really grand entrance, but it is not just the number of people that makes it so grand; it is the significance of His act. In this His third entry into Jerusalem, Jesus comes as the King of His people. It is like a head of state who arrives in a visiting country and presents his credentials at the capital. But here Jesus isn't just a visiting head of state; He is the King who has come to His own kingdom.

But Jesus knows there is treachery in the hearts of His subjects. Those who receive Him with shouts of acclamation on Sunday will be yelling something quite different at Him by Thursday, because He disappoints them. He lets them down. They think they are getting one thing, and they get another. They don't like the radical difference between their expectations and reality. Let's look at those differences.

THE KING COMES TO WAVING PALMS

During the two hundred years before Christ, waving leafy branches from the many palm-like trees in Israel had been a nationalistic symbol, like waving a flag. It demonstrated the people's hopes for a national liberator, a redeemer, someone who would rescue them from foreign oppression. About one hundred and fifty years before Christ, a leader called Simon Maccabeus had driven the Syrian forces out of Israel. When he did so, he was celebrated with music and with the waving of palms, much like the tattered Stars and Stripes that were waved in the faces of the Tories at Bunker Hill. They were a defiant symbol of courage and national hope.

The Israelites were expressing more than patriotism on Jesus' arrival. They were demonstrating hope in the midst of political and military oppression. They shouted, "Hosanna!" literally, "Give salvation now!" It was a moral and spiritual call to arms for every Jew, a call for liberation. Politically, it was a freedom song. It was the "We Shall Overcome" of the first century. It comes from Psalm 118, which is part of the "Hillel" psalms. Psalms 113–118 were shouted, recited, and musically portrayed during the great feasts in Jerusalem, and particularly at the Passover Feast. It was really kind of a college fight song or perhaps a national anthem with religious overtones. It was a bit like our singing "God Bless America." It was familiar and stirring music that would muster the resolve of the people in the midst of the difficult circumstances in which Israel now found itself.

But above all, Psalm 118 was a promise that the Messiah, a great Redeemer who would lead His people, would come. The multitude shouts from Psalm 118:26, "Blessed is the one who comes in the name of the LORD," and then add words that are not directly in Psalm 118: "Even the king of Israel." Psalm 118 probably was a song originally shouted about King David, a psalm that was a symbol of Israel's hope that they would have another king like David, one who would stand up to all of the Goliaths and enemies of God's people and would lead Israel to victory.

So Psalm 118, as the people came to understand it, was calling for a combination of a religious Messiah and a folk hero who would be a political liberator. The problem is that they sought to use their religion as a handmaiden for a larger political end and to advance their political ends by reinterpreting the kingdom of God in political terms. When they did so, they actually created a form of idolatry that is condemned again and again by the Old Testament prophets. Jesus will never tolerate this mixture of politics and religion, this lethal combination that inevitably leads to loss of the spiritual.

During every national election process, I feel obliged to gently and lovingly warn our congregation about the particular dangers of buttressing political ambitions with spiritual truths. I love politics. In another life I could easily have been fully engaged in politics, and I urge the members of our church to exercise any particular political interest they might have. If they want to run for city council, the school board, or Congress, our church will pray for them and encourage them in every possible way. But no one will be endorsed from the pulpit. To do so introduces a danger that the uniqueness, essence, and purity of the gospel would be compromised. This isn't some theoretical distinction between politics and religion. If we compromise the power of the gospel by whittling it to fit any particular political theory, cause, or person, then inevitably we make the gospel subservient to that political end, and we create an idol. We compromise the power and the beauty of the gospel to transform us and make us new. A gospel watered down so that it can be defined in political terms cannot change hearts. It might change someone's politics or the way they vote, but it is not going to change their heart. In this passage, the crowd (the political liberals, in this scenario) and the leaders (the political conservatives) both want to use Jesus to further their own agendas.

You say, "Okay, Skip, I appreciate the political lecture, but where is this going? This is not my problem." But it is your problem and mine. There is a principle always at work in our hearts: the temptation to use the gospel to promote something else. We want Jesus for what He gives us, for how He'll bless us—for the healing He might bring, for rescue from a difficult financial situation, or help for a son or daughter in trouble. Those are all legitimate concerns, but if we don't keep our priorities aligned, the desire to be blessed quickly becomes the main agenda, and Jesus becomes simply the servant of that agenda.

The controlling issue in many Christians' lives is a personal agenda, and they want Jesus to fit into their plans, their hopes, their ambitions. In the end, then, there are only two choices: *either we use Jesus for our ends or Jesus uses us for His ends.*

THE KING COMES ON A DONKEY

Jesus deals with the crowd's efforts (and ours) to use Him in a remarkably simple word picture. He gets on a donkey and rides it in fulfillment of what had been written in Zechariah: "Fear not, daughter of Zion; behold, your King is coming, seated on a donkey's colt" (Zech. 9:9, quoted in John 12:15). The huge crowd at the Passover seriously misunderstands the meaning of Christ's kingship. They are on the verge of marrying politics and religion in a way that will inevitably compromise the very gospel that Jesus comes to bring. How does Jesus tell 2.7 million people that? There is no microphone, no amplification. He portrays it visually before them all by this simple but profound act of mounting a lowly beast of burden.

Jesus finds a young donkey and sits on it *after* the people have already started shouting, "Hosanna!" Note the sequence here, particularly in verse 14. A clear translation would say: "First, Jesus walked in to the 'Hosannas' and the waving palms; and then He got on a donkey and rode it the rest of the way into Jerusalem."

This is different than our usual picture of Him riding the donkey the whole time past the palms and the "Hosannas." The addition of the donkey *after* the "Hosannas" is deliberately calculated by Jesus to redefine the crowd's view of the liberation that He has come to bring.

The donkey completely destabilizes the expectations of the crowd. D. A. Carson says, "to report the ride on the donkey immediately after the acclamation of the crowd has the effect of dampening down nationalistic expectations."[1] He has crawled onto a beast of burden instead of a warhorse. If Jesus wanted to take advantage of this opportune political moment, He would have mounted a flashing white steed. Jesus demonstrates to them that He is not the nationalistic leader who will bring political liberation from the Romans. Jesus says, "I am a King, but I am not that kind of king. I do bring liberation, but it is not the kind you expect."

The leaders have their expectations destabilized, too. They are worried. Pilate and the Jewish leaders are threatened by Jesus' popularity already, let alone these shouts that He was about to be made a king. The leaders are sensing dangerous mob-controlled dynamics. What happens if 2 million people suddenly decide to make Jesus king? Jesus is destabilizing the fragile *quid pro quo* arrangement between the Jewish Sanhedrin and the Roman authorities. The Romans let the Jewish leaders run the local governments and give them almost all the religious freedom they want. In return the Jews must stop local insurrections, pay taxes to Caesar, and, most importantly, let no one challenge both the political and the religious supremacy of the Roman emperor. Jesus is a threat to this arrangement.

Jesus is playing a political card here as He comes into Jerusalem. There are definite political overtones to His plan as His arrival creates tremendous stress in the relationship between the Jewish leaders and the Roman authorities. "The world has gone after Him," they say (John 12:19), sensing that the masses are moving in His direction. The irony, of course, is that the world really isn't going after Jesus at all. The world which He loves, which He came for, actually hates Him, and soon enough it will turn against Him and then against those who follow Him.

The disciples themselves are confused about what kind of king Jesus is. Verse 16 says that they understand this incident, namely, His getting on a donkey, only later, after His glorification. Every time the crowd or the leaders or the disciples think they have Jesus figured out, He surprises them. No one yet fully understands that Christ's kingdom is spiritual, heavenly, and eternal.

Maybe you are tempted to think, *I know. Jesus brought a spiritual kingdom, and that kingdom is nice, but it is not as powerful as the kingdom we hope the president (or some other political figure) is going to bring.* Don't we automatically think that the kingdom represented in the politics of this world really is the one with teeth, the one with real power and presence, and that whatever the kingdom of God is, it is a little vague? The kingdom of God is not vague at all! It is far more real and far more enduring than any kingdom man could ever devise. Why? Christ's kingdom has lasted longer and will last longer than any of them; and Christ's kingdom challenges every human political kingdom. In the end it is the conscience of them all. It demands every kingdom be true to its own principles, and again and again they all fail. The kingdom of God is the undoing of the powers of this age.

THE GRAND EXIT

Where is the "triumph" in the Triumphal Entry? Do the armies come? Is the Roman kingdom overthrown? Do the Romans flee? Where is the triumph? John's intention in this passage is dripping with beautiful irony. The triumph of the story is actually not in the grand entry but in the grand exit. By coming the way He did with palms and shouts, Jesus fulfills the prophecy of the coming King and Messiah; but then He goes way beyond them. He presents Himself officially as the head of state, knowing that the leaders of that state want Him killed. But He is a better politician than anyone else here—better than Pilate, better than the Jewish leaders—because He forces the issue at the Passover, right at the critical time when a lamb is going to be offered as the sacrifice for the sins of God's people.

Jesus enters on a donkey, and He exits the city as the Lamb of God. He enters on a donkey to say that all of their thinking about this kingdom is inadequate, but then He exits the city as the One who is the focal point of all of the promises of all of Scripture, of all of the kingdom hopes as the One who would die for the sins of His people. He comes in His own time, one He controls, precisely at the time when the Passover lamb is going to be sacrificed. He enters Jerusalem as a King, knowing that five days later He will exit Jerusalem, carrying His cross, as the Lamb of Sacrifice. The exclamation when He leaves the city is a metaphorical, "Christ, our Passover, has been sacrificed for us!" And then the real Hallelujah begins.

Jesus comes to Jerusalem as a King to offer Himself to death as the Lamb of God. The only princely anointing that He gets is the perfume that Mary has poured on His feet. The only crown He receives is the crown of thorns stuck maliciously onto His brow. The only cloak He gets is the castaway of some soldier that is used to mock Him. He is the King who has absolute authority over the torture that He is given moment by moment. He is the King who has precise authority over every act of maliciousness that the people of Jerusalem perform on His body. Earlier Jesus has said, "I lay down My life that I may take it again. No one has taken it away from Me, but I lay it down on My own initiative. I have authority to lay it down, and I have authority to take it up again" (John 10:17-18).

He is the King with all authority in heaven and earth. Not one bit of His authority was ever taken from Him. But how did He use that authority? He used it to give up all of the power and prerogatives that were His by right, and to become a bleeding sacrifice for our sins. He is the King who is the eternal Lamb of God, who never loses control.

There is a wonderful rhythm to this. Jesus enters the city as a King; He exits the city as a Lamb; and then He leaves the world as the King of glory, going back to His Father's throne. He is given that throne of all glory and honor because of His perfect obedience as the Lamb of God.

What are your expectations of Jesus? What do you want out of Him? Do you want Him to fix your marriage? Good, He might just do that. But the only way He will fix your marriage is if you submit your marriage to Him. Do you want Him to bless you financially because you are in deep difficulty? Well, He might or might not do that, because He has larger ends in mind for your life. You cannot manipulate this King of glory. You cannot make Him do what you want Him to do any more than you could make Him the King or the Lamb.

All of us must face the reality of shattered expectations even as the writer, John, himself did. The beloved disciple, the one who was the closest friend of Jesus, who had seen Jesus suffer, die, rise again, and ascend to heaven, later had a vision that knocked him off his feet. It was totally unexpected: "[I saw] one like a son of man, clothed in a robe reaching to the feet, and girded across His breast with a golden girdle. And His head and His hair were white like white wool, like snow; and His eyes were like a flame of fire; and His feet were like burnished bronze, when it has been caused to glow in a furnace, and His voice was like the sound of many waters. And in His right hand He held seven stars; and out of His mouth came a sharp two-edged sword; and His face was like the sun shining in its strength. And when I saw Him, I fell at His feet as a dead man" (Rev. 1:13-17). John, who knew Him, who loved Him, who leaned his head upon His breast, sees a vision of the exalted King, and he cannot take it in. He falls at the feet of the Lord as a dead man.

Is that not the appropriate response for every one of us who would be confronted with a vision of the glory and power and honor of the King of kings and the Lord of lords? Do we not then need the Lord to say to us what He says to John: "Do not be afraid; I am the first and the last . . . and I have the keys of death and of Hades" (Rev. 1:17-18)?

You will come to honor and revere Christ as King only when you first honor and revere Him as the Lamb slain for you. Otherwise His kingship will scare you to death, and there will be no recovery from that death. But if you know Him as the Lamb of God, then He will, just as He does for John, reach down and pull you to your feet and say, "Don't be afraid. I have conquered death and hell for you. I am the eternal Lamb of God, and I have given My lifeblood for you. Now, come and honor Me as the King, who became the Lamb, who again became the King, and who reigns forevermore."

25

THE HOUR OF GLORY

Now there were certain Greeks among those who were going up to worship at the feast; these therefore came to Philip, who was from Bethsaida of Galilee, and began to ask him, saying, "Sir, we wish to see Jesus." Philip came and told Andrew; Andrew and Philip came, and they told Jesus. And Jesus answered them, saying, "The hour has come for the Son of Man to be glorified. Truly, truly, I say to you, unless a grain of wheat falls into the earth and dies, it remains by itself alone; but if it dies, it bears much fruit. He who loves his life loses it; and he who hates his life in this world shall keep it to life eternal. If anyone serves Me, let him follow Me; and where I am, there shall My servant also be; if anyone serves Me, the Father will honor him. Now My soul has become troubled; and what shall I say, 'Father, save Me from this hour'? But for this purpose I came to this hour. Father, glorify Thy name." There came therefore a voice out of heaven: "I have both glorified it, and will glorify it again" (John 12:20-28).

DURING A TRIP TO CHINA a few years ago, the group with which I was traveling met with ten pastors who, by virtue of their gifts and God's providence, had risen to places of responsibility in the underground church of China. Among them they represented 20 million Chinese Christians. These dear people were all in prison within a year of our meeting with them.

Where is Jesus? Jesus is at the right hand of God; Jesus is in our hearts; and Jesus is in a dirty prison on the outskirts of Beijing on any given Sunday, leading His people in worship.

This particular passage is one that we might have a tendency to read over quickly and then move beyond. It seems to be a transition from the very significant events we have been examining to Jesus' final discourses beginning in chapter 13. This little passage is caught in between and is easy to miss altogether. But we must not miss it. It is an important hinge, because in it we learn a lot about China, and about the deepest concerns and motivations of our own hearts.

John 12:20 tells us the Jews were going up to Jerusalem at Passover time, and "going up" was quite literal. The Sea of Galilee is 680 feet below sea level. Jerusalem is seventeen miles away from the Sea of Galilee and 2,500 feet above sea level. One climbs rapidly to go from the sea to the city; but figuratively speaking as well, there is another sense of "going up" to Jerusalem. We might say today that someone is going up to Washington to be a congressman. The psalmist says Jerusalem is where the tribes go up to praise the name of the Lord (Ps. 122:4).

THE GREEKS COME

There are others who are going up to Jerusalem—not just Israelites, but also Gentiles, non-Jewish people who were generally Greek, from all over the Roman Empire. They are going for the Passover festivities. These people were possibly attracted to the Jewish religion by its monotheism. That was very attractive to these Greeks, who had a panoply of gods who didn't seem to help them out very much. They were attracted to the One God of Israel and were called "God-fearers."

In China today there is quite a movement of what is called "culture Christians"—not "cultural" Christians, the way we might use the term today. These intellectuals realize the intellectual, moral, and spiritual bankruptcy of modern China, and that fifty years of communism has done nothing to improve that country. They see the value of the Christian faith in its capacity to shape culture, its ability to give a culture coherence and meaning. They don't personally believe in Jesus Christ, but they believe in Christianity, and they are very motivated to see it affect the nation in which they live.

Perhaps they are similar to these Greeks who were coming up to Jerusalem. They have heard about Jesus, and they approach Philip the disciple, perhaps because he has a Greek name, and they say, "We wish to see Jesus." That is interesting. They could see Jesus just by standing on the street corner. Obviously they don't want just to *see* Jesus but to *talk to* Him as well. They want to have an interaction with Him. Maybe they want to invite Him to preach to them or to teach them. Most likely they realize that their own system of religion is bankrupt, and they are looking for alternatives. "We wish to see Jesus," they say. The term *wish* is very interesting. It means "earnestly desire." They *really* want to talk to Him.

Philip seems unsure of what to do. He has blown it once before. You remember at the feeding of the five thousand, when Jesus tests His disciples by asking, "How are we going to feed this many?" Philip responds, "Well, two hundred denarii wouldn't be enough to feed this crowd" (see John 6:7). Then, of course, Jesus feeds them anyway. Philip had missed the mark on that question. He doesn't want to blow it again, so he goes to Andrew, the levelheaded, resourceful disciple. Andrew was the one who took the little bag of lunch to Jesus, which Jesus then used to feed the crowd. Andrew was one of those of whom Jesus said, "You will be fishers of men" (see Matt. 4:19). He was always bringing people to Jesus. He brought Peter to Jesus.

Jesus' answer to the Greeks' request seems totally unrelated to the question: "And Jesus answered them, saying, 'The hour has come for the Son of Man to be glorified'" (John 12:23). That answer doesn't make any sense to us until we begin to pick the phrase apart. "Hour" in the Gospel of John is always a reference to the Cross. Remember at the wedding in Cana, Jesus tells His mother, "My hour has not yet come" (2:4). Or later in chapter 7, as His enemies are seeking to seize Him, Jesus says essentially the same thing: "My time is not yet at hand" (7:6). But now He says, "The hour has come." And in 13:1 we find, "Now before the Feast of the Passover, Jesus knowing that His hour had come that He should depart out of this world . . ."

THE HOUR COMES

Here in this passage is the hinge of history. The hour is upon Jesus, but now He calls it the "hour of glory." Now is the hour for the Son of Man to be glorified. How could *glory* mean "the Cross"? If the *hour* is the *hour of glory*, how could it be possible that the *glory hour* is something that Jesus thinks of as a time of triumph? We think of glory as fame. You get your fifteen minutes in the spotlight. But for God, *glory* is literally "weight."

The word for *glory* in the Hebrew language of the Old Testament is *kābôd*, meaning "weight" or "heaviness." The glory of God is weighty.

It is substantial. The glory of God is solid and heavy—something that will last forever. It is the weightiness of His being, of His nature. Most of all, in terms of us, the glory of God is His weighty presence with us.

In the Old Testament, God's presence was in the tabernacle and temple. That is where God's glory was shown. In the New Testament, the glory of God is in His Son. The glory of God is demonstrated in the Old Testament in a place of sacrifice—in the tabernacle or in the temple. In the New Testament the glory of God is shown in the place of sacrifice, namely, the body of Christ. The body of Christ is the heaviest thing in the world. The cross of Christ is the weightiest thing that a human being can ever know.

The glory of Christ is shown in His loneliness as He lived out His life before men, among them but apart from them. Most of all it is shown in His death for His people on the cross, a place known for its shame. Only the worst of criminals would be hung on a cross. Only the despicable enemies of the empire would die this horrible death, but we understand that the death of Christ on the cross manifests His weight, the presence of His glory.

When Judas sneaks out to betray Jesus, Jesus says, "Now is the Son of Man glorified, and God is glorified in Him" (John 13:31).

The Cross is the hour of the fullest expression of Christ's glory. It is, as D. A. Carson puts it, "the supreme manifestation of Jesus' glory. . . . It is not just that the shame of the Cross is inevitably followed by the glory of the exaltation, but that the glory is already fully displayed in the shame."[1]

Jesus is glorified because He refuses to seek His own glory. He Himself said elsewhere that if you seek for your reward the approval of men and you get it, then you have your reward (Matt. 6:2-5). Jesus seeks His reward, His glory by pursuing what pleases His Father, and this subordination of the Son to the Father culminates in the spectacular act of self-sacrifice on the cross.

THE WORLD COMES

When Philip and Andrew told Jesus, "There are Greeks here who want to see You" (see John 12:20-22), Jesus responded in a way that was surprising to them: "The hour has come for the Son of Man to be glorified"

(v. 23). But what was mysterious to them was very clear to Jesus, because He understood that the Greeks represented this truth: not only was the Cross coming to Christ, but the world was coming to Christ. The Greeks represented all those who were not Jewish. Jesus saw in this very moment the fulfillment of the prophesy of Isaiah: "I will also make You a light to the nations so that My salvation may reach to the end of the earth." (Isa. 49:6).

Interestingly, Caiaphas, the high priest, says in the previous chapter that Jesus was actually the One who "was going to die for the nation, and not for the nation only, but that He might also gather together into one the children of God who are scattered abroad" (John 11:51-52). Caiaphas, of all people, unwittingly gave this prophecy.

In 12:19 the Pharisees are frustrated about Jesus and His continuing ministry. Exasperated, they say, "Look, the world has gone after Him." And Jesus Himself has said, "I have other sheep, which are not of this fold; I must bring them also" (10:16).

Where was the Cross in relation to the city of Jerusalem? Outside the city. Why? To demonstrate that the glory of the Cross was intended to extend to all the earth. The light that will come out of Christ's death is not just for Jewish people; it is also for the world of non-Jewish people.

THE SEED MUST DIE

Many churches have a "missions moment" during the worship service when a missionary will speak or a community outreach will be featured; but in Jesus' thinking, the "missions moment" is the time between His cross and the time when His feet, once nailed to that cross, will touch down again on this earth. Missions is really an era during which God's plan continues. Jesus knows that the Greeks' coming is a sign that the great ingathering of the new people of God is about to take place. It will be necessary for a seed to die so that a great oak tree might rise over earth and give shade and life and salvation to many.

Jesus offers an agricultural analogy in John 12:24: "Truly, truly, I say to you, unless a grain of wheat falls into the earth and dies, it remains by itself alone; but if it dies, it bears much fruit." The husk that surrounds the seed must die and fall off in order for the seed to sprout the shoot; and when the seed sprouts its shoot, the seed itself dies. The seed is the source of life, becoming a new shaft of wheat, but it must give up its life to do so. Jesus is to die so that the life of God might sprout out of Jewish provincialism and go to the world. Do you remember what God told Abraham? "In your seed all the nations of the earth shall be blessed" (Gen. 22:18). And as Paul points out in Galatians 3:16, the word "seed' is singular. Jesus is the true seed of God who must die in order that new life for a world of Greek people can sprout out of Him.

LOSING AND SAVING

Powerfully and amazingly, Jesus applies this truth to us: "He who loves his life loses it; and he who hates his life in this world shall keep it to life eternal" (John 12:25). *Hate* is a relative term indicating a level of priority. You must love something else ahead of your own life. It doesn't mean you hate yourself; it means you love something else first. If you hold onto your own life first, it is like taking a fistful of wet sand from the beach, squeezing it, and trying to hold onto it. What happens? It oozes out of the crevices between your fingers.

Do you know how hunters trap monkeys in Africa? They place a banana in a wide-bottomed, narrow-necked jar that is tied to a tree. The monkey sees the banana and sticks his hand in the jar. He grabs the banana and then tries to pull it out. But he can't get it out because his fist won't pass through the narrow neck of the jar. That monkey wants that banana so much that he will not let it go. He will hold onto it until the trappers come and take him away to the zoo. That is what Jesus says we are like when we hold onto our life and do not expend it for Him and for better realities than our own comfort, enjoyment, and pleasure. In the memorable words of Jim Elliot, martyred missionary to the Auca Indians of South America, "He is no fool who gives up what he cannot keep to gain what he cannot lose." We are not foolish if we give up what we will never get to keep anyway. We will not get to keep our life and all of our "stuff" anyway. Let's give it up, to gain what we can never lose—the glory of God and the promise that He is about bigger and better things in our lives.

The words *lose* and *destroy* are the same in Greek. So when Jesus says, "He who loves his life, loses it," He also suggests that, "He who loves His life, destroys it." When you hold onto your life, you end up destroying it. You end up betraying the very thing that you want, the very happiness you hope to have.

Verse 26 defines losing our life in terms of serving Christ. "If anyone serves Me, let him follow Me; and where I am, there shall My servant also be; if anyone serves Me, the Father will honor him." Where is Christ? Where do you follow Him? He has not left us in doubt, because in other parts of the Gospel accounts He clearly tells us He is where there are hungry people, particularly brothers and sisters in Christ. He is where there are lonely people or strangers. He is where there is a brother without adequate clothing. He is where there is a sister who is in the hospital. He is where there are prisoners in jail cells (Matt. 25:34-36).

The Lord said we are to be the salt of the earth. Then why do we just keep salting the salt? We are to spread out. We must follow Christ both individually and corporately as a church to where He is showing His splendor and His glory to some Greek somewhere—maybe in China, maybe in post-Christian France, in Muslim Egypt, or in the glass and steel towers of a big American city. If we begin to think about the Greeks of the world, we will inevitably think less of our own pleasure and more about the glory of God and the Cross.

One summer, between years at college, I went back to my hometown, and I found a remarkable thing going on—a revival. The gospel was spreading like wildfire through that community, and it did so for about five years. Guess who was at the forefront of this revival: eighth-grade girls who had decided that instead of getting up at six o'clock in the morning and spending an hour putting on makeup, they would get together at the junior high school and pray. They didn't just pray for their friends; they didn't just pray for their school; they prayed for their whole community. They prayed that the gospel of the Cross would run like fire through town, and God honored their prayers.

There is a wonderful story in *Let the Nations Be Glad!* by John Piper. He tells of a man in Haiti named Edmund. The church there was having a Thanksgiving festival, and each Christian in the church was invited to bring a love offering. When they opened one particular envelope, they found thirteen dollars in it. The people counting the offering were just stunned because thirteen dollars was three months of wages in Haiti. They were dumbfounded. Who gave this large sum? Recognizing

Edmund's handwriting on the envelope, but knowing he hadn't seen Edmund in church, the pastor went to see him. He asked, "Edmund, why didn't you come to church today for the big celebration of all these gifts being given?" Edmund replied, "I had no shirt to wear." He had literally sold his shirt (as well as his horse!) to be able to give this gift.[2]

To you who are older: do you find the word *retirement* in the Bible? It isn't there. Oh, there are changes of occupations, but ultimately Christian people just develop and move from one opportunity to another to serve the Lord. My father in the faith and friend Edmund Clowney, whom I mentioned in chapter 19, is well into his eighties, and in the last year he has moved to Charlottesville, Virginia, to assist in the teaching ministry of Trinity Presbyterian Church, which I had the privilege of pastoring from 1976 until 1992.

Joel Williams, a real friend (and surrogate grandfather to our children), is a member of our church in Dallas. He has been retired for many years now but he recently said to me with deep conviction, "I now know what everything I've done in my life up to this point is for. I now know that what I want to do with the rest of my life is to serve the Lord in this church."

Another close friend in Dallas, Bud Smith, was quite successful in business. He is now "retired." He has helped many Christian ministries with his time, energy, and resources because it is how he gives his life away to the kingdom.

Let me tell you about a man who is younger. He is very successful. He has started, operated, and sold more businesses than I can count. And now he says to me with a little glint in his eye and a smile on his face, "Hey, Skip, what am I going to do now?" And then he says, "What are *we* going to do, Skip? Come on, the world is waiting, Skip. Come on, how do we turn this church into a real engine to serve the world?"

There is the story of a man named John G. Paton, an older Christian gentleman, who decided in his second or third retirement to go as a missionary to the South Sea islands. A friend who was about his age warned him, "You will be eaten by cannibals," to which Mr. Patton replied, "You are advanced in years now, and your own prospect is soon to be laid in the grave, there to be eaten by worms; I confess to you, that if I can but live and die serving and honoring the Lord Jesus, it will make no difference to me whether I am eaten by Cannibals or worms; and in

the Great Day my resurrection body will arise as fair as yours in the likeness of our risen Redeemer." John Piper, who gives us this particular
illustration, adds, "When the world sees millions of 'retired' Christians
pouring out the last drops of their lives with joy for the sake of
unreached peoples and with a view toward heaven, then the supremacy
of God will shine. He does not shine as brightly in the posh, leisure-
soaked luxury condos on the outer rings of our cities."[3]

Another friend caught me one day and said, "You are performing
a wedding Saturday night, aren't you, Skip?"

I said, "Yes."

He said, "You better be ready. There are going to be lots of people
there who don't know The Story."

His friends who don't know the story were on his heart. What is on
your heart? Is it your glory, your comfort, your life, your time? Or is it
the glory of Christ in the Cross?

Are you retired? Perhaps you should start using those "advantage
miles" that you have been saving up all these years. Perhaps you should
reconsider the way you are spending all that money you made in the
stock market in the 90s. You may want to consider where the glory of
God is shining brightly in this world. And you just might want to seek
it out.

26

A LONG OBEDIENCE IN THE
SAME DIRECTION[1]

"Now My soul has become troubled; and what shall I say, 'Father, save Me from this hour'? But for this purpose I came to this hour. Father, glorify Thy name." There came therefore a voice out of heaven: "I have both glorified it, and will glorify it again." The multitude therefore, who stood by and heard it, were saying that it had thundered; others were saying, "An angel has spoken to Him." Jesus answered and said, "This voice has not come for My sake, but for your sakes. Now judgment is upon this world; now the ruler of this world shall be cast out. And I, if I be lifted up from the earth, will draw all men to Myself." But He was saying this to indicate the kind of death by which He was to die. The multitude therefore answered Him, "We have heard out of the Law that the Christ is to remain forever; and how can You say, 'The Son of Man must be lifted up'? Who is this Son of Man?" Jesus therefore said to them, "For a little while longer the light is among you. Walk while you have the light, that darkness may not overtake you; he who walks in the darkness does not know where he goes. While you have the light, believe in the light, in order that you may become sons of light." These things Jesus spoke, and He departed and hid Himself from them (John 12:27-36).

WHEN MY SON CHRIS was two years old, he was just learning the difference between obedience and disobedience. One area of "learning" involved his climbing on a chair and from the chair onto the kitchen table. A second, and by far the most serious, was throwing everything—the cup, the bowl, the spoon—to the floor from his high chair when he had decided he was finished with his meal.

This was a matter of authority: who was in charge? It was a test not only of my son's obedience but of my fathering. Finally there came a moment of real crisis. I have since called it the "Nag's Head Standoff," because it took place in Nag's Head, North Carolina, on the Outer Banks, where we've gone every summer for twenty years for a family vacation. In the beach house where we were staying, my son had just thrown everything off the high chair again. I was determined that he was not going to get out of that high chair until he said, "I'm sorry." We wasted a perfectly beautiful beach afternoon as we sat for *three hours* in that kitchen while Dad waited for the magic words.

Now Chris has gotten older and the stakes have gotten higher. The issue of obedience is still a dramatic watershed issue in his life and in mine. Time and time again, not only for my children but also for me, there are moments when we say, "I am either going to obey, or I am not."

Though the word *obedience* does not appear in it, John 12:27-36 is really all about the obedience of another Son. But there is a vast difference between the obedience of my Christopher and the obedience of the Christ for whom he was named. Jesus Christ never once disobeyed His Father.

THE COST OF JESUS' OBEDIENCE

Obedience for Jesus is always pointing toward His Passion. The issue is whether or not He will be obedient even to the end; and the cost of obedience for Jesus is remarkable. The Gospels describe this cost in different ways. We remember His emotional agony in the Garden of Gethsemane, where drops of blood mingled with sweat on His brow indicate His anxiety at the prospect of what is ahead.

In John 12 there is the honest statement that His soul has become troubled. Jesus asks almost rhetorically, "What shall I say, 'Father, save me from this hour?'" (v. 27). The question reflects Jesus' human nature understandably shrinking from death. On the one hand, what He wouldn't have given if God had said, "Yes, I'll save You from this hour. Full stop on the plan of eternity. I've changed My mind. We are going to do it a different way, My Son." In his troubled state, it is fair to say that Jesus would have welcomed a reprieve.

We want to say, "Well, He was the Son of God. He knew this was the plan and He had to do it." Yes, but we are dealing with the mystery of the person of Jesus: that though He was God, He was fully man. The divine nature of the person of Jesus cannot cancel out the human nature. He was fully God, but He was also fully man. In His humanity He suf-

fered as any of us would suffer at the prospect of the kind of death that
awaited Him. You say, "Oh, He knew what would become of it. He
knew He would hang on the cross for so many hours, that He would be
dead for about seventy-two hours, and that He would rise again." But
His knowing all this in His divinity did not negate the genuine suffering
He experienced.

This is a mystery. There were creeds and councils in the ancient
church that worked this out with great difficulty. The Nicene Creed says
that Jesus was truly man, through and through. His humanity was not
like a Halloween costume with His deity underneath. He was at one and
the same time in His earthly being both God and man. In the fullness of
His humanity, He experienced the complete and full agony of One who
had to suffer. He was one hundred percent God, but He was one hundred percent man. Many people try to minimize Jesus' suffering by saying that it couldn't have been as bad as ours would be, due to His deity.
But that is a denial of an incredibly important truth that Christians
affirm when they say that He was truly man. Nothing compromised His
humanity, so His obedience was very, very costly.

THE CONSEQUENCES OF HIS OBEDIENCE

One of the first results of Christ's obedience was that the Father was glorified. When Jesus says, "'Father, glorify Thy name,' There came therefore a voice out of heaven: 'I have both glorified it, and will glorify it
again'" (John 12:28). The obedience of Jesus Christ glorifies the Father
because it vindicates His name. God had promised that He was going
to redeem humanity when He said He would send the seed of the
woman who would crush the head of the serpent (Gen. 3:15). In order
for God to be glorified, that promise had to be fulfilled, and Jesus Christ
is the fulfillment. God is glorified by Jesus' obedience because Jesus' obedience makes good the promises of God. God cares about the vindica-
tion of His name.

Another consequence of Christ's obedience is that the world is judged
by it. "Now judgment is upon this world; now the ruler of this world shall
be cast out" (John 12:31). The world will condemn itself by its treatment
of the Son. "He who believes in Him is not judged; he who does not believe
has been judged already, because he has not believed in the name of the

only begotten Son of God" (3:18). Unbelief brings judgment. If we do not see the Cross as being for us, then we do not have its benefits; the work of Christ does not avail for us. That is judgment indeed. There is much in the Gospel of John about God's judgment; for instance, "He who rejects Me, and does not receive My sayings, has one who judges him; the word I spoke is what will judge him at the last day" (12:48).

Many people are offended by the idea that God is a Judge. How can a God of love be a God of judgment? But if there is no Judge, then ultimately there can be no definition of right or wrong in the world. In any courtroom in this country, the judge's bench is always raised up. It is always above eye-level, in order to demonstrate that the judgment seat is *above us,* that we are *under* the law and subject to its judgment. Imagine a trial with no judge on the bench. Imagine going into the courtroom of life and there is no Judge. Would that really make us happy? If there is no Judge, there is no basis for saying what is right and wrong or that life really matters—that the good we do, the people we are, the things we strive for make any difference.

But there is a Judge, and there are two principles by which judgment takes place: first, the judgment of God focuses on our hearts; and secondly, the judgment of God is based on our knowledge of the truth.

JUDGMENT FOCUSES ON THE HEART

In John 12, Jesus is dialoguing with the religious leaders as we read, "Nevertheless many even of the rulers believed in Him, but because of the Pharisees they were not confessing Him, lest they should be put out of the synagogue; for they loved the approval of men rather than the approval of God" (vv. 42-43). These rulers are "semi-believers." These are people who obey the Ten Commandments—not perfectly, but fairly well. They pray regularly, come to synagogue, do the right thing, seek to be kind to people. But something is wrong. All of their outward obedience doesn't count because of what is going on in their hearts. Jesus says to them, "You do the right thing but for the wrong reason. You are prideful. You want the approval of men."

Doesn't that sound like us, if we are honest? Why do we smile at certain people? Why do we pat them on the back? I am not saying there is no such thing as genuine friendliness; but we spend a lot of time "buttering people up" just because we want their approval. Jesus says people are not judged on the basis of outward performance but on the content of their hearts. These leaders knew God's attitude on this from their Old Testament Scriptures: "For man looks at the outward appearance, but the LORD looks at the heart" (1 Sam. 16:7).

But what about all the places in the New Testament that seem to say that God will judge on the basis of what we do? For example, Romans 2:6 says God will render to every man according to his works. Jesus says in John 5:28-29, ". . . an hour is coming, in which all who are in the tombs shall hear His voice, and shall come forth; those who did the good deeds to a resurrection of life, those who committed the evil deeds to a resurrection of judgment." That sounds a lot like judgment based on works.

We can resolve this dilemma by use of a metaphor, one that the Lord Jesus Himself gives us in Matthew 7. Teaching about trees and fruit, He says, "You will know them by their fruits" (v. 16). Jesus was talking about good fruit versus bad fruit, but it is also true that we judge whether or not a fruit tree is alive based on whether or not we see any fruit at all coming from it. Fruit is produced from a heart that is alive. If we do not have a live tree, we cannot have live fruit.

Our house in Virginia sat on a beautiful wooded lot. The previous owners of our house had planted about ten apple and pear trees along the back of the property. Every June, I would see the fruit coming out on the trees, and by the end of July it was just begging to be picked. But one summer I saw there were no leaves and no fruit on one of the trees. What conclusion did I draw? The tree was dead. It was incapable of bearing fruit, and if our hearts are dead, they are incapable of bearing fruit.

What if I had decided to fix that tree by taking some apples from the good trees and stapling them on the bad tree? Then I could say, "How nice. Now all the trees are bearing fruit." That is actually what many try to do who seek to perform well and do the nice, right, sweet Christian thing, but do so out of a heart that is really dead.

Does the fruit *cause* the life of the tree? Of course not, but the fruit is an *indicator* of the life that is there. So Jesus says we will be judged on the basis of whether or not we fed the poor, clothed the naked, visited the prisoner, or ministered to the sick, because these outward actions reveal the inward condition of our hearts. A self-centered, self-righteous heart cannot produce the works of true obedience; but a heart that has been changed by the Lord will be demonstrated by the fruit it produces.

Remember the story of the prodigal son in Luke 15? There are two sons. One is disobedient and leaves home. One stays home and obeys. You would think, based on everything I have said, that the one who would be rewarded would be the one who obeys. But he isn't, because his obedience is dead obedience coming out of a dead heart. When the other son truly repents and returns to the Lord, he produces fruit—the fruit of repentance, fruit of a heart that has really changed, fruit of a new life. But the elder brother, who stays home, who is really like the Pharisees, does the right things for the wrong reasons. To look at him is to look at a dead apple tree with live apples stapled onto it.

JUDGMENT FOCUSES ON KNOWLEDGE

God judges on the basis of our hearts, but He also judges on the basis of what we know. Jesus says, "He who rejects Me, and does not receive My sayings, has one who judges him; the word I spoke is what will judge him at the last day" (John 12:48). Many other times in the Gospel of John it is clear that the Son is a Judge, but He says here that the instrumentality of His judgment is His Word. We will be judged on the basis of what we know, on the words that we have heard. We have all been asked about the plight of people in remote places who have never heard the name of Jesus Christ. Upon what basis will they be judged? Paul says very simply in Romans 2 that they will be judged only according to what they know, not according to what they don't know. What do the unreached peoples of the world know? And what do *you* know? Paul says that every person knows there is God (Rom. 1:18-19), so we will be judged at least on that basis.

Maybe all someone knows is the Golden Rule: Do unto others as you want them to do unto you (Matt. 7:12). That person will be judged on the basis of what he or she knows. The question is, Have we done what we know? What we know will rise up on the last day of judgment and say to us, "You knew Me, but you didn't do Me." That is the basis of judgment.

Francis Schaeffer once said that it is as if at the moment of birth everyone is given an invisible portable tape recorder that is hung around his or her neck. It is voice activated by only the wearer's voice, and only a word of moral judgment about other people activates it. So, for example, when someone says, "Can you believe what she said? . . ." the tape recorder begins recording. When I say, "I can't believe the memo this guy sent me. This is the sloppiest thing I've ever seen in my life . . ." the tape recorder goes on. Schaeffer says, "On the day of judgment God doesn't say a word. He simply pushes the play button on the tape recorder, and I am judged by my own words."

Are we terrified yet? Isn't it terrifying to know that judgment is going to be on the basis of what is in our hearts instead of on outward behavior? Isn't it terrifying to know that the instrumentality of the judgment is our own words?

Isn't it amazing to know that Jesus Christ, who never spoke a moral judgment from a wicked or self-righteous heart, and whose words and life were pure, steps in between you and God at the very moment that the Lord reaches down and pushes the play button? He takes the tape recorder off of your neck and He puts it around His own, and He receives the judgment that you deserve. That is the gospel.

The King of kings and the Lord of lords, who was perfect from all eternity, who Himself designed the world with all of the moral principles that make it work, is the One who takes upon Himself all the moral wickedness of His people. And it crushes Him, and He dies for them.

THE OTHER HALF OF THE GOSPEL

Is your obedience to the Lord important? Yes. But much more important than your obedience to the Lord is His obedience to the Father. Not only did Jesus die for you, He lived for you. The perfect life that Jesus Christ lived is given to you as you trust in Him, so that when God the Father looks at you, He sees the perfect righteousness of His Son. The theological term for this is *imputation;* Christ's righteousness is imputed to you. When God the Father flicks on the tape recorder, He hears the words of His loving Son that He has heard from all eternity: "Father, accept them in My name, in My place." Our obedience means nothing if the Son of God was not perfectly obedient, receiving upon Himself the judgment He didn't deserve out of that perfect obedience in order to give us the merits of His perfect life before God His Father.

Why did Jesus die? Most Christians, whether old or new to the faith, would say, "He died for my sins." True. But here is the real question: Why did Jesus live? Christians give a variety of answers to that question. One answer might be, "He lived to show me how to live, to be an example I could imitate." That is true enough. Another answer would be, "He came to teach very important things for me to know." That is true as well. Another answer might be, "He lived as a man so that He could die as a man." It is true that He could die only if He had lived, and since it is centrally important that Jesus died, it is therefore necessary that He lived.

Some people would say that Jesus was born to die. But that statement by itself is misleading. It tends to relegate His life to second place, making His life a means to an end. But the witness of God's Word is that the life of Christ is as important as His death. Jesus died the death that we could not die, but He also lived a life that we could not live. We talk about Christ's substitutionary death, but it is also true that He substituted His life for our lives.

By Christ's death, God forgives our sins; but it is also true that by Christ's life, God gives us an altogether new life, a new righteousness. This is what you might call the other half of the gospel. It is Christ's righteousness, an alien or foreign righteousness that is not intrinsic to us but is from Jesus Christ's perfect life. Jesus gives us the merit of both His death and His life.

When Barbara and I were married, we chose for our call to worship a passage from Isaiah 61: "I will rejoice greatly in the LORD, My soul will exult in my God; for He has clothed me with garments of salvation, He has wrapped me with a robe of righteousness, as a bridegroom decks himself with a garland, and as a bride adorns herself with her jewels" (v. 10). If you are married, you probably gave a lot of time and attention to your clothing on your wedding day. You didn't throw on the first thing you found in your closet and head off to the church. This passage from Isaiah tells us that it is God who has taken the trouble with our dress. He has clothed us well for the wedding day of our marriage to His Son as our great Bridegroom. He has adorned us in the clothes of His Son's own perfectly earned righteousness.

Where do we get those good clothes? We can't rent them from a tuxedo service or buy them at a bridal shop. We get them by faith, by believing, by trusting Christ, that His life as well as His death was for us. "For as through the one man's disobedience the many were made sinners, even so through the obedience of the One the many will be made righteous" (Rom. 5:19). Jesus is what we are not. We are like Adam; we have disobeyed, and by our disobedience we have earned ill-fitting, dirty clothes. But Jesus is the perfect One, the only man who has ever been perfectly obedient to His Father; and His Father credits Him with perfect goodness. Then by faith we receive that perfect goodness from Jesus. That is the other half of the gospel—why Jesus lived as well as died.

The early church fathers and the councils went to great trouble to define the nature of Christ's humanity in relation to His deity, in order that our salvation may be whole. If we don't understand Christ's humanity, we don't have His life; and if we don't understand His divinity, we don't have the merit of His death.

TEMPTED LIKE US

Of all the places where the New Testament speaks of our receiving the benefits of Christ's life, perhaps the most poignant is Hebrews 4, which deals with, of all things, temptation. Every one of us is tempted; sometimes it seems that we are tempted constantly. "Since then we have a great high priest who has passed through the heavens, Jesus the Son of God, let us hold fast our confession" (v. 14). Jesus is the High Priest who prays for us right now in heaven. "For we do not have a high priest who cannot sympathize with our weaknesses, but One who has been tempted in all things as we are, yet without sin. Let us therefore draw near with confidence to the throne of grace, that we may receive mercy and may find grace to help in time of need" (vv. 15-16).

Jesus Christ, in the fullness of His humanity, has been tempted with every temptation that is common to mankind. Think of the most despicable temptation you have ever had, one that you are utterly ashamed of. Do you believe that Jesus Christ experienced that temptation, yet without sin? If you don't believe that, then you don't understand His full humanity. In the fullness of His humanity He experienced every temptation we have experienced.

The important distinction is, "Yet without sin." Martin Luther reportedly said of temptation, "I cannot keep sparrows from flying about my head, but I can keep them from making a nest in my hair." The temptations that Jesus experienced were the birds that were circling, but He didn't let them nest in His hair like we do. That is an important difference.

The sin that we experience in conjunction with temptation comes out of our fallen nature. Jesus didn't experience that, but He did experience the temptation. You say, "Wait a minute. Whatever Jesus experienced must have been different than what I have experienced because He was the Son of God."

Who experiences that unrelenting, unremitting full weight and anguish of a temptation that gnaws at you, begs at you, claws at you unremittingly? Who experiences it fully and completely to the very end? The one who doesn't give in to it! The minute you give in to a temptation, it goes away. You have satisfied the temptation. That is what we all have done from time to time and in many ways. Jesus never acted on the temptation, so He, and only He, experienced the full, unremitting weight of that temptation.

Never let go of the truth that Jesus was completely human. The early church battled over this for a couple of hundred years in order to get it straight. A lot of people in those days wanted to cancel out Jesus' humanity and keep His divinity. They wanted to say He wasn't fully human, but the early church fathers came to understand that Jesus lost nothing of His deity in order to assume all of His humanity.

When Paul says that Jesus emptied Himself (Philippians 2) when He became a man, it doesn't mean He emptied Himself of His divinity. He emptied Himself of the "perks" and the prerogatives of His divinity. He emptied Himself of its splendor. He was like the royal son who disavows all of the king's wealth but doesn't cease for one second to be the king's son.

Whatever Jesus experienced in and by His obedience, particularly in the midst of temptations, was not *just* what we experience. It is actually *more*, worse than what we experience. We must always say that His humanity is never qualified nor negated by His deity, and His deity is never qualified nor negated by His humanity. He faced the full difficulty of obedience like no human being ever has done before, because He never gave in.

When we think about obedience, the first thing we think of is not

Jesus' obedience, is it? We think of ours, or of our child's. Naturally, we think of ourselves, and we think about our own temptations and our own struggles and failures. Our conscience tells us again and again that we have not been obedient. We know that Romans 5:19 is true: "For as through the one man's disobedience the many were made sinners, even so through the obedience of the One the many will be made righteous." We know that we are the "sons [and daughters] of disobedience," as Paul describes in Ephesians 2:2.

We all fail like Adam failed, yet the promise is that we can somehow succeed in the test of obedience. The critical thing is how. This is where many Christians get off the track and lose the way in their growth in Christ. They begin to take the Avis approach to obedience: "I need to try harder." Others try the Nike approach to obedience: "Just do it." But moralistic obedience isn't ever going to work. We try hard and then we fail. We try a little harder and then succumb. We work a little, pray, and then fail again because we haven't understood the relationship between Christ's active obedience and our ability to be obedient. That is the critical connection we need to make.

OUR NEW IDENTITY

Christ's obedience gives me my righteousness. It provides me the standing of being absolutely righteous in God's sight, so that when God looks at me He doesn't see my sin; He sees the righteousness of His own beloved Son.

I have a new identity. I am to begin to understand myself not as Skip, the sinner, but as Skip, the one who has received the righteousness of Christ. As I grow as a Christian, as I really begin to understand this new identity, I no longer think of myself as a person who is automatically going to fail at every turn. I no longer see myself as a sinner. Oh, I am a sinner, and I do fail, but my primary identity has shifted. I have been given a new nametag that says, "Righteous one, made righteousness by the righteousness of Christ." That is my deepest and truest identity. Now I grow up into my identity.

The New Testament basis of behavior and morals is this: *Become who you are.* You have been given a brand-new identity in the righteousness of Christ; now live that way. Another approach is to call it the indicative-imperative method of living. The indicative is the statement of who you are. The imperative is the command that flows out of your new identity. The New Testament never says, "Go be good." It says go and live in a good and kind way that is in keeping with the identity that you have been given.

I received a new identity in 1992: I became a Texan. Do you know what? After several years, I am becoming proud of that fact. I am beginning to think like a Texan. I'm beginning to feel like a Texan. I have been given an altogether new identity and now I am gradually growing up into living that identity.

The apostle Paul says this in Ephesians 4 and 5 and many other places. All throughout the New Testament there is the indicative-imperative: become who you are. For example: "That, in reference to your former manner of life, you lay aside the old self, which is being corrupted in accordance with the lusts of deceit, and that you be renewed in the spirit of your mind, and put on the new self, which in the likeness of God has been created in righteousness and holiness of the truth. Therefore, laying aside falsehood, speak truth, each one of you, with his neighbor, for we are members of one another" (Eph. 4:22-25). We have been given an honorable, righteous identity, so we speak the truth.

Later, Paul says, "And be kind to one another, tenderhearted, forgiving each other" (v. 32a). That is the imperative; where is the indicative? "Just as God in Christ also has forgiven you" (v. 32b). Our identity is those who are forgiven; so we go and forgive.

Paul goes on to say, "Therefore be imitators of God, as beloved children; and walk in love, just as Christ also loved you, and gave Himself up for us, an offering and a sacrifice to God as a fragrant aroma" (5:1-2). Our identity is those who have been loved sacrificially; so we go and love others sacrificially. As we gradually realize that God reckons us as having the perfection of His Son, our wills are changed so that we want to do what God wants us to do. Then the Lord has won the victory. He has captured our hearts, and when this happens, the devil gets scared. There is nothing the devil fears more than our desires changing so that we want to be the people the Lord has made us to be.

The Screwtape Letters, by C. S. Lewis, is a series of letters written by an older devil, Screwtape, to a junior devil named Wormwood, containing advice about how to trip up us humans. One of the letters says this: "Do not be deceived, Wormwood. Our cause is never more in danger than when a human, no longer desiring, but still intending, to do our Enemy's [God's] will, looks round upon a universe from which every trace of Him seems to have vanished, and asks why he has been forsaken, and still obeys."[2] When the going gets tough, yet a human being still says, "I know I have a new identity and I am going to live in the midst of it," watch out, devil, because your cause is really in danger.

THE COSTLY WEIGHT OF OBEDIENCE

There is a big difference between the obedience of grunting and the obedience of grinning. What is described by Lewis, and certainly in Scripture, is not a moralistic obedience. It is rather the new obedience that grows out of understanding the indicative and imperative of the gospel: "I just can't believe that Jesus died for me. He did *what* for me? I can't believe that. Oh, Lord, it is too good to be true. It makes me want to be a different person."

Gospel or evangelical obedience is not primarily *imitating* the obedience of Christ but *standing* in it, realizing that we are dressed in the obedience of Christ, the merit that Christ's obedience won.

R. A. Torrey, a great preacher who was also an avid mountain climber, reportedly told this story. While climbing in the Swiss mountains, he looked over to another peak not far away and saw a group of five climbers roped together, making their way up the mountain. Then a hideous and awful thing happened. All of a sudden, the last man in the group, number five down below, lost his footing. He fell and hurtled down into space, and because all the men were bound together, the fourth man was jerked off the incline when the fifth man's weight caught him, and he went down, too. Then the third one went, and then the second one. The first man, the leader and strongest in the group, saw all of this happening. He dug his pickax in with all his might and held on. Torrey saw the sickening sight of the man's body snap when the weight of all four of the other men hit him. Torrey found out later that the man's ribs had been crushed and he was bleeding severely from his sides, but somehow he had held on. As a result, the next man down was able to gradually get his footing. And then number three was able to get his footing. And then number four and five. And they all survived.

Jesus experiences the full weight of the cost of obedience. It snaps His body. But He stands firm, even when we do not. His obedience allows us to gain our footing. He goes the distance. He receives in His own body the awful cost of obedience, but He stands firm, and He is able to give the merit of His obedient life to all who stand in Him, all who believe in Him. Have you embraced this benefit of God with a believing heart? Have you displayed the obedience of faith, which is trusting in Christ to do in His life as well as in His death what you could never do for yourself?

Make no mistake. We have slipped off the mountain, we are careening down, we are falling to our deaths, but Jesus holds His ground, and only if we are tethered to Him will we not fall to our eternal deaths. We are saved not just by Christ's death but by His life, by His perfectly obedient life. "For if while we were enemies, we were reconciled to God through the death of His Son, much more, having been reconciled, we shall be saved by His life" (Rom. 5:10).

From his deathbed, the last words of J. Gresham Machen, founder of Westminster Theological Seminary, were these: "Thank God for the active obedience of Jesus Christ." You would think he might have said, "Thank God that Jesus died for my sins," which would be true enough. I'm sure he was thankful for that. Or, "Thank God that He gave me faith to believe and trust in Him." He could have said that. But he didn't say those things. Christ's active obedience to the point of death is our hope, our life, our future. Because of it we can stand before the Father, clothed in the merit of Christ's perfect obedience as if we had been obedient ourselves.

In John 19:23-24 we read, "The soldiers therefore, when they had crucified Jesus, took His outer garments and made four parts, a part to every soldier and also the tunic; now the tunic was seamless, woven in one piece. They said therefore to one another, 'Let us not tear it, but cast lots for it, to decide whose it shall be'; that the Scripture might be fulfilled, 'They divided My outer garments among them, and for My clothing they cast lots.'" Christ was stripped of His garments so that we might be clothed with His righteousness. He was naked. When you and I were with Adam in the garden after the Fall, we were naked and we were ashamed. God clothed us with animal skins, which were the precursor of the sacrifice by which we would be clothed with the righteousness of His Son.

When Jesus hung naked on the cross, He wasn't ashamed. Oh, He was suffering greatly because of His obedience, but He knew that His nakedness meant that you and I would be clothed in His righteousness.

Take the clothing and put it on, and walk about in it for the rest of eternity.

PART IV

*The Ministry of the Son of God
to His Disciples*

27

THE ORDER OF THE TOWEL

Now before the Feast of the Passover, Jesus knowing that His hour had come that He should depart out of this world to the Father, having loved His own who were in the world, He loved them to the end. And during supper, the devil having already put into the heart of Judas Iscariot, the son of Simon, to betray Him, Jesus, knowing that the Father had given all things into His hands, and that He had come forth from God, and was going back to God, rose from supper, and laid aside His garments; and taking a towel, He girded Himself about. Then He poured water into the basin, and began to wash the disciples' feet and to wipe them with the towel with which He was girded. And so He came to Simon Peter. He said to Him, "Lord, do You wash my feet?" Jesus answered and said to him, "What I do you do not realize now, but you shall understand hereafter." Peter said to Him, "Never shall You wash my feet!" Jesus answered him, "If I do not wash you, you have no part with Me." Simon Peter said to Him, "Lord, not my feet only, but also my hands and my head." Jesus said to him, "He who has bathed needs only to wash his feet, but is completely clean; and you are clean, but not all of you." For He knew the one who was betraying Him; for this reason He said, "Not all of you are clean." And so when He had washed their feet, and taken His garments, and reclined at the table again, He said to them, "Do you know what I have done to you? You call Me Teacher and Lord; and you are right, for so I am. If I then, the Lord and the Teacher, washed your feet, you also ought to wash one another's feet. For I gave you an example that you also should do as I did to you. Truly, truly, I say to you, a slave is not greater than his master, neither is one who is sent greater than the one who sent him. If you know these things, you are blessed if you do them" (John 13:1-17).

A FEW YEARS AGO, Barbara and I went to the high school graduation of a young man we knew quite well. We felt proud of Jonathan, having watched him grow up into a fine young man. In fact, he gave the valedictorian speech that night, and we had the privilege of hearing him give what I felt to be one of the most well-crafted addresses I had ever heard.

The reason I tell you this is that Steve, his dad, a good friend of mine, said right before the commencement began, "One of the neat things that happened in the last couple of weeks is that my son asked for my help with this speech." I saw a father brimming with pride as his son spoke. But the pride wasn't that he had helped with the speech; the pride was in his son, and the joy was in the result. I saw on this father's face his delight to be his son's servant.

Many of us, of course, would say that it would be our delight to serve our children if they asked us. But the further out from the centers of our lives we go, this idea of learning how to serve and care for one another gets a bit harder.

John 13:1-17 is a marvelous and familiar passage. Jesus teaches quite dramatically about how we are to serve one another. He portrays what He means and bids us to follow His example. That's what Steve did when he coached his son behind the scenes, in effect saying, "Follow my example. Do it as I might do it. But *you* do it."

Some churches have taken this example of Jesus' servanthood so literally that they have raised footwashing virtually to the level of a sacrament as they hold services where people wash one another's feet. While footwashing is not a sacrament, it is certainly not wrong to do. The danger is that some people might feel they are discharging their duty in obeying the Lord by that actual physical act of footwashing. But what does the Lord bid us do in this passage? What does it mean to open our lives to other people? What does it mean to go beyond the confines of our own concerns and begin to serve one another?

THE CULTURAL CUSTOM OF FOOTWASHING

The example itself centers around the cultural custom of having one's feet washed by a servant upon arrival at a place where there was going to be a meal served, in a home or in a public gathering place. Walking, of course, was the most common form of transportation. The streets were dusty, so guests for a meal would arrive with dirty feet in need of washing. Most Jews would no more think of sitting down to dinner without having their feet washed than you or I would consider working in the garden all day and sitting down to eat before washing our hands.

In Old Testament times, hospitality was much more of a require-ment incumbent upon people, so hosts would be expected to provide a servant who would wash guests' feet in the same way as we offer guests the opportunity to freshen up before sitting down to a meal. In private homes in that day, there would be a servant placed at the door with a basin of water at his side and a towel in his hand to rinse and dry each guest's feet. The lowliest servant of the house would be given this task.

We have noted previously that Jews who were servants to other Jews would never be expected to wash feet. Only Gentile slaves would have to do it. It is remarkable when John the Baptist says he is not fit to untie the thong of Jesus' sandal. He is saying he would gladly touch Jesus' feet, gladly undo the thong of His sandal, but feels unworthy to do even that. Remember how shocked everyone was when Mary of Bethany anointed, touched, and caressed Jesus' feet? It is clear that Peter, James, John, and the other disciples do not have John the Baptist's or Mary of Bethany's insight or devotion.

The disciples arrive at rented quarters for a meal. Rented quarters meant there was no servant there to wash feet. Maybe they were having a discussion as they arrived, as they did when they argued about which one of them was the greatest (Luke 22). Perhaps, as James and John did in Mark 10, they were asking Jesus if they could sit on His right hand and left hand in glory. The disciples want to be in the spotlight—the antithesis of the servant who would wash feet.

As they arrive, there stands the basin and the towel by the door, and there is this awkward moment as the disciples undoubtedly maneuver for position as far away from the basin and towel as possible. Peter was probably thinking, *Let Bartholomew do it.* Or maybe Bartholomew was thinking, *Oh, John hasn't carried his weight lately; he ought to do it.* Judas, whose self-serving led him to an ultimate act of betrayal for a few pieces of silver, is also present. So the setting may have been one of self-exaltation, posturing, and positioning of oneself.

As I think about this text, I am amazed at how I camouflage these impulses to exalt myself in my own heart and life. I have learned how to do it, because I am a good Christian guy. But even among Christians we sometimes see this maneuvering for position. We want the "glory spots." We want to be known for our goodness or our good deeds.

THE "EXAMPLE" OF JESUS

Everyone sits down, ignoring both custom and their own dirty feet. Then one of them rises. Jesus lays aside His garments, takes the towel, and girds Himself about with it. Then He pours water into the basin and begins to wash the disciples' feet and wipe them with the towel. This is, of course, the remarkable example of our Lord's servanthood.

But the most remarkable aspect of this story is what Jesus knows as He begins the footwashing. He knows, for instance, that the hour for His own departure has come, and that the Cross is imminent (John 13:1). Jesus also knows that He loves His disciples. The second part of verse 1 says, "Having loved His own who were in the world, He loved them to the end." He loves them despite their self-seeking and attempts to glorify themselves.

In the Gospel of John the word *love* appears six times in the first twelve chapters, and in chapters 13–17 it appears thirty-one times. These chapters contain the last conversation that Jesus has with His disciples, and He cannot help but express again and again His love for them. "He loved them to the end." That means not just to the end of His earthly life but to the end of His earthly strength. He was willing to be utterly used up out of love for His disciples.

Jesus also knows that the Father has given Him all things, that He has come forth from God, and that He is going back to God (see John 13:3). He knows the Father has given Him authority over everything in heaven and earth. He knows that He is the eternal Son of God. He knows what Paul later describes in Ephesians 1:20-22, that He will soon be sitting far above all rule and authority and power and dominion and every name that is named. Or, as Paul said in Colossians 1:16-18, He knows He is the Creator of all things and is before all things and that in Him all things hold together.

At the very moment that Jesus is washing the disciples' feet, He is holding together the molecules of the water in the basin and the bodies of His vainglorious disciples. The King of kings and Lord of lords rises from supper, lays aside His garments, takes a towel, girds Himself, and washes feet.

Imagine it. The supper has been served, and the feet are still dirty. Jesus stands up and proceeds to take His outer clothes off. Don't miss the detail. When He takes His outer clothes off He is laying aside His glory as the Son of God. It reminds us of the Christmas carol line, "Mild he lays his glory by."[1] Jesus takes off His glory like it was a coat and throws it aside. In fact, Jesus becomes practically naked. He strips down to a loincloth. This is the Son of God, the King who has the right to wear the royal robes that the Father has given Him from all eternity.

Don't miss this. It is the Incarnation. When God becomes a man, He lays His glory by to take up the towel of cleansing, then girds Himself with the towel. The towel was long enough for Him to wrap it around Himself, tie it in a knot, and wipe feet with the ends. Let's not run too quickly beyond that word *gird*. It is not a word we hear often these days, but it is a rich biblical idea with quite a pedigree.

Girding denotes that an important action is to follow. For example, in the Old Testament Aaron girds himself with special garments when he enters the holy place of the tabernacle (Lev. 16:4, NASB). When a person was going on an important journey, he would be girded, that is, he would arrange his clothing in the most convenient way for travel. When a soldier was going to war, he would gird on his sword, as it says in Psalms 45:3, a prophecy of Christ Himself: "Gird Thy sword on Thy thigh, O Mighty One, in Thy splendor and Thy majesty!" When one was preparing to warn someone of a fault or a sin or bad news, he would gird himself, perhaps with sackcloth (see, e.g., 2 Sam. 3:31; Jer. 4:8). When preparing to eat the Passover meal, the book of Exodus says that the people should gird themselves to eat (Ex. 12:11).

Jesus is girding Himself for a very important action. He is not girding Himself with the elaborate garments of a priest, though a priestly sacrifice is about to be made (Jesus' sacrifice of Himself). He is not girding Himself for war, though the greatest warfare ever against sin and Satan is about to take place at the Cross and empty tomb. He is not girding Himself to mourn, though agony and grief lie just ahead. He is not girding Himself to eat the Passover meal. No, He *is* the Passover meal, the Passover Lamb.

Jesus is girding Himself for the cleansing of His disciples from the deep, indelible stain of sin on their hearts.

PETER'S RESPONSE

The disciples sit in stupefied silence as Jesus begins to wash their feet. And then He comes to Peter. "Lord, do you wash my feet?" says Peter. "Never shall You wash my feet!" (John 13:6, 8). The original language is an emphatic double negative. Peter was a man of "nevers," wasn't he? "I will *never* deny You" (see Matt. 26:35). And at Christ's prediction at the Cross, he says, "This shall *never* happen to You" (Matt. 16:22).

Perhaps, with Peter, we need to learn to humble ourselves before God. But while that is important, it is not really the main message here. The main issue in this passage is that God humbles Himself before us. In God's humility, our pretensions are silenced. Our religious posturing is seen for what it is. What do you think the disciples talk about as they watch, disbelieving, as the Lord of glory stands up, takes off His garments, kneels down, and begins to wash their feet? Do you think they start talking with one another about how great they are?

They are silenced.

We want to say, "Lord, I will humble myself before You; but don't *You* humble Yourself before *me*. To understand the implications of that costs me too much. I can't take it."

But the Lord makes it clear that if we do not see Him humbling Himself to cleanse us, then we cannot know Him. He says, "If I do not wash you, you have no part with me" (John 13:8). If we do not allow ourselves to be washed by Jesus Christ, which is to say, if we do not understand that the Lord of glory comes to cleanse us from the inside out, then we do not have any part in His inheritance.

Peter then responds as we would expect, with wholehearted renunciation of his previous refusal: "Lord, not my feet only, but my head, my hands—every part of me" (see v. 9). This is the right response.

What is *our* response to the cleansing power of Jesus Christ in our lives? Is it to say, "Yes, Lord, I just have a little sin today. I need just a little dab there." No, the right response is to take a "gospel bath." It is to recognize that we need to be overwhelmed by the wonder of the gospel. "Oh, Lord, not just my feet: my head, my hands, every part of me." It is to recognize that sin has us in its grip so deeply that we need to take a gospel bath every day, that we need to have our hearts cleansed again and again.

A RULE OF GOSPEL-CENTERED LIVING

Some scholars say this passage means that, having been cleansed once thoroughly and completely, we have need only to come day by day and ask for forgiveness. That seems to be what the Lord suggests in verse 10: "He who has bathed needs only to wash his feet, but is completely clean; and you are clean, but not all of you." If we have confessed our sins, put our faith in Christ, and know ourselves to be new creatures in Him, then we don't need to come and confess our faith in Christ day after day, though it is true that we do need to come each day to confess the sins of that day. But having said that, we need to remind ourselves every day of the wonder of what Jesus did for us. If there are not at least seasons of renewal in our lives where we find ourselves in wonder at what He did for us on the cross, then we need to take a daily gospel bath all the more.

The normal Christian experience is typified by periods in our lives when we confess our sins day by day in a fairly mechanical way. But those normal periods should be punctuated by extraordinary periods of repentance—times and seasons when the Lord again brings the gospel to our hearts by Word and Spirit. He reminds us of how much we need Him to gird Himself and cleanse us, and of how much awe that should strike in us. Out of that wonder comes a new season of repenting, believing, and gospel faithfulness.

I would imagine that when Jesus sat down after washing those feet, He did not say much at all for a while. The statement had been made with an eloquence that could not be surpassed.

Jonathan Edwards, the great philosopher, theologian, writer, and pastor of the 1700s, and one of my heroes, tells a story in his memoirs about riding on a horse for exercise and recreation in the woods of Massachusetts, as he would often do. He says that there sometimes came a point on these rides when he would realize how much Jesus had done for him, how much his heart had been cleansed, but how much dirt was still there. Then he would take another gospel bath, he reported, "which continued . . . about an hour; which kept me the greater part of the time in a flood of tears, and weeping aloud."[2]

We modern Americans don't know much about the preciousness of the cleansing work of our Savior. We want to leave that in the past.

"Jesus died for me, and I'm going to heaven. Now let me get on with my Christian life."

"But before you get on with your Christian life," Jesus says, "today you need to remember again what I did for you."

When were you saved? You weren't saved five years ago, or ten years ago, or twenty years ago at camp or at Sunday school. You were saved at Passover in A.D. 33 on a hill outside of Jerusalem, and you need to live there every day. Only then can you live in the present. Only then can any of us begin to obey what the Lord tells us to do: "Truly, truly, I say to you, a slave is not greater than his master; neither is one who is sent greater than the one who sent him" (John 13:16).

If we follow Jesus' footwashing example, three results will become apparent:

First, we will see ourselves as sent on a mission. Jesus says, "As I was sent, so you are sent" (see 13:14-16; cf. 20:21). There will be a quality of "sentness" about our lives. Being a missionary doesn't always mean that we go on mission trips, although some people do. It may mean we are sent to the hospital to care for a friend who is lonely. We are sent next door with a pot of soup when someone is sick. We are sent to care for one another as the Lord has cared for us, as the Lord gave up His rights. We think we have the right to our own happiness, but if we are sent, perhaps we are to do more than nap or watch the game on TV on a Sunday afternoon. We have been commissioned, initiated into the fraternity of the water basin, the order of the towel.

The *second* thing we will know is that our service will ultimately cost us nothing less than it cost Jesus, which is everything. We play games here. We want to follow Christ, but we want to take the part of the example that we want and leave the rest aside. Dietrich Bonhoeffer said, "When Christ calls a man, He bids him come and die."[3] I am convinced that the most subtle temptation of our lives is not this or that obvious or gross thing but the desire to be normal. Jesus calls us to lives that are not normal. It is not the normal life of having rights, of doing what we want to do, of building up our own prosperity, of being the person we want to be.

The *third* result of following Jesus' example is that we are blessed. He says in verse 17, "If you know these things, you are blessed if you do them." We know the Lord's companionship in the order of the towel.

When you have done something for someone and they thank you, can you say, "It was my pleasure," and mean it? "For the joy set before Him [Jesus] endured the cross," we are told in Hebrews 12:2. When we thank Jesus for dying for us, He says, "It was My pleasure," which doesn't mean that He didn't suffer or that there wasn't pain, but that there was a greater pleasure. When you are washed by Christ and then go out after Him, imitating Him, isn't it your joy to do it? You are not building up "brownie points" for yourself before God or man. You don't even care about that. When we follow Christ's example, we don't get normal; we get Him. He blesses us. His presence is our joy.

Do you want to be normal, or do you want to have Christ? Every follower of Christ should have one situation in his or her life where he or she is ridiculously, absurdly, irrationally giving himself or herself away. Have you ever been to the hospital in the middle of the night wearing your pajama top because you got a call that a friend needed you? Have you ever done anything like my dear friend who, when a neighbor down the street was dying of cancer, went to his home every night the month before he died to lift him into bed? Have you ever cared for special needs children in your congregation so those children's moms and dads can have an hour of worship—as eighteen people do at our church Sunday by Sunday?

No, you don't want to be normal. You want to take a gospel bath. And then out of that gospel cleansing you want to find a way to give away your life, don't you? Don't be normal. Be a Christian.

28

A PLACE PREPARED

"Little children, I am with you a little while longer. You shall seek Me; and as I said to the Jews, I now say to you also, 'Where I am going, you cannot come.' A new commandment I give to you, that you love one another, even as I have loved you, that you also love one another. By this all men will know that you are My disciples, if you have love for one another." Simon Peter said to Him, "Lord, where are You going?" Jesus answered, "Where I go, you cannot follow Me now; but you shall follow later." Peter said to Him, "Lord, why can I not follow You right now? I will lay down my life for You." Jesus answered, "Will you lay down your life for Me? Truly, truly, I say to you, a cock shall not crow, until you deny Me three times" (John 13:33-38).

"Let not your heart be troubled; believe in God, believe also in Me. In My Father's house are many dwelling places; if it were not so, I would have told you; for I go to prepare a place for you. And if I go and prepare a place for you, I will come again, and receive you to Myself; that where I am, there you may be also. And you know the way where I am going." Thomas said to Him, "Lord, we do not know where You are going, how do we know the way?" Jesus said to him, "I am the way, and the truth, and the life; no one comes to the Father, but through Me" (14:1-6).

IN 1986, I HAD THE unique experience of being on loan from the church I served in Virginia to the U.S. Department of State in their South African Working Group, a special project that pulled together people from all parts of the government as well as outside the government to focus on a particular problem: South Africa. For six months I worked in Washington, visited South Africa and, together with a number of other people, sought solutions to the difficult and problematical situations in that country at that time.

One time our group went to the White House for a briefing. We met in the Roosevelt Room, a conference room immediately across the hall from the Oval Office. After the meeting, the senior State Department official who was responsible for my appointment to the group marched me right into the Oval Office. President Reagan was not there at the time, but there was still a tremendous presence in that room, an aura to the place where such important conversations and decisions occur.

It was only because I was with my friend that I could go right into the Oval Office. Likewise, some of us assume that we have the right to go right into heaven. There is much hope that we will go in, but it is presumptuous to think that we can go right in, unless we go with a certain Friend.

THE PRESUMPTION OF POSITION

There are actually two forms that this presumption can take. One form is observed in the Jewish leaders of New Testament times. Jesus alludes to this in John 13 when He begins this discussion with His disciples. He says in verse 33, "Little children, I am with you a little while longer. You shall seek Me; and as I said to the Jews, I now say to you also, 'Where I am going, you cannot come.'"

The Jews' response had been, "Where does this man intend to go that we shall not find Him?" (7:35). They are presumptuous, assuming that there is no place that Jesus can go that they can't go. After all, they are Jewish leaders. They are the achievers, the ones who have made it, the kingpins in the social order. Their educational objectives have been met. They are professionals. They presume that they have every right to go to heaven. These leaders assume that their position in life guarantees them a reservation in heaven, just like a prominent person might assume that he can walk into a restaurant that requires reservations months in advance and get any table he wants.

We see the presumption of position more than you might think among Christians.

"I'm a good Christian."

"I go to the right church."

"I serve the Lord."

"Of course, I'll go to heaven!"

This is very dangerous thinking.

THE PRESUMPTION OF PERSONAL ABILITY

The second kind of presumption is seen in Peter in this conversation. It is not the willful presumption of position but the naïve presumption that personal ability will enable him to follow Jesus. Jesus says, "Where I go, you cannot follow Me now; but you shall follow later" (John 13:36).

Peter quickly answers, "Lord, why can't I follow you right now? After all, I am willing to lay my life down for you" (see v. 37).

But Jesus knows what Peter is made of, and He responds with a rhetorical question in verse 38: "Will you lay down your life for Me? I assure you that before the rooster crows, you will deny Me three times."

Peter's good intentions when his stomach is full, the candlelight is burning softly, and the fellowship is sweet will not hold up among the mean-spirited accusers a little later in the garden.

D. A. Carson comments on this passage: "At this point in his pilgrimage, Peter's intentions and self-assessment vastly outstrip his strength."[1] It is one thing to have good intentions; it is another thing to have the personal ability to fulfill them. Peter will learn that he cannot do what he presumes he can do. He actually has no ability *not* to deny Christ. He is hopelessly lost in the presumption of his own ability.

Peter needs to realize that the issue isn't that he, Peter, will lay down his life for the Lord, but rather that the Lord will lay down His life for Peter. Jesus' question silences Peter. He says nothing. In fact, he doesn't say anything for the next five long chapters in John, which, for Peter, is a record! The next time he speaks is outside Pilate's house when a servant girl says, "Aren't you one of those who were with Him?" and Peter answers, "I am not" (see 18:25ff.).

It is humbling for Peter and for us to begin to understand that we need to live in our limitations, not in our strengths. That may sound bizarre to you. You might say, "Wait a minute, Skip. I didn't get where I am today by focusing on my limitations but by focusing on my strengths."

Your strengths will inevitably disappoint you. I promise you that.

I got one of those sappy "Dear Pastor" birthday cards for my last birthday. To make matters worse, it was a card that had the "as you are growing older" line in it. It was all I could do to open it. It even had flowers on the front. Inside I found a prayer presented as coming from a pastor: "Lord, help me to see my life not in terms of my limitations but in terms of my achievements."

I looked at that, and read it again: "Lord, help me to see my life not in terms of my limitations but in terms of my achievements."

I read it four times and said, "That's wrong! Hallmark got it all wrong." I was preparing in my mind the letter that I was going to write.

Anyone who takes the existence of God seriously must learn to live his life in light of his limitations. We are limited and God is not, and we need to learn that our limitations become the doorway to knowing God's grace. It is in the midst of my limitations that I call out to God; and then I begin to know Him.

THE PROMISE OF A PLACE PREPARED

Amazingly, after Jesus questions Peter with a rebuke, He does what the Lord alone would do in this situation. He begins to comfort Peter and the other disciples, who are worried about Jesus saying that He is about to leave them. Jesus says, "Let not your heart be troubled" (John 14:1). He encourages and comforts the disciples as He Himself is facing the most incredible trouble. Jesus has every right to be troubled, but instead He comforts His disciples in their trouble as they grapple with what it means that He is going away. Jesus meets Peter's presumption with the peace of a double promise: one, the promise of a *place prepared* for them; and, two, the promise of a *way provided.*

First, Jesus promises His followers, "In my Father's house are many rooms; if it were not so, I would have told you. I am going there to prepare a place for you" (v. 2, NIV). To understand this promise, we need to understand how Jesus thought about time. For Him, the most important time was the future. It wasn't the past, although He drew upon the whole history of Israel to point to His purpose and His calling. It wasn't the present, though He called upon His followers to love God and obey Him in the present. The pivotal point of history for Jesus Christ is always the future. The eschatological center of Scripture is the future. Everything points to the future. That is where the whole momentum is pushing. "I go to prepare a place [a *future* place] for you. . . . I will come again [*in the future*], and receive you to Myself" (vv. 2-3).

Our hope is anchored not in the past, as much as we cherish the past and know our life in Christ is anchored in the reality of the cross and the empty tomb; our truest hope is yet in the future. Our hope is not in the present, either. The present is here today and gone tomorrow. Real hope is not determined by past or present accomplishments but by the amazing promise of the future. It is a place prepared.

This same promise is ours when we consider the most serious of personal issues in our lives such as the loss of loved ones. If they are in Christ, they are alive with Christ and experiencing what is future to us. They are living in that great promise of the future which belongs to those who know the Lord of the future, the Lord of Sabbath Rest.

Paul puts it this way: "If we have hoped in Christ in this life only, we are of all men most to be pitied" (1 Cor. 15:19). The one who has Christ in his or her life merely because of what He adds to it right now, with no orientation to the future, is to be pitied. It is incomprehensibly pitiable to put one's hope in Christ only for this life, for all the joy and purpose that Christ gives our lives now. It is but the echo backwards of a greater joy that we will one day know. But if we are honest, many of us do measure our lives now in terms of what Jesus, religion, faith, or anything else for that matter, gives us right now. So when it comes to losing loved ones, we have no choice but to measure our loss in terms of the "hereness" and the "nowness" of it.

That we do this is understandable. The ache of longing, the missing, the desperate, unquenchable thirst of the absence of one we love— there are times when it is more than we can bear. So what Jesus says in this passage is very practical, because He is saying that the future is a more certain truth than anything we see now. The future is more certain than the chair you sit on, your physical body in the chair, or the book you are holding right now. This is no platitude. Our departed loved ones are experiencing our future, and while our knowledge of this does not lessen our loss, it does put perspective on it.

When Barbara and I visited Rome several years ago, we found a cemetery right off the Via Veneto in the middle of the city. On a sign at its entrance is a message spoken, as it were, by its inhabitants, that says, "What you are, we used to be. What we are, you will one day be." What is future for us is present for them.

Scripture stretches our imaginations into the future by the use of images—snapshots of heaven. It is like peeping through a keyhole in a doorway; we get just small glimpses of life, light, peace, a wedding feast, the wine of the kingdom, the kingdom to come, a heavenly city—and here, in this passage, the Father's house of many rooms.

The Father's house is heaven, and in heaven there are many rooms. From the perspective of the future, the present will seem so small, so trifling, so inadequate to satisfy our deepest longings. The unqualified truth of the Scripture is that if we base our hope for happiness on what we are achieving or will achieve now, we will surely be disappointed.

When Jesus talks about the future, He talks about a reality that is so far beyond what we can imagine that we cannot take it in. He knows that His disciples are thinking He is promising too much, and that is why He says, "If it were not so I would have told you" (John 14:2). Jesus stakes the extravagant promise of the future on the credibility of His own Word. He is either saying, "Heaven is a magnificent place I am preparing for you," or, the alternative: "I am a liar." We must all pick one of these possibilities or the other.

All of the Bible's images of our future in heaven, including this one, are concrete. We think of heaven as abstract, ghostlike, somehow less real than this existence. But the Bible presents heaven as a place *more* real than this existence, a place where the senses are more attuned, more alive to the taste of the finest wine, the aroma of the feast, the sound of a thousand choirs, the sight of a million angels.

This is the theme of C. S. Lewis's wonderful book *The Great Divorce.*[2] In it Lewis takes us on an imaginary bus trip to heaven with a group of prim and proper English tourists. The minute they get off the bus in heaven for their brief, temporary tour, they appear ghostlike. Lewis describes them as transparent compared to everything else in heaven, which is solid and real. The visitors from London take off their shoes to go walking on the pretty green grass in the park, but the grass is so real and so strong that it hurts their tender, ghostlike feet. He calls the people who dwell in heaven "solid people," and the earthlings are the "ghosts." Lewis is teaching that heaven is more real than earth.

Lewis often talked about inns. He once remarked, "Our Father refreshes us on the journey with some pleasant inns, but will not encourage us to mistake them for home."[3] God gives us beauty beyond our imagining here, but all this beauty is just a foretaste of the greater and more magnificent beauty that awaits us. It is intended to whet our lips, to make us long for that greater beauty.

Sometimes I get up before sunrise and turn on a light and read. After reading awhile I look up and realize the sun has come up. The sunlight is flooding the room, and the light I turned on is now weak and feeble by comparison. I don't need it anymore. There will be a day when all the beauty that we see in this earth will pale by comparison to the beauty that we will see that day. For the Christian, death is turning off the lights because the dawn has come, and the sunlight is fair and bright as it casts its glow upon the most beautiful person we will ever see.

I have perhaps said more than the Bible says about heaven, yet I hope I have been consistent with the Word. The Bible is reluctant to talk about heaven. It speaks in snapshots—no MGM-length movie. There is a reason for that. Paul says, "Things which eye has not seen and ear has not heard, and which have not entered the heart of man, all that God has prepared for those who love Him" (1 Cor. 2:9).

The Promise of a Person Provided

If Jesus and the Scriptures are reticent to say much about heaven, they are not reticent to speak about the way to get there. Not only has a place been provided, so has the way. It is the promise made by Jesus in John 14:6: "I am the way." Jesus has said He is ready to go and prepare a place, and then He'll come again for His followers (vv. 1-3); and then He adds, "You know the way where I am going" (v. 4). The earnest disciple Thomas asks, "Lord, we do not know where you are going, how do we know the way?" (v. 5). And Jesus gives His famous answer: "I am the way, and the truth, and the life" (v. 6).

Truth and *life* are words we are pretty familiar with by now in the Gospel of John. Jesus is the truth because He accurately explains the truth of God to us. He is the life because He has God's life in Himself and He bestows that life to us. "I am the way, and the truth, and the life" includes an element of irony, however, because the One who says He is the way will hang immobile on a cross a few hours after He makes this statement. The One who says He is the truth will see the lies of men enjoying an apparent great victory over Him. The One who says He is the life will have His lifeless body sealed in a tomb.

When Jesus says He is the way, He means two things: 1) He is our pilot; and 2) He is our powerful friend.

Our Pilot

Several years ago, a member of our church who is a commercial pilot called me and asked, "What are you doing at midnight tonight?"

I said, "Hmm. I guess I'll be in bed sleeping."

He said, "No, you won't. Get Chris and one of his buddies. We are going to DFW [the Dallas-Fort Worth airport] to fly a 767."

He took Chris, his friend, Will, and me out to his airline's simulators that are used to train the pilots. After the pilots were all done for the day, we got in the simulator, which recreates the setting of any airport in the world, the precise details of what it is like to approach that airport. Different kinds of weather, wind speed, runway patterns—all the possible conditions are programmed in by computer. The most amazing thing was how well Chris and Will knew, almost by instinct, how to fly. I think that had something to do with years of video games. I, on the other hand, hadn't had that valuable video experience and crashed and burned every time. The toughest part of flying is landing, and only a skilled pilot, after many years of video training, can land a 767 on its wheels, like Chris did repeatedly, instead of on its wings, like I did repeatedly. Landing on the runway at Dallas in fog and wind is tricky business. It is even dangerous.

Landing in heaven is tricky business, and it is also dangerous. Yes, heaven is dangerous if you don't have the right pilot, because it is full of God's glory, His perfection and His holiness. It is full of angels who cry out day and night, "Holy, holy, holy, is the Lord God, the Almighty" (Rev. 4:8). Heaven isn't daffodils and tulips; it is fire and glory, and if you do not have a pilot who can bring you safely in, you will crash and burn in a consuming fire that is God. If Jesus is your pilot, then, the author of Hebrews says, "We have confidence to enter the holy place by the blood of Jesus, by a new and living way which He inaugurated for us through the veil, that is, His flesh, and since we have a great high priest over the house of God, let us draw near with a sincere heart in full assurance of faith, having our hearts sprinkled clean from an evil conscience and our bodies washed with pure water" (Heb. 10:19-22). Jesus has already endured the terror of landing in the midst of the storm of God's just anger against sin. He has already experienced the wind shear of God's wrath that we deserve. And He has passed through the veil into a new and living way which is His flesh, which suffered the terrors of God for us.

Was Jesus successful? That depends on how you measure success. I measure success by making heaven a safe place for me to go. There is no man or woman in the history of the world who could do that except One, One who could render a dangerous place a safe place—full of delight, beauty, and wonder. Heaven is a safe place, because of our very competent Pilot.

Our Powerful Friend

But Jesus is not only our pilot who guides us to heaven; He is also our powerful friend who brings us with Him, right into the heavenly center of the universe. "If I go and prepare a place for you, I will come back and take you to be with me that you also may be where I am" (John 14:3, NIV). Because we are with our powerful friend, we can go with Him anywhere He goes, including the place He has prepared.

This is the great teaching at the heart of the New Testament—the doctrine of our union with Christ. We have been united with Christ in His death and in His resurrection. "For if we have become united with Him in the likeness of His death, certainly we shall be also in the likeness of His resurrection" (Rom. 6:5). Not only did Jesus die and rise again for us, but the massive truth of our union with Christ says that when He died, we died with Him; and when He rose, we rose with Him. He was our representative. Somehow, mysteriously, I was with Jesus when He died and when He rose. His past is my past, and His future is my future. Jesus lives, and so shall I!

When the great Christian scientist Sir Michael Faraday was dying, journalists questioned him about his speculations on life after death. "Speculations!" Faraday cried out, "I know nothing of speculations. I am resting on certainties." Faraday knew that His Redeemer lived, and he would too.

Once an old, dying man was asked what he thought of death. He said, "It matters little to me whether I live or die. If I live, Jesus will be with me. And if I die, I will be with Jesus."

In 1986, I could walk into the Oval Office only because I had a powerful friend. And it will be only because of another powerful Friend that

I will be allowed to enter heaven. When Jesus says, "I am the way," He is not showing us the path we walk but a person we cling to. We do not want to walk the path Jesus walked. It was a path through a garden of terrors to a garbage dump where He hung like a criminal on a cross. The whole point of the gospel is that, if we believe in Jesus, we won't have to walk that way. If we go the way Jesus went, we will not make it.

Our way is not a path; it is a person. We go to Jesus and we go with Jesus. There is no other way.

The question is whether you are on the way, or in the One who *is* the way. If you say, "I am on my way to heaven because _____," and fill in the blank with anything except the name of Jesus Christ, you are not on the way to heaven. And if you were to get there in any other way than through the name of Jesus, you would burn up as you landed. But if you are *in, with, and attached by faith to* the One who says He is the way, then you have a Pilot and a powerful Friend who assures you a landing at the most important airport in the universe—and an entrance into the most important room in all of heaven and earth.

That is why Jesus says, "Believe in God, believe also in Me" (John 14:1). He means "Believe *into*"—believe in such a way that you are attached to Jesus, united to Him, so that where Jesus goes, you go. His death avails for you. His life is given to you. His promise of heaven is yours.

29

THE DISCLOSURE

"If you love Me, you will keep My commandments. And I will ask the Father, and He will give you another Helper, that He may be with you forever; that is the Spirit of truth, whom the world cannot receive, because it does not behold Him or know Him, but you know Him because He abides with you, and will be in you. I will not leave you as orphans; I will come to you. After a little while the world will no longer behold Me, but you will behold Me; because I live, you shall live also. In that day you shall know that I am in My Father, and you in Me, and I in you. He who has My commandments and keeps them, he it is who loves Me; and he who loves Me shall be loved by My Father, and I will love him, and will disclose Myself to him." Judas (not Iscariot) said to Him, "Lord, what then has happened that You are going to disclose Yourself to us, and not to the world?" Jesus answered and said to him, "If anyone loves Me, he will keep My word; and My Father will love him, and We will come to him, and make Our abode with him. He who does not love Me does not keep My words; and the word which you hear is not Mine, but the Father's who sent Me.

"These things I have spoken to you while abiding with you. But the Helper, the Holy Spirit, whom the Father will send in My name, He will teach you all things, and bring to your remembrance all that I said to you. Peace I leave with you; My peace I give to you; not as the world gives, do I give to you. Do not let your heart be troubled, nor let it be fearful" (John 14:15-27).

"But I tell you the truth, it is to your advantage that I go away; for if I do not go away, the Helper [*paraklete*] shall not come to you; but if I go, I will send Him to you. And He, when He comes, will convict the world concerning sin, and righteousness, and judgment; concerning sin, because they do not believe in Me; and concerning righteousness, because I go to the Father, and you no longer behold Me; and concerning judgment, because the ruler of this world has been judged" (16:7-11).

"These things I have spoken to you, that in Me you may have peace. In the world you have tribulation, but take courage; I have overcome the world" (16:33).

AS HE IS ABOUT TO LEAVE His disciples, the Lord promises that He will nevertheless return to disclose Himself to them. The prospect of Jesus' departure obviously causes the disciples to be deeply troubled, and

Jesus wants to reassure them, so He tells them about the Holy Spirit. He wants them to understand that He is going away, but that the third person of the Trinity, who has been hinted at throughout the Old Testament and has been discussed before by Jesus, is about to come to be with them forever.

THE *PARAKLETE* DISCLOSES JESUS

English translations use words such as *Helper* (NASB, ESV) or *Counselor* (NIV) to translate the Greek term Jesus uses in this passage to describe the Holy Spirit, but such words are too weak in the English language to describe Him. *Helper* sounds like an "assistant." The Holy Spirit is *not* Jesus' assistant; He is the third person of the Trinity. He is God. The word *Comforter* (KJV) can also be misleading. Indeed, the Holy Spirit does comfort, but that is not all He does; He does much more than that.

In order to capture the essence of Jesus' teaching about the third person of the Trinity, we've got to use the Greek word from the text—*paraklētos,* or, in English, *paraklete.* That is the name Jesus gives the Holy Spirit. It is made up of two parts: *para* and *kaleō. Para* means "alongside," like parallel lines. *Kaleō* means "to call." So to *parakaleō* someone means "to come alongside, to be with," to, as it were, "be his companion." The verb *kaleō,* "to call" in the Greek language, is used with different prefixes a number of times. One of them is *pros.* If you *proskaleō* someone, you tell him to "come and stand before" you. You summon him to stand there, usually to bawl him out. But if you *parakaleō* someone, you come alongside him to be his friend, to be an encourager, to care for him.

In Luke 15, when the father hosts a banquet for the prodigal son who has returned, the older brother gets upset. The father had never thrown a party for him although he was always a good boy and stayed home and did the right thing. His father does something that a father in the ancient Near East would *never* do—he *parakaleō*'s his older son. He loses face by beseeching his son. He comes alongside him. The son actually *proskaleō*'s his father; he *summons* his father. He stands before his father and rebukes him. But the father moves to his son's side.

When Jesus comes to His people, He has every right to come as a righteous Judge and to *proskaleō* us, to stand before us and summon us to account. But nowhere in the Greek New Testament is that word used of Jesus coming to His people. Instead, the word that is used here and elsewhere is that He comes *alongside* us. He beseeches us. He comes as our friend. He stands together with us.

The term *parakaleō* actually has the overtones of being an "advocate," like an attorney who arrives in a difficult situation and gives legal counsel. That is why the word is sometimes translated from Greek to English as "advocate." But what is the particular kind of advocacy the Holy Spirit provides? The answer is in John 14:21: "[I] will disclose Myself to him." This is the promise Jesus makes His followers about what He will do in a near-future time. He promises that, even though He will not be present with them in the flesh, He will *disclose* Himself to them. And that is a promise that He kept at Pentecost fifty days after His own resurrection, when the Holy Spirit came.

Other roles of the Holy Spirit include that of teacher and reminder of Jesus' words (15:26); and 16:14 says, "He shall glorify Me; for He shall take of Mine, and shall disclose it to you." The Holy Spirit's job is to put a spotlight on Jesus, to glorify Jesus. What is the purpose of spotlights or footlights on a stage? To better reveal what is happening there. Such lights do not call attention to themselves; they are invisible to the audience. The Holy Spirit is like a spotlight shining in our hearts, revealing Jesus or whatever else is there as well. Later in John 16, we learn that the Holy Spirit comes to convict us of sin, of righteousness, and of judgment (vv. 8-11). He convicts us of what is in our hearts that is wrong; but He also reveals what is right there, the One who is right. He discloses Jesus; He glorifies Jesus.

In the Old Testament, this disclosing that glorifies happens in what is called "theophanies." Theophanies in the Old Testament are when Jesus Christ in His preincarnate form appears precisely at times when God wants to speak of His own glory. One of the most notable times this happens is in Exodus 33. Moses is on his face before the Lord and is having a difficult dialogue with Him, because Moses is saying that he cannot lead His people out of Egypt unless the Lord goes with him. The Lord says He will do as Moses asks because He is pleased with him and knows him, and Moses replies, "Show me Thy glory" (Ex. 33:18).

That word *show* is precisely the same word in the Greek version of the Old Testament as the word here in John 14 when Jesus says, "The

Holy Spirit will *disclose* Me in your hearts." Moses is saying, "Disclose Your glory to me." And the Lord responds, "I Myself will make all My goodness pass before you, and will proclaim the name of the LORD before you; and I will be gracious to whom I will be gracious, and will show compassion on whom I will show compassion." But then He adds, "You cannot see My face, for no man can see Me and live!"

So how is Moses going to see God's glory? The Lord goes on to explain, "Behold, there is a place by Me, and you shall stand there on the rock; and it will come about, while My glory is passing by, that I will put you in the cleft of the rock and cover you with My hand until I have passed by. Then I will take My hand away and you shall see My back, but My face shall not be seen" (see Ex. 33:19-23).

"But wait a minute," you say. "I thought God the Father didn't have a body."

He doesn't. Who is it that appears to Moses to reveal the glory of God? It is Jesus Christ, in a preincarnation appearance. When the Father displays His glory to Moses, He shows him a preview of Jesus. Jesus discloses the Father's glory. And when Jesus discloses His own glory here in John, it is the Holy Spirit who shows that glory to us. The Holy Spirit shows us the glory, the perfection, the wonder of who Jesus Christ is. That is His "job."

Jesus Makes His Home with Us

What are the indicators that the Holy Spirit is disclosing Jesus and His glory to us? The first indicator is that Jesus makes His home with us. In John 14:17, Jesus says that the Spirit will abide with us and be in us. *Abide* means "to make a home." Then verse 18 says that the Lord will not leave us as orphans but will come to us. That brings to mind the language of the apostle Paul in Romans 8, where he says that we "have received a Spirit of adoption as sons by which we cry out, 'Abba! Father!'" (Rom. 8:15). The Holy Spirit brings us to our true family by bringing us to the Father and to the Son, who make their home with us.

This is what Jesus promises in John 14:23: "If anyone loves Me, he will keep My Word; and My Father will love him, and We will come to him and make Our abode with him." We become a part of the holy, Trinity family. We call out "Father" for the first time in our lives. We know God not as distant and holy only, but as close and caring as a father.

Because many of us did not come from homes where everything was right—and indeed none of our homes were perfect—there is a yearning within every one of us for a perfect family. That is why we who are parents now are trying to do a better job of it than our parents did. We want to "do a family" right. But there is only one right family in all the universe, one family untainted by the sin of selfishness. That family is God the Father, God the Son, and God the Holy Spirit. And you are adopted into that family when Jesus makes His home in your heart by the Holy Spirit.

There were a lot of orphans in the ancient world, and there are a lot of orphans today in many Third World countries. The Lord promises that we will no longer have the vulnerability, the exposure, the lack of emotional validity in our lives that orphans suffer. We will be drawn into the heart of our Father's love, and it is a perfect love.

The language Jesus Himself uses when He says that He is going to reveal Himself in our hearts is the language of fatherhood. It is the language of family. That is what He chose, and that is what you and I want. "I will not leave you as orphans. . . . He who loves Me shall be loved by My Father. . . . And We will come to him, and make Our abode with him" (vv. 18, 21, 23). Don't you long for that? Don't you want to be a part of a perfect family?

Jesus Makes His Truth Live in Us

There is a second thing that the Holy Spirit does. He comes alongside us and discloses Jesus and His glory so that Jesus makes His truth live in us. Jesus calls the Holy Spirit "the Spirit of truth": "I will ask the Father, and He will give you another Helper [*paraklete*], that He may be with you forever; that is the Spirit of truth, whom the world cannot receive, because it does not behold Him or know Him" (John 14:16-17).

We already know that Jesus speaks the truth and never lies, but the Holy Spirit does more than just speak the truth as opposed to a lie; He gives us invaluable information. And the source of that information is Jesus Himself: "I have many more things to say to you," Jesus says, "but you cannot bear them now. But when He, the Spirit of truth, comes, He

will guide you into all the truth; for He will not speak on His own initiative, but whatever He hears, He will speak; and He will disclose to
you what is to come" (16:12-13).

The Holy Spirit takes the words of Jesus that we now have contained in Scripture and brings them to our remembrance. It is His job to
highlight. We have seen that the Holy Spirit is like a spotlight or a floodlight on a stage, showing Jesus there; He is also like a yellow marker,
marking the words of Jesus, bringing them to our hearts, and remind-
ing us of their truth.

The Spirit's work is *not* to bring us new revelation. When people say
to me, "Well, God told me this morning that . . ." I listen, and if they
say the words of Scripture, the words that Jesus has already said, then I
pay attention. But if they say new words, I say, "Wait a minute. The
Holy Spirit's job isn't to say anything new. He is to remind us of the best
that has ever been spoken, God's own words." It is not just Jesus' own
words, but the whole of Scripture. He teaches us in all of it.

The Holy Spirit is the Spirit of truth who helps us understand the
meaning of what we read or hear. But the Holy Spirit doesn't just give
us words or "factoids" or send an auto-reply e-mail with the message
of the day. No, as the *paraklete,* the One who comes alongside, He gives
us Jesus Himself, the infallible Interpreter of His own words. This is an
amazing promise.

When you open your Bible and pray earnestly, "Lord, show me
Your truth," Jesus doesn't just illumine your mind by flicking on a light
switch in your brain, or in some mechanical way. He illumines your
mind personally. He *comes* to your mind and heart and leads you in your
Bible study. Jesus is the best Bible study leader you will ever have.

Jesus Makes Us Holy

A third mark of the Spirit disclosing Jesus to us is that we begin to care
about our character. Jesus said, "If you love Me, you will keep My commandments. And I will ask the Father, and He will give you another
Helper [*paraklete*], that He may be with you forever" (John 14:15-16).

When the Holy Spirit discloses Jesus in our hearts, we begin to care
in a new way about keeping the Lord's commandments. Before the dis-
closure, we cared about our behavior but not about our character. Like

Willy Loman in *Death of a Salesman,* we cared about our morality due to our fear of the consequences if others found out what we were truly like on the inside.

If there were an overhead projector in your church that flashed upon it every thought you had between the time you got up and the time you arrived at your worship service, I guarantee you wouldn't want anyone to see that projection. I wouldn't want anyone to see mine! I would be ashamed of it. But the question is, Would I be ashamed of it for the wrong reason or for the right reason? Would I care more what others think or would I realize that I live my life *coram Deo,* before the face of God? Would I care most about what *He* thinks?

This is the question I have been asking myself recently in a way I have never asked it before: Do I really care what God thinks about what is going on in my heart, or do I care more about what our congregation thinks? If the answer is that I care more about what the members of our church think, I am living in the fear of man, and the Bible calls the fear of man a snare (Prov. 29:25).

When the Holy Spirit discloses Jesus to us, we become less fearful about others knowing of our sins and shortcomings. They don't have to know all the details, but it is okay if they know that we are not as good as they thought we were. We care about our character and the behavior it produces, not out of fear of others but because it is before God's face that we live our lives.

If I focus too much on my behavior, it may be because I am full of pride. Some people are fearful when they look at their own lives, and they say, "I'm not as bad as that guy!" If we live out of our relative moral accomplishments, if we are prideful about the way we behave or what we do, even for the Lord, in due season the Lord will smash that pride.

He will make us face our worst fears. He will bring us to a place where the fear of man nearly overwhelms us as we dread being found out. If pride is the problem, He will bring us to the place where we see our pride for what it is. He will disclose the gospel in our hearts by bringing Jesus there, and then we will begin to live out of a humility that acknowledges our need for Him.

Finally, we want to keep the Lord's commands out of love. The text says, "If you love Me, you will keep My commandments. And I will ask the Father, and He will give you another Helper . . ." (John 14:15-16a).

Your motives become "gospelized"; they are transformed. Jesus doesn't give a *condition* here; He doesn't say, "If you keep My commandments, if you do the right thing, then God will love you and send the Spirit to you." We already know we can't keep those conditions. It is better to understand verse 15 this way: "If you keep My commandments, it demonstrates a heart change so great that you are beginning to love the Lord more than any other thing." Jesus is describing not a set of conditions but an essential relationship. Jesus' followers will love Him and will keep His commands, and Jesus will send a *paraklete* who will enable Jesus' followers to love Him more and to want more to keep His commands. And so it goes. It is a relationship. When the Holy Spirit begins to disclose Jesus to us, we start to do gospel work in our hearts about fear and pride, and we begin to love Jesus more than our sin, and we begin to be new people.

Make this prayer of A. W. Tozer your own:

> Father, I want to know Thee, but my coward heart fears to give up its toys. I cannot part with them without inward bleeding, and I do not try to hide from Thee the terror of the parting. I come trembling, but I do come. Please root from my heart all those things which I have cherished so long and which have become a very part of my living self, so that Thou mayest enter and dwell there without a rival. Then shalt Thou make the place of Thy feet glorious. Then shall my heart have no need of the sun to shine in it, for Thyself wilt be the light of it, and there shall be no night there. In Jesus' name. Amen.[1]

Herman Dooyeweerd was a Dutch theologian with a tremendous mind who had an ongoing theological dispute with one of my seminary professors, Cornelius Van Til. It was a dispute over a very technical issue that lasted for many years. They wrote letters back and forth and various documents and articles on the subject. When they were both frail, old men, Van Til had one last exchange with Dooyeweerd, explaining once again his position, why he thought he was right and Dooyeweerd was wrong. He ended this last exchange with the words, "Soon we shall meet at Jesus' feet."[2]

Even if we disagree or don't understand one another, the common denominator of our lives is that we are going to meet at the feet of Jesus because we all need the gospel. The Cross is the greatest leveler in the history of the world because it shows us our tremendous need. I have a lot more in common with the most despicable sinner in this world than I do with a saint in heaven, and I need to be honest about that because out of that honesty comes the humility that allows me to appreciate and enjoy all that the Cross means. Need is the nemesis and antidote to pride. Pride says, "I can do it," like the "little engine that could." That story that we all read to our children is great for teaching kids that they can get dressed by themselves and eat their own breakfast; but that is no way to run a life, because you and I are not the little engine or the big engine that could.

Jonathan Edwards said, "Pride is the worst viper in the heart; it is the first sin that ever entered into the universe. . . . and is the most secret, deceitful, and unsearchable in its ways of working. . . . It is ready to mix with every thing."[3] Pride is hard to recognize, subtle as it mixes with all kinds of things, some of which are good, and then it oozes out. We have learned to disguise our pride quite well. We are very sophisticated. We know how to disguise it with syrupy words, with nice smiles, with, "Oh, don't you look nice today," when we are really saying, "I look better than you today." When the Holy Spirit begins to disclose Jesus to us, we gradually stop living out of our accomplishments and start living out of a humility that is honest about how susceptible we are to fear and pride. The work of the Holy Spirit is to make us honest, and that is a great work.

Conviction Experienced

When the Holy Spirit discloses Jesus to us, three important things happen: "But I tell you the truth, it is to your advantage that I go away; for if I do not go away, the Helper shall not come to you; but if I go, I will send Him to you. And He, when He comes, will convict the world concerning sin, and righteousness, and judgment; concerning sin, because they do not believe in Me; and concerning righteousness, because I go to the Father, and you no longer behold Me; and concerning judgment, because the ruler of this world has been judged" (John 16:7-11).

When the Holy Spirit comes, He will convict the world of its sin, its righteousness, and its judgment. Conviction of *sin* is not man-made guilt but the weight of God pressing on our souls so that there is nowhere to hide. Have you ever experienced the conviction of the Holy Spirit that something you have done, said, or been is wrong? You want to say, "Lord, I've done that before and You've never put Your finger on it. Why are You putting Your finger on it now?" The Holy Spirit circles around you. He is tightening the circle of your freedom to operate without Him, and He is putting His finger on something you need to address.

David was a man of great stature, but he was embarrassingly honest about his own sin. When God was dealing with David, David had nowhere to go, and he spoke out. So, for example, he said, "When I kept silent about my sin, my body wasted away through my groaning all day long. For day and night Thy hand was heavy upon me; My vitality was drained away as with the fever heat of summer" (Ps. 32:3-4).

Dallas has some humid days in the summer, but I try to get some exercise anyway by jogging. The air can be like a heavy weight, bogging me down, keeping me from moving. That is what God the Holy Spirit is like when He moves into our hearts to convict of sin. He will not let us go. He will put His finger on something and keep it there until we cry out to Him for mercy.

Secondly, the Holy Spirit convicts the world of its *righteousness*. He teaches us about the kind of righteousness that we cling to out of fear and pride, the kind of righteousness we grab for ourselves to create an image before men and God. The Holy Spirit reveals it to our hearts for the "filthy garment" that it is (Isa. 64:6), and He begins instead to show us the glory and beauty of that only robe of righteousness in which we dare be caught, the perfect righteousness of Jesus Himself (Rom. 5:19).

Third, the Holy Spirit convicts the world of its *judgment*. Jesus has already commanded in John 7 that we stop judging by the way things look and start judging by a deeper standard. Judging by mere appearances is no way to make a right judgment. Apart from Christ, judgment is always going to be based on the wrong things, and therefore it is profoundly wrong and even morally perverse. The Holy Spirit convicts the world of its false basis of judgment. It is false, Jesus says, because the ruler of this world has been judged (16:11). In the triumph of Christ, the false one, the liar, the accuser who wants to hold up to us false standards of judgment has been defeated. Do you evaluate yourself by your appearance? Your wealth? Your standard of living? Your success? The opportunities that you have? The clubs to which you belong? The accuser lies and tells us to see ourselves in this way. Jesus comes to reveal him as the liar.

When the Holy Spirit comes to convict the world of its sin, its righteousness, and its judgment, His work is full of grace. It isn't done out of meanness. He does it because He is full of the love of Jesus. The Holy Spirit's grace-filled work happens so that we can see our sin for what it is, so that we can see our horrible weakness and the inadequacy of our own righteousness. We must note the superficiality of the world's judgment and feel the weight of the judgment of God.

WORLDLY SORROW VS. GODLY SORROW

When the Holy Spirit begins to disclose Jesus to us, He does it out of love, so that we will shift our basis of evaluation of ourselves and others. He radically reorients us so that instead of basing our behavior on what others think, we care more about what God thinks.

When this happens, it produces what the Bible calls godly sorrow. In 2 Corinthians 7:8-11 Paul contrasts godly sorrow to worldly sorrow, which is sorrow for the consequences of our bad behavior, sorrow that comes from fear of what others think or from injured pride.

After David had fallen into the terrible sins of adultery and murder, he penned Psalm 51, where he says, "Against Thee, Thee only I have sinned, O God" (v. 4). I read that and think, *Wait a minute, David, there are a few other people involved here. How about Bathsheba? How about Uriah, her husband, whom you arranged to have killed?* No, using the primary meaning of sin, David sinned against one alone—he sinned against God. That doesn't mean we don't hurt other people with our sin or that we don't need to make amends for the hurts our sin causes to others. But first things first; it is God with whom we must reckon. It is God whom we have grieved, and if we truly have godly sorrow, we care about that. And godly sorrow, Paul says, is good because it leads to repentance, to real change.

Godly sorrow changes the way we read John 14:21: "He who has My commandments and keeps them, he it is who loves Me; and he who loves Me shall be loved by My Father, and I will love him, and will disclose Myself to him." If we truly have come to know godly sorrow, we could read that verse like this: "If you keep My commandments, it demonstrates a change of heart in you. It demonstrates the conviction of the Holy Spirit and the graciousness of the new birth, which together reorder your affections so that now you love the Lord more than other things." Jesus is describing the consequences of a radically reordered relationship with God. Jesus' followers will love Him, and they will keep His commandments, and Jesus will send a *paraklete*, the Holy Spirit, and that will enable Jesus' followers to love Him even more and to keep His commandments even more.

JESUS MAKES HIS PEACE OUR PEACE

"Peace I leave with you; My peace I give to you; not as the world gives, do I give to you. Let not your heart be troubled, nor let it be fearful" (John 14:27). When the Holy Spirit comes alongside, He discloses Jesus, and Jesus says to every storm, "Peace! Be still!" (Mark 4:39, ESV). Only the power of the gospel can bring that peace. Nothing in the world can bring it. Sometimes the storm is caused because we have looked to the world to give us its peace. The world's peace is to believe that we are well thought of or to take pride in our accomplishments or possessions. But a gnawing fear tells us that peace is not really ours. We never have enough acceptance, and we never have enough possessions, if that is the basis of our peace.

When wealthy old John D. Rockefeller was asked, "How much money does it take to make a man happy?" he answered, "Just a little bit more."[4] That is what we all say if we base our peace on our accomplishments or possessions or the way other people think of us. But the gospel tells us that pursuing peace in that way not only doesn't give the peace we want, it is also *sin* to pursue it in that way.

Saint Augustine said, "My sin was this, that I looked for pleasure, beauty, and truth not in Him but in myself and His other creatures, and the search led me instead to pain, confusion, and error."[5] Sometimes our worlds come crashing down not because of our sin but because of circumstances. Tribulations beyond our causing bring storms upon us over which we have absolutely no control. Sometimes in the crashing, the Spirit, amid our fear and pride, whispers to us, "No matter how much you have, it won't be enough. No matter how many people you impress, it will never be enough." Sometimes the Holy Spirit shouts at us, "In Me you may have peace. In the world you have tribulation, but take courage; I have overcome the world" (John 16:33). That verse reminds me of the old spiritual, "Nobody knows the trouble I've seen, nobody knows but Jesus." It is enough to know He knows, and He gives His peace when our world falls apart.

I used the simile of a spotlight or a floodlight to describe the Holy Spirit disclosing Jesus in our hearts. Sometimes we think that it should be like the floodlights in a dark stadium. When the switch is thrown, the lights flood the field. It doesn't happen that way very often. Actually, it is more like the floodlights are on a rheostat. The Lord turns them up gradually and slowly—which is good, because we probably couldn't stand what would go on in our hearts if He turned the searchlight of the Holy Spirit on full blast. Eventually, the light of the Holy Spirit will completely flood the stadium of our hearts, and Jesus will be seen there. Jesus will take up His home there, He will open His Word to us, He will make us holy, and He will give us His peace forever.

30

"THAT THEY MAY ALL BE ONE"

"I do not ask in behalf of these alone, but for those also who believe in Me through their word; that they may all be one; even as Thou, Father, art in Me, and I in Thee, that they also may be in Us; that the world may believe that Thou didst send Me. And the glory which Thou hast given Me I have given to them; that they may be one, just as We are one; I in them, and Thou in Me, that they may be perfected in unity, that the world may know that Thou didst send Me, and didst love them, even as Thou didst love Me. Father, I desire that they also, whom Thou hast given Me, be with Me where I am, in order that they may behold My glory, which Thou hast given Me; for Thou didst love Me before the foundation of the world. O righteous Father, although the world has not known Thee, yet I have known Thee; and these have known that Thou didst send Me; and I have made Thy name known to them, and will make it known; that the love wherewith Thou didst love Me may be in them, and I in them" (John 17:20-26).

SOMETIMES CHRISTIAN FELLOWSHIP in the church isn't all that it is cracked up to be. It can be difficult! If we are honest, sometimes our Christian fellowship looks more like a bad wreck at the Indy 500 than a Sunday school pageant.

There is a little poem that goes this way:

To be with the saints in heaven,
Ah, it will be great glory;
But to be with the saints on earth,
Well, that's another story.

We all recognize a great truth in that little ditty, but our relationships on earth in the body of Christ are supposed to be reflections of what they will one day be, even though we know that is not always true.

In Jesus' prayer to His Father, He is asking that that would in fact be the case, that our relationships with one another would reflect the kind and style of relationships that we will one day have with one another when we are in glory. C. S. Lewis said that if we could see one another right now filled with the glory that we will one day have when we are in heaven, we would be sorely tempted to fall down on our knees and worship one another.[1]

John 17 is the *real* "Lord's Prayer." The one that we call the Lord's Prayer is really the disciples' prayer. Jesus prays His prayer on Thursday night just before He goes into the trials, the scourging, the mocking, and ultimately His death on Good Friday. Just hours before He faces His own death, the Lord Jesus Christ prays for us.

John 17, a wonderful prayer, is divided into three parts: a prayer for Christ's own glory (vv. 1-12); a prayer for the disciples who are with Him at the time (vv. 13-19); and then a prayer for those who will believe in Him through the word of these disciples (vv. 20-26). *We* are those who will "believe . . . through their word" (v. 20).

Jesus is praying for you and for me, which is a remarkable thing in and of itself. Presumably, in addition to praying for you and me and for the specific things that are on our minds and hearts, He is praying for us concerning the things mentioned in these verses. So it behooves us to look at these verses closely and to understand how the Lord Jesus is praying for us *right now.*

Verses 20-26 mention four things that Jesus is praying for us: *first,* that we may be one; *second,* that we might prove the gospel to be true; *third,* that we might behold His glory; and, *fourth,* that we might know His name.

THAT WE MAY BE ONE

Three times in verses 21-23 of John 17, Jesus prays that those who believe in Him may be one. He prays that we may be perfected into a unit, completely knit together.

Verse 21 describes that unity in a specific way: "That they may all be one; even as Thou, Father, art in Me, and I in Thee, that they also may be in Us." It is a most remarkable truth that the measure of our unity in the body of Christ is the unity that exists between God the Father and God the Son.

We are in Christ. Christ is in us. Christ is our representative. When Jesus died, we were united with Him in His death. When Jesus rose, we were united with Him in His resurrection. What Jesus did, we did. In the mystery of God's economy, somehow we were with Jesus when He died and when He rose; His death was our death, His life was our life. And because we were there, each of us individually united to Jesus, we are united with one another. The basis of our Christian unity is not the fact that we happen to be members of the same church or send our kids to the same schools or hang out in the same places and go to the same grocery stores. The basis of our unity is nothing less than the cross of Jesus Christ.

Throughout his letters the apostle Paul wrestles with the question, "How in the world are we ever going to get Jews and Gentiles together with their racial, economic, and worldview differences?" His answer isn't that they *will be* brought together but that they *have already been* brought together by the cross of Jesus Christ. He writes in Ephesians 2: "For He Himself is our peace, who made both groups into one, and broke down the barrier of the dividing wall, by abolishing in His flesh the enmity, which is the Law of commandments contained in ordinances, that in Himself He might make the two into one new man, thus establishing peace, and might reconcile them both in one body to God through the cross" (vv. 14-16).

We are one new race of people. There is a new humanity: Christians. This union is not something that we work at or accomplish ourselves. It is something that God has accomplished and done, and as Christians we are to be characterized as those who live out of the reality of the Cross together.

Jesus is not praying that we will *build* unity with one another. He is describing a state of affairs. We *are made one* by the Cross just as the Father is one with the Son. The measure of our oneness is the oneness God the Father has with God the Son. In a certain way it is correct to say that we don't build unity in the church. Church members may say, "We are going to build unity around here." We don't build unity, but on the other hand, we don't destroy it either. We can't destroy it. It is a given. It is made by the Cross. We can neither build upon the Cross nor undo the Cross. We either operate on the truth of the Cross or we don't, and that is what He is calling us to do in His prayer. We will be those who move in obedience to what has already been accomplished by Jesus for us, that unity that is created and measured by the unity of the Father with the Son.

Here is a thought worth pondering: the doctrine of the Trinity is at stake in the way we relate to one another. That God the Father and God the Son are united into one is demonstrated visibly in the world by the way that *we* relate to one another. The greatest truth of all, the one upon which our whole notion of God hangs, the truth of the Trinity, is demonstrated or not demonstrated by the way in which we love and care for one another. Either our relationships show the oneness that God has with His Son, or our relationships deny that oneness. *Our relationships either speak the truth about God or lie about Him.* We are not changing anything about God, but we are either speaking the truth about Him or we are telling an untruth about Him, the One who is perfect in love and unity.

Jesus prays in John 17:24, "That they may behold My glory, which Thou hast given Me; for Thou didst love Me before the foundation of the world." This is high ground. God the Father loved God the Son, and God the Son loved God the Father from before the foundation of the world. Now we are given the privilege of looking through a peephole into this love and communion which God the Father has had with God the Son forever. That means that when we love each other, we are showing something about the deepest essence of God's eternal being and love. When we fail to love each other, we are lying about the deepest essence of God's eternal love and being.

This is why Jesus says, "I do not ask in behalf of these alone, but for those also who believe in Me through their word" (v. 20). We can't have unity without truth. They are a one-two punch. There will be no real unity in the church or ultimately anywhere else unless it is built around something that is true. This is why Jesus prays that His disciples be sanctified in the truth (v. 17). Who God the Father is, who God the Son is, who God the Holy Spirit is, and their union and communion with one another become the only basis of the disciples' unity. That truth is the basis of our oneness with one another.

If this is true in our relationships with one another as Christians, then it is a hundred times true in our marriages. The primary fellowship that many of us will have is with one person. In our marriage we actually demonstrate or fail to demonstrate eternal truths about God. That is why in Ephesians 5 the apostle Paul sees our marriages as windows through which the world will see something of the wonder and reality of the way God the Father has loved God the Son and the way God the Son has loved His bride, the church.

When I perform a wedding I always say at the beginning, "We are gathered together in the sight of God and in the face of this company to join together this man and this woman in holy matrimony, which is an honorable estate instituted by God and signifying to us the mystical union that exists between Christ and His church; and therefore it is not to be entered into lightly or unadvisedly but advisedly, soberly, discretely, and in the fear of God." Marriage is serious business because it demonstrates spiritual, eternal truths. Therefore any kind of infidelity, whether it is the gross, physical kind or the internally disloyal kind is a denial of the existence and essence of God's being. That's how much God has invested in our marriages. When I fail to love my wife, Barbara, when I allow distance or bad temper or any shadow of deceit or dishonesty to creep across my heart and linger there in my relationship to her, I am telling a lie about Jesus. In our unity or disunity the demonstration of the integrity of the Trinity's character is at stake.

THAT WE MAY PROVE THE GOSPEL TO BE TRUE

There is something else at stake in our unity as believers, and that is why Jesus prays that we may prove the gospel to be true (John 17:21, 23). We are commanded by Jesus in His farewell address in these chapters of John that we are to love one another. He says three different times, "I give you a new commandment. This is it. Pay attention. I give you a new commandment, that you love one another" (see John 13:34, 35; 15:12). Anything Jesus says three times, we ought to listen to. He says it three times in a row. But the second time He says it, He conjoins it with a specific result that will follow if we obey that commandment. He says, "As you love one another, the world will know that you are My disciples" (see John 13:35). People will recognize us as Jesus' followers by the way we treat one another.

It is not just the truth of the Trinity but the truth of the gospel that will be demonstrated by our love for one another. Jesus says that people will understand or fail to understand the truth of the gospel itself based on what they observe in our relationships.

Look again at 17:21: "That they may all be one; even as Thou, Father, art in Me, and I in Thee, that they also may be in Us; that the world may believe that Thou didst send Me." He repeats the same truth again two verses later: "That the world may know that Thou didst send me" (v. 23). Why did God the Father send the Son? In order that He would be flesh and grow up as a man, live as a man, understand us in all our foibles and faults and sins, but then even more, die as a man. Only flesh can die, so only because of the Incarnation can Jesus Christ die. If there is no death of Jesus, there is no relief from our sins, and we are still in our sins, and we are lost, and we are foolish to waste our time thinking about these things when we could be on the golf course.

Jesus says that the pagan, unbelieving world is given the right to evaluate the truth of whether or not God the Father sent God the Son in the Incarnation based on what they see in our relationships. It is absolutely staggering that the eternal and perfect God would hang the truth of His gospel on us and the way we treat one another. But that is precisely what He does.

Friendships that are because of Jesus Christ are better than gospel tracts, better than witnessing programs, maybe even better than sermons. Our friendships in Jesus become the most powerful witness the Lord can ever have, and it is even clearer when the gospel itself has given rise to friendships that wouldn't otherwise be there, in relationships that would have no reason to exist if it weren't for Jesus.

Lem Tucker was my roommate in graduate school. He was a strong, massive guy who had played quarterback for William and Mary. When he finished school he went to Jackson, Mississippi, to be the president of Voice of Calvary Ministries. In 1976, I flew to Jackson to visit Lem, and the first words he said as I got off the airplane were, "Welcome to Jackson. You have just flown into 1950." I didn't understand what he meant until I noticed the way people were looking at us. You see, Lem was an African-American, and in the mid-seventies in Jackson people weren't used to seeing a white man and a black man ride around in a car or eat in a restaurant together.

My friendship with Lem taught me a lot about the gospel, how it can rub people the wrong way and what the unity in the body of Christ is supposed to look like. By being brothers, Lem and I were in our own small way shouting the truth that God the Father sent God the Son, because there really wasn't any other reason why Lem and I would be together, much less be brothers, much less love each other.

A few years later, Lem died at the age of thirty from a rare form of cancer. There were hundreds and hundreds of people at his funeral. Half of them were white and half of them were black, and at that funeral service, the gospel was heard.

THAT WE MAY BEHOLD HIS GLORY

Jesus prays, "Father, I desire that they also, whom Thou hast given Me, be with Me where I am, in order that they may behold My glory, which Thou hast given Me; for Thou didst love Me before the foundation of the world" (John 17:24). The glory of God is what God the Father has given God the Son. And He gave it together with His love before the foundation of the world.

Glory means two things in this context: first, it means "the perfection of God's own being." Everything that God is and has, all of His being, all of His perfection, He gave to His Son. The second thing that *glory* means in the Gospel of John is the obedience of Christ's going to the cross and, therefore, His wounds. Jesus is praying that we would see His perfection and His wounds.

Think about that. Your Savior is praying right now that you would see His perfection and His wounds. He is not simply praying that we would see it *now,* though He is in a certain way. We won't see it perfectly now, in this world. He is praying, rather, that we will see His perfection and His wounds when we are with Him in glory.

Yes, this is nothing less than a prayer from your Savior's lips for a glorious death for you. He is praying that when that moment comes for you and for me, it will be a moment filled with glory. Yes, death is the enemy. Death is not to be welcomed. And yes, death is going to be defeated ultimately by the resurrection of Christ. True enough. But for every one of us, there will come a moment when we pass from this existence to another existence, and He is praying that that moment will be filled with glory.

I know a man who prays every day that when he gets old and close to the time of his death, he will not dishonor the Lord with his speech. He has seen a number of older people begin to say things dishonoring to the Lord when life gets difficult. He prays that when he comes to that moment in his life he will not do that. He is praying, and we should pray, not that we would despise death, even though it is unnatural, but that as we walk through it we would enjoy what the Puritans described as an "abundant entrance." Sweet is the death of those who savor the Lord Jesus their whole life long, because they know that death is only going to give them more of their Savior—and more of Him is what they want.

James Montgomery Boice, noted author, church leader, and senior minister of Tenth Presbyterian Church in Philadelphia, died in the year 2000 as a relatively young man. He received the diagnosis of terminal liver cancer just two hours before he stepped into the pulpit on Good Friday to preach about the crucifixion of Jesus Christ. In his last year, Jim wrote a number of hymns. As he was lingering near the time of his death, some of the staff members and elders of his church came to his bedside and sang some of his hymns with him.

Here are some lines from one of those hymns, called "Hallelujah" and based on Romans 8:38-39:

What can separate my soul
From the God who made me whole,
Wrote my name in heaven's scroll?
Nothing. Hallelujah!

Victors we're ordained to be
By the God who set us free.
What can therefore conquer me?
Nothing. Hallelujah!

We face death for God each day.
What can pluck us from his way?
Let God's people ever say,
"Nothing. Hallelujah!"[2]

An assistant pastor who was there said later that when they sang, "What can separate my soul," Jim raised his weakened arm and held his fist to heaven as he proclaimed, *"Nothing!"* Nothing can separate us from the glory of God that is in Christ Jesus. I wish for you such an abundant, glory-filled entrance. But more important than *my* wishing it for you, Jesus wishes it for you. And He prays for it for you.

THAT WE MIGHT KNOW HIS NAME

In John 17:26, Jesus says, "I have made Thy name known to them, and will make it known . . ." We know that in Scripture a name means more than just a label or word that we use to identify someone. To name someone is to attribute the worth and value of that name to him or her. When we name a child after a beloved relative or friend, that is what we are doing. My daughter, Carey Elizabeth, is named to attribute to her the worth of a lovely lady named Elizabeth who is now in heaven.

Baptism is rightly understood as a naming sacrament. When we baptize children or adults, we pronounce the name of God upon them. As a minister, I baptize them in the name of the Father and of the Son and of the Holy Spirit. By naming them with that name, I am asking that the worth, the value, the truth about the triune God would be upon and in them so that they would know God as Father and live as a child of His, know Jesus as Savior and trust and believe that Jesus is Savior and Lord, and know the Spirit as *paraklete*—Helper, Friend, Counselor, Guide. When we baptize people, we are baptizing them in the hope and belief that they will live up to the name that is being given at baptism, and especially that they would live up to the name of Jesus, because in baptism we take the name of Christ upon ourselves—*Christian, Christ's one, bearer of Christ.*

Christ's name becomes our name. We are adopted into the Father's family. Our family name becomes *Christian,* which means we are all in the same family. Now, in families there can be squabbles, right? And sometimes in a family things can get a little tense and a little bit ornery, can't they? But in the end, family is *family,* and the loyalty is sure and secure. When the name of Christ becomes your last name, you take an oath that you will be loyal to those who have the same name.

Baptism involves taking an oath, but so does the Lord's Supper, where we have communion with the Lord and communion with one another. The Word of God tells us that if you are at odds with any other member of your church, you are duty bound by virtue of blood-oath in the name and by the blood of Jesus to go to that person and settle the matter before you take the Lord's Supper.

It is a family prayer that Jesus has given, a prayer that we might be one; that we might prove the truth of the gospel by our oneness; that we would behold His glory; and that we would know His name. Imagine that. Imagine that the Lord is praying these things for us right now. Isn't that remarkable? If that is what He is praying for us, I guess we had better do it.

PART V

The Passion and Resurrection of the Son of God

31

LAST WORDS

But there were standing by the cross of Jesus His mother, and His mother's sister, Mary the wife of Clopas, and Mary Magdalene. When Jesus therefore saw His mother, and the disciple whom He loved standing nearby, He said to His mother, "Woman, behold, your son!" Then He said to the disciple, "Behold, your mother!" And from that hour the disciple took her into his own household.

After this, Jesus, knowing that all things had already been accomplished, in order that the Scripture might be fulfilled, said, "I am thirsty." A jar full of sour wine was standing there; so they put a sponge full of the sour wine upon a branch of hyssop, and brought it up to His mouth. When Jesus therefore had received the sour wine, He said, "It is finished!" And He bowed His head, and gave up His spirit (John 19:25-30).

IT IS TRADITIONAL TO SPEAK of the seven sayings of Jesus from the Cross. The Gospel of John reports three of those sayings.

"HERE IS YOUR MOTHER"

First, Jesus turned to his mother and said, "Woman, behold, your son!" Then he said to John, "Behold, your mother!" (see John 19:26-27).

A mother is about to lose her son. She is presumably a widow, in a day when there were no nursing homes, no social security plans, no pensions, no investments upon which Mary could live comfortably for the rest of her days. It would be incumbent upon the family to provide for her. One of the last things Jesus does before He dies is to tenderly arrange for ongoing care for His mother. But it is interesting that He speaks to John, the beloved disciple, not to His own brothers or cousins. Why doesn't He do that which would be most natural, instead of speaking to John?

The reason is very simple, yet profound and highly important to the church of the Lord Jesus Christ: at the Cross, all of our relationships are rearranged. At the Cross, all of our loyalties are undone and then put back together again. At the Cross, we have an altogether new family. At the cross of Jesus Christ, all of the old loyalties of our life become new, and most of the old things that we have clung to are discarded. There is a rearrangement of the way we think about even those who are closest to us.

We are so used to thinking as Americans; we think of the Cross in very individualistic terms. Jesus died for *me*. Of course, that is true, but Jesus didn't just die for *me*; He died for *us*. And the "us" that Jesus died for is the family of His people, an altogether new set of relationships. Now, no loyalty is to be ahead of our loyalty to our brothers and sisters in the Lord. No membership in any fraternal organization, no club membership, no professional allegiance, and not even any blood family ties now hold first place for the people of God. We are God's people, and we are made new at the Cross, where we see the lengths to which Jesus went to make space for us in His own heart. He bids us at that same Cross to go to great lengths to make space in our hearts for one another in Christ.

Christians are not always the easiest people to love. I am a "professional" Christian, so I ought to know. There are Christians whom I would call "VLPs"—"very lovable people," and then there are Christians I would call "VUPs"—"very unlovable people." The question I must answer when confronted with a VUP is, Do I make room for this person in my life? I do so on the basis of only one issue: at the Cross, Jesus broke down the barrier between us. He has created a new race of men and women, a new family of His people. The Cross rearranges all of my relationships.

The church is an organism first, not an organization. We lay the stress in the wrong place when we care too much about dotting the *i*'s and crossing the *t*'s on our charts and graphs, on our plans and programs. All of that means precisely nothing if we cannot look any Christian in the eye and say, "My dear brother for whom Jesus died," "My beloved sister . . ." and treat them as more beloved than blood brothers or sisters. The world cries out to see that.

Jesus Himself said, "By this will all men know that you are my disciples," by whether or not the Cross has so rearranged your loyalties, "if you have love for one another" (13:35). "Greater love has no one than this, that one lay down his life for his friends" (15:13). Maybe in other cultures much more often, but not so much in our culture do we find that we lay down our lives for one another. Where we have to go to see it, of course, is to the Lord Himself.

"I AM THIRSTY"

Jesus does not just rearrange our relationships at the Cross, He also asks us the question, What do you thirst after? He says, "I am thirsty" (John 19:28). Throughout Scripture, thirst is a metaphor for a deep, inward spiritual emptiness and need. Without God we will die, because the Bible says that what we most thirst for and need at the center of our lives is not stuff but God. The question always is, What do I drink to fill that deep and profound thirst within me?

Jesus was dying. He was terribly thirsty. The hot, arid, Middle Eastern sun was beating down upon Him. People in the ancient Middle East knew something about death by dehydration that we may not know. In the first stages of dehydration, one feels an inward caving in or longing. But then as the thirst goes on, it actually becomes a deep and profound burning inside. Our bodies are 98 percent water. When they do not have water to replenish what they themselves are, every molecule begins to cry out. Spiritually speaking, if God is not at the center of our souls then we do not have that which can ultimately meet our thirst and quench it. The real danger of that thirst is eternal death in hell.

C. S. Lewis gives us a wonderful way to understand hell when he says, "Heaven is the place where man says to God, 'Thy will be done,' and hell is that place where God says to man, 'Thy will be done.'"[1] Hell is the place where we get more and more of what we have been seeking to quench our thirst. Hell is the place where we get more than we ever wanted of those things that we are trying to stuff into our souls.

Jesus tells the remarkable little parable in Luke 16 about a poor man, Lazarus, who is the servant of a wealthy man. Both of them die within a short period of time; Lazarus goes to heaven and the rich man goes to hell. From hell the rich man prays to Father Abraham, who is in heaven with Lazarus, "Father Abraham, would you send Lazarus down to dip his finger and give me just a little taste of water, because it is so hot down here?"

It is interesting that there is no sign of repentance in what the rich man says. In fact, he is still giving Lazarus orders as if he were still his servant. "Fetch me water," he says (see v. 24). There is no sign that he understands that the things he has been seeking to fill his soul will not satisfy him at all.

When Jesus says, "I am thirsty," I don't think He means physical thirst, because in the whole Passion account we never once hear Jesus complaining about any of the physical torture and agony into which He is placed. He is blindfolded and beaten with the fists of soldiers. He is scourged with a whip made with bits of metal and glass fragments tied into straps that are laid repeatedly across His back. There is a crown of thorns meanly pressed into His brow until He bleeds. Never once does He complain. Never once does He say, "It hurts." So when He says, "I am thirsty," He is saying, "I am thirsty with a thirst that every sinner deserves to experience forever." He means that He is going to hell, that He is now like the rich man in hell, with no one to bring Him water.

In speaking of His thirst, perhaps Jesus is thinking of Psalm 22: "I am poured out like water, and all my bones are out of joint. My heart is like wax; it is melted within me. My strength is dried up like a potsherd, and my tongue cleaves to my jaws; and Thou dost lay me in the dust of death" (vv. 14-15). Jesus understands His thirst biblically. In fact, the larger context of Jesus' remark about His thirst reads, "in order that the Scripture would be fulfilled, [Jesus] said, 'I am thirsty.'" Psalm 22 begins this way: "My God, my God, why hast Thou forsaken me?" (v. 1; quoted in Matt. 27:46; Mark 15:34). This thirst is not primarily physical but comes about because the Son of God has now been put into hell, a hell which He does not deserve. You and I deserve that unquenchable, unremitting, agonizing thirst because we have sought to fill our lives with anything and everything but Him.

Those of us who grew up on the ocean know that sometimes you get thirsty while sailing or boating. If you run out of water, the last thing you want to do is to put your mouth down into the salt water. It will only increase your thirst and accelerate the process of dehydration. Every one of us puts our mouth down into the salt water of whatever we use to meet our deepest needs. Jesus Christ became for you that One who thirsted unto death. He descended into hell, as the Apostles' Creed says. It was as if He was placed into the position of eternal separation from God that you and I deserve.

Look to Jesus and say, "You are the only One who can satisfy my deepest need. I know, Lord, even this day I will find yet more ways to stick my mouth into the salt water of this world. Nevertheless, Lord, forgive me. And nevertheless, Lord, I come to you as one who believes that You took my place and thirsted for me and descended into hell for me so that I might have life evermore." If you say that in faith, then you are at one with Him, despite the fact that your sins are many.

"IT IS FINISHED"

You may know that "It is finished" (John 19:30) is one Greek word—*tetelestai*—in the original New Testament. Perhaps it is better translated, "it is accomplished." There is a problem with the English translation because it sounds rather passive, as if Jesus isn't doing anything. In actual fact, He is quite active. We get an idea of it in the stem of the word, *telos*, which means "design" or "plan." The idea is not so much that something has happened to Jesus as it is that He is accomplishing something toward an objective, toward a plan that He has in mind. *Tetelestai* is perhaps better translated, "I have finished, I have accomplished."

That is actually a remarkable thing for Jesus to say. On the Cross, He cannot move. His hands and feet are nailed in a stationary position. He cannot even wipe the sweat from His forehead. And yet He says, "I have accomplished everything. I have done it all." The moment when Christ has absolutely no ability to do anything becomes the moment in which He declares that He has done everything. At the moment in which He seems absolutely helpless and defeated, He is actually saying, "I have accomplished the most important victory that could ever be accomplished."

This wonderful Greek language tells us even more. The particular tense of this verb conveys the meaning that He has done it perfectly, completely. What has He done? First Peter 3:18 summarizes it this way: "Christ died for sins once for all, the righteous for the unrighteous, to bring you to God" (NIV). He has closed the infinite gap that exists between human beings and God, between finite and sinful human people and the infinite and perfect God. "It is finished" is actually a great summary statement of the whole gospel. There is nothing left to do.

When Buddha died, it is reported by tradition that his last words were, "Strive without ceasing." Jesus' last words were, "I have done it." Religion tells us to finish the work—to go out and do something and be something. Jesus says, "Receive the finished work." Jesus says, "Before you contemplate doing anything as a Christian, be careful to do nothing," because He has accomplished it all. Be careful that you do not assume that anything you would *do* is the rightful and legitimate expression of your faith. Be careful that you do not understand *doing* as the sum and substance, as the heart and kernel of your faith. "No," Jesus says, "I have done it all."

Do you believe that? I don't believe that. Oh, I believe it, but in countless ways in my life, again and again, I find myself saying, "I don't believe it." It is kind of like a fellow I used to know. He didn't wear his seatbelt. One day while riding in the car I said to him, "You know the statistics are against you. You should wear your seatbelt."

He said, "Oh, yes, I believe those statistics. I believe it is important to wear my seatbelt, but I just don't do it."

A year later I got into the car with him again and the first thing he did was snap on his seatbelt. I said, "A year ago you wouldn't put on your seatbelt. What happened?"

He said, "A friend of mine was badly injured in an accident six months ago. Ever since then, I wear my seatbelt."

Did he not believe that seatbelts save lives and keep people from injury a year ago? He believed it, but he didn't believe it. Now he really believes it.

That is true for all of us. Do you believe that Jesus finished the work that was to be done on the cross for you? Yes, you believe. But do you believe it? Perhaps not.

THREE KINDS OF BELIEVERS

There are at least three kinds of Christian people who believe but don't believe.[2] The first is one who suffers from an inferiority complex. He says, "I know I am a terrible sinner. I know I am a person for whom Christ died." But he is trying to finish Christ's work because he feels so inadequate, so unworthy of what Christ has done. He keeps trying to improve on what Jesus has done because he can't really believe He did it for him. He keeps beating himself up out of his sense of inferiority and does not recognize the fact that Jesus has already been beaten up for him. There is no more beating up to be done.

The second kind of person who believes but doesn't believe is just the opposite. This person has a superiority complex. He feels morally superior to other people. There are a lot of Christians like that.

Let me give you a couple of tests to see if you are such a person. Can you stand being around people who either doctrinally or morally don't get it? Can you tolerate being around people who have all kinds of inadequate beliefs? Do you think of yourself as the doctrinal police out there to correct everyone, to shake your finger and tell people where they are wrong? Or, on the moral side of things, do you find yourself saying, "I can't stand to be around such a person?" If so, you may be guilty of this kind of moral superiority.

Here's another test: Do you hold grudges? If someone wrongs you, can you forgive him or her? If you can't, then you really don't believe that Jesus has done it all. If you really believe that Jesus has done it all, then there is nothing left for you to hold against that person. We all stand as equal before the Cross, and we are all going to mess up. But if you hold grudges against other people, then you are putting yourself above them.

So on one hand there are wimpy Christians and on the other hand there are proud Christians. There is one final category of Christians who believe but don't believe: addicted, driven Christians. These are Christians who are addicted to their own activity for the Lord. They need to fill up the empty emotional gaps in their lives with frenetic behavior. Any pop psychologist will tell you that such people don't like themselves and if you don't like yourself, it is because you don't believe that the work is finished.

As a pastor, I tell you gently but directly that there are many, many Christians who are wimpy Christians, proud Christians, or addicted Christians because we don't get it. We don't see that Christ has done it all, and we keep trying to finish the work that has already been finished. We keep trying to complete what Jesus has fully, completely, absolutely, once and for all accomplished.

What we need to learn to do is nothing.

32

JOSEPH OF ARIMATHEA

And after these things Joseph of Arimathea, being a disciple of Jesus, but a secret one, for fear of the Jews, asked Pilate that he might take away the body of Jesus; and Pilate granted permission. He came therefore, and took away His body. And Nicodemus came also, who had first come to Him by night; bringing a mixture of myrrh and aloes, about a hundred pounds weight. And so they took the body of Jesus, and bound it in linen wrappings with the spices, as is the burial custom of the Jews. Now in the place where He was crucified there was a garden; and in the garden a new tomb, in which no one had yet been laid. Therefore on account of the Jewish day of preparation, because the tomb was nearby, they laid Jesus there. Now on the first day of the week Mary Magdalene came early to the tomb, while it was still dark, and saw the stone already taken away from the tomb. And so she ran and came to Simon Peter, and to the other disciple whom Jesus loved, and said to them, "They have taken away the Lord out of the tomb, and we do not know where they have laid Him." Peter therefore went forth, and the other disciple, and they were going to the tomb. And the two were running together; and the other disciple ran ahead faster than Peter, and came to the tomb first; and stooping and looking in, he saw the linen wrappings lying there; but he did not go in. Simon Peter therefore also came, following him, and entered the tomb; and he beheld the linen wrappings lying there, and the face-cloth, which had been on His head, not lying with the linen wrappings, but rolled up in a place by itself. So the other disciple who had first come to the tomb entered then also, and he saw and believed. For as yet they did not understand the Scripture, that He must rise again from the dead. So the disciples went away again to their own homes (John 19:38–20:10).

COME MEET JOSEPH OF ARIMATHEA and sit down for a few minutes with him, if you will. He has an amazing story to tell you!

"I am so glad that this weekend is over. I mean, I'm glad that Friday is over. It has not been easy. In fact, it has been the most difficult time of my life. Do you have a few minutes? I would like to tell you about what has happened to me in the last few days.

"Let me begin by telling you who I am. My given name is Joseph, and I am from the small town of Arimathea, which is about twenty miles northwest of Jerusalem. I was born there and grew up there, but came to the big city. I like the small town, and I like having a house out in the country, but I like the bright city lights, too. And the city has been good to me. I suppose that I like the idea of making a lot of money in the city but then retreating to my country place where I can be a big fish in a little pond.

"I don't believe in overdone modesty, so I will tell you straight out that I am a wealthy man. But I will also tell you that I did not inherit a thing. My father was a solid, substantial working man; but he didn't leave me very much. I have always had a good feel for real estate and finance, and this Roman peace that we have been enjoying has provided some economic stability for us. Business has been good, and I have done well.

"But there is more to my life than making money. I am—though possibly not for much longer—a member of the Council of the Seventy. My participation in the life of the temple and my work on behalf of the preservation of our Jewish traditions and hopes has always been one of my most important concerns. At least I would have said that until two days ago.

"As the legislature and the Supreme Court of Israel, the Sanhedrin has been the most relevant force in trying to preserve our sense of Jewishness in the midst of the Roman occupation. With the Roman infringement on so much of our way of life, the Sanhedrin has come to represent the bulwark of Judaism against the crush of the culture all around us. The people count on us to hold to all that is good about being Jewish. And until this last week, I have been most proud to be one of the Seventy.

"But it is not just the maintaining of our Jewish institutions that interests me. I have been waiting for something, or should I say some-one, all my life. Perhaps you think I sound too simple and pious putting it that way, but hear me out. Whatever else it means for us to say that we are Jews, it means at least, and perhaps most of all, that we are waiting for the Messiah, that we are those who understand that history is going somewhere. We are those who believe that God has intervened in history, that in times past He sent us messengers and prophets and leaders, the likes of Abraham and Moses and even the stern Isaiah, to remind us that He intervenes in our lives. This world is not what the Romans would have you believe it is, not the inevitable click, click of time and event endlessly going on, independently of God. No, the world is the place into which God intends to come and live among His people. So I have been waiting for the fulfillment of the promise of the prophets, waiting for the One who would redeem us like Moses redeemed our ancestors from Egypt, waiting for the One who would be David's greater son, who would slay all the Goliaths of our lives.

"I am going to tell you something that will shock you. I believe that that rabbi who was executed by the Romans the day before yesterday with those two other criminals on Golgotha hill was the Promised One. Actually, I have believed that for some time. But I am ashamed to tell you that I was afraid to make my belief public for fear of the Sanhedrin—and particularly of Caiaphas—and what they would say.

"You see, I think there is something of a tragedy in the making here, the likes of which the world has never known. If the Sanhedrin, which is intended to protect the interests of Judaism, does not understand what it means for us as a people to hope for the Messiah, then they have no real purpose as an institution. But something has gone wrong with the Sanhedrin. It has become defensive and self-protective and so concerned with maintaining its own position before the people and in the face of Roman threats that it is reluctant to make any move that might compromise its position.

"And I, too, know what it would mean if I were to openly confess faith in this Rabbi. You see, He is from Nazareth, and we know that nothing good comes out of Nazareth. We know that no well-educated, cultured person capable of being the Messiah would come from Nazareth. We also know that this Rabbi did not have the formal education required of one to lead us.

"But I think that the council has fallen into grave error, and I am a part of that. Our hopes as Jews have become too political, too centered on the expectation of a Messiah who will somehow liberate us from Roman captivity. But no, we have not read carefully the promises of our own prophets, which point us to a kingdom quite different than we might expect.

"Now you were not there Friday, were you? You did not see the way He died, did you? I left the council chambers when the vote was being taken to turn this Jesus over to Pilate for execution. I made some lame excuse to Caiaphas. I told him that my mother was sick in Arimathea, and I had to go home. I knew that if I had been there, I would have had to say something. I knew I would have to tell them that I thought what we were about to do was the most tragic error of all human history. But I had no courage. And so I let it go. Oh, I tried to justify myself, thinking that my presence in the council would have made no difference at all in the final vote. But if the truth be known, I was afraid.

"But I did go to Golgotha. Being quite sure that no other members of the Sanhedrin would care to be there, I knew they would not see me. You know, I am absolutely appalled at the way we Jews say we know the teaching of our own Scriptures, and yet we have been blinded. We cannot even see the most obvious things. Do you not remember that passage by Isaiah where he speaks of the Messiah who is to come? He says of Him that He has no stately form that we should want to look at Him, that He has no appearance that we should be attracted to Him, that He was despised and forsaken of men, a man of sorrows, and acquainted with grief, and One from whom men are likely to hide their face. That is what I saw yesterday. That is what I saw out there at Golgotha—One who had no majesty, One who was in anguish, One who was forsaken even by those who said they were His disciples, One who was sorrowful and in grief. I wanted to hide my face from Him. And yet do you not remember what Isaiah says about Him? 'Surely our griefs He Himself bore, and our sorrows He carried. . . . He was pierced through for our transgressions, He was crushed for our iniquities.'

"Now I must tell you that I believe this Galilean somehow bore my griefs and sorrows as He died. Somehow I feel that my transgressions—including the worst of the lot, my treacherous silence about Him—were the cause of His being crushed and bruised.

"I saw Him yesterday, overburdened with affliction, yet He did not open His mouth. He was like a lamb led silently to slaughter. Remember what that wild man from the desert, the fellow named John, said about Him? He called Him the 'Lamb of God who takes away the sin of the world.' That kind of Messiah is not the One the Sanhedrin wants. But that is the kind of Messiah I want.

"I knew then that, though it was tragically too late, I had to do something. He died quickly, more quickly than Pilate expected. As I watched Him go, I knew that there would not be the means or the ability to provide a proper burial for Him. You probably know that the final execution of a condemned man in our society is not the end of his humiliation. The Roman law necessitates the loss of all honor in death for a criminal.

"The people who are sentenced to death in this culture forfeit their property and are forbidden a proper burial. Usually the criminal's body is left on the cross to rot in the midday sun or to be eaten by vultures. The release of the corpse for burial might be given at the whim of the magistrate—in this case, Pilate—and usually even a criminal's body would be given over to his family for burial, but not a burial with honor. No public ceremony or mourning can ever accompany the burial of an executed criminal.

"The problem was that the family of this now dead Galilean was incapable of action. His mother, whom I saw at the execution, was emotionally exhausted and had to be led away by one of the followers of Jesus. I think it was John who took her away. His brothers were nowhere to be seen. His other disciples had run away. If I were to request permission to bury the Galilean, it would be tantamount to my confession of His being the Messiah. I was very much afraid, and thought of many excuses why I should not go to Pilate. I knew it would be only a matter of time before the council heard of my actions and knew I was in fact not in Arimathea but was actually His disciple. But I must tell you something: there is a poverty to all of my riches if they make me unable to say what I really believe.

"There is a subtlety to all of this. In our culture it is very easy, indeed very proper to be appropriately religious; but the kind of commitment that Jesus demanded is too costly for many. And those of us who have wealth and position and country homes and status, all of those to lose, we choose a safer route. Many of us want a little religion, but we don't want it to ask too much of us.

"I have come to the place of wanting poverty in my life. Now I don't mean that I want to be stripped of all my material goods. I just mean this: if my abilities, my status, or my wealth somehow stand in the way of my knowing this Jesus, then take it all away. I know now that all of my riches and all of my position in this world matter little compared to what He has done.

"So I went to Pilate. He knew me, of course, and he knew of my connections with the Jewish power structure of the city. It struck him as odd that I would be seeking the body of someone who was executed for treason. He was puzzled and even confused at my interest. I am quite sure he is suspicious about my desire to give Jesus a burial. But it was late. Time was moving quickly. I had to hurry. You see, it was already moving toward sundown and the beginning of the Sabbath, and the Jewish law prohibits any burial proceedings on the Sabbath.

"So when Pilate approved, I immediately sent my servants to Golgotha. I collected certain things we would need: sponges, cloths, soap, and, above all, the linen shroud that I had been saving for my own burial. I sent for Nicodemus, a fellow member of the Sanhedrin who also was a secret disciple. He was the one who had had that conversation with Jesus, something about a new birth. Nicodemus brought burial spices, and together we met my servants at the place of execution.

"I am not so old as to be ready to die. But somehow I did have that linen shroud, and that tomb. In fact, it was a brand-new tomb, just carved out of a quarry near the garden outside the city gates and near Golgotha. We quickly carried the body of Jesus to the garden to complete our task before sundown. Although the washing of the body is considered a very important part of Jewish burial, there was too little time. So we rapidly wrapped His dirty, bloody body in the shroud and laid it in the tomb. Nicodemus had brought a mixture of spices—myrrh and aloes. The myrrh is a pungent and powerful spice. And the aloes is a strong perfume. We had about eighty pounds of them. You know, only the wealthiest people could be buried with this amount of very costly spices. But we determined to do for Jesus in His death what we had never done for Him in His life.

"Hastily we placed the body in the tomb and rolled a specially carved disc-like stone into the doorway. Though the stone was quite heavy, it was readily rolled downhill into place. But rolling it the other way, well, that would be quite impossible, humanly speaking.

"So now I wait, expecting any moment to receive a message from Caiaphas, summoning me before the council. They will strip me of my position. They will even use their influence to deprive me of my business holdings and investments. There is even a real chance that they will expel me from the temple. So you must go now if you do not want to be identified with me and therefore with Him. I would not try to implicate you in my own confession of faith in Jesus—that is something you alone must decide—whether or not you will be identified with this Galilean, even at the cost of public esteem and popularity, even at the cost of being publicly scorned.

"There is, of course, the middle way, the way that I chose for some time, the secret way of being His disciple. That way, I suppose, is also open to you. But it is not the way I recommend. It leaves you vulnerable to the accusation of your conscience, that you are a hypocrite. And it leaves you vulnerable to *His* accusation that you publicly denied Him. In fact, although I would say that you may begin as a secret disciple, you may not continue very long as a secret disciple. Didn't He say something about the danger of hiding your light under a basket? No, the cost of being a secret disciple will in the long run, as you stand before a Judge far greater than Pilate or Caiaphas, be far worse than the cost of some risk to your status or possessions.

"But there is a more positive way to put this. When I was a secret disciple, I enjoyed certain benefits the world gives its own. They are not bad things. But they are not, as I have discovered, good enough to be the center of my joy. I have found something, no, *someone* who is the pearl of great price, the treasure that has so much value that He is worth the loss of all things if it comes to that.

"But there is something else, something quite disturbing and thrilling. There was a stir among His followers this morning. They are saying that Mary Magdalene came to His tomb while it was still dark and that the stone was rolled away from the entrance. Now as I have already told you, I rolled that stone downhill and into place. I know that no human being could roll it back. But Mary said that He was not there. Apparently Mary went and found Peter and John, who came running to the tomb and confirmed that He was not in it. They saw the blood-soaked linen in which I had wrapped Him.

"I do not understand what this might mean. I prepared His body for burial, not for resurrection. I examined the dead body of the Galilean more closely than any other human being, and I will tell you this: if His dead body, which I touched with my own hands, the blood of which is smeared into my white linen shroud, is somehow no longer dead but splendidly alive, then there has been exerted on His body a life-giving power that has never been seen in the history of the world.

"Until Friday, I felt as unclean in my soul as that stained and dirty linen cloth. My conscience was eating away at my peace. I tried appeasing my conscience by staying busy with my business and with my work with the Sanhedrin. I tried to reassure myself that all was well. But in the silence I knew that nothing could take away the soil in my soul. I felt condemned by my sly diplomacy, by trying to be a secret disciple and somehow still curry the favor of the Sanhedrin. I felt that I was on the side of Judas because I betrayed Jesus again and again by my silence.

"But no longer. If the rumors are true, if Jesus lives, then by the strength and power of that new, unique life He declares that His blood is sufficient to cleanse my guilty conscience. I cannot imagine it.

"I used to fear the criticism of my peers. I should have dreaded, instead, the rightful condemnation I deserved from God for all the secret wrongs of my heart. But the blood of Christ cries out, announcing God's love. And the cry of love is much louder than the cry of condemnation. Now I fear no condemnation, for the principle of the Spirit of life has set me free from the principle of sin and death.

"I see something now that all of my education and all of my wealth and all of my upbringing could never teach me. I see that I am much worse than I ever thought. But I am also much more loved than I ever dreamed. The secret sins of my heart whisper to my conscience, but the wonder of God's love in the blood of His Son is shouted from the cross to set me free. Love and blood are stronger than sin and death.

"The metaphor for my life is that expensive linen shroud in which I wrapped the body of the now-risen Jesus. The linen was dirty, soiled with my sin. But now it is drenched in the blood of Jesus—the blood that shows how much I am loved.

"Jesus could have kept the secret of His love for me, but He didn't. He was publicly mocked, spat upon, and beaten. He was publicly and wrongfully executed on that Roman cross. Jesus made no secret of His sacrifice for me, and I will not keep the secret that His blood and His new life are of infinite value to me. Others may flee or compromise, straddle the fence, balance their agendas, and serve two masters, knowing Jesus but keeping Him a secret from other parts of their lives and from other people; but I will no longer do that. No. I won't, because He is now alive.

"And now I must go and find Him. I will fall before Him and beg Him to forgive me for the treachery of my silence and the double-mindedness of my heart. I will follow Him, and He will be my Lord and my Life and my Hope and my Glory forever. For, you see, I was lost in my double-mindedness and my secrecy. In my lostness, He found me and loved me to the end. Oh, I am going to go, and I am going to find Him. And I am going to follow Him forever. Do you want to come with me?

33

THE THREE MARYS

Now on the first day of the week Mary Magdalene came early to the tomb, while it was still dark, and saw the stone already taken away from the tomb. And so she ran and came to Simon Peter, and to the other disciple whom Jesus loved, and said to them, "They have taken away the Lord out of the tomb, and we do not know where they have laid Him" (John 20:1-2).

But Mary was standing outside the tomb weeping; and so, as she wept, she stooped and looked into the tomb; and she beheld two angels in white sitting, one at the head, and one at the feet, where the body of Jesus had been lying. And they said to her, "Woman, why are you weeping?" She said to them, "Because they have taken away my Lord, and I do not know where they have laid Him." When she had said this, she turned around, and beheld Jesus standing there, and did not know that it was Jesus. Jesus said to her, "Woman, why are you weeping? Whom are you seeking?" Supposing Him to be the gardener, she said to Him, "Sir, if you have carried Him away, tell me where you have laid Him, and I will take Him away." Jesus said to her, "Mary!" She turned and said to Him in Hebrew, "Rabboni!" (which means, Teacher). Jesus said to her, "Stop clinging to Me, for I have not yet ascended to the Father; but go to My brethren, and say to them, 'I ascend to My Father and your Father, and My God and your God'" (20:11-17).

WOMEN ARE VERY IMPORTANT in the Scriptures, particularly in the Gospel of John. There are three specific women who stand out there like stars, and they all have the name "Mary." Let's look at these three Marys as a way of thinking about the role of women in our lives and about the work of the gospel in the lives of women.

MARY OF MAGDALA

First, let's look at Mary of Magdala, who is often called Mary Magdalene and is the Mary mentioned in these passages from John 20. Magdala was a small town just a few miles north of the city of Tiberias, which is on the west coast of the Sea of Galilee, or as John would call it, the Sea of Tiberias. It was a small town, like a suburb of a larger town, and a very wealthy community.

Traditionally, this Mary is thought of by many in the church as a woman with a checkered past. Looking at the scriptures concerning her a little more closely, however, I discovered that there is absolutely no clear biblical evidence to support that assumption. A tradition grew up, particularly through the Middle Ages, that made her a woman of ill repute. But in actual fact, she was probably not that kind of woman.

The Gospels tell us little about Mary Magdalene, but they do tell us two things. Firstly, she was a woman who, along with other women, supplied the needs of Jesus and some of His disciples; she gave to them out of her own resources, so she was probably a woman of independent means, maybe very wealthy. Secondly, we note that she had a problem. It wasn't a problem with men. In some ways it was a much worse problem. It was a problem with demons.

Demons Then and Now

In Luke 8:1-2, we read, "Soon afterwards, . . . He began going about from one city and village to another, proclaiming and preaching the kingdom of God; and the twelve were with Him, and also some women who had been healed of evil spirits and sicknesses: Mary who was called Magdalene, from whom seven demons had gone out . . ."

We do not know what these seven demons were like nor the nature of the hold that they had upon Mary. We do know this, though: at no time in human history, either before or since the Lord Jesus Christ walked the earth, was there ever so much report of demonic activity as there was when He was here. There were apparently a lot more demons in Palestine in the time of Christ than there are in Dallas or Chicago today. Why? Because the critical moment in salvation history is during Jesus' days on earth. He comes to bring the kingdom of God, and the devil and all of his minions are lined up against this kingdom. They would like to do anything to derail Jesus. That is why the devil takes Jesus to the wilderness and tempts Him. That is why there are so many demons around Him all the time. They know that in Jesus Christ the kingdom of God has been announced and introduced, and they will do anything to stop Him.

Luke 8:1 says that Jesus was going around proclaiming the kingdom. In the very next verse, Mary is noted as having had seven demons. It is the proclamation of the kingdom—that there is a King whose name is Jesus, the Lord of lords—that makes the devil spitting mad. In his anger, he unleashes the full fury of his forces against Jesus, knowing that if he can derail Jesus at this point, he will derail the coming of God's kingdom.

We all have our images of demon possession, don't we? Maybe you have seen something in your life that you would equate with demon possession. Maybe your image comes out of the movie *The Exorcist*. Actually, a more reliable source is the Scripture itself. Take one example that we do have a bit of a description of: the Gadarene demoniac.

The Gadarene demoniac was a crazy man who lived on the eastern shore of the Sea of Galilee. He ran around naked, cutting himself on the rocks, scaring people to death. He had no personal autonomy, no freedom. He was held in bondage until Jesus spoke the Word to him, cast the demons out, and freed the man—freed him to sit at Jesus' feet, freed him to listen to the Word of God in the fellowship and company of God's people.

Maybe Mary was convulsed like the Gadarene. Maybe she was possessed by her possessions, by her preoccupations, her autonomy, her addictions, her willfulness, her physical appearance. Maybe the demonic powers of the universe had their grip on her through these preoccupations. We don't know. We do know that, after meeting Jesus, she demonstrated the power of a changed life.

A Changed Heart and Life

Mary of Magdala is a wonderful demonstration of a woman whose life has been changed by the gospel. We see evidences in this Mary in at least three ways.

First, Mary uses her wealth for the Lord and His disciples. One of the clearest marks that the gospel has gotten hold of us is that the Lord has gotten hold of our checkbooks. When there are changes going on in our hearts that are gospel-rock changes, we think about what we own differently.

The *second* thing that happens to this woman as a result of this changed life is that she becomes the first witness to the resurrection of our Lord. Women are the first witnesses to the Resurrection in all the Gospels, and Mary of Magdala is always present. She is the only person present in all four of the Gospel accounts of the Resurrection. She is the first; she is honored by the Lord to be His first witness as a result of the gospel change in her life.

And *third,* she is also probably the first missionary Jesus appoints. In John 20:17 Jesus says to her, "Stop clinging to Me," and then He says, "Go to My brethren . . ." He tells her to *go.* He tells her to be a missionary, to go take the Word of truth and the Word of life in Christ to the disciples themselves.

Do you remember how Mary came to be the first to see her risen Lord? After reporting to the disciples that the tomb is empty, Mary returns to the tomb. She is crying. She meets the Lord there. Confused, she thinks He is the gardener. She can't recognize Him. Maybe she is blinded by her tears. Then He speaks her name, "Mary" (which brings to mind something else He said: "My sheep know the sound of my voice"—see 10:4, 27). The minute Mary hears His voice, she turns and says, "Rabboni."

Verse 17 is a difficult passage to understand. Mary clings to Jesus, and He says, "Stop clinging to Me, for I have not yet ascended to the Father." I think He is saying, "Mary, you need to understand that a new era has begun. The Cross and the Resurrection have moved us into an altogether new way of thinking. I am about to ascend to My Father and to your Father. Therefore, go and tell My disciples that everything is new. Go, Mary, be the missionary that I have appointed you to be by virtue of your changed life." In the history of missions, women play an absolutely central role, and Mary of Magdala could be considered the first missionary.

The Source of Change

Here is a gospel challenge. The Lord might use our wealth for Christ, or use us to be a witness to Christ, or use us to be a missionary for Christ in ways that we perhaps have never thought of before. Mary knew the source of change in her life. She knew that the source of change was not her own attempts to be a virtuous woman. She knew that the source of change in her life was not that she had joined the right charitable organizations and was doing good for her community. That was not her identity. It could have been. It probably was back in Magdala. It may have been part of the demons' grip upon her—she was enslaved to all this activity. Who knows? We do know there were seven strong demons that held her. And we know that Jesus, with the power of His Word, changed all that. And in doing so, He made her useful. When the Lord changes us, He makes us useful.

No doubt there was a humbling for Mary in this. These demons, whatever they were, had a grip on her heart, and that undoubtedly worked itself out in all kinds of selfish ways in her life. Her view of her life, her beauty, her possessions, her status, her memberships—Jesus changed it all. He changed it all by His gospel power, and He gave Mary freedom from all of these enslavements. He also gave her a brand-new primary affection—her love for Him—and she was never the same. By His gospel power, Jesus changes women and men and causes them to turn their lives around so that they use their wealth differently, speak about Christ differently, even give their lives to His work in a different sort of way.

You cannot be useful to the Lord unless and until the Lord has changed you by His gospel. Until you believe in the finished work of Christ for you on the cross, you cannot be useful to Him. That is the lesson for Mary of Magdala.

MARY OF BETHANY

If Mary of Magdala shows us the usefulness of a changed life, then Mary of Bethany shows us the *worship* of a devoted life. Mary of Bethany is the sister of Martha and Lazarus from Bethany, another suburb of a different city, Jerusalem.

We looked at Mary of Bethany earlier. Let's just review what we learned. In John 12:3, Mary uses a pound of very costly, genuine spikenard ointment to anoint the feet of Jesus, then she wipes His feet with her hair. It is a tremendous act of devotion that follows the raising of Lazarus. By this act of devotion, Mary demonstrates that there are no conditions to her love.

First, the cost of the perfume is three hundred denarii, almost a year's wages for a typical family. This Mary is probably not as wealthy as Mary of Magdala. She pours all the perfume out in extravagant devotion.

Second, there is no limitation to her service. She touches His feet. No one in the Mideastern culture of that day would ever touch anyone else's feet. The lowest of Jewish slaves was not expected to touch the feet of his master, because the feet were just untouchable.

Third, she lets down her hair. Women did not let their hair down publicly in that culture, only in private when they were expressing intimacy, love, and devotion. Mary really understands what devotion is all about. When Mary is criticized by the onlookers about her act of devotion, Jesus says, "She has done it for My burial" (see v. 7). Jesus knows that Mary knows why she is doing it, which means that Mary understands what Jesus is about to do: He is about to go to the cross for her. How does she know what Jesus is going to do? Every time you see Mary of Bethany in the Gospels, where is she? She is sitting at the feet of Jesus, learning the gospel from Him.

This is reflected back in John 11, where Lazarus is raised. When Martha says, "Lord, if you had been here, my brother would not have died," Jesus responds with a sermon—"I am the resurrection and the life." A few lines later, Mary says the same thing, "Lord, if you had been here, my brother would not have died." Jesus doesn't say a word. He weeps with her. Why the difference? Jesus knows that Mary already knows. She already knows the gospel, already knows what is about to happen. What we find in this Mary is the worship of a devoted life.

Women, how devoted are you? In asking this, I don't want to make you feel guilty. I am not talking about the length of your quiet time or about your Christian activities; I am asking you whether the gospel has so changed the texture of your heart that you want to worship. Have you "let your hair down" in devotion before the Lord?

MARY OF NAZARETH

Mary of Nazareth, the mother of Jesus, shows us the *submission* of a consecrated life. There is deep, deep submission to the Lord shown in this Mary's life. As you'll recall from Luke 1, the angel comes to her, announces that this great and marvelous thing is going to happen, that she is going to be with child though still a virgin, and that she is going to give birth to this One who is going to be the Messiah. While she asks questions about it, at the end of the day, when the angel is done with his statement, Mary says, "Behold, the bondslave of the Lord; be it done to me according to your word" (Luke 1:38). Then she proceeds to give one of the most eloquent, beautiful, masterful poems that has ever been written in the course of human history, the Magnificat. Here are just a few lines:

> "My soul exalts the Lord,
> And my spirit has rejoiced in God my Savior.
> For He has had regard for the humble state of His bondslave;
> For behold, from this time on all generations will count me blessed"
> (Luke 1:46-48).

What a submitted woman! What happens, though? In John 2, at the wedding in Cana, when the wine gives out, the mother of Jesus says to Him, "They have no wine." Jesus says to her in what seems to be a strong rebuke, "Woman"—He doesn't even call her "Mother"— "Woman, what have I to do with you? My hour has not yet come."

Jesus isn't being mean or disrespectful to His mother; He is saying to her, "Do you know, Mother, who I am? Do you know that your son must become your Lord?"

The deepest submission of a mother's life is when she comes to the place where she must give her children to the Lord, when she must allow the Lord to rearrange all the relationships in her family, when she must allow the Lord to become more important to her children than she is.

Mothers, the deepest challenge is not to love your children, but to see your children through the gospel. *The deepest challenge of your life is not to make idols of your children.*

I will never forget a moment many years ago at a missions conference at our church. A dear woman walked into the last meeting of that conference, and before the service even started, she started weeping. I went to her and said, "Cindy, why are you crying?"

She replied, "This conference has shown me that I need to give my children up to whatever the Lord has for them." The deepest submission of Mary's consecration was to give her son to His calling and to rearrange her heart around His gospel.

Being Gospel Women and Men

Mary of Magdala shows us the usefulness of a changed life, Mary of Bethany shows us the worship of a devoted life, and Mary of Nazareth shows us the submission of a consecrated life. It is important that you see these women for what they were: they were not notable primarily for being moral women or virtuous women; they were gospel women, women who understood the gospel. Out of that came rearranged virtues, rearranged morals, a new way of thinking about everything.

Has the Lord Jesus Christ rearranged your life? Has the gospel changed everything? Has it realigned your priorities? Is it chipping away at your idols? Is it uncovering the sins of your heart? Is it loosening the grip that the demons of this world have on you?

In our local newspaper there is a column that features a person from the community every week, and it lists all the things he or she does. Often, with women particularly, that list is a long list of good things, memberships and offices held in a variety of societies, auxiliaries, service groups, boards, and community and school projects. Are you willing to let Jesus rearrange such priorities? Are you ready for the gospel to undo your life, even your family's, and then put it back together?

34

THE GLORIFIED BODY

Then the disciples went back to their homes, but Mary stood outside the tomb crying. As she wept, she bent over to look into the tomb and saw two angels in white, seated where Jesus' body had been, one at the head and the other at the foot. They asked her, "Woman, why are you crying?" "They have taken my Lord away," she said, "and I don't know where they have put him." At this, she turned around and saw Jesus standing there, but she did not realize that it was Jesus. "Woman," he said, "why are you crying? Who is it you are looking for?" Thinking he was the gardener, she said, "Sir, if you have carried him away, tell me where you have put him, and I will get him." Jesus said to her, "Mary." She turned toward him and cried out in Aramaic, "Rabboni!" (which means Teacher). Jesus said, "Do not hold on to me, for I have not yet returned to the Father. Go instead to my brothers and tell them, 'I am returning to my Father and your Father, to my God and your God.'" Mary Magdalene went to the disciples with the news: "I have seen the Lord!" And she told them that he had said these things to her (John 20:10-18, NIV).

I'VE BEEN TRYING TO EXERCISE more lately due to a renewed commitment to physical fitness, but I admit that I lack the commitment of my son and daughter, who occasionally go running together at midnight. My goal is at least an attempt to recapture some past level of fitness from younger days, but they work out to build up their bodies for future use. John 20:10-18 is a passage about the condition of our bodies in the future, and it causes us in a quite remarkable way to look to the future for our deepest identity.

These mysterious verses take us to issues of the future and our identity as they relate the post-resurrection meeting of Jesus and Mary Magdalene, perhaps the same woman mentioned in Luke 7 who came to Simon's house, anointed Jesus' feet with perfume, and wiped her tears off of them with her hair. We don't know for certain, but some scholars suggest it is she. (Scholars generally agree that the anointing in Luke 7 is different from the anointing by Mary of Bethany, recorded in John 12 and elsewhere, which we have considered in two previous chapters.)

The resurrection of Jesus Christ is a physical event; it happened in history. It isn't the projection of people's imagination, it isn't a hope for remembrance, it isn't rebirth in spring, it isn't gladiolas and lilies at a holiday. It is a solid, historical, actual physical happening. A dead man rose; lungs that were not breathing started to breathe; a brain with no activity started to produce brain waves again, forty hours after its death.

It is remarkable how much attention John gives to the precise physical details of the Resurrection. There were two angels—not three, not one, but two. They were wearing white, not turquoise or maroon. They were seated, not standing or kneeling. They were seated one at the head and one at the foot of where Jesus had lain, not at His sides. It is the third day—not the second, not the fourth. It happens at dawn, not mid-morning or evening. It happens at a specific tomb. A parallel account tells us that this Mary grasps Christ's feet, just as the woman of Luke 7 did. She grasps His feet, not His arms or hands.

John Updike writes, in "Seven Stanzas at Easter":

Make no mistake: if He rose at all
it was as His body;
if the cells' dissolution did not reverse, the molecules
    reknit, the amino acids rekindle,
the Church will fall.

It was not as the flowers,
each soft Spring recurrent;
it was not as His Spirit in the mouths and fuddled
    eyes of the eleven apostles;
it was as His Flesh: ours.

The same hinged thumbs and toes,
the same valved heart
that—pierced—died, withered, paused, and then
    regathered out of enduring Might
new strength to enclose.

Let us not mock God with metaphor,
analogy, sidestepping transcendence;
making of the event a parable, a sign painted in the
        faded credulity of earlier ages:
let us walk through the door.

The stone is rolled back, not papier-mâché,
not a stone in a story,
but the vast rock of materiality that in the slow
        grinding of time will eclipse for each of us
the wide light of day.

And if we will have an angel at the tomb,
make it a real angel,
weighty with Max Planck's quanta, vivid with hair,
        opaque in the dawn light, robed in real linen
spun on a definite loom.

Let us not seek to make it less monstrous,
for our own convenience, our own sense of beauty,
lest, awakened in one unthinkable hour, we are
        embarrassed by the miracle,
and crushed by remonstrance.[1]

THE WHOLE TRUTH

The Resurrection is real, it is concrete, it actually happens; but that makes us ask an important question about this passage: Why doesn't Mary recognize Him? She has spent a great deal of time with Him. Cleopas and his friend on the road to Emmaus didn't recognize Jesus because they were not expecting to find Him there. They thought Jesus was dead and gone. Their hopes were dashed. But not only does Mary not expect to see Jesus alive at the tomb, she doesn't really understand what, or whom, she is looking for. When Jesus asks her whom she is looking for, He is not just making conversation. He implies, "What do you expect to come here and find?" He is saying, "There is more here than you think, Mary. There is more here than a physical resurrection."

Once an Islamic friend from Indonesia said to me, "You Christians believe in the resurrection, don't you?"

I said, "Yes, we do!"

"You believe that Jesus actually physically rose from the dead, right?"

"Yes!" I answered.

He said, "No big deal!"

"I beg your pardon?"

He said, "In Indonesia, we have resurrections all the time, no big deal. It's a wacky world, and strange things happen all the time. People who are sick and supposed to die get better. Miracles happen, absurd things happen. And you know what, Skip? Dead people rise."

Apparently there are accounts in Indonesia and other places of dead people being raised. Though I do not give such accounts much credibility, they do point to an important truth. The simple fact of the physical resurrection is not the whole truth. Mary didn't recognize Jesus because she didn't understand the whole truth about the Resurrection. She saw only, as it were, the half of it. She saw the physical resurrection and was in awe of it when she realized who it was. But she didn't really recognize the Lord. Later, Mary goes back and tells the disciples that she has seen the Lord. But the Lord she saw was not just a man raised from the dead.

We rightly stress the very compelling historical evidence of the Resurrection. In trying to help people understand the truth of the gospel, we must emphasize that the Resurrection actually took place. But we must go one step further.

THE GLORIFIED BODY

This same body that had nail marks on its hands and ate fish on the seashore appeared and disappeared after the Resurrection. It went through closed doors and rose into the clouds. Jesus had additional powers given to Him as the resurrected Christ. Those properties are summarized in the word *glorified*. We speak of the body of Jesus as the glorified body with magnificent new properties. It was a body so remarkably new that Mary and others did not recognize Jesus after His resurrection.

The glorified body has more to it than just a physical body. In 1 Corinthians 15:42-44 (NIV) Paul says, "So will it be with the resurrection of the dead. The body that is sown is perishable, it is raised imperishable; it is sown in dishonor, it is raised in glory; it is sown in weakness, it is raised in power; it is sown a natural body, it is raised a spiritual body." The body of Jesus Christ was no longer simply and only a physical body. Do Christians make a lot of the fact that Jesus was born in the flesh like us and identified with us in our flesh? Of course we do. The Incarnation is absolutely critical to all that it means to be a Christian. But the marvelous thing that happens as a result of the resurrection of Jesus Christ is that *more* happens. The eternal glory that God had given to His Son is given back to the Son in His resurrection, so that He is quite literally filled with a light and a splendor and a beauty and a wonder that His body simply did not have before.

This is the only way I can explain some of the mystery of this passage. If this is the same Mary as in Luke 7, it is amazing that He would tell her, who had touched His feet and wiped them with her hair, not to touch Him. "Don't you see I am completely different now?" He implies. Then He says this very curious thing: "I ascend to My Father and your Father, to My God and your God." Why doesn't He just say, "I ascend to *our* Father?" We understand that Jesus' relationship with the Father as His only begotten Son is different than ours. We are adopted sons and daughters of God; true enough. But He is talking about something more—His glorified state, which is altogether new and different. Therefore, even more so His relationship with His Father is radically different than the one that Mary could have at that moment. Jesus has received a glorified body. He has become the second Adam.

And someday, according to the Bible, we too will have a glorified body. The New Testament talks about Jesus as a leader of a new race. His resurrection means power and dominion have been restored to Him and, therefore, the capability of being an altogether new person who is a leader of a race of people. Paul says in 1 Corinthians 15:45-47, 49 (NIV): "'The first man Adam became a living being'; the last Adam a life-giving spirit. The spiritual did not come first, but the natural, and after that the spiritual. The first man was of the dust of the earth, the second man from heaven. . . . And just as we have borne the likeness of the earthly man, so shall we bear the likeness of the man from heaven."

Not only does Jesus have a glorified body; the promise is that so, too, will we! Just as we have borne the likeness of the earthly man, so shall we bear the likeness of the Man who is from heaven. The promise of the Christian gospel is that although your body disintegrates in the grave, although the molecules die, the amino acids decompose, and you become real dust, Jesus Christ will return and you will be literally, physically raised from the dead just as Jesus Christ was. Your body will be reknit. Your flesh will be reattached to your bones. You will rise up, and you will live again. But you will not be simply a resurrected version of your old self. You will be, if you are in Christ, a glorified being. You will be filled with splendor, life, and all that it means to be in the train of the second Adam. You will be filled with the glory that belongs to Jesus.

What will your glorified body be like? I don't know. (I know mine will have lots and lots of rippling muscles!) John tells us in his first letter, "Dear friends, now we are children of God, and what we will be has not yet been made known. But we know that when he appears, we shall be like him, for we shall see him as he is" (1 John 3:2, NIV). We will be filled with the same splendor and glory that Jesus has. We know that when we see Him, we will see Him as He is and we will understand ourselves to be like Him. Isn't that absolutely amazing?

LIVING FOR THE FUTURE

The meaning of this for you and me is that we live in the future. The critical center of a Christian's life is not the past. Of course, we look to the past to rejoice in what the Lord accomplished for us in space and time at the Cross. And yes, we live in the present. But it is really to the future that we belong. In a certain way the center point of the Bible is the future, not the past or the present. Just like the title of the movie, we live "Back to the Future"—or, perhaps more accurately, back *from* the future. We live our lives now in light of what we are becoming.

What is the specific implication of this for Christians? What is one thing that will not be there in our glorified bodies? Sin. Just as there will be no more decay, no more loss, no more sickness, no more death, there will also be no more sin, for sin is the root cause of all of these struggles. Sin will be done away with once and for all. And we have a down payment on this sinless future glory right now. The Holy Spirit has come—the seal of the King is on our very souls.

Therefore I say to you in the name of the Risen One, live like the person you truly are and are becoming. Just as the sin that adheres to your earthly body is going to be done away with, so is your mortal body itself. Put away those wrong thoughts, words, and actions that do not please the Lord. They are not who you really are. They are not part of your true identity. The ethic of the New Testament is to become who you are. You are a new person in Christ, now live that way. You have been raised with Christ, now live that way. You are on your way to having glory like the glory of Jesus, now live that way. Live back from the future. Live in the present as you will someday be. This is the best way to deal with sin. Just saying we are not going to do those bad things anymore will not work. There must be motive, and the motive that will help us become the people we truly are is to recognize that we are not the people we once were. You are being filled with splendor and light. You are on your way to glory, so live that way. Stop living for yourself and start living for the Head of your race.

When does Mary recognize Jesus? When He says her name. Jesus says that His sheep will know His voice, He will call them by name, and they will follow Him. The only way to know that you are on your way to glory by being raised up from the dead in a glorified body is if the glorified One has called you. How do you know if He has called you? You are responding; you are rising in faith this very moment if you believe these words. The voice of the Shepherd is in the voice of these words, calling to you from His own truth, beckoning you to Himself. He is calling you by name, and with that life-giving call He beckons you to respond in faith to all that He has done for you. He has died for you, yes, but He has also risen for you to new glory. Heed His call. Respond in faith to the wonder of what the Risen One has done for you. He is glorified, and He is giving you the promise that you will share in that glory with Him, that your very being will be aflame with resurrection, light, and glory and power—and probably a few muscles, too!

35

THE STRANGER ON
THE SHORE

After these things Jesus manifested Himself again to the disciples at the Sea of
Tiberias, and He manifested Himself in this way. There were together Simon
Peter, and Thomas called Didymus, and Nathanael of Cana in Galilee, and the
sons of Zebedee, and two others of His disciples. Simon Peter said to them, "I
am going fishing." They said to him, "We will also come with you." They went
out, and got into the boat; and that night they caught nothing. But when the
day was now breaking, Jesus stood on the beach; yet the disciples did not know
that it was Jesus. Jesus therefore said to them, "Children, you do not have any
fish, do you?" They answered Him, "No." And He said to them, "Cast the net
on the right-hand side of the boat, and you will find a catch." They cast therefore, and then they were not able to haul it in because of the great number of
fish. That disciple therefore whom Jesus loved said to Peter, "It is the Lord."
And so when Simon Peter heard that it was the Lord, he put his outer garment
on (for he was stripped for work), and threw himself into the sea. But the other
disciples came in the little boat, for they were not far from the land, but about
one hundred yards away, dragging the net full of fish. And so when they got
out upon the land, they saw a charcoal fire already laid, and fish placed on it,
and bread. Jesus said to them, "Bring some of the fish which you have now
caught." Simon Peter went up and drew the net to land, full of large fish, a hundred and fifty-three; and although there were so many, the net was not torn.

Jesus said to them, "Come and have breakfast." None of the disciples
ventured to question Him, "Who are You?" knowing that it was the Lord.
Jesus came and took the bread and gave it to them, and the fish likewise. This
is now the third time that Jesus was manifested to the disciples, after He was
raised from the dead. So when they had finished breakfast, Jesus said to Simon
Peter, "Simon, son of John, do you love Me more than these?" He said to Him,
"Yes, Lord; You know that I love You." He said to him, "Tend My lambs."
He said to him again a second time, "Simon, son of John, do you love Me?"
He said to Him, "Yes, Lord; You know that I love You." He said to him,
"Shepherd My sheep." He said to him the third time, "Simon, son of John, do
you love Me?" Peter was grieved because He said to him the third time, "Do
you love Me?" And he said to Him, "Lord, You know all things; You know
that I love You." Jesus said to him, "Tend My sheep. Truly, truly, I say to you,
when you were younger, you used to gird yourself, and walk wherever you
wished; but when you grow old, you will stretch out your hands, and someone else will gird you, and bring you where you do not wish to go." Now this
He said, signifying by what kind of death he would glorify God. And when He
had spoken this, He said to him, "Follow Me!" (John 21:1-19).

IN *THE LION, THE WITCH, AND THE WARDROBE,* by C. S. Lewis, Aslan the lion inspires great love and fear in four children who find themselves in Narnia. But before they first meet Aslan, when they first hear of him from a character named Mr. Beaver, Lewis says:

> None of the children knew who Aslan was any more than you do; but the moment the Beaver had spoken these words, everyone felt quite different. Perhaps it has sometimes happened to you in a dream that someone says something which you don't understand but in the dream it feels as if it had some enormous meaning—either a terrifying one which turns the whole dream into a nightmare or else a lovely meaning too lovely to put into words, which makes the dream so beautiful that you remember it all your life and are always wishing you could get back into that dream again. It was like that now. At the name of Aslan each one of the children felt something jump in his inside.[1]

A little later, one of the children, Lucy, discovers that Aslan is, in fact, a great lion, and in her fear of Aslan she asks Mr. Beaver, "Then, he isn't safe?"

"Safe?" he responds. "Who said anything about safe? 'course he isn't safe. But he's good."[2]

The risen Christ isn't safe; the risen Christ is dangerous because He is going to find you out. And He is going to pursue you with the vigilance of love. And He is going to make you into something that you are not because He loves you.

Aslan, of course, is Lewis's portrayal of Christ. In the language of Narnia, the loving and terrifying picture that Lewis paints is of a lion who is at once gentle, kind, and approachable, yet ferocious. The girls get on his back and ride like the wind, holding onto his mane. They smell the delicious sweetness of his breath and yet they know all the while that there is something so ferocious about him, so terrifying that there is both a deep desire to draw near and an uneasy urge to pull away at the same time.

That is Jesus. That is not Jesus your buddy; that is not Jesus your golf partner; that is not Jesus, God of the gaps, there when you need Him, when everything else just doesn't quite work right and you can't figure it out yourself. No, this is the loving and terrifying risen Savior. Is

He good? No doubt. Is He safe? Never. It is risky business to know this risen Savior, and it is downright dangerous to follow Him.

This passage from John 21 has an incredibly eerie quality about it. Can you envision the misty, dewy, early morning on the Sea of Galilee? Do you sense the strangeness of it? We see the risen Lord's goodness, but we see how unpredictable He is, how we can't control Him, how He is not the God who is going to fit into our pocket or our fishing boat.

Why does Jesus appear in this way at this time after the Resurrection, as a stranger out of nowhere on the shore? About two weeks have passed since His resurrection. The disciples have returned to the northern part of Israel, by the Sea of Galilee, because that is where Jesus had said He would meet with them. But He didn't say exactly where, and He didn't say when or what for. There is a cryptic uncertainty, a mystery about this promise.

What does the risen Christ want from these disciples? What does the risen Christ want from us? Clearly the disciples didn't have much to do, except to wait for further instructions; and the instructions come in this passage. We have to hunt for them, but they are there, very clearly so. The risen Christ who meets His disciples on the shore wants three things: He wants to enter our everyday working lives; He wants us to follow Him; and He wants our love.

THE STRANGER WANTS OUR LABOR

Seven of the disciples are walking together by the Sea of Galilee, or, as John calls it here, the Sea of Tiberias. Perhaps they were at the port of Tiberias itself, a beautiful vacation spot in Israel today and perhaps then as well. It was not a bad place to wait for what was next. But even a vacation gets boring after a while, especially if, like these disciples, you feel a little lost and disjointed, maybe even hopeless. What were the disciples thinking? Two weeks had gone by. Yes, they had seen Jesus once or twice in those two weeks, but surely they wondered, "Lord, what's next?"

Perhaps some of the disciples were reflective and thoughtful. Some had time to kill. Maybe they would get a good book and stick their feet in the spa waters. But not Peter, whose motto was, "When in doubt, do something." He decided that waiting for Jesus would probably not be incompatible with trying his hand at his old trade—fishing. Some think that Peter had given up on Jesus, that he had thought it was all lost and there was nothing else to do but go back to work. I don't think that is quite fair. In his restlessness Peter is doing what he knows and needs to do. He is a fisherman.

The strength of Peter's personality draws the others along with him. After fishing through the night with no catch to show for it, as the light breaks they see someone on the beach who calls out to them, "Do you have any fish to go with My bread?"

They can see the stranger only faintly in the misty dawn light, but apparently they can hear Him well enough. "No," they say, disappointed that they hadn't caught any fish.

The stranger on the beach responds, "Cast your nets on the other side of the boat."

When they do, they are unable to haul in the net because of the large number of fish they catch.

Christian singer Michael Card wrote a song many years ago about this passage entitled "Stranger on the Seashore." It begins this way:

> In the early morning mist
> They saw a Stranger on the sea shore
> He some how seemed familiar
> Asking what the night had brought
> With taught anticipation then
> They listen to His order
> And pulling in the net
> Found more than they had ever caught.*

The disciple John says, "It is the Lord." Maybe it is his great love for Jesus that makes him the one who is so perceptive to see first that it is the Lord. We can imagine John standing in the prow of the boat, shading his eyes, trying to see the figure on the shore through the mist.

But Peter is a different sort, so when he hears it is Jesus, he grabs his shirt, ties it around his waist, jumps into the water and swims ashore.

---

*Michael Card, "Stranger on the Seashore," © 1982 Singspiration Music (ASCAP) (admin. by Brentwood-Benson Music Publishing, Inc.) and Mole End Music (Admin. by Word Music, Inc.). All Rights Reserved. Used by Permission.

In his song, Card then says this:

The one He loved first recognized
The stranger there was Jesus
And he alone remembered
This had happened once before
The one who had denied Him
Who had once walked on the water
Jumped in and swam to Him
To be confronted on the shore.

Meanwhile the others come in the boat more slowly. They see a fire with fish roasting on it. Why does Jesus ask for fish if He already has them? But now He tells them to bring the fish that they have just caught, and again, Peter takes the lead. He drags the heavy net ashore. And then the oddest detail is recounted: the fish are counted—one hundred and fifty-three of them. Such a huge catch, yet amazingly, the net hasn't ripped open.

It is a simple but remarkable fact that the first thing Jesus does *not* do as He meets with these disciples in history's first prayer breakfast is give them a sermon on the doctrinal meaning of the Resurrection. No, the first thing He does is bless the work of everyday fishermen.

Though the text does not say this specifically, we can imagine that the Lord says, "Peter, count them." And in front of the Lord of glory, Peter counts the fish, "135, 136, 137 . . ." Why? As the resurrected Christ, Jesus has authority over everything in heaven, on earth, and under the sea. He already knows how many fish are there. But it is into the everyday work of our lives that the risen Christ wants to come.

Jesus comes to find Peter this day at his place of work. Post-resurrection, the disciples are not at the temple, or a prayer meeting, or a church committee meeting. Jesus meets us in the ordinary routines of our lives: taking care of our children and our grandchildren, making sales calls, phoning potential investors, coaching a Little League baseball team, doing homework, answering phone or e-mail messages. The greatest heresy in the history of the Christian church is platonic dualism, which puts all of life into two categories, one spiritual and one material. Platonic dualism says spiritual things are church things, the rest of everyday life is material, and the Lord really only cares about the spiritual things. Not true, and if there was ever a passage in the Bible that makes it abundantly clear that it is not true, it is here.

The work of our lives is not separate from what the Lord cares about. He involves Himself with fish, lots of fish, large fish, small fish, a hundred and fifty-three fish, plus the ones He already has that He is cooking on the fire. If Christ is truly risen, then He is at this moment no farther from us than He was from those disciples on the beach. He enters the marketplace as well as the worship place, and if He comes out of the tomb at all, He comes out of it as the Lord of all. He is no less the Lord of our working lives than He is of our prayer lives, and He will not be content to stay in some religious compartment of our lives. He is not safe because He will intrude Himself into all the parts of our lives.

Jesus doesn't need the work of our lives any more than He needs anything else from us, yet He commands us to bring Him our fish. He holds all the power and authority and is complete in Himself, but the risen Christ asks for our labor. And He is somehow pleased with it. The Lord values our work. He sees our work as part of His creative endeavor. In our work we become creators made in the image of the Great Creator, and our work is beautiful to God because it is a created thing that imitates His great work of the creation of heaven and earth.

A teacher once told me how in his early days of teaching he prepared every lesson carefully and prayerfully. He was nervous. He needed help in the classroom every day. But now, many years later, he is quite casual about it. He has done it a lot. Most of us, if we are honest, would say, "We don't need the Lord in the daily routines of being homemakers or bankers or surgeons or even ministers." This disconnectedness in our life from the risen Christ is grievous to Him. He wants us to offer our labor to Him. If we don't, we deny His resurrection authority and power in all of life.

All of our life's work will be counted, "135, 136, 137 . . ." But the object of the count is whether or not it is done as honoring to Him. Do you name your clients before Him in prayer? Do you read a story to your grandchild purposefully?

God loves our work, but most of us make our work an idol. When we separate our work from God, when we treat our work as something that He doesn't care about, it becomes idolatrous in our hearts. It becomes the basis of our living.

What is the very first thing that God gave man to do after He created him in His image and gave him a spouse? He put him to work in the garden. Work was good before the Fall, but afterwards becomes corrupted. Man has to earn his living by the sweat of his brow, but work is still good. Work is to be *a legitimate expression of* our identity, but it is not our identity, and therein lies all the difference. When we make work our identity, we make it an idol. When you say, "I am what I do," or, "I am my success," then what happens when you cease to be a success? What happens when you are too old to work or you get fired? Are you still your work? Do you see the balance that the risen Lord of glory wants? We love our work and we should, but we must not idolize it. We must count out our clients, count out our fish to Him. He is pleased as we do that, but not if we make it an idol.

THE STRANGER WANTS TO LEAD US

Later, after Jesus and His disciples finish eating, Jesus confronts Peter on the issue of leading and following: "Truly, truly, I say to you, when you were younger, you used to gird yourself, and walk wherever you wished; but when you grow old, you will stretch out your hands, and someone else will gird you, and bring you where you do not wish to go" (John 21:18).

Imagine strong, vigorous, young Peter hearing those words. He has just hauled in one hundred and fifty-three big fish. Peter wants to be on the front lines. He is disposed by nature to be a leader. It is now time to lead, as far as he is concerned. "You have already told me I have a job to do, Lord; let's get to it." But the Lord tells Peter, "There will come a time when all you can do is follow. Down the line, Peter, things are going to change. You will be forced into the background. Others will lead. In fact, others will lead you, Peter, when you are old and feeble. They will take you where you do not necessarily want to go. So follow Me." Perhaps Peter is reminded of words Jesus has said earlier: "If anyone serves Me, let him follow Me; and where I am, there shall My servant also be; if anyone serves Me, the Father will honor him" (12:26).

Jesus is saying that to follow Him will always mean a death of sorts, a loss of our own prerogatives to do what we want. Peter may think he is going out to be a triumphant church leader, but no, he is going to the cross. He is going to the place where he must learn *who* leads his life and sets its tempo and type of service. The risen Lord's command to follow is an absolute trade-off. Either we learn on our own to lead, and fail, as Peter did, or we follow quite simply by surrendering leadership to Christ's risen power and authority.

The chorus of "Stranger on the Shore" says this:

> You need to be confronted
> By the Stranger on the shore
> You need to have Him search your soul
> You need to hear the call
> You need to learn exactly
> What it means for you to follow
> You need to realize that He's asking for your all.

THE STRANGER WANTS OUR LOVE

Jesus also wants what a man of action finds the most difficult to give. At the end of the meal, Jesus turns to Peter and asks, "Simon, son of John, do you love Me more than these?" (John 21:15). Jesus uses his birth name, not Peter, the rock, the apostle, the one upon whom the great confession of the church would begin to be built. This is Simon, stripped of everything, being asked, "Do you love Me?" Will he still boast of his allegiance to Christ as he did before (Mark 14:29)? Will he brag that his love is greater than that of the other disciples?

Jesus is asking Peter if he is still struggling for control. Peter, the man of action, knows how to live his life only if he is in control; and Jesus tells him he can't be in control, by asking him the question over which Peter has no control. Peter cannot love apart from the quickening love of Christ in him. He cannot call up love. Oh, he can fish. He can lift heavy nets. He can lead the troops, maybe. But he cannot love the risen Savior until the risen Savior has loved him first. In His risen glory, Jesus is so close and yet so far away. No one, not even Peter, dares to ask Him the burning question, "What do You want from me?"

"Do you love Me, Simon?" is a question that cuts through all of Peter's pretensions and attempts to control. It cuts to the heart of the failure in his denial of Christ, which had been motivated by his sinful "me-and-what-I-want" thinking.

"Peter," the Lord says, "I know what you can do and what you cannot do. I do want your fish. I do want you to follow. I know that you are a man of action. But Peter, you will inevitably fail Me because you are a son of Adam. Every son of Adam who has ever lived has failed Me."

Jesus knew what was in Peter's heart: failure, fear, uncertainty, tentativeness, selfishness. But He waits for the answer nonetheless.

"Yes, Lord; You know that I love You." Peter croaks it out as best he can, and the Lord answers, "Tend My lambs." Here, despite his three-fold denial, Jesus restores to Peter his apostolic authority. He is giving him his job back, restoring him to his position of responsibility. But note the order. *The restoration of Peter's heart must precede the restoration of his service.* "Peter, you can't fix your denials. You can't make the past right by your own effort. Don't you see that you can only accept My love and respond with a heart that is seared with failure but healed with love? I know you want to go fishing for Me, Peter. But, Peter, are you ready simply to do nothing except receive My love and love Me back?"

"But, Lord, here are my fish."

"Do you love Me?"

"But, Lord, look what I can do for You."

"Simon, do you love Me?"

Together with Peter, we, too, must learn to "do nothing" for Jesus. He keeps pressing the hot, surgical knife into our hearts. He drives us to the place where either by inward or by outward failure we realize again that we cannot do anything for Him, and that we need to receive His love.

I had lunch recently with two bright, competent men who were used to being quite able to handle every situation in their lives. We discussed the areas in our lives where we were learning that we just weren't able to fix everything—places where we needed the love and power of the risen Christ. The conclusion we came to was this: by the confession of our inability, we come to the beginning of our ability. God's power truly is perfected in weakness, as Paul tells us in 2 Corinthians 12:9. Perhaps it is a child whose sickness we cannot cure. Perhaps it is a profession that has run out of gas. Perhaps it is a marriage that is failing. Like Peter, we must stop trying to run our lives in our own power and boastfulness, and we must let the risen Lord heal our broken hearts with the same power that was exerted when He was raised from the dead. Are we living in the grace of Christ and feeding from it daily?

Who is this Stranger on the shore? He is the risen King of glory. And He is very, very good, but He is not at all safe, not at all.

You need to be confronted
By the Stranger on the shore.
You need to have Him search your soul,
You need to hear the call.
You need to learn exactly
What it means for you to follow.
You need to realize that He's asking for your all.

36

A Pattern for
Beloved Disciples

But Thomas, one of the twelve, called Didymus, was not with them when Jesus came. The other disciples therefore were saying to him, "We have seen the Lord!" But he said to them, "Unless I shall see in His hands the imprint of the nails, and put my finger into the place of the nails, and put my hand into His side, I will not believe." And after eight days again His disciples were inside, and Thomas with them. Jesus came, the doors having been shut, and stood in their midst, and said, "Peace be with you." Then He said to Thomas, "Reach here your finger, and see My hands; and reach here your hand, and put it into My side; and be not unbelieving, but believing." Thomas answered and said to Him, "My Lord and my God!" Jesus said to him, "Because you have seen Me, have you believed? Blessed are they who did not see, and yet believed." Many other signs therefore Jesus also performed in the presence of the disciples, which are not written in this book; but these have been written that you may believe that Jesus is the Christ, the Son of God; and that believing you may have life in His name (John 20:24-31).

THERE IS SOMETHING PARTICULARLY appealing about John, the apostle. He apparently outlived all the other apostles. His letters in the New Testament are some of the last documents in the Bible to be written. We love old John. He is so warm. There is a universal appeal to his Gospel because we sense his passionate commitment to Jesus and to the truth. He wants to persuade his readers to feed off of the very truths that he is relaying. We sense that he himself is partaking of the very truth as he communicates it to us. He wants us to taste and see that the Lord is good, just as he has.

In John 20:30-31, the summary verses of this Gospel, John says that these things were recorded in order that we might believe that Jesus is the Christ, the Son of God. But in this context, just before these verses, we have this amazing account of Thomas, who is a doubter just like all of us. The shadows of doubt crossed Thomas's heart just as they cross our hearts. We need to be renewed again and again in the truth that we say we believe about who Jesus is. Thomas was apparently a left-brain type. He wanted to touch, to see; he wanted technical, scientific evidence.

THE TRUTHFUL AND PASSIONATE WITNESS

John wants us to believe just as Jesus wants Thomas to believe. Remember in chapter 1 we discussed how John sees himself in three specific ways, and the ways he sees himself are the ways that he wants us to see ourselves. He very deliberately, self-consciously writes this apologetic, this banner that he lifts high for Jesus Christ. As a truthful and passionate witness to the events and meaning of Christ's life, death, and resurrection, he calls on his readers to respond with like passion and love for the truth. John is not neutral about Jesus Christ. He profoundly cares that people understand, and telling us about Thomas is another example of this great concern. Jesus cares deeply that Thomas will come to believe in Him. Jesus goes the extra mile to reach out to Thomas, particularly in his doubt and his insecurity, in order that he might cross the line to faith.

Jesus goes after the unbeliever. That is a revolutionary thought that should motivate a revolutionary pattern of life for us. Jesus doesn't care just about us and the church. His parables tell us that He cares about the lost coin, the lost sheep, the lost son, lost people. He cares passionately about people in diverse cultures. He cares that they would come to believe.

We began this study of John by looking at the author in the light of his own description of himself as the beloved disciple (13:23). Rather than being a sign of arrogance, we saw that this is precisely the right way for John, and all Christians, to think. John is just making it personal. He is saying that the love of Jesus is for us. It is not abstract. It is not just for the world. Paul says in a similarly personal way in Galatians 2:20b, "I live by faith in the Son of God, who loved me, and delivered Himself up for me."

That is why Jesus reaches out to Thomas and tells him to touch. "Thomas, don't doubt. I love you. Thomas, what is it going to take to get you to understand that the Messiah is standing right in front of you?"

SEEING OURSELVES AS JOHN SAW HIMSELF

After reading through this entire book on the Gospel of John, how do you see yourself? Like John did? Do you live at the intersection of passion and truth? He lived there because Jesus had changed His life. The gospel is a transforming power. The gospel doesn't come to us as just something to believe. It changes lives and makes us new people.

I am passionate about that which really affects my life. I have a new passion for football because I have a son who plays football. I wasn't so passionate about football a few years ago, but I am passionate about football now. It touches my life now. Where does Jesus touch your life? Where is the gospel changing you? That is where you are likely to find the source of both truth and passion.

How is Christ at work in your heart today? If there is no evidence of transforming power there, if Jesus isn't rearranging the furniture of your life somewhere in a way that may be uncomfortable, then ask yourself the question: Have I ever understood that the gospel that saves me is the gospel that changes me? We cannot believe in that gospel without being on the road to change.

Is there any change particularly in the deepest dispositions of your heart and life, those things that you don't think can change? What about those habits, attitudes, and responses that you describe as "just the way I am"? Is it a problem with anger, with food, with alcohol, with wanting what others have, with looking at things you shouldn't look at? No, it is not just "the way I am"—not if you are in Christ. You are a new person. You have been given an altogether new life. You have been brought into union with Jesus Christ. You are made new by the gospel; now live that way.

But you say, "I can't. I don't know how to change."

Cry out to God, and say, "Lord, help my unbelief. Lord, show me the wounds you endured for me; show me where they touch my heart."

Pray that prayer, and be passionate about it.

SEEING OURSELVES AS EVANGELISTS

As John was, we need to become culturally aware communicators and advocates. When we speak of Christ to others, we must not only read the gospel right; we must also read the culture right. John did a lot of cultural exegesis. He understood the culture of the world to which he was writing. He understood the Jews; he understood the Greeks. He was thinking about urban, educated people. He was thinking about his audience when he wrote this book. Are you thinking about the people to whom you need to speak about Christ?

When I was younger, I had a zeal for speaking the gospel to the lost. When I was first out of seminary and first doing the work of ministry, I used to pray every morning, "Lord, lead me to someone this day who does not know the gospel's truth." That needs to be my prayer every day. It is a prayer that will lead us to a diverse selection of people needing to hear of Jesus.

The health of a church is measured by the cultural diversity that constitutes it. You only know you are a beloved disciple when you see that the breadth and length and height and depth of the love of God and the extending grace of God goes far beyond the likes of you or me. It goes to people of every tribe and every tongue. The kingdom of God is a grand and glorious place, and there are a lot of beloved people in it. And a lot of them don't look like you or me, thanks be to God.

If we are disciples who love the truth, and whom Jesus loves, our lives will reflect the pattern of love and truth, truth and love, interwoven to make the whole. Love and truth are inseparable. We cannot give someone the truth if we do not love them; and if we do not give someone the truth, we do not love them.

Jesus loves us so much that He makes us face the truth about ourselves and about Him, and telling His truth causes us to see it more clearly in ourselves. In our early enthusiasm for Christ, we may blurt out our first attempts at witnessing and almost right away sense opposition. But that opposition should reveal more clearly our own unrighteousness before Him and our dependence on Him. Then the truth of the gospel can dig even deeper into our hearts, and the result is refreshed joy and hope in the Lord, which leads us on to more and better witnessing. Is this the pattern of your life?

Unfortunately, the more common pattern for most lives is something like this: we grow up, get educated, get a job, get married, get a family, get successful at work and life, get some fun, get retired. The call of John's Gospel is to a life much deeper, much more God-glorifying and much more joyful.

SEEING OURSELVES AS BELOVED DISCIPLES

The issue is this: do you say that the Christ is this man, Jesus? Does the love and truth of this God/Man overpower you? Are you swept up, overwhelmed, as a small boat in a mighty storm? As the great old hymn describes it:

> O the deep, deep love of Jesus! Vast, unmeasured, boundless, free;
> Rolling as a mighty ocean in its fullness over me.
> Underneath me, all around me, is the current of thy love;
> Leading onward, leading homeward, to thy glorious rest above.
>
> O the deep, deep love of Jesus! Spread his praise from shore to shore;
> How He loveth, ever loveth, changeth never, nevermore;
> How He watches o'er His loved ones, died to call them all His own;
> How for them He intercedeth, watcheth o'er them from the throne.
>
> O the deep, deep love of Jesus! Love of every love the best:
> 'Tis an ocean vast of blessing, 'tis a haven sweet of rest.
> O the deep, deep love of Jesus! 'tis a heav'n of heav'ns to me;
> And it lifts me up to glory, for it lifts me up to thee![1]

Let the mighty love of Jesus roll over you, turn your life upside down, then restore it in the wholeness that only the truth of His life, death, and resurrection can provide. Are you so profoundly aware of your sin and inadequacy that the wonder of the grace of God amazes you? Does the truth that God reached out and saved even you seal your heart to the reality that *you* are the object of God's love in Christ Jesus? You are a beloved disciple if you are a disciple at all. Be overwhelmed by His love, overjoyed by His truth, and give Him all the glory He is due.

NOTES

CHAPTER 1: THE BELOVED DISCIPLE

1. D. A. Carson, *The Gospel According to John* (Grand Rapids, Mich.: Eerdmans, 1991), 76.

CHAPTER 2: THE WORD

1. D. A. Carson, *The Gospel According to John* (Grand Rapids, Mich.: Eerdmans, 1991), 114.
2. Dallas Willard, unpublished lecture, 1998.
3. F. F. Bruce, *Second Thoughts on the Dead Sea Scrolls* (London and Grand Rapids: Eerdmans, 1956), 134; quoted in Leon Morris, *The Gospel According to John* (Grand Rapids, Mich.: Eerdmans, 1971), 87, note 44.

CHAPTER 3: THE TRUE LIGHT

1. C. S. Lewis, *Mere Christianity* (New York: Macmillan, 1952), 35.

CHAPTER 4: THE WORD MADE FLESH

1. G. K. Chesterton, "The Wise Men," in *As I Was Saying: A Chesterton Reader,* ed. Robert Knille (Grand Rapids, Mich.: Eerdmans, 1985), 306.
2. Quoted in Philip Schaff, *Creeds of Christendom,* 3 vols. (New York: Harper, 1878–1882), 2:62-63.
3. Attributed to John Francis Wade, "O Come, All Ye Faithful," *Trinity Hymnal* (Philadelphia: Great Commission Publications, 1961), 208.
4. John Donne, "Christmas Day, 1626," in *Sermons of John Donne,* ed. Evelyn M. Simpson and George R. Potter (Berkeley: University of California Press, 1962), 7:279.

CHAPTER 6: "COME AND SEE"

1. John Calvin, *John,* The Crossway Classic Commentaries, Alister McGrath and J. I. Packer, eds. (Wheaton, Ill.: Crossway, 1994), 42.
2. Wayne Grudem, *Systematic Theology* (Grand Rapids, Mich.: Zondervan, 1995), 692.
3. Calvin, *John,* 41.

CHAPTER 7: THE NEW WINE

1. The Form of Solemnization of Matrimony, *The Book of Common Prayer* (New York: Seabury, 1953), 300.
2. D. A. Carson, *The Gospel According to John* (Grand Rapids, Mich.: Eerdmans, 1991), 171.
3. Ibid.

4. George Herbert, "The Agony," in *The Complete English Poems,* ed. John Tobin (London: Penguin, 1991), 33.

CHAPTER 8: THE NEW TEMPLE

1. D. A. Carson, *The Gospel According to John* (Grand Rapids, Mich.: Eerdmans, 1991), 179.
2. Ibid., 181.
3. Ibid., 182.

CHAPTER 9: THE NEW BIRTH

1. D. A. Carson, *The Gospel According to John* (Grand Rapids, Mich.: Eerdmans, 1991), 185.
2. John Calvin, *Commentary Upon the Acts of the Apostles,* ed. Henry Beveridge, in *Calvin's Commentaries,* vol. 19 (Grand Rapids, Mich.: Baker, 1999), 132.
3. Charles Spurgeon, *The New Park Street Pulpit,* vol. 1 (London: Banner of Truth, 1963), sermon 52.

CHAPTER 10: THE (REAL) NEW AGE

1. Edmund Morris, *Dutch: A Memoir of Ronald Reagan* (New York: Random House, 1999).
2. D. A. Carson, *The Gospel According to John* (Grand Rapids, Mich.: Eerdmans, 1991), 212.
3. J. I. Packer, *Knowing God* (Downers Grove, Ill.: InterVarsity, 1973), 136.

CHAPTER 11: WATER, WORSHIP, WITNESS

1. Charles Spurgeon, *Faith's Checkbook* (Chicago: Moody, n.d.), 94 (July 6).
2. Tim Keller, unpublished sermon, January 10, 1999.

CHAPTER 12: A SIGNPOST TO HOME

1. D. A. Carson, *The Gospel According to John* (Grand Rapids, Mich.: Eerdmans, 1991), 237.
2. Jonathan Edwards, "Pardon for the Greatest of Sinners," in *The Works of Jonathan Edwards,* vol. 2 (Peabody, Mass.: Hendrickson, 1998), 112 (doctrine III., 4).
3. Elizabeth Clephane, "Beneath the Cross of Jesus," *Trinity Hymnal* (Philadelphia: Great Commission Publications, 1961), 251.

CHAPTER 13: THE CONFLICT

1. D. A. Carson, *The Gospel According to John* (Grand Rapids, Mich.: Eerdmans, 1991), 243.
2. Shab. 23:1; 2:5; 14:4; quoted in Leon Morris, *The Gospel According to John* (Grand Rapids, Mich.: Eerdmans, 1971), 305, note 25.
3. William Barclay, quoted in Leon Morris, *Gospel According to John,* 311.
4. Carson, *Gospel According to John,* 251.

5. G. Campbell Morgan, quoted in Morris, *Gospel According to John,* 299.
6. Carson, *Gospel According to John,* 255.

CHAPTER 14: A SIGN OF PROVISION

1. Augustine, *Tractates on the Gospel of John* (Washington, D.C.: Catholic University of America Press, 1994), tractate 24.
2. John Calvin, *John,* The Crossway Classic Commentaries, Alister McGrath and J. I. Packer, eds. (Wheaton, Ill.: Crossway, 1994), 148.
3. Leon Morris, *The Gospel According to John* (Grand Rapids, Mich.: Eerdmans, 1971), 343.
4. R. F. Bailey, *Saint John's Gospel* (London, 1957), quoted in Morris, *Gospel According to John,* 346-347.
5. Calvin, *John,* 149.
6. Martin Luther, "Letters . . . to Philip Melanchthon (August 1, 1521)," in *Luther's Works,* ed. Gottfried G. Krodel, vol. 48 (Philadelphia: Fortress, 1963), 282.

CHAPTER 15: "THE WILL OF HIM WHO SENT ME"

1. D. A. Carson, *The Gospel According to John* (Grand Rapids, Mich.: Eerdmans, 1991), 291.

CHAPTER 16: THE PAST, PRESENT, AND FUTURE WITH JESUS

1. John Calvin, *Institutes of the Christian Religion,* Library of Christian Classics, ed. John T. McNeill, trans. Ford Lewis Battles (Philadelphia: Westminster, 1960), book 4, chapter 17, see pages 1359-1428.

CHAPTER 17: RIVERS OF LIVING WATER

1. Arthur Bennett, ed., *The Valley of Vision* (Edinburgh: Banner of Truth, 1977), 96.
2. John Bunyan, *Pilgrim's Progress,* ed. James Blanton Wharey (Oxford: Oxford University Press, 1960), 263.
3. William Wordsworth, "Rob Roy's Grave," *Wordsworth's Poetical Works* (New York: Oxford University Press, 1965), 231.
4. C. John Miller, *Outgrowing the Ingrown Church* (Grand Rapids, Mich.: Zondervan, 1986), 24.

CHAPTER 18: "I AM"

1. C. S. Lewis, *Mere Christianity* (New York: Macmillan, 1952), 55.
2. Flannery O'Connor, "A Good Man Is Hard to Find," in *Flannery O'Connor: The Complete Stories* (New York: Farrar, Straus, and Giroux, 1971), 132.
3. Rudolf Otto, *The Idea of the Holy* (London: Oxford University Press, 1977).

CHAPTER 19: TRUTH THAT FREES . . . AND MAKES YOU ODD!

1. Peter Berger, in Peter Berger, Brigitte Berger, and Hansfried Kellner, *The Homeless Mind* (New York: Vintage, 1973), 77.
2. Ibid., 77-78.

3. Ibid., 78.
4. The following illustration is taken from Os Guinness, *Time for Truth* (Grand Rapids, Mich.: Baker, 2002), 12.
5. Ray Price, quoted in Joe McGinniss, *The Selling of the President* (New York: Trident, 1969), 193.
6. Flannery O'Connor, personal correspondence, widely attributed.

CHAPTER 20: BLINDING LIGHT

1. Leon Morris, *The Gospel According to John* (Grand Rapids, Mich.: Eerdmans, 1971), 476.
2. D. A. Carson, *The Gospel According to John* (Grand Rapids, Mich.: Eerdmans, 1991), 375.

CHAPTER 21: THE TRUE AND GOOD SHEPHERD

1. D. A. Carson, *The Gospel According to John* (Grand Rapids, Mich.: Eerdmans, 1991), 385.
2. C. S. Lewis, *The Weight of Glory* (New York: Macmillan, 1949), 4.

CHAPTER 22: "LAZARUS, COME FORTH"

1. D. A. Carson, *The Gospel According to John* (Grand Rapids, Mich.: Eerdmans, 1991), 415.
2. Ibid., 416.
3. John Calvin, *John,* The Crossway Classic Commentaries, Alister McGrath and J. I. Packer, eds. (Wheaton, Ill.: Crossway, 1994), 281.
4. B. B. Warfield, *The Person and Work of Christ* (Philadelphia: Presbyterian & Reformed, 1980), 117.
5. William Williams, "Guide Me, O Thou Great Jehovah," *Trinity Hymnal* (Philadelphia: Great Commission Publications, 1961), 598.

CHAPTER 23: THE ANOINTING

1. Frances R. Havergal, "Take My Life, and Let It Be," *Trinity Hymnal* (Philadelphia: Great Commission Publications, 1961), 585.

CHAPTER 24: "BEHOLD, YOUR KING COMES"

1. D. A. Carson, *The Gospel According to John* (Grand Rapids, Mich.: Eerdmans, 1991), 433.

CHAPTER 25: THE HOUR OF GLORY

1. D. A. Carson, *The Gospel According to John* (Grand Rapids, Mich.: Eerdmans, 1991), 437.
2. John Piper, *Let the Nations Be Glad!* (Grand Rapids, Mich.: Baker, 1993), 107.
3. Ibid., 111.

CHAPTER 26: A LONG OBEDIENCE IN THE SAME DIRECTION

1. The title of this chapter is taken from the title of a book by Eugene Peterson (*A

Long Obedience in the Same Direction [Downers Grove, Ill.: InterVarsity, 1980]).

2. C. S. Lewis, *The Screwtape Letters* (New York: Macmillan, 1946), 47.

CHAPTER 27: THE ORDER OF THE TOWEL

1. Charles Wesley, "Hark! the Herald Angels Sing," *Trinity Hymnal* (Philadelphia: Great Commission Publications, 1961), 203.

2. Jonathan Edwards, *The Works of Jonathan Edwards,* vol. 1 (Edinburgh: Banner of Truth, 1984), xlvii.

3. Dietrich Bonhoeffer, *The Cost of Discipleship* (New York: Macmillan, 1949), 7.

CHAPTER 28: A PLACE PREPARED

1. D. A. Carson, *The Gospel According to John* (Grand Rapids, Mich.: Eerdmans, 1991), 486.

2. C. S. Lewis, *The Great Divorce* (New York: Macmillan, 1946).

3. C. S. Lewis, *The Problem of Pain* (New York: Macmillan, 1940), 115.

CHAPTER 29: THE DISCLOSURE

1. A. W. Tozer, *The Pursuit of God* (Camp Hill, Pa.: Christian Publications, 1982), 30.

2. Cornelius Van Til, "Response" to Herman Dooyeweerd, "Cornelius Van Til and the Transcendent Critique of Theoretical Thought," in *Jerusalem and Athens: Critical Discussions on the Theology and Apologetics of Cornelius Van Til,* ed. E. R. Geehan (Philadelphia: Presbyterian & Reformed, 1971), 127.

3. Jonathan Edwards, *The Distinguishing Marks of a Work of the Spirit of God,* in *The Works of Jonathan Edwards,* vol. 2 (Peabody, Mass.: Hendrickson, 1998), 274 (section 3, "Practical Inferences").

4. John D. Rockefeller, cited in Os Guinness, *Doing Well and Doing Good* (Colorado Springs: NavPress, 2001), 60.

5. Augustine, Confessions, I, 20.

CHAPTER 30: "THAT THEY MAY ALL BE ONE"

1. C. S. Lewis, *The Weight of Glory* (New York: Collier, 1980), 18.

2. James Montgomery Boice, "Hallelujah," *Hymns for a Modern Reformation* (Philadelphia: Tenth Presbyterian Church, 2000).

CHAPTER 31: LAST WORDS

1. C. S. Lewis, *The Great Divorce* (New York: Macmillan, 1946), 72.

2. I am indebted to Tim Keller for these insights.

CHAPTER 34: THE GLORIFIED BODY

1. "Seven Stanzas at Easter," from *Telephone Poles and Other Poems* by John Updike, copyright © 1959 by John Updike. Used by permission of Alfred A. Knopf, a division of Random House, Inc.

CHAPTER 35: THE STRANGER ON THE SHORE

1. C. S. Lewis, *The Lion, the Witch, and the Wardrobe* (New York: Macmillan, 1951), 64.
2. Ibid., 75.

CHAPTER 36: A PATTERN FOR BELOVED DISCIPLES

1. Samuel Trevor Francis, "O the Deep, Deep Love of Jesus!" *Trinity Hymnal* (Philadelphia: Great Commission Publications, 1961), 535.

GENERAL INDEX

abortion, 205
Andrew,
   and the feeding of the multitude,
     158, 265
   as wedding guest, 75, 78, 80
   calling of, 66
Aristotle, 245
Aslan, 372
Augustine, 157, 322

baptism, 57, 59, 62, 111, 333
Barclay, William, 150
Barna Research Group, 202-203
Berger, Peter, 203
Boice, James Montgomery, 332
Bonhoeffer, Dietrich, 298
Bruce, F. F., 29
Buddha, 341-342
Bunyan, John, 190

Caiaphas, 267, 347, 348, 350
Calvin, John, 66, 71-72, 98, 158, 161,
   176, 234, 244
Card, Michael, 374-375, 378, 380
Carson, D. A., 20, 25, 76, 85, 89, 90,
   96, 112, 137, 146, 151, 152, 167,
   234, 244, 259, 266, 303
Charlie, Bonnie Prince, 179
Cheng, Nien, 207-208
Chesterton, G. K., 46
China, 131, 207-208, 214, 263-264
Clephane, Elizabeth, 138-139
Clowney, Edmund, 214, 270
conflict management, 143-144
conversion, 70, 101, 225
cultural complexity, 21

Dalí, Salvador, 47
David, 85-86, 257, 320-321, 347
devil, theology of, 17
Disney World, 201-202
docetism, 47
Donne, John, 50, 245
Dooyeweerd, Herman, 318

Edwards, Jonathan, 138, 199-200,
   297, 319
Eidson, Jim, 99
Elliot, Jim, 268

Faraday, Sir Michael, 309
Feast of Tabernacles, 83, 183
feet, 246, 249-250, 292-297, 359-360
Ferguson, Sinclair, 106
footwashing, 292-296
foyer, 23, 31
fruit, 276-278

God,
   as Judge, 276
   as personal, 26, 196
   personal relationship with, 26
   sovereignty of, 167
grace, 22, 23, 50, 79-80, 101, 122-
   123, 127, 138-139, 162-164, 170
   common, 36
   expectant, 71-72
   for Peter, 71
   in stages, 68
   irresistible, 69-71
   personal, 69

heaven, 306
Herbert, George, 81

Heston, Charlton, 256
Hobbes, Thomas, 245
Holy Spirit, 62, 70, 92, 100, 115, 166-
    167, 182-189, 191, 232, 312-323,
    333, 368
home, 137-139
humility, 104-106, 187, 317, 319

imputation, 279
irony, 37, 40, 135, 147, 161, 221,
    259, 260, 307

John,
    as the beloved disciple, 20-22, 261-
        262, 337, 382
John the Baptist, 28, 56, 110-114,
    116, 152, 184, 293
    as the best man, 111-113
    witness about himself, 57-59
    witness about Jesus Christ, 59-62,
        67
Jesus Christ,
    as Bible study leader, 316
    as Creator, 26-27
    as flesh, 34, 47-48, 50-51, 156,
        169, 173, 177, 198, 210, 330,
        367
    as Friend, 309-310
    as I AM, 195-196, 198
    as King, 260-262@Index2:
    as Lord of the new age, 114-115
    as Peace, 322-323
    as personal, 69, 196, 231, 316, 382
    as Pilot, 308-309
    as the Bread, 49, 156, 163, 168,
        173, 177-178, 193, 199, 241
    as the Bridegroom, 78-80, 113,
        116, 280
    as the Good Shepherd, 199, 228-
        236
    as the Light, 31, 32-34, 40, 221,
        225
    as the Revelation of God, 28-31
    as the Sabbath breaker, 147-148
    as the Son of God, 21, 56, 62, 67,
        76, 107, 150, 150-153, 168-
        169, 184, 223, 224, 242-243,
        245
    as the Tabernacle, 48-49

as the Word, 24-26, 46-47
as Truth, 208-210
baptism of, 184
hometown of, 134
manner toward mother, 75-76
name of, 333
obedience of, 151, 168-170, 235,
    261, 274-276, 279, 282-283,
    285-286, 331
on a donkey, 258-260
rejection of, 37-40, 137
resurrection of, 364-367
thirst of, 339-340
witness to himself, 67
Joseph of Arimathea, 345-353
Josephus, 255
Judas, 160, 248, 250, 252, 253, 266,
    293, 352
Julian of Norwich, 51

Keller, Tim, 122

"Ladybug," 102-103
Landry, Tom, 232
language,
    analysis, 45
    crisis of, 44-45
    of family, 315
    spoken by John, 16
Lazarus, 77, 99, 152, 238-244, 247,
    255, 360
Lazarus (the servant), 339-340
Lehrer, Jim, 109
Lewis, C. S., 34, 197, 234, 284-285,
    306, 326, 339, 372
Lincoln, Abraham, 202-203, 206
Loman, Willy, 317
Lord's Supper, 176-179
Luther, Martin, 163, 281-282

Maccabeus, Simon, 256
Machen, J. Gresham, 286
Martin, Steve, 73
Martha, 238-242, 244, 245, 247, 252,
    253, 360
Mary of Bethany, 247-254, 293, 359-
    360, 362
Mary of Magdala, 355-359, 362

Mary the mother of Jesus, 75-77, 337, 349, 360-361, 362
McGinnis, Joe, 205
Miller, Jack, 191
"missions moment," 267
Morris, Edmund, 109, 117
Morris, Leon, 159
mourning, 240, 244, 349

Narnia, 372
Nathanael,
    as wedding guest, 75, 80
    calling of, 66, 69
The New York Times, 175-176
Nicodemus, 95-107, 110, 114, 115, 121-123, 127, 186-187, 221, 350
Nixon, Richard, 205

O'Connor, Flannery, 198, 209, 213
oddness, commandments of, 213-215
Otto, Rudolph, 198-199
Oval Office, 301-302

Packer, J. I., 115
palms, 255-256, 258
Paton, John G., 270-271
Peter,
    and the washing of feet, 296
    as a fisherman, 373-374
    as wedding guest, 75, 80
    calling of, 66, 69
    denial of, 303
    grace for, 71
    personality of, 374
    presumption of, 302-304
    restoration of, 378-379
Philip,
    and the feeding of the multitude, 159
    and the Greeks, 264-265
    as wedding guest, 75, 78, 80
    calling of, 66
Phillips, J. B., 150
Picasso, Pablo, 204
Pilate, 206, 259, 348, 349, 350, 351
Piper, John, 189-190, 269, 271
photograph, 35, 40-41, 102
politics, 252, 205, 257-260
Powlison, David, 219

Price, Ray, 205-206

Qumran community, 190

regeneration, 99-107
Reagan, Ronald, 109-110, 302
retirement, 270
revival, 269
Rockefeller, John D., 322
Rose, Dr. Ed, 238
Rousseau, 245
Ryan, Barbara, 23, 27, 38, 48, 50, 114, 123, 146, 228, 238, 280, 291, 305, 329
Ryan, Bekah, 237-238
Ryan, Carey, 27, 48, 333
Ryan, Christopher, 48, 178, 273-274

Sabbath, 16, 143, 147-150, 217, 222, 350
Samaritan woman, 119-124, 127-130, 146, 187
Schaeffer, Francis, 34, 205, 278-279
sickness, 218-220
Smith, Bud, 270
Sons of Thunder, 15
Spurgeon, Charles, 105, 122

temptation, 281-282
testimony, 17, 55-56, 211
theophanies, 313-314
Thomas, 382
Torrey, R. A., 285-286
Tozer, A. W., 318
Trinity, 27
    as a family, 315
    as demonstrated by believers' relationships, 328-329
    as relationship, 26
    conversation of, 26, 166-167, 170
    "true," meaning of, 35-36
Tucker, Lem, 330-331

unity, 326-331
Updike, John, 364-365

Van Til, Cornelius, 37, 318

Warfield, B. B., 244

wedding, 38, 78, 111, 113, 271, 329
    clothes, 115, 280-281
    feast (banquet of the Lamb), 116-
        117, 162, 305
    in Cana, 73-80, 97, 112, 146, 239,
        265, 361
    of Christ with church, 78-79
Willard, Dallas, 27
Williams, Joel, 270
Williams, William, 244
witness, pattern of, 66

Wordsworth, William, 191
work, 374-377
worship, 86-94, 124, 126, 129, 253
    at the temple, 84-85
    of Mary of Bethany, 251-253, 359-
        360

Zaccheus, 231

Scripture Index

Genesis
22:18   268

1 Samuel
16:7   277

2 Kings
4:38a, 44-44   158

Nehemiah
9:19b-20a   189

Job
14:14   244

Psalm
22:1   126
22:14-15   340
22:15   126
32:3-4   320
33:6   46
51:4   321
69:5-6   86
86:11   208
118   256-257

Isaiah
11:1-4a   183-184
25:6   79
40:11   229
42:1   184
49:6   267
53:2   49
53:5, 6, 12   61
55:1   117

55:1-2   80
60:1   31
60:1-3   29-30
60:3   36
61:10   280

Jeremiah
2:13   123
31:12   79

Ezekiel
34:3   230

Daniel
12:2   241

Joel
2:28-29   185

Nahum
1:6   126

Zechariah
9:9   258

Malachi
3:1, 2   87

Matthew
1:4   49
4:4   163
26:39   168

Mark

6:34   159

Luke

1:17   58
1:46-48   361
4:18-19   184
22:44   168

John

1:1   207
1:1-8   23
1:3   26
1:4   27, 28
1:5   28
1:6-7   28
1:10   36
1:11   39, 223
1:11-12   137
1:12-13   70
1:14-18   43
1:18   55
1:19-34   55
1:23   58
1:27   59
1:30   59
1:35-51   65
1:37   67
1:38   67
1:39   69
1:42   69
2:1-11   73
2:5   75
2:11   80
2:12-22   83
2:23   135
2:23–3:21   95
3:3   98
3:7   97
3:8   99
3:14-16   106
3:16   103
3:17   104
3:18   275-276
3:19   29
3:19-20   98, 225
3:20   104
3:22-36   109

4:4-42   119-120
4:43-54   133
4:45   134
4:48   136
5:2-3, 5-9, 14-24, 143
   27, 30, 44
5:16   149
5:18   149
5:19   151
5:24-26   246
5:28-29   277
5:47   153
6:1-15   155
6:2   157
6:16   193
6:19-20   193
6:26   157
6:28-35, 51-59   173
6:30-31   177
6:35   49, 163, 193
6:38   169
6:38-40   165
6:41   193
6:51   179-179
6:52   193
6:54   179
6:58   179
6:66-69   193
7:1-13, 37-39   181
7:12   193
7:16   193
7:29   193
7:33   193
7:35   302
7:37   188
7:43   193
8:12   67, 193
8:13   211
8:14   193
8:18-19   201
8:24-25a   193
8:28a   193
8:31-36, 43-47   201
8:33   211
8:35   213
8:58   193
9:1-41   217-218
9:30   223
9:35   223

.39	224
10:1-18	227
10:9	229
10:10	62
10:14-15	231
10:29	229
11:1-6, 17-27, 38-44	237
11:3-4	242
11:25-26	241
11:27	245
11:40	242
11:45-47, 53; 12:1-8	247
11:51-52	267
12:12-16	255
12:20-28	263
12:23	265
12:23-24	50
12:24	267
12:25	268
12:26	269, 377
12:27-36	273
12:31	275
12:32	49
12:42-43	276
12:48	276, 278
13:1-17	291
13:23	15, 20
13:31	266
13:33-38	301
13:36, 37, 38	303
14:1-6	301
14:3	309
14:6	49, 229
14:15-27	311
14:15-16	316
14:16-17	315
14:21	321
14:23	314
14:26	189
15:4	68
16:7-11	311, 319
16:12-13	316
16:33	311
17:20-26	325
17:20	328
17:21	326, 330
17:24	328, 331
19:23-24	286
19:25-30	337
19:38-20:10	345
20:1-2	355
20:10-18	365
20:11-17	355
20:24-31	381
20:30-31	15
20:31	18, 74
20:28	49
21:1-19	371
21:18	377
21:24	16
21:24-25	15

Acts

2:24	243
16:14	70

Romans

1:3-4	243
5:19	168, 283
5:20	163
6:5	309
8:30	70
14:17	161

1 Corinthians

2:9	307
3:6	92
6:11-12	93
6:13-15	93
6:14	244
6:16-20	93
10:3-4	162
11:25-26	176
15:19	305
15:42-44	366-367

2 Corinthians

4:6	28, 49
6:16	92

Galatians

2:20b	382

Ephesians

2:14-16	327
4:22-25, 32	284
5:1-2	284
5:10	286
5:25	235

Colossians

1:15	43
1:16	26, 37
2:9	49

Hebrews

1:2	26
1:3	27, 35, 44
4:14, 15-16	281
5:7	168
10:12	49
10:19-22	308

1 Peter

1:23, 24b-25	
2:24	
2:25	2
3:18	34

1 John

3:2	368

Revelation

1:10, 13-17a	91
1:13-17	262
1:17-18	262
4:8, 11; 5:6, 9-14	91-92
21:22	90